Copyright Industries and the Impact of Creative Destruction

This b ght
durati the
UK b py-
right. to
analys , in
order and
the gr op-
ment the
digital ght
protect lar.
Using of
the du ook
publish hat
would ive
industr

This of
Intelle

Jiabo l A.

Birmingham | Bristol | Chester | Guildford | London | Manchester | Leeds

Routledge Research in Intellectual Property

Copyright Industries and the Impact of Creative Destruction

Copyright expansion and the publishing industry

Jiabo Liu

Routledge
Taylor & Francis Group

LONDON AND NEW YORK

First published 2013
by Routledge
2 Park Square, Milton Park, Abingdon, Oxfordshire OX14 4RN

Simultaneously published in the USA and Canada
by Routledge
711 Third Avenue, New York, NY 10017

Routledge is an imprint of the Taylor and Francis Group, an informa business

First issued in paperback 2015

British Library Cataloguing in Publication Data
A catalogue record for this book is available from the British Library

Library of Congress Cataloguing in Publication Data
A catalog record for this book has been requested

ISBN 978-0-415-52388-2 (hbk)
ISBN 978-1-138-78656-1 (pbk)
ISBN 978-0-203-07658-3 (ebk)

Typeset in Garamond
by RefineCatch Limited, Bungay, Suffolk

To my mother and father, who give me strength and confidence

And Xinyan, my wife, who loves and directs me in all aspects of my life

Contents

List of tables

List of figures

Foreword

This book has been many years in preparation. It is the fruit of several years of discussion between Jiabo and me during his studies for his PhD in Law at the LSE. It is a book that for many reasons I imagined may never quite come to fruition and thus I am extremely pleased to be writing this foreword to the published edition. My doubts about this project never related to Jiabo's talents or drive, they were related instead to the unique nature of Jiabo's thesis and the investigation of it. The study of the nexus of law and economics is driven by a few basic assumptions and schools. Dominant among them is, of course, the Chicago School of neoclassical law and economics and at its heart the Coase Theorem as applied to legal transactions: the pursuit of efficiency becomes the root of legal foundations. Particularly badly served from within this School is the Law of Intellectual Property, and in particular Copyright Law. It is not the place of a foreword to disagree with the standing of classic works such as *The Economic Structure of Intellectual Property Law* by William M. Landes and Richard A. Posner but if I may point out a weakness of this work, common to almost all works in the field, the authors start from some basic principles, primarily that intellectual property law does encourage investment in innovation and the arts, and then examine how to make it most efficiently serve those ends through the application of secondary resources and available statistics. This I may term is the Chicago Orthodox approach to the study of the economics of intellectual property law. Alternate approaches are developing, including Lawrence Lessig's 'New Chicago School' and Neil Netanel's critical approach. This text departs from the traditional legal analysis by taking questioning these underlying assumptions, in the style of Lessig and Netanel, but by reference to original data analysis. By removing assumptions about the efficiency or otherwise of copyright law the author allows himself to critically examine both the role of copyright and copyright law to one sectorof the copyright industries, the book publishing industry, using the experiences of the UK book publishing industry during a thirty year period 1976-2006. In so doing Jiabo gives us a unique insight into how major changes in copyright law affect the industry which is so reliant upon it for its business models. The period studied includes at least two major disruptive events in UK copyright law – the passing of the Copyright, Designs and Patents Act 1988 and the extension of the period of copyright protection via the Duration of Copyright and Rights in Performances Regulations 1995. These are seen as major disruptive events, events of natural copyright expansion and are generally seen in the orthodox literature as being of benefit to the copyright industries, including the book publishing industry

Jiabo's work though starts with few assumptions. He assumes, by taking a Schumpeterian approach that the copyright industries will develop through processes of development and destruction. From this viewpoint a new perspective on the efficiency of copyright law develops – is it a tool to encourage investment in creative outputs, or is it a defence mechanism which inefficiently is used to protect entrenched interests against the march of technology or markets through continual expansion of the portfolio of rights possessed by the entrenched industry representatives? Jiabo analyses the development of the UK book publishing industry throughout the thirty years of his survey sample, and though key events such as those mentioned above to test these opposing thesis. Do the established players of the industry invest further following periods of copyright expansion? Does copyright expansion prevent (or at least delay) innovation or 'creative destruction'? For the first time full industry data is examined to divine an answer to these questions. This is research led thinking not orthodoxy clothed in the data which best establishes the author's point of view. This to me is the key contribution of this work. I have sat for several hours discussing with Jiabo what he expected to find. He did have expectations, but he clearly was not bound by them. What, I asked, if the data departs from your expectations – 'then clearly I need to refocus' was the answer. I'm not going to give away the final results of his investigations but I will say the data told a story different from the one Jiabo first discussed in my office in London in autumn 2005.

This book should be the first of a new body of literature: one where lawyers discussing the economics of any area of law are held by the same standards of rigorous independent data analysis as economists. Further, it is time lawyers and economists talked about this more freely between the disciplines. This is a book which will appeal to both.

The book is a testament to Jiabo's drive and commitment to the project. We spent several years working on this jointly as supervisor and supervisee. Commitments at home meant Jiabo was often several thousands of miles (and several time zones) away not only from me but from the sources of his data. Despite challenges which would have led other candidates to reconsider the project Jiabo remained positive and committed. This book is the fruition of his energy and commitment.

Andrew Murray, Professor of Law, LSE

Preface

This book originated with my doctoral study in law at the London School of Economics. Even before the central topic of my PhD thesis was finalised, I was already excited about what I was pursuing. In an institute where Schumpeter, Popper, and Coase studied or taught (or both), I felt fortunate to trace their paths and to enhance their perspectives for exploring the present world of intellectual property rights in general, and copyright in particular. Eventually, when adapting my PhD thesis into a book, I felt relaxed in explaining the features of the book.

This book addresses the broad issues regarding (but not limited to) the relationship between copyright expansion and the growth of copyright or creative industries under the forces of creative destruction. A variety of audiences, such as professors, postgraduate students, entrepreneurs, practitioners, or policy-makers in the copyright or creative industries, or whoever may develop stakes in copyright, intellectual property rights, or 'law and economics' in general, may find their concerns being explored in one way or another in the book. Of course, facing such a diverse readership, this book cannot examine their wide concerns in a way that suits everyone. What the author can do is to place the issues or concerns, from promising research devices to practical policy advice, into perspective and to represent the meanings and insights behind these specific issues or concerns.

The research in this book is designed as a classic econometric analysis of the relationship between copyright expansion in duration and the growth of the UK book publishing industry as a typical copyright industry and as the cradle of modern copyright law under Schumpeter's framework. The research sticks to Popper's scheme of scientific discovery.[1] Certainly, scientific research had advanced before Popper's scheme. Nevertheless, it was Popper who redefined the classical process of scientific discovery and reinforced the vitality of theoretical construction and clarification for empirical assessment as the key component of scientific research. Following Popper's path, unlike many existing empirical researches that focus heavily on the quantitative section, this book instead accentuates theoretical construction and clarification before conducting empirical assessment. To rephrase Schumpeter's words, this book is 'a theoretical, historical and statistical analysis'[2] of the central subject.

Perhaps I should appreciate the British-style doctoral thesis for its advantage in systematically endorsing a theoretical exploration, historical enquiry, and empirical assessment of these specific issues.

As the 'spirit of informationalism', which analogises Max Weber's vision of the 'spirit of capitalism',[3] Schumpeter's vision of creative destruction is more relevant than ever in the new economy of the twenty-first century.[4] Without Schumpeter's direction, the studies of legal issues, growth issues, and business strategies in all information industries reliant on intellectual property rights would lose more inspiring perspectives and visionary prospects. Once upon a time, Schumpeter categorised the role he played in his academic world was to 'open doors'.[5] This book not only draws on Schumpeter's theory of creative destruction to analyse the implications of copyright law and policy on the book publishing industry, but also models Schumpeter's role to 'open doors' for future empirical research and policy analysis in the large field of intellectual property rights from more diverse perspectives of law and economics.

Notes

1 K. Popper, *The Logic of Scientific Discovery*, London: Hutchinson, 1959. *Conjectures and Refutations: The Growth of Scientific Knowledge*, London: Routledge & Kegan Paul, 1963.
2 The subtitle of Joseph Schumpeter's *Business Cycles: A Theoretical, Historical, and Statistical Analysis of the Capitalist Process* 2 volumes, New York: McGraw-Hill, 1939.
3 M. Castells, *The Rising of the Network Society* 2nd edn, Malden, MA: Blackwell, 2000, p. 215.
4 T. McCraw, *Prophet of Innovation: Joseph Schumpeter and Creative Destruction*, Harvard University Press, 2007, pp. 495–503.
5 Ibid, p. 203.

Acknowledgements

This book is adapted from my PhD thesis. I should like to express my profound gratitude to all who supported, encouraged, advised, and assisted me in the whole process of my researching and writing. First and foremost, I would like to thank my doctoral supervisor, Professor Andrew Murray at the London School of Economics, who generously offered me his cerebral suggestions, comments, and advice for researching my thesis and writing this book. His professional supervision directed and challenged me to engage in an ever-improving research project. Without his instructions, my thesis and this book would not have been possible.

When proposing the research design for my PhD thesis, many exceptional faculty members at the London School of Economics provided their valuable advice and comments. Colin Scott, Anne Barron, and Dev Gangjee in the Law Department offered their generous suggestions and comments. They upgraded my research design to a higher and more practical level. Meanwhile, at the early stage of my research, when I still felt somewhat uncertain about the research topic and design, the endorsement and advice of Professor Danny Quah in the Economics Department encouraged me to continue my efforts.

I am grateful to Professor Ruth Towse and Professor David Evans for their inspiring suggestions and comments when examining my thesis, which were very instructive in strengthening and restructuring my thesis and this book for further amplification and rigour.

I am indebted to many other excellent professors and scholars from diverse institutions for their encouragement, advice, suggestions, and assistance. The list should include the following individuals: Professor Neil Netanel at UCLA School of Law, Professor Mark Schankerman at the London School of Economics, Professor Graeme Dinwoodie and Dr Mark Rogers at the University of Oxford, Professor Lawrence Lessig at Harvard Law School, Professor Tim Wu at Columbia Law School, Professor Robert Yaffee at New York University, and Mr Tony Clayton, Director of the UK Intellectual Property Office. I appreciate the assistance and services of the British Library of Political and Economic Science, the British Library, the University of Oxford Library, Key Note Ltd, and Mrs Rachel Yarham, Doctoral Programme Administrator of the Law Department at the London School of Economics.

Both the readers and I are indebted to Katie Carpenter and Stephen Gutierrez, the editors of Routledge Books, Daria Renshaw, copy-editor, Melvyn Dyer, project manager at RefineCatch Ltd, and three anonymous reviewers, for their outstanding editorial assistances and revealing comments.

My infinite debt is to my wife, Xinyan Jiang. Her intelligence, care, and love inspire me to think deeply and encourage me to accomplish everything I would not have thought possible myself. Without her inspiration, encouragement, and support, I would not find my way in all aspects of my life.

I remember with appreciation Professor Baoyinhuriyakeqi (Baoyin Chen), my former supervisor at Peking University Law School, who guided me into law's empire. His long list of readings was my first roadmap for exploring the field of law. His legacy of sincerity and talent still heartens me.

No matter how many people I may still fail to mention when expressing my thanks, my gratitude to my parents can never be forgotten. During my early years, when China was still isolated from the West, my parents told me that, besides Beijing, there were other large cities in the world such as Moscow, Paris, New York, and London. They rarely provided me with formal knowledge but always gave me confidence and encouraged me to do the right and best thing all the time. Today they are watching me doing my best abroad.

Of course, I am fully responsible for all errors or deficiencies. All the feedback, encouragement, suggestions, comments, and advice from others can only reduce those errors or deficiencies.

1 Introduction

This book aims to investigate the impacts of creative destruction on the copyright or creative industries and related broad issues. Principally, the book is designed to examine the extent to which the forces of creative destruction can affect the relation between copyright expansion – the legal extension of copyright duration as an enduring means of copyright protection – and the growth of the UK book publishing industry as a typical copyright industry and as the cradle of modern copyright law. To explore the context of the purpose, this introductory chapter states the legal and policy issues concerning copyright expansion, addresses the main subject (research purpose and research question), defines the main terms, demonstrates the corresponding contributions, and presents the outline of the book.

1.1 Legal and policy issues

Copyright, as one type of intellectual property right or 'property right in innovation', is designed to protect an individual's (being a legal or natural person) exclusive ownership over the reproduction or distribution of their creative or innovative expressions – or put simply, their creative outputs.[1] Copyright expansion has been recorded within the literature for decades.[2] There has been particular focus on the duration of copyright protection, the 'most straightforward' area for copyright expansion,[3] which it has been noted 'has always increased rather than decreased'.[4] Technological advances in general, and in particular digital technology,[5] have been widely perceived as the key reason for triggering copyright expansion.[6] The copyright industries have vigorously compelled such expansion.[7] It is widely argued that since the digital revolution began, these industries have used their lobbying powers for copyright expansion in order to further their proprietary interests in the new environment.[8] This raises questions such as: 'Does copyright expansion stimulate or restrict the growth of copyright industries as information technology advances'? 'What is the relation between copyright expansion and the growth of copyright industries'? 'What forces could affect the relation between copyright expansion and the growth of copyright industries'? These questions and related issues in the growth of UK copyright industries are addressed in this book through both a theoretical enquiry and an empirical quantitative assessment on the growth of the UK book publishing industry as a typical copyright industry and as the cradle of modern copyright law.

To examine these questions and related issues, this book pursues a Schumpeterian approach in analysing the relation (interaction or correlation) between copyright expansion and the growth of the UK book publishing industry. One of the most influential economists of the twentieth century,[9] Joseph Schumpeter, contributed his exceptional ideas and approaches to many aspects of economic analysis, mainly to the themes of economic development or industrial growth (such as capitalism's progress and creative destruction), entrepreneurship (such as competition and innovation), the business cycle, and democratic theory. Only certain facets of economic development or industrial growth and entrepreneurship in his theory are explored for the research in this book. His main works addressing these facets include *The Theory of Economic Development* in 1911, *Business Cycle* in 1939, and, perhaps the most prominent one, *Capitalism, Socialism and Democracy* in 1942.[10]

Schumpeter had made strong efforts to identify the complex or dynamic factors in the course of capitalist progress and to examine the long-term effects of these factors on economic development and industrial growth. He conceptualised the process of capitalist development in which the complex or dynamic factors shall exert their long-term effects on economic development and industrial growth as a course of 'creative destruction'. Among these complex or dynamic factors, concentrating industry structure, dynamic competition, technological innovation, and entrepreneurship have been identified as the powerful forces in development and growth.[11] In Schumpeter's scheme, a system of property rights and proprietary ownership should by no means play a crucial role in developing economy and growing industry as classical and neoclassical economists would advise. Rather, Schumpeter emphasised the forces of creative destruction and their dynamic roles in reinforcing the efficiency and effectiveness of development and growth. Following Schumpeter's reasoning, for a plausible understanding of intellectual property and related issues, intellectual property should be placed in the context of creative destruction forces – industrial structure, competition, innovation, and entrepreneurship – and be examined as one of the growth-promoting issues rather than as a resource-allocating problem.

Under Schumpeter's framework, the theoretical enquiry and empirical quantitative assessment in this book explain why whether copyright expansion promotes or precludes the growth of copyright industries depends on many factors or conditions. Among these factors or conditions, the forces and process of creative destruction – industrial structure, competition, innovation, and entrepreneurship – as defined by Schumpeter, are the crucial ones. The research in this book endeavours to investigate these crucial factors or conditions of creative destruction and their impacts on the relation (interaction or correlation) between copyright expansion and the growth of the UK book publishing industry as a typical copyright industry and as the cradle of modern copyright law.

1.2 Main subject of the book

The purpose of this book is to examine the extent to which the forces of creative destruction can affect the relation (interaction or correlation) between copyright expansion – the legal extension of copyright duration as an enduring means of copyright protection – and the growth of the UK book publishing industry at the firm and industry levels. The primary concern of this book is the relation between copyright expansion and the growth of the UK book publishing industry, with the focal point being the role of copyright expansion in growing the industry. Considering that 'the publisher is the real player in the legal and commercial game'[12] of book publishing, and the main beneficiary and driving force behind copyright protection and expansion,[13] a research study at both the firm and industry levels can address the research question, the primary concern, and the focal point from a broad perspective.

Of course, there are many aspects of copyright expansion. This book concentrates solely on one aspect of copyright expansion – expansion in duration – for consideration. First and foremost, copyright expansion in duration has drawn more extensive concerns among diverse groups than any other aspects of copyright expansion in both the UK and the US.[14] Addressing their concerns in systematic research can reinforce the conversations among these diverse groups for future explorations of the concerned issues. Second, compared with other aspects of copyright expansion, copyright expansion in duration is an unambiguously defined legal policy under a series of international conventions and national statutes.[15] An empirical study focusing on its effects on the copyright industries in the process of creative destruction can provide some pragmatic advice for future policy initiative and legislation design. Third, unlike other aspects of copyright expansion, copyright expansion in duration affects almost all players (from individuals to institutions) in the copyright industries. An investigation of this unique aspect can offer some reciprocal insights for all players in the field.

Although the examination of copyright growth from a Schumpeterian standpoint, as conducted in this book, is a new research inquiry, the relation between intellectual property rights and economic development in general, and between copyright and industrial growth in particular, have long been of concern among academic scholars, business leaders, and policy-makers.[16] Inquiry into the relation between intellectual property rights and economic development has also been conducted in many studies.[17] Similarly, the role of copyright law in the growth of copyright or information industries has been examined in some research.[18] Kamil Idris, former Director General of the World Intellectual Property Organization (WIPO), presented a strong and policy-oriented statement on the relation between copyright and industrial growth:

> Copyright laws provide the framework by which business and persons involved in the cultural industries can make important business decisions,

can rely upon and expect consistency and reliability for their operations and investments, and can compete fairly. The results have been spectacular. Economic benefits made possible because of copyright and related rights laws are evident in each of these industries; there has been measurable growth and development; an ever-expanding range of products and services; greatly enhanced creativity and innovation; and hope about the future; and the ability to tackle and satisfactorily resolve any and all problems.[19]

Idris took an over-optimistic view of the role of copyright law in economic development and industrial growth. In reality, the relation between copyright and industrial growth is more complicated than the linear and smooth copyright-growth parallel Idris portrays. Nevertheless, Idris's message at least conveyed a noteworthy observation – a coherent connection between copyright, creativity (both individual and industrial), and industrial growth in the cultural or copyright industries – even if how to explain the dimension and direction of such a connection is another matter. According to Idris, while addressing the cultural or copyright industries, 'the term "industry" is construed as covering not only the enterprises in a certain activity or business, but also the many individual creators, authors, artists, and performers who take part in commercial cultural activities both worldwide and locally, and the communities that they have come to constitute ... Creativity and innovation are at the heart and soul of the copyright industries'.[20] Indeed, some scholars share Idris's viewpoint on the interaction between copyright, creativity, and industrial growth in the cultural or copyright industries.[21] Even the market process in the copyright industries has been termed 'the creation and distribution of these creative works'.[22] Thus, creativity (both individual and industrial) and industrial growth should be the two sides of one coin in the cultural or copyright industries. Accordingly, the question of whether or not copyright law in general, and copyright expansion in particular, would promote the growth of cultural or copyright industries can be examined against the theoretical foundation of copyright justification on account of the assumed connection among copyright, creativity, and industrial growth in the cultural or copyright industries.

1.3 Definitions of terms

The main terms of this research are defined as follows:

The *copyright industries* include newspapers, periodicals, book publishing, radio and television broadcasting, music record and tape production, motion picture production, distribution and exhibition, theatrical productions, advertising, computer programming, and software development. In many senses, the terms 'copyright industries', 'cultural industries', and 'creative industries' should be interchangeable expressions.[23]

Creative destruction refers to a process by which innovative forces (technological and organisational innovations) obliterate existing institutional arrangements[24] of industrial or economic systems and re-orient industrial growth or economic development in an accelerated, unstable, and inflexible way.[25]

Creativity refers to all original activities in processing information, growing knowledge, generating products, providing services, and managing organisations.[26]

Industrial organisation is a field of economics that investigates how the firms make their business decisions on account of certain industry or market structures.[27] On some occasions, industrial organisation as a concept might encircle the contents of industry or market structures.[28]

Industry structure, or *market structure* in a broader sense, refers to an interactive arrangement of competition and monopoly in terms of concentration, entry and exit barriers, product differentiation, and information diffusion in diverse industries or markets.[29]

Innovation refers to the exploration, discovery, development, improvement, adoption, and commercialisation of new processes, products, organisational structures and procedures.[30] In general, there are two types of fundamental innovations – technological and organisational innovations.[31]

1.4 Contributions of the book

The research in this book contributes to the current study of copyright protection and expansion in several ways. First, a systematic examination of the relation between copyright expansion and the growth of the UK book publishing industry as a typical copyright industry, and as the cradle of modern copyright law from a Schumpeterian perspective, is generally lacking. This research attempts to fill the void. Meanwhile, a Schumpeterian standpoint will enrich the future explorations of the broad issues with regard to antitrust measures, competition, and copyright expansion in the information age. Moreover, an empirical quantitative assessment of the relation between copyright expansion and the growth of UK book publishing industry as a typical copyright industry, and as the cradle of modern copyright law in the process of creative destruction, will elaborate on some informative legal or policy implications for dealing with copyright law's perennial dilemma – to 'determine where exclusive rights should end and unrestrained public access should begin'.[32]

1.5 Outline

This book consists of seven chapters.

Chapter 1, 'Introduction', states the legal and policy issues concerning copyright expansion, addresses the main subject (research purpose and research question), defines the main terms, demonstrates the corresponding contributions, and presents the outline of the book.

Chapter 2, 'The pros and cons of copyright duration', reviews the historical development of UK copyright expansion and explores the legal and economic concerns on copyright protection in general, and copyright expansion in duration in particular, in order to examine the research question in perspective.

Chapter 3, 'Copyright in the digital age', further explores the essential issues on copyright protection and expansion that are addressed in Chapter 2 by reviewing the digital context of copyright protection and expansion under some specific industry or market structure from a Schumpeterian perspective.

Chapter 4, 'Theoretical perspective', examines Schumpeter's theory of creative destruction and its role in investigating the dynamic interaction between copyright expansion and the growth of the copyright industries. The applicability of a Schumpeterian growth model and a Schumpeterian method of inquiring into the copyright-growth relation under the forces of creative destruction is appraised.

Chapter 5, 'Empirical research on UK book publishing', conducts an empirical quantitative assessment based on the theoretical framework constructed in Chapter 4. The assessment is specifically formatted as an estimate and analysis of the extent to which the forces of creative destruction can affect the relation between copyright expansion and industrial growth in UK book publishing at the firm and industry levels. Correspondingly, the relation between copyright expansion and the growth of the UK book publishing industry and the role of copyright expansion in growing the industry are estimated and analysed.

Chapter 6, 'Policy implications of empirical research', reflects on the research (empirical assessment and analysis) conducted in Chapter 5, and addresses the policy implications of the research in tackling the relation between copyright expansion and industrial growth in the UK copyright industries in general, and in the UK book publishing industry in particular.

Chapter 7, 'Conclusion', presents the closing remarks on the theory, research, and policy implications in this book.

Notes

1 P. Goldstein, *Copyright's Highway: from Gutenberg to the Celestial Jukebox*, New York: Hill and Wang, 1994, pp. 3–36. J. Litman, 'Revising Copyright Law for the Information Age', in A. Thierer and W. Crews (eds), *Copy Fights: the Future of Intellectual Property in the Information Age*, Washington DC: Cato Institute, 2002, p. 131.
2 L. Lessig, *Free Culture: How Big Media Uses Technology and the Law to Lock Down and Control Creativity*, New York: The Penguin Press, 2004, pp. 130–139. See also his *The Future of Ideas: the Fate of the Commons in a Connected World*, New York: Vintage Books, 2001, pp. 106–107.
3 N. Netanel, 'Copyright and a Democratic Civil Society', *The Yale Law Journal*, vol. 106, 1996, 298.
4 L. Bently and B. Sherman, *Intellectual Property Law* 2nd edn, Oxford University Press, 2004, p. 152.
5 J. Litman, *Digital Copyright*, Prometheus Books, 2001, p. 114.
6 The literature on copyright expansion in both duration and scope in light of information technology is plentiful. For a resourceful treatment, see Netanel,

op. cit., 1996, pp. 283–387. See also R. Ku, 'The Creative Destruction of Copyright: Napster and the New Economics of Digital Technology', *University of Chicago Law Review*, vol. 69, 2002, pp. 263–322. R. Spinello and H. Tavani (eds), *Intellectual Property Rights in a Networked World: Theory and Practice*, Hershey, PA: Information Science Publishing, 2005, Chapter I. HMSO, *Gowers Review of Intellectual Property*, Norwich, UK: Crown Copyright, 2006, pp. 26–33. Online. Available <http://www.cipil.law.cam.ac.uk/policy_documents> (accessed 28 November 2010).

7 N. Netanel, 'Locating Copyright Within the First Amendment Skein', *Stanford Law Review*, vol. 54(1), 2001, 1–86. See also his *Copyright's Paradox: Property in Expression/Freedom of Expression*, Oxford University Press, 2006. Lessig, op. cit., 2004, pp. 133–135, 232–236.

8 Lessig, op. cit., 2004, pp. 133–135, 232–236. See also Lessig 2001, pp. 106–107. R. Towse, *Creativity, Incentive and Reward: an Economic Analysis of Copyright and Culture in the Information Age*, Cheltenham, UK: Edward Elgar, 2001, p. 5.

9 N. Rosenberg, *Schumpeter and the Endogeneity of Technology: Some American Perspectives*, New York: Routledge, 2000, pp. 1–3. A. Roncaglia, *The Wealth of Ideas: A History of Economic Thought*, Cambridge University Press, 2005, p. 416.

10 Roncaglia, op. cit., pp. 416–420.

11 J. Schumpeter, *Capitalism, Socialism and Democracy* 3rd edn, New York: Harper & Row, 1976[1942], pp. 81–106. J. Schumpeter, translated by R. Opie, *The Theory of Economic Development: an Inquiry into Profits, Capital, Credit, Interest, and the Business Cycle*, Harvard University Press, 1962[1911], pp. 128–156.

12 S. Vaidhyanathan, *Copyrights and Copywrongs: the Rise of Intellectual Property and How It Threatens Creativity*, New York University Press, 2001, p. 40.

13 IIL, *The IViR Report*, Institute for Information Law, University of Amsterdam, 2006, p. 13. HMSO, *Gowers Review*, 2006, p. 15. S. Breyer, 'The Uneasy Case for Copyright: A Study of Copyright in Books, Photocopies, and Computer Programs', *Harvard Law Review*, vol. 84(2), 1970, 292. H. MacQueen, *Copyright, Competition, and Industrial Design*, Edinburgh University Press, 1995, pp. 14–15.

14 Lessig, op. cit., 2004, pp. 228–241; 2001, pp. 106–107. MacQueen, op. cit., pp. 8–9. Andrew Porter, 'Plan to Extend Copyright on Pop Classics', *The Sunday Times*, 5 June 2005. Online. Available <http://www.timesonline.co.uk/tol/news/uk/article530132.ece> (accessed 10 March 2011). D. Cronin, 'Proposed EU Copyright Term Extension Faces Vocal Opposition in Parliament', Intellectual Property Watch, 27 January 2009. Online. Available<http://www.ip-watch.org/weblog/2009/01/27/eu-copyright-term-extension-meets-vocal-opposition-in-parliament> (accessed 10 March 2011). M. Kretschmer *et al*, 'Creativity Stifled? A Joint Academic Statement on the Proposed Copyright Term Extension for Sound Recordings', *European Intellectual Property Review*, vol. 30(9), 2008, 341–347. PwC, *The Impact of Copyright Extension for Sound Recordings in the UK: A Report for the Gowers Review of Intellectual Property prepared by PwC on Behalf of the BPI*, PricewaterhouseCoopers LLP, 2006, p. 13.

15 H. MacQueen, C. Waelde, G. Laurie and A. Brown, *Contemporary Intellectual Property: Law and Policy* 2nd edn, Oxford University Press, 2011, p. 117.

16 Michael Ryan systematically addressed this concern among diverse interest groups. See his *Knowledge Diplomacy: Global Competition and the Politics of Intellectual Property*, Washington, DC: Brookings Institution Press, 1998, pp. 3–19, 50–53. See also S. Alikhan and R. Mashelkar, *Intellectual Property and Competitive Strategies in the 21ˢᵗ Century*, New York: Kluwer Law International, 2004. For more literature on the relation between intellectual property and economic development, see K. Maskus (ed), *The WTO, Intellectual Property Rights and the Knowledge Economy*, Northampton, NA: Edward Elgar, 2004. C. Greenhalgh and

M. Rogers, *Innovation, Intellectual Property, and Economic Growth*, Princeton University Press, 2010.

17 R. Sherwood, *Intellectual Property and Economic Development*, Boulder, CO: West-view Press, 1990. D. Gould and W. Gruben, 'The Role of Intellectual Property Rights in Economic Growth', *Journal of Development Economics*, vol. 48, 1996, 323–350. K. Idris, *Intellectual Property: A Power Tool for Economic Growth* WIPO Publication No. 888, Geneva: World Intellectual Property Organization, 2002. S. Sell, *Private Power, Public Law: the Globalisation of Intellectual Property Rights*, Cambridge University Press, 2003. D. Richards, *Intellectual Property Rights and Global Capitalism: the Political Economy of the TRIPS Agreement*, New York: M E Sharpe, 2004. R. Cellini and G. Cozzi (eds), *Intellectual property, Competition and Growth*, New York: Palgrave Macmillan, 2007.

18 Gould and Gruben, op. cit., pp. 323–350. Towse, op. cit., 2001. R. Towse (ed), *Copyright in the Cultural Industries*, Cheltenham, UK: Edward Elgar, 2002.

19 Idris, op. cit., p. 231.

20 Ibid, p. 189.

21 Towse, op. cit., 2001, p. 1. Towse, op. cit., 2002, pp. 9–31.

22 M. Nadel, 'How Current Copyright Law Discourages Creative Output: The Overlooked Impact of Marketing', *Berkeley Technology Law Journal*, vol. 19(2), 2004, 787.

23 This classification is adopted from S. Siwek, 'The Measurement of "Copyright" Industries: The American Experience', *Review of Economic Research on Copyright Issues*, vol. 1(1), 2004, 17–25. Alikhan and Mashelkar, op. cit., pp. 89–102. Idris, op. cit., pp. 189–231.

24 For a brief treatment of the difference between 'institutional arrangement' and 'institutional environment', see N. Mercuro and S. Medema, *Economics and the Law: From Posner to Post-Modernism*, Princeton University Press, 2006, pp. 247–248.

25 This definition is developed on the basis of Schumpeter's *Capitalism, Socialism and Democracy* 3rd edn and other works that analyse Schumpeter's theory; for instance, L. McKnight, P. Vaaler, and R. Katz (eds), *Creative Destruction: Business Survival Strategies in the Global Internet Economy*, The MIT Press, 2001, pp. 3–17. J. Ellig and D. Lin, 'A Taxonomy of Dynamic Competition Theories', in J. Ellig (ed), *Dynamic Competition and Public Policy: Technology, Innovation, and Antitrust Issues*, Harvard University Press, 2001, pp. 16–21.

26 This definition is drawn mainly from the perspective of psychology. The differ-ence is that legal scholars, especially scholars of intellectual property rights, are interested in novel and innovative activities in expressions under copyright laws, while psychologists in general emphasise the mental or emotional processes of creativity. There are abundant psychological researches on creativity. I use the following works as references not because they are authorities but due to their legible treatments of creativity in perspectives. See T. Amabile, *Creativity in Context*, Boulder, CO: Westview Press, 1996. J. Getzels and I. Taylor (eds), *Perspectives in Creativity*, Chicago: Aldine, 1975. K. Gilhooly, *Thinking: Directed, Undirected and Creative*, New York: Academic Press, 1982.

27 This definition is developed on account of the works of P. Ghemawat, G. Mankiw, and O. Shy. P. Ghemawat, *Games Business Play: Cases and Models*, The MIT Press, 1997, pp. 1–11. G. Mankiw, *Principles of Economics* 3rd edn, Mason, OH: South-Western/Thomson Learning, 2004, pp. 267–268. O. Shy, *Industrial Organization: Theory and Applications*, The MIT Press, 1995, pp. 1–7.

28 This way of defining 'industrial organization' is drawn mainly from Timothy Sturgeon's exploration of the Schumpeterian perspective on industrial organiza-tion. T. Sturgeon, 'Modular Production Networks: A New American Model of Industrial Organisation Grasping Opportunity, Meeting Challenges of New

Technology Revolution', *Industrial and Corporate Change*, vol. 11(3), 2002, 451–96. See also Shy, op. cit., pp. 1–7.

29 This definition is developed on the basis of R. Grant, *Contemporary Strategy Analysis: Concepts, Techniques, Applications* 4th edn, Malden, MA: Blackwell Publishers, 2002, pp. 70–71. Meanwhile, J. Stiglitz also provides a sufficient treatment of industry or market structure. See his *Economics* 2nd edn, W W Norton & Company, 1997, Chapters VIII–XX.

30 This definition is adopted directly from T. Jorde and D. Teece (eds), *Antitrust, Innovation, and Competitiveness*, Oxford University Press, 1992, p. 48.

31 The meaning of 'technology' could be wide-ranging from a Schumpeterian perspective. See Luis Béjar, 'The Evolutionary Approach to Technological Change: A Framework for Microeconomic Analysis', in K. Nielsen and B. Johnson (eds), *Institutions and Economic Change: New Perspectives on Markets, Firms and Technology*, Northampton, NA: Edward Elgar, 1998, p. 60. Paul Krugman has also explored the concept of 'technology' 'in the broad sense'. According to him, technology should define 'not just new kinds of hardware, but also "soft" innovations like just-in-time inventory management'. See his *Peddling Prosperity: Economic Sense and Nonsense in the Age of Diminished Expectations*, New York: Norton, 1994, p. 59. Esben Andersen identified five types of innovation – product, process, organisational, market, and input innovations – under Schumpeter's framework. E. Andersen, *Schumpeter's Evolutionary Economics: A Theoretical, Historical and Statistical Analysis of the Engine of Capitalism*, London: Anthem Press, 2009, p. 269. In this book, technological and organisational innovations take account of the five types. For further reference, see Oliver Williamson, *The Economic Institutions of Capitalism*, The Free Press, 1985, Chapter XV.

32 Netanel, op. cit., 1996, p. 292.

2 The pros and cons of copyright duration

This chapter explores the legal and economic concerns regarding copyright protection in general and copyright expansion in duration in particular in order to examine the research question: to what extent can the forces of creative destruction affect the relation (interaction or correlation) between copyright expansion in duration and the growth of the UK book publishing industry at the firm and industry levels? For this purpose, this chapter reviews the historical development of UK copyright expansion. After this review, the legal arguments and economic justifications of copyright protection and expansion are elaborated upon.

2.1 Historical development of UK copyright expansion

This section offers a tentative exploration of the historical development of UK copyright expansion in duration as, in Schumpeter's terms, an 'adaptive response'[1] to the pressure of creative destruction in the UK book publishing industry. In Schumpeter's system, the process of creative destruction has in general persisted, with a periodic and recurrent transition among various modes of industry or market structure (from perfect competition, monopolistic competition, and oligopoly, to monopoly or in a reverse order) owing to innovative forces. For the most part, the process has proceeded with four 'destructive' paths as follows:

- The Destruction of Traditional Industry Structures
- The Destruction of Traditional Regulatory Approaches
- The Destruction of Traditional Competitive Positioning Strategies
- The Destruction of Traditional Technological Assumptions[2]

Among the four destructive paths, 'the destruction of traditional industry structures', replacing an identical and monopolistic arrangement of entry, production, and distribution with a diverse and competitive scheme, should be the decisive route for the whole process of creative destruction. Of course, the four paths shall not necessarily proceed in parallel. They should overlap without a clear-cut boundary in the whole process of creative destruction.

The growth of the UK book publishing industry follows a process of creative destruction. Three forces of creative destruction – technological innovation, dynamic competition, and concentrating industry structure – introduced in Chapter 1.1, play certain roles in interacting copyright expansion and the growth of the book publishing industry. In particular, the development of the UK publishing industry has substantiated the above four destructive paths in the process of creative destruction, which has evolved in company with copyright expansions, particularly the extensions of protection duration, in 1814, 1842, and 1911 respectively.

2.1.1 Copyright expansion before the 1814 Act

The history of the UK book publishing industry indicates that the industrial progression in this field embarked on a process of creative destruction in the seventeenth century, and that the Statute of Anne in 1710 was a resultant institutional arrangement of this first round. The starting point of the first round was the termination, in 1694, of the Licensing Act of 1662. The ending point was the creation of the Statute of Anne in 1710. Although the London publishers under the Stationers' Company engaged in a rigorous campaign for perpetual copyright after 1694,[3] through this statute Parliament granted both authors and publishers a limited term of copyright for their creative works – limited to 28 years after a work's publication, being a maximum of two 14-year terms.[4] In consequence, the movable-type printing – as a new technological innovation – eventually advanced the new institutional arrangement in the Statute and constructed a broad platform for both authors and publishers, both the incumbent and the insurgent, and both innovators and imitators in the publishing industry.[5] Their dynamic interactions under the new technology brought about a need for overhauling the existing way of industrial organisation and mode of industry or market structure.

Moreover, this statute marked the early legislative effort to 'regulate the challenges posed by the development of the moveable type printing press' and to contend with technology-motivated social change.[6] With the passage of the Statute of Anne, on the one hand, chaotic competition in the UK publishing industry was transformed into regulated competition. On the other hand, an absolute monopoly for the Stationers' publishers was reduced to a limited monopoly.[7] This transformation initiated the dynastic interactions among copyright expansion, growth, industrial organisation, and industry or market structure in the development of UK publishing industry under a process of creative destruction.

In 1711, immediately after the passage of the Statute of Anne, the bookseller cartel entrenched their practice of coordinated financing. Meanwhile, around 1718, they undertook a new practice, 'trade sale' – a private auction of copy-owning shares inside the conger members – to protect their position as shareholders in the book trade.[8] It seemed that the industry structure of London publishing, largely an oligopolistic alliance of booksellers as copyright holders, which was termed the 'share-book system', had not been destroyed; rather, it had been sustained with the authorisation of the first British copyright legislation.[9]

Nevertheless, this kind of industry structure did not last long. Eventually, the competitive environment changed. The Statute created a new institutional arrangement and a more competitive environment for the business operations of publishers. With more innovations, both technological[10] and organisational,[11] in book publishing and trading appearing since 1710, the traditional industry structure was unlikely to remain the same. The crucial development of creating a more competitive environment and destroying the old industry structure was a continuing challenge to the share-book system endorsed by the copy-owning and wholesaling congers under the Stationers' Company in London. One such challenge came with the emergence of provincial publishers and publishers from Scotland. To contain the competition, London publishers under the Stationers' Company appealed to Parliament seeking a perpetual copyright for their publications rather than the limited one stipulated in the 1710 Statute.[12]

However, Parliament rejected their petition. As a result, they had to resort to the courts in order to pursue permanent copyright protection under the common law.[13] During the eighteenth century, as their Scottish counterparts' challenge to their dominance in the industry became apparent, London publishers took further legal actions seeking to uphold their oligopolistic positions.[14] The case of *Tonson v Collins* in 1761 was the first key battle in which the incumbent publishers secured their copyright as a perpetual legal right under the common law.[15] Eight years after *Tonson v Collins*, the ruling of *Millar v Taylor* in 1769 reinforced copyright as a perpetual common law right.[16] At that moment, it seemed that a new copyright institution had been established. Nevertheless, it was far from an uncontested position. Five years later, in 1774, after a three-week hearing in *Donaldson v Beckett*, the House of Lords abandoned the institution of perpetual copyright under the common law.[17]

The case of *Donaldson v Beckett* 'proved to be the definitive turning point in modern copyright law'.[18] Since then, the notion of perpetual common law copyright has been consigned to history. Even at the time when the case was heard in the House of Lords, it had already 'excited a certain amount of public interest'.[19] The verdict of the House of Lords led to wide-scale repercussions in both England and Scotland. For London's establishment of book publishing and trading, it was a dark message. However, in Scotland, it caused celebrations in the street. Because copyright was reconfirmed as a limited statutory right, 'the public domain' had been clarified and created through free choice 'in a competitive context'.[20] The verdict of *Donaldson v Beckett* pressed forward the break-up of the monopolistic power of the Stationers' Company and related industry structure, and in essence authenticated the eventual end of such power and structure. It marked an end to the second round of the process of creative destruction in the British publishing industry.

In short, the House of Lords' decision in *Donaldson v Beckett* 'reversed not merely a decision of the Court of Chancery but the entire tradition of the law of copyright'.[21] With the destruction of the monopolistic power of the Stationers' Company, innovative forces (technological and organisational innovations) advanced; traditional regulatory approaches, competitive positioning strategies, and technological assumptions had been gradually weakened and destroyed after two rounds of creative destruction in the publishing industry after the Statute of Anne. Accordingly, a new institutional arrangement and environment had been created.

The 'destruction of traditional regulatory approaches', replacing an established regulatory framework that limits competitive entry and promotes monopolistic practices with a framework that advances competition, was clear. Both the Statute of Anne in 1710 and the decision of *Donaldson v Beckett* in 1774 rejected perpetual common law copyright and endorsed copyright protection in a limited term. In summer 1774, a few months after the decision of *Donaldson v Beckett*, a Bill proposing to repeal *Donaldson v Beckett* and to ratify a perpetual statutory copyright failed to pass through the House of Commons. In 1775, the House of Lords ruled directly against the Stationers' Company's monopoly claim. A Bill attempting to repeal the Lords' ruling failed again in the Commons.[22] These legal changes endorsed by both Houses conveyed a clear message to all players in the publishing business – the state would no longer support a regulatory regime for the long-term constraint of competitive entry and other competitive practices.

In fact, the Scottish publishers' challenge was merely one of the forces that destroyed the traditional industry structures and regulatory approaches in the UK publishing business at the time. Many innovative forces (both technological and organisational innovations) had also played diverse roles in the renewal of industry structures, regulatory approaches, competitive positioning strategies, and technological assumptions. Historically, credit and venture capital were considered to be the driving forces behind economic development and industrial growth.[23] In the eighteenth century, Britain underwent a 'financial revolution'[24] after the Bank of England was established in the late seventeenth century[25] and the Act of Bankruptcy was enacted in the early eighteenth century.[26] Application of bank credit and risk capital was one type of organisational innovation in British publishing.[27] Indeed, even if the banking system was still at the pre-modern stage in the eighteenth century, the utilisation of bank credit and venture capital still opened up a new channel for sponsoring the publishing business and raising more competitive book publishers.[28] Another noteworthy organisational innovation was the development of independent book publishing. In the first half of the eighteenth century, collective publishing within the copy-owning and wholesaling congers under the Stationers' Company was still the main pattern of book publishing. However, a number of established publishers, in addition to the Scottish publishers, gradually started to change their business directions and withdraw from collective publishing practice.[29] This independent line of book publishing further weakened the market power of the Stationers' Company and fostered a more competitive environment.

Meanwhile, many other innovations in the production and distribution of the publishing business also strengthened the transformative path of industry structures and regulatory approaches in the field. Technological innovations in papermaking in the late eighteenth century had enhanced book production[30] and reinforced the competitive context following *Donaldson v Beckett*. Experiments in papermaking mechanisation were made in the 1780s. Consequently, paper was produced on a much larger scale and at a lower cost[31]: the cost of book production was reduced accordingly. Although the prices of new books were not immediately reduced, the prices of non-copyrighted books started to fall in the early nineteenth century.[32] Meanwhile, during that period, some publishers tried price-discrimination strategies to attract customers when facing a strict copyright system.[33] These measures might not notably transform publishing industry structures but could still smooth competitive entry and slash monopolistic power to some extent. At the end of the eighteenth century and the beginning of the nineteenth century, mechanical papermaking was commercialised.[34]

Alongside technological innovations such as mechanised papermaking, organisational innovations in the production and distribution of published works had also boosted the transformation of industry structures and regulatory approaches. On the production side, children's books as new products had emerged from the middle of the eighteenth century.[35] At the same time, other new products, such as newspapers, magazines, novels, and travel books, were gradually created and developed.[36] Such diversity of product characteristics opened up a new market for publishing enterprises and led to a new way of industrial organisation and new mode of industry structure.[37] The innovations with regard to the distribution of publishing business were also influential for updating the field. One of the main innovations in this regard was the improvement of the wholesale system. From the late eighteenth century, some large wholesale houses were established. They gradually replaced joint wholesaling and revolutionised book distribution.[38] Unlike joint wholesaling, a large wholesale house was both a new creation of a competitive book market and a channel for facilitating competitive transactions in the book trade. Not only did the few members of the copy-owning and wholesaling congers established under the Stationers' Company benefit from the establishment of these large wholesale houses, their benefits extended to the entire book trade. Another innovation in book distribution, which also emerged in the late eighteenth century and related to large wholesale houses, was remaindering. This business practice was designed to clear out the wholesale houses for new books by reducing the prices of the books in current storage. Such practice inspired a new business strategy that sought the long-run returns at marginal profits.[39]

In general, all of these innovations – technological and organisational – enhanced 'a process of qualitative change' in Schumpeter's terms[40] and, in effect, intensified a process of transforming industry structures and regulatory approaches in the publishing world. As the transformation continued, the 'competitive positioning strategies', the practical measures for pursuing favourable market positions, had to adjust to a new competitive environment in the publishing industry. In such a new competitive context, a perpetual copyright was no longer a realistic expectation, and the monopolistic power of copyright had been constrained.[41] As a result, Schumpeter would predict that firms in the field should abandon old-fashioned competitive positioning strategies that rely on the protected market positions and adopt new competitive positioning strategies that tackle continual innovations for the new way of production or distribution, new products, and new markets. Under the circumstances, entrepreneurship became a necessity for business surviving and thriving.[42]

Indeed, following the Statute of Anne, especially after *Donaldson v Beckett*, was an era brimming with a 'more entrepreneurial climate' in publishing.[43] Accordingly, as societal and judicial attitudes to competition and entrepreneurship changed, 'at the turn of the eighteenth and nineteenth centuries, there were firms which could be labelled as "publishers" in the modern sense'.[44] The publishing business had become a new avenue of enterprise for new players in their new roles.[45]

In a more competitive climate, 'the destruction of traditional technological assumptions', challenging the conventional views on the relation between technology and economic development (or industrial growth), should be inevitable. When technological innovations facilitated the destruction of traditional industry structures, regulatory approaches, and competitive positioning strategies, the destruction would simultaneously remodel the views on the technology-growth relation (technological assumptions) and encourage a more suitable environment for broadening the function of technological innovations in the industry. In other words, the remodelled views on the technology-growth relations should specifically concentrate on the role of technology in 'opening up new opportunities rather than offering complete, final solution'.[46] In this regard, competition and entrepreneurship should be the key for maximising the function of technological innovation in the process of economic development or industrial growth.

The development of the British publishing industry, especially the progress after the Statute of Anne, witnessed the strength of the remodelled views on the technology-growth relation over the traditional insights into that relation (technological assumptions), either from an endogenous or an exogenous perspective.[47] Gutenberg's contribution to the improvement of movable-type printing technology in the mid-fifteenth century showed less of a profit incentive. In contrast, William Caxton's introduction and application of printing technology in England in the late fifteenth century were clearly business motivated.[48] However, for Caxton, entrepreneurship rather than technological capacity played a crucial role. 'It is not his technical competence that marks him out. It is his commitment to publishing in English, thus starting the long process of reducing a chaos of inflections and dialects to a simpler, common tongue.'[49] The Statute of Anne was itself an institutional reform on account of technological innovation. In turn, it gave rise to a new Schumpeterian technological assumption: technological innovation equalises the competitive entrance into the publishing market for both imitators and creators but only those with entrepreneurship can prolong a competitive advantage.[50]

Overall, the eighteenth century was a transformative era for the British publishing industry. By the end of the century, 'the United Kingdom was both a European power and a trading nation with a rapidly developing global empire'.[51] The emerging Industrial Revolution was reshaping British industries and society. While free trade as an economic doctrine continually spread, protectionist and mercantilist policies that endorsed state and guild monopolies eventually lost ground. Trade guilds, such as the Stationers' Company, gradually waned.[52] As a series of innovations (technological and organisational) advanced, the process of creative destruction in the industry recurrently advanced. With the two rounds of the process, traditional industry structures, regulatory approaches, competitive positioning strategies, and technological assumptions in the publishing field were overhauled. A new copyright regime, institutionalised principally in the Statute of Anne and *Donaldson v Beckett*, had been established. As modern publishing firms were constructed and the market was widened, the industrial organisation and the industry or market structure had experienced dramatic reorganisation. The British publishing industry entered the nineteenth century in a more dynamic climate. In this new sphere of competition and innovation, entrepreneurship and creativity had become a crucial factor for business survival and revival in the industry.[53]

Entrepreneurship was, of course, not just the privilege of publishers. Authors at a time of competition and innovation or, in other words, at a time of dynamic or Schumpeterian competition, had also realised their own entrepreneurial spirits. Indeed, as early as the middle of the eighteenth century, authors had already started to negotiate for the more favourable contractual arrangements with publishers.[54] As for publishers, facing the legal changes in copyright and corresponding dynamic process[55] of creative destruction,[56] respecting and advocating authors' copyright may help them to pursue their own interests in the long run. First, with the end of perpetual copyright protection, incessant collaborating with authors for new books or other new forms of publications that possessed a new term of protected copyright became a necessary survival strategy for publishers.[57] Second, as the dynamic process of creative destruction in publishing advanced, publishers faced intensive uncertainties and risks. Accordingly, they needed distinct creative works from a variety of authors in order to diversify their risks. Rallying around authors and consolidating authors' copyright was a realistic approach to sharing out risks in investment.[58] Third, because of both the end of perpetual copyright protection and the progression of creative destruction, extending copyright terms for coping with the future's uncertainty became a viable way to preserve both authors' and publishers' interests. Thus, under the pressure of creative destruction, authors and publishers would cooperatively stand up for copyright expansion. 'The great copyright debates of the nineteenth century, both domestic and international, were largely driven by the authors with the support of the publishers.'[59] What came next, the Copyright Act of 1814, was an adaptive response to the pressure of creative destruction. 'It is an essential feature of law and the legal system to be able to adapt in response to the pressure of change.'[60]

2.1.2 Copyright expansion under the 1814 and 1842 Acts

The Copyright Act of 1814 doubled the original duration of copyright protection and expanded it to 28 years or the author's natural life since the book's publication.[61] An expansion to 28 years within a 100-year period may not seem noteworthy. However, this legislation can be seen as the cumulative result of a long-lasting process of creative destruction at the dawn of the Industrial Revolution. The period from 1814 to 1842 witnessed many changes following the above-mentioned four paths of creative destruction in the UK publishing industry.

The publishing industry continued to fight to reform copyright law after the passage of the 1814 Act. The period of less than 30 years from 1814 to 1842 witnessed remarkable progress in both technological and organisational innovations in the UK publishing industry. Since its invention in 1776, the steam engine[62] had been improved and applied in a number of fields, and had enhanced the course of mechanisation in the printing/publishing industry. The mechanisation of book production, mainly the innovations in typesetting, printing, and binding, had brought about substantial transformations in the publishing field[63] since the passage of the 1814 Act. That same year, *The Times* introduced steam-engine printing technology into newspaper production.[64] In the 1820s, the Albion, an improved hand-printing machine, became popular in England.[65] The mechanisation of bookbinding also emerged. These and other related technological innovations made the publishing industry 'more cost-effective'.[66] Accordingly, transaction costs and other costs in the production process were reduced by varying degrees,[67] which in turn affected organisational innovations, especially those in the financial reform and distribution/production processes of publication.[68] Papermaking mechanisation, after being commercialised at the end of the eighteenth century and beginning of the nineteenth century, still played a notable role in advancing the publishing industry, particularly its production process, after 1814.[69]

Meanwhile, since the early nineteenth century, steam-engine locomotives and railway systems had started to modernise UK transportation.[70] As a result, the distribution system in the publishing field was gradually revolutionised.[71] As to other types of organisational innovations, such as new financial practices in the publishing field, the period following the Copyright Act of 1814 was also a significant era. The legislature in 1826 initiated a process of stabilising the financial institutions that smoothed business transactions among publishers.[72] All of these technological and organisational innovations had further transformed the business climate of the UK publishing industry following the 1814 Act. The 1814 Act itself had been a substantial force behind the climate of change.

Clearly, the Copyright Act of 1814 was not only an adaptive response to the pressure of creative destruction but also a legal action elevating the process. Since authors had emerged as one of the main forces in the publishing process under the 1814 Act, competition in the publishing market had further intensified. In the 1830s, 'The trade itself was changing: more publishers, more titles, an increasing market and more bookshops were all factors which militated against a restrictive regime'.[73] As innovations diffused and the financial resources for publishing were widely available, monopoly and oligopoly in the field became more and more difficult. Accordingly, the industry structure in publishing continued diversifying and the course of reforming the traditional industry structure sustained. The change of industry structure provided an opportunity to reassess the regulatory approaches in the area. The adjustment of the copyright registration system reflected a change in regulatory approaches after the 1814 Act. Although the 1814 Act 'was the first statutory recognition of the author as a party in the process of writing and publishing',[74] and the traditional regulatory approaches had been overhauled in many aspects, the existing copyright registration system still 'had grown up from the old privileges of the Stationers' Company' and 'the number of deposit copies associated with registration had long been controversial'.[75] Such regulatory arrangement was no longer able to cope with the more competitive industry structure. As a reforming response, the Copyright Act of 1836 started a process of deconstructing the old regulatory regime through adjusting the old copyright registration system that required a legal deposit in publishing.[76]

The transformations of industry structure and regulatory framework in the UK publishing industry further prompted the destruction of the traditional competitive positioning strategies in the field after the 1814 Act. Facing much harsher and dynamic (or Schumpeterian) competition, changes to the publishing trade in early nineteenth-century Britain necessitated new entrepreneurial publishers. As noted by Feather, the industry 'was largely dominated by "new" publishers who were not hidebound by the old traditions of the trade for which some still hankered'.[77] To adapt to a new and expanding mass market, these entrepreneurial publishers further adopted new competitive positioning strategies under a dynamic or Schumpeterian competition. Rather than solely relying on the protected interests under the 1814 Act, they built up or consolidated their market positions through diversifying or renovating their products and cooperating with a variety of authors. Books, magazines, and newspapers were all their concerns. Fiction and non-fiction, academic and non-academic publications were all included for pursuing profits. Partnership with authors as a strategic endorsement was also established.[78]

As the industry structure and regulatory framework in the UK publishing industry had further transformed since the 1814 Act, and the new competitive positioning strategies had emerged, technological assumptions accordingly adjusted to the new environment. For publishers, especially for new entrepreneurial publishers, technological innovations not only promoted efficiencies but also provided opportunities for their business development. The progression from an assumption of technological efficiency to technological opportunity indicated an ongoing process of creative destruction. These new entrepreneurial publishers were not only concerned with technological capacities but also with technological probabilities.[79] When those in other fields such as in the printing sector were worried about the risk of technological changes,[80] these entrepreneurs' openness towards technology in the publishing field showed an interest in reinvigorating the sector.[81] The reformation of technological assumptions under their entrepreneurship shed light on the modernisation of the British publishing industry.

Overall, the ongoing process of creative destruction in the UK publishing industry since the Copyright Act of 1814 furthered the course of marketisation, mechanisation, and modernisation in the field. Although the 1814 Act as 'the first substantial revision of the Statute of Anne'[82] consolidated authorial copyright and extended the term of the right, the realisation of the author's financial interests would depend on the effects of the legislation on industrial growth under the forces of creative destruction. Indeed, the renovations of the industry structures, regulatory frameworks, competitive positioning strategies, and technological assumptions in the UK publishing industry – as the four paths of creative destruction – had brought to the surface concerns about the copyright-growth relation and revived the disagreements among a variety of players who had a stake in copyright issues since the 1814 Act.

In Schumpeter's account, the competition between innovators and imitators in the process of creative destruction shapes the pattern of industrial growth to different degrees. The progress of the UK publishing industry since the 1814 Act had, more than ever, attested to Schumpeter's view. This is not to say that the growth of the publishing industry before the 1814 Act was due to a lack of competition regarding copyright protection among players. Rather, such tensions had been enduring throughout the whole course of development. What made the period following the 1814 Act significant was the far-reaching impact of competition among players, resulting from the enormous efforts of Thomas Talfourd as Member of Parliament for Reading, on copyright issues in the publishing industry at that time.[83] The 1842 Copyright Law, by stipulating further copyright expansion, was a result of the ongoing competition between innovators and imitators in the process of creative destruction.

Of course, besides the ongoing process of creative destruction in the economic arena, the political reforms in the 1830s also fortified the competition among players over the copyright issues in the publishing field. The

Great Reform Act of 1832 and other reforming legislation created a liberal public space for both the general public and the players in the publishing industry. As the political environment changed, many political institutions had become more open and responsive.[84] British society as a whole in the first four decades of the nineteenth century not only enjoyed a steady economic growth[85] but also experienced a stately political transformation. Accordingly, the pressures to transform laws in general, and copyright law in particular, became inevitable in the reforming period.[86] After the enactments of both the 1814 and 1836 Copyright Acts, 'in the mid-1830s, it might have seemed that the general climate of opinion was favourable to the further development of copyright law'. In time, Talfourd launched a campaign to expand authors' copyright duration and drove 'the further development of copyright law' in May 1837.[87] In 1842, his sixth Bill became statute. Under the new Copyright Act, copyright protection was expanded 'for the author's life-time and forty-two years thereafter'.[88]

The Copyright Act of 1842 was a milestone. It 'was to remain the basis of British copyright law until 1911, and indeed to exercise immense influence through the British Empire and the rest of the world'.[89] It also proposed important content for the 1956 and 1988 Acts.[90] In essence, it was a product of compromise. Both authors and the trade benefited from the new legislation to a different extent.[91] Moreover, this new legislation created a platform for addressing the international issues of copyright in the future and 'made it possible for the United Kingdom to become part of a network of international protection for copyright and other intellectual property'.[92] Over 60 years later, the Copyright Act of 1911 endorsed the copyright protection model institutionalised in a series of international copyright agreements,[93] of which the primary one was the Berne Convention of 1886.[94] Following the Berne Convention, the Copyright Act of 1911 expanded the duration of copyright to the author's lifetime plus 50 years.

2.1.3 Copyright expansion under the 1911 Act

The progression from the Copyright Act 1842 to the Copyright Act 1911 does not merely entail an expansion of copyright duration from the author's natural life plus 42 years to the author's lifetime plus 50 years. An eight-year expansion would by no means be significant. Since 1842 Britain had followed a path of unprecedented transformation and progress. 'Until the middle of the nineteenth century, information didn't move all that much faster than man.'[95] Since the middle of the century, the pace of information transmission and the advance of technological networks such as the railway had been no more than a partial picture of the whole Industrial Revolution. Nevertheless, for the publishing industry, which is in general perceived as 'a popular information and entertainment industry',[96] the impacts of technological and organisational innovations in information and communication had been more profound as the process of creative destruction was proceeding since the middle of the Victorian age.

In the process of creative destruction, the interaction between technological innovations and organisational innovations is straightforward. Technological innovations provide a material foundation for organisational innovations. In turn, organisational innovations establish a wide platform for diffusing technological innovations. Under some circumstances, the imitators of technological innovations might become the innovators of organisational innovations.[97] In other situations, technological innovators would learn how to finance or trade their knowledge through imitating others' organisational innovations. The 1840s – the decade in which the British public, who were concerned with book publishing, continued debating the issues surrounding Talfourd's Copyright Bill and Parliament eventually passed it – was critical for both technological and organisational innovations in the UK publishing industry.[98] Since the 1842 Copyright Act, both the authorship (the innovators with regard to copyright) and entrepreneurship (either innovators or imitators of technological and organisational innovations with regard to copyright) had been encouraged or motivated to a great extent.[99] Accordingly, the interaction between technological innovations and organisational innovations within the industry had become more palpable.

The technological innovations in book publication started to have far-reaching effects and created the real prospect of organisational innovations, such as cheap print identified as 'the information price revolution',[100] and related business opportunities in general.[101] In particular, the mid-nineteenth century saw printing technology advancing.[102] Power presses were introduced.[103] Steam presses began to have a strong impact on the UK publishing industry and promoted a series of organisational innovations such as the part-book and cost-saving production methods.[104] Photography, invented in 1839, and lithography, which were created as technological innovations, transformed certain areas of publishing and initiated a new era for the book trade.[105] In the meantime, railways in Britain began to expand at a remarkable rate during this period.[106] As a result, a national market was established in stages. In the 1870s, the publications for mass education, academic communities, and non-fiction as organisational innovations boomed and transformed the publishing market.[107] In 1895, a new brand of typesetting mechanisation advertised as 'Linotype' was introduced into Britain.[108]

Technological and organisational innovations were able to build a basis of flexibility and economies of scale into the publishing market.[109] Correspondingly, the industry structure in the area under pressure from these innovations would continue on a course of transformation. Indeed, the publishing industry structure in the UK experienced an undulating reconstruction process after the 1842 Copyright Act. The 1842 Act protected the property ownership of copyright but in no way ensured a sensible commercial interest from the property. The Act itself, as previously noted, was the antithesis of the Victorian mainstream, which embraced the principle of the free market. However, a copyright-type monopoly would not impede the mechanism of the free market. Rather, an author-oriented legislation like the 1842

Act can only diversify the marketplace and smooth the market process in publishing as technological and organisational innovations bridged rather than divided the link between authorship and entrepreneurship.[110] Meanwhile, these innovations also pressured authors and publishers to commercialise existing copyright works and to exploit new opportunities.[111] Thus, an institutionalised copyright expansion in the 1842 Act enhanced the level of competition in the market under the pressure of creative destruction. In fact, after the 1842 Act, the UK publishing industry was so contestable that the Booksellers' Association, facing severe competition, still made efforts to establish 'a general system of fixed prices for books'.[112] This encountered strong opposition from the mainstream and eventually failed. In 1852, the Booksellers' Association itself lifted restrictions on competition as an enduring aspect of free-market industry structure renovated.[113]

The reformation of a free-market industry structure after the 1842 Act continued the process of reconstructing the regulatory regime in publishing that the Copyright Act of 1836 had started.[114] As previously stated, one path of the process was to adjust the old copyright registration system. Nevertheless, this adjusting process took considerable time. In 1911, the old copyright registration system was finally abolished under the new Copyright Act.[115] Of course, the eventual abandonment of the copyright registration system was just one of the developments in the period from 1842 to 1911.[116] This period also saw other aspects of the reconstruction of the regulatory regime in the UK publishing industry, for which the revocation of tax on paper and the formation of the Net Book Agreement were central. The market climate that echoed the 1842 Act and the reformation of industry structure after the Act compelled the need for change. As the publishing market was getting larger, freer, and more competitive, the tax on paper became a bottleneck for the further growth of the industry. Facing such paper duties, a loose alliance encompassing the groups from free trades, social liberals, philanthropists, and publishers was formed to fight the same tax but for different purposes. This was the same alliance that worked for the reforms of copyright law, including the enacting of the 1842 Act, in the 1840s. In 1861, the tax on paper was eliminated.[117]

With the reformation of a free-market industry structure, plus the end of tax on paper and the ongoing reform of the old copyright registration system, market mechanisms in the publishing field worked more efficiently. However, the market forces in an open and unregulated environment also engendered uncertainties and risks for publishers, authors, and booksellers. The failure of price-fixing efforts in 1852 had not convinced the players in this field that an unrestricted trade could be in their best interests. After the aborted price-fixing attempt, publishers – in spite of their opposition to price fixing – started to seek a new regulatory approach to protecting their interests in a marketplace with intensive competition and soaring risk. In 1890, Frederick Macmillan, a young but well-established publisher, proposed that a publisher should be able to impose a fixed or 'net' book retail price with which a bookseller could enjoy a discount but could not sell the book for any less. This proposal received positive responses from booksellers and publishers. In 1899, the Net Book Agreement was finalised.[118]

In general, in the period from the 1842 Copyright Act to the 1911 Copyright Act, the developments of industry structure and regulatory framework as the paths of creative destruction in the publishing industry adhered to a conviction of *laissez faire* and minimal government. Meanwhile, during the same period, new trends of competitive positioning strategies surfaced under a robust market mechanism within the publishing trade. One of the new directions was an ongoing convergence of strategic business partnership among publishers, booksellers, and authors from reforming the Copyright Law in 1842 to reaching the Net Book Agreement at the end of the nineteenth century. Publishers, booksellers, and authors all realised their 'mutual interdependence'[119] within the publishing industry and engaged in 'dealing fairly with the different interest groups within it and around it'.[120] This strategic convergence scheme can swing the market positions or partnerships among players in the field and would in turn foster a recurrent adaptation of structural and regulatory arrangements as a process of prolonging creative destruction. In particular, when plunging into a mass market with cheap print,[121] this strategic convergence scheme should play a more significant role than ever in ameliorating the industry structure and regulatory approach in the field.

In such a larger, freer, dynamic, and more competitive publishing marketplace, the technological assumption in the field tended more towards a technology-opportunity premise than a technology-efficiency inducement. The succession of motive power in printing/publishing from water and steam to electricity[122] resulted in a factory system that broadened the scale of both printing and publishing operations. Eventually, printing and publishing operations proceeded more independently and, in the Victorian era, each became a distinct industry.[123] The progression of motive power, the formation of the factory system, and the separation between printing and publishing overhauled the technological assumption in publishing, and expanded the publishing business domestically and internationally in the late nineteenth century.

On the whole, 'the British book trade in the nineteenth century became a modern industry in every way'.[124] As the dynamic process of creative destruction advanced alongside the Industrial Revolution, technological forces, social forces, and market forces interacted and exerted diverse effects on the growth of the Victorian publishing industry. The doctrine of *laissez-faire* and minimal government intervention became the mainstream in the business community, and the publishing industry was no exception. In a freer and more competitive publishing market, organisational and technological innovations were vital for business operation and growth. More and more, while the industry structure had been reconstructed and the regulatory approach had been adapted, competition strategies were renovated and technological assumptions remodelled. As the market broadened and toughened, the issues of literary property – mainly copyright concerns – surfaced as one of foremost legal battles of the century. In the first half of the nineteenth century, the duration of copyright had twice been expanded. In the latter part, as the national publishing market matured, international commerce became essential for British publishers and authors.[125] In 1886, as a founding member, the UK signed the Berne Convention, an international copyright treaty that stipulated the principle of national treatment and the minimum protection of copyright duration as author's life plus 50 years.[126] The Berne Convention was a reaction to the internationalisation of forces that steered the interaction between domestic and international publishing markets. At the turn of the twentieth century, the Net Book Agreement came into effect and framed a constant arrangement for publishing business operations.[127] All of these events or actions were not accidents but an adaptive response to the pressure of creative destruction in the industry while the major players in the field – publishers, booksellers, and authors – apprehended their mutual interests and assumed the interaction among copyright expansion, industrial growth, innovation, and profitability. The Copyright Act of 1911 followed the same path and 'rationalised the pre-existing law',[128] including the Copyright Acts of 1814 and 1842.

2.1.4 Copyright expansion under the 1988 Act

In the late twentieth century, 'a symbiotic relationship between technology and copyright law'[129] was further revealed in the UK publishing industry. Although the technological change in the field in the first part of the twentieth century was inconsequential, 'from the mid-1950s onwards, however, a series of technical innovations wrought profound change on the business of publishing in almost every aspect'.[130] Especially in the late twentieth century, the application of digital technology in publishing greatly transformed many aspects of the business processes, such as (but not limited to) standardisation, financial management, records management, and stock monitoring.[131] Certainly, the UK publishing industry is not the only industry that has been modernised by digital and other general-purpose technologies.[132] In fact, these general-purpose technologies have revolutionised the whole information industry, which includes not only publishing but also the audio recording and movie-making industries. As a result, a convergence occurred between the UK information and media industries.[133]

Meanwhile, since the mid-1980s, the UK publishing industry has gradually faced challenges from the force of globalisation as well.[134] The copyright expansion in the UK Copyright, Designs and Patents Act 1988 and the Duration of Copyright and Rights in Performance Regulations 1995, which implements the EU Duration Directive that endorses copyright expansion in the UK, were the obvious indications of both digitalisation and globalisation.[135] At the end of the twentieth century, 'British publishing was part of the global network of media, entertainment and leisure industries, as well as the burgeoning information industry in its multiple manifestations'.[136] Under the forces of digitalisation and globalisation, 'the rosy Schumpeterian picture', as Landes and Posner termed,[137] in the UK publishing industry in the period from 1911 to 1996, became much clearer.[138]

2.2 Legal arguments for copyright expansion

Chapter 2.1 reveals that copyright expansion is a series of legal responses to the complex or dynamic forces of creative destruction in the UK book publishing industry. In a broad sense, the legal arguments for copyright expansion could, of course, include legislative and judicial reasoning for sustaining diverse purposes – economic, moral, governmental, or social – for the legal extension of copyright term. However, in a narrow sense, the legal arguments for copyright expansion refer to the legislative and judicial perspectives on the governmental purpose of extending copyright term. In this regard, the legal arguments for copyright expansion contain regulatory and harmonisation arguments for extending copyright term.

2.2.1 *Regulatory argument for copyright expansion*

In the early sixteenth century, long before the Statute of Anne, British writers, publishers, and booksellers already took collective action to 'prevent free-rider[s] in the publishing industry through the creation of a quasi-proprietary publisher's copyright in printed texts'.[139] Their actions had a profound impact on the evolution of UK copyright law and remained unchallenged for a long period until digitalisation, as a new and innovative force, came to light.[140] Copyright expansions in the United Kingdom, particularly the extension of protection duration in 1814, 1842, and 1911, also reflected this initial activity to a different extent, while these statutory expansions have evolved as responses to the pressure of creative destruction in the UK publishing industry.

Meanwhile, once these legal or policy initiatives have been institutionalised in the common law or in a legislative process, the legal institutions will serve as a regulatory regime and an intermediate factor that relays the market process. As a regulatory regime, copyright institutions serve to 'regulate the commercial exploitation of intellectual products'.[141] According to Professor Wu, the role of copyright law as a regulatory regime is to regulate the 'competition among rival disseminators'[142] and 'among natural rivals in the world of packaged information'.[143] Moreover, 'as the pace of technological change accelerates, copyright's role in setting the conditions for competition is quickly becoming important, even challenging for the primacy the significance of copyright's encouragement of authorship'.[144] Explicitly, with the advance of technological innovations, the weight of copyright's authorship function as a goal of rights protection yields to the importance of copyright's regulatory function as a mean of rights protection. Accordingly, the neoclassical doctrine that 'regulation is undesirable' should be re-examined as a technological progression likely to cause 'a high degree of regulation flux'.[145]

Copyright's dual role as both the *goal* and the *mean*, as identified by Wu, is indeed a reflection of the substance–procedure distinction of rights protection. This dual role is, at the least, no less creditable than the idea–expression dichotomy for analysing the rationale of copyright law. Copyright law as a regulatory regime has been designed to achieve certain goals such as encouraging authorship and promoting creativity or growth in the market process of information products. Of course, whether or not these goals are achievable, and whether or not the process engenders substantive protection, is another matter – and is the ongoing subject matter of this book. Placing copyright expansion in the market process and analysing its role in regulating a dynamic competition will be the first step to understanding the goal–mean dual role of copyright protection. In particular, the applicability of this dual role in exploring the UK publishing industry should be considered. Combining Lessig's modalities of regulation and Murray's view of regulatory mechanism under Schumpeter's scheme of creative destruction will help explain the regulatory argument of copyright expansion in the industrial organisation and in the growth of the UK publishing sector.

In *Code and Other Laws of Cyberspace*, Lessig outlined a regulatory model based upon four modalities of regulation that he used to explain the interaction between constrictive protection of creative property and cultural development in the information age. In the model, four modalities or constraints that regulate people's activities are identified: law, norm, market, and architecture. Law, with an emphasis on copyright law, regulates behaviours through threatening punishment. Norm restricts people by endorsing communal values. Market confines human actions under certain cost structures, while architecture restrains individuals by way of technological encroachment.[146] According to Lessig, these four modalities interact. Restrictions or freedom under one modality may be underpinned or undermined by another or others. Among all of the four modalities, 'law has a special role in affecting the three'.[147] More importantly, all of the four modalities can change and 'we must track these changes over time'.[148] In other words, the process of the interaction among four modalities would need more attentions.

Lessig further explored the applicability of his model in the copyright industries, especially in the content industry. He singled out copyright expansion in duration and scope as one dramatic aspect of the US copyright law as a regulatory regime in US copyright industries over the past 210 years.[149] Corresponding with this change in the 'law' modality is the industrial concentration of the copyright industries.[150] As a result, a strong 'market' modality could strengthen copyright's legal institution and right-holders' market power. In the meantime, the 'architecture' modality also becomes more robust with the advance of technology. Lessig did realise that the changing technology would have 'a profound effect on the content industry's way of doing business'[151] but 'the way of doing business' itself should be a big concern. He insisted that, while the changing technology enfeebled an existing 'way of doing business', the government should not accordingly endorse a strong 'architecture' modality for maintaining the old 'way of doing business' that the copyright holders pushed for.[152] Instead, to put up with the changing technology, according to Lessig, 'an adjustment to restore the balance that has traditionally defined copyright's regulation – a weakening of that regulation, to strengthen creativity'[153] – is needed. Eventually, Lessig pursued a constitutional check-balance approach to scrutinising the regulation of the copyright industries in a free market. 'In a free society, with a free market, supported by free enterprise and free trade, the government's role is not to support one way of doing business against others. Its role is not to pick winners and protect them against loss. If the government did this generally, then we would never have any progress . . . A world in which competitors with new ideas must fight not only the market but also the government is a world in which competitors with new ideas will not succeed.'[154]

Obviously, what Lessig sought was a complete market with perfect competition for the copyright works. However, this type of market may not exist. The appeal of Lessig's framework is that it can inspire a cohesive exploration of the interaction between copyright expansion, market power, technology, and the firm's strategic operation ('way of doing business'), and a consistent investigation into the process of interaction in the copyright industries. What is further needed is an analytic framework for outlining the mechanism of the process of interaction in order to analyse the reciprocal response between the copyright industries and copyright expansion, the goal–mean dichotomy of copyright's role, and, eventually, the relation between copyright and industrial growth. Murray's and Scott's view of regulatory mechanism can serve the purpose.

Murray and Scott offered an analytic framework of regulatory mechanisms in the new media based upon Lessig's modalities of regulation.[155] In their terms, the diverse and interlocking way of regulating signals the control issues in the new media. They identified four institutional arrangements of a regulatory regime – *hierarchical*, *competition*, *community*, and *design* through a renovation of Lessig's four modalities of regulation – and defined three essential elements of regulatory control – *standard setting*, *information gathering*, and *behaviour modification* – under each institutional arrangement of a regulatory regime. For example, under the hierarchical arrangement corresponding with the 'law' modality in Lessig's account, standard setting is instituted under law and other formalised rules, information gathering is performed by certain agencies or third parties, and behaviour modification is achieved through enforcing law and rules. Under the competition-based arrangement corresponding with the market modality in Lessig's account, standard setting is initiated by the price–quality ratio, information gathering is monitored by the demand side, and behaviour modification is achieved through the aggregate of decisions on the demand side.[156]

According to Murray and Scott, an extensive application of their above review of Lessig's four modalities of regulation to institutional choices is necessary for an understanding of how to choose proper institutional arrangement(s) under a regulatory regime for public policy objectives. They argued that no single institutional arrangement under a regulatory regime alone, whether it be *hierarchical*, *competition*, *community*, or *design*, could serve to achieve a public policy objective. Instead, hybrid forms of these institutional arrangements will be desirable. They accordingly presented a variety of hybrid forms that join these institutional arrangements together in diverse ways. Within each hybrid form, hierarchical arrangement is deployed as an instrument to stimulate diverse types of industrial growth in the context of competition, community, or design in the new media industries. Among these hybrid forms, a combination of hierarchical and competition arrangements is initiated in the new media industries. Under this hybrid form, a hierarchical arrangement of regulation is applied to some large or dominating firms in these industries, while other small or less powerful firms are still controlled by market elements. Thus, a competitive space is still located in an industrial continuum from a hierarchical arrangement at one end to a market arrangement at the other end.[157] The *standard setting, information gathering,* and *behaviour modification* in the hybrid arrangement are complicated with the conflicts between the incumbent and the insurgent, market entry and market barriers, and innovators and imitators. This type of competitive space can be classified as a contestable market as defined in William Baumol's presidential address at the 94th meeting of the American Economic Association in 1981. In a contestable market, the pressure from potential entrances can sustain the competitive nature of a market with no perfect competition.[158]

In *The Regulation of Cyberspace*, Murray further specified the framework and placed it into a broad perspective on the interaction among regulation, technology, and social change.[159] According to him, 'Traditional regulatory discourse has been informed by an understanding of law and society'.[160] After reviewing five models of a regulatory regime – *Public Interest, Capture/Cyclical Model, Economic Theory, Public Choice Theory,* and *Historic Institutionalism,* Murray identified their common weakness – a general assumption shared by all five models – that the change to the regulatory settlement should be the outcome of a change in policy. This assumption, according to Murray, is no help for understanding the drive of regulatory change. To understand this drive, especially the drive for change in the new media, Murray proposed a new model through differentiating socio-legal modalities of regulation in the physical space from socio-technological-legal modalities in the information space. Socio-legal modalities of regulation can be categorised using Lessig's model of four modalities of regulation and encompass three of them – law, market, and norms. The fourth modality – architecture – consists of environmental modalities.[161] That is, socio-legal modalities of regulation can be considered as one component of Lessig's model, with environmental modalities as another. Environmental modalities have been applied in some areas of regulatory policy such as transport policy, while socio-legal modalities were employed in the communications industries.[162] Meanwhile, socio-legal modalities of regulation can also be classified as a competition-based institutional arrangement under a regulatory regime in the Murray–Scott model. Under the competition-based arrangement of regulation, the drive behind the changes to the regulatory settlement should not be the outcome of a change in policy. Rather, the competition between regulators and regulatory modalities thrust the changes in the regulatory settlement.[163]

A subsequent question is 'Which force functions behind the competition between regulators and regulatory modalities?' Murray implied that technological innovation would be the driving force. However, both systems of modalities – socio-legal and environmental modalities of regulation respectively – fail to include technology as an analytic element for exploring regulation. Accordingly, both fail to recognise technological innovation as the driving force behind the competition between regulators and regulatory modalities. Integrating the two systems and taking technology into account as an endogenous factor in the evolution of regulation is a necessary step for examining the trends and changes in regulation. For this consideration, Murray resorted to a socio-technological-legal theory for envisaging the interaction between regulation, competition, and technology in the information market.[164] Of course, Murray's framework is designed to understand a special information space – cyberspace. Is his framework applicable to the copyright industries? The answer should be positive. The new media industries should belong to the copyright industries in particular, or to the information industries in general.

Lessig's model of modalities, the Murray–Scott model, and Murray's integrative framework of regulatory mechanism are compatible with Schumpeter's scheme of creative destruction. Schumpeter considered 'the interaction between institutional forms and entrepreneurial activity' as 'a major topic for further inquiry' and stressed 'the "shaping" influence of the former and the "bursting" influence of the latter' as a starting point.[165] It seemed that, through highlighting the 'shaping' influence, Schumpeter regarded institutional forms as regulatory regimes that guide the actions of entrepreneurs and their firms. In the meantime, entrepreneurial activity under the pressure of creative destruction, including (but not limited to) technological and organisational innovations, would also disturb the existing institutional arrangements and demand new ones. In particular, when realising the depressing performance of market forces and related institutions under a dynamic competition, Schumpeter left a 'space for a more general theory of regulation'.[166] Wu took up the 'space' through a specific regulation/competition theory of copyright law and defined the function of copyright law as regulating the 'competition among rival disseminators'[167] or managing the 'competition among natural rivals in the world of packaged information'.[168] Murray's integration extended Wu's framework and specified the change and complexity of a regulatory regime while taking account of technology as an essential element in regulatory settlement.[169]

Historically, regulation is 'part of the tradition of the British system of common law'.[170] With the advance of technology, under the pressure of creative destruction, the change of regulatory regimes and reconstruction of market institutions took place in diverse ways in the UK communications industry.[171] As explored in Chapter 2.1, the same trend has proceeded in the UK publishing industry as well. That is, both industrial fields have witnessed 'a process of adaptation of regulatory regimes to a series of technologies that have affected industry or market structure and regulatory rules and institutions. The Internet is the latest in the series and the process of rethinking regulation is ongoing'.[172] Under the circumstances, both the 'shaping' influence of institutions and the 'bursting' influence of entrepreneurial activity in Schumpeter's terms become imperative in these industries. To survive or thrive, it has become a norm for the firms to 'compete through the regulatory process for the market structure and rules that suit their interests'.[173]

Both 'regulating the competition among rival disseminators' and 'competing through the regulatory process' are cohesive courses in the regulatory process. The competition between regulators and regulatory modalities – specifically, the regulatory competition among diverse institutional arrangements of regulatory regimes – synthesises the two courses under the pressure of creative destruction in the information industries. To achieve a regulatory settlement, the cooperation among diverse institutional arrangements of regulatory regimes may also be necessary from time to time. However, 'the harnessing of one regulatory modality through the application of another is more likely to lead to further regulatory competition, due to the complexity of the network environment'.[174] Thus, under the pressure of creative destruction, a certain type of competition can still be sustained and the anti-competitive effects can be minimised in the information market. Of course, a regulatory competition under the special industry or market structure and institutional environment is expected to be a biased one. As Murray put it, 'It is highly unlikely that content producers, media corporations and copyright holders will allow for a neutral system designed to protect cultural property and creativity at the cost of loss of control over their products'.[175]

In the UK publishing industry, copyright was initially favourably biased towards the established guilds by regulating the challenge from new technology and related socio-economic interests. Copyright expansion in scope served the same policy goal.[176] By the same token, this will be true of copyright expansion in duration. No matter what their position, the firms in the copyright industries, like those in the other information industries, should confront both the 'shaping' influence of institutions and the 'bursting' influence of entrepreneurial activity from other firms within the conflicting institutional arrangements or modalities of regulatory regimes under the pressure of creative destruction. Copyright expansion in duration will subject entrepreneurs and their firms' conduct to the governance of regulatory rules in Fuller's terms[177] under the conflicting institutional arrangements or modalities among hierarchy, competition, community, and design by means of standard setting, information gathering, and behaviour modification. This is the mechanism depicted in Murray's framework that can translate legal and regulatory arrangements into entrepreneurial strategies and the firm's activities. A socio-technological-legal theory is indeed a mirror of Schumpeter's perspective of creative destruction that refracts the dynamic reality of the information space and will serve the common goal for exploring the regulatory competition and its complexity in a process of creative destruction. In this sense, a socio-technological-legal theory is no different from an economic-technological-legal theory that could also be inspired by Schumpeter's perspective of creative destruction.

In brief, placing the legal issues on copyright expansion into the perspective of regulatory modalities and mechanism will shed light on an investigation into legal arguments for copyright expansion and the copyright-growth relation from Schumpeter's perspective. However, this approach is not to simply equalise a legal expansion of copyright with a government's regulation in a narrow sense. Rather, from a broad sense, copyright expansion will exert a regulatory effect on the entrepreneurs and their firms in the copyright industries. From a European approach to regulation and Fuller's view of law, as Murray explored,[178] copyright expansion as an institutional arrangement under a regulatory regime can mutate entrepreneurial activities and firms' actions under the 'shaping' influence of institutions and the 'bursting' influence of entrepreneurial activity in Schumpeter's account. No matter how imperative marginal effect and profit maximisation will be, no matter whether or not a firm is involved in a legal dispute over copyright,[179] a firm in the copyright industry should function as a creative or innovative institute to cope with both the 'shaping' influence and the 'bursting' influence. Of course, the function of copyright expansion is intricate under the complex interaction among regulation, technology, and socio-economic changes in a process of creative destruction.

2.2.2 Harmonisation argument for copyright expansion

In Chapter 2.1, one of the rationales behind UK copyright expansion in duration, copyright expansion as an adaptive response to the pressure of creative destruction, is explored against the historical background of the UK publishing industry from a Schumpeterian perspective. The historical logic of UK copyright expansion, which still persists under the contemporary UK copyright regime, reveals the essence of copyright protection *per se*. Clearly, the need to expand the term of copyright indicates that perpetual copyright has been consigned to history, and a limited term for copyright can afford the space for balancing public interests and private incentives. As perpetual copyright became history, legal pragmatism surfaced as the guiding principle for pursuing a longer but still limited term of copyright.[180] Of course, under the current UK copyright system, as information technologies advance, the legal rationales behind the statutes, court cases, and international treaties involving the relation between copyright expansion and the growth of copyright industries can be expected to change to some extent.[181] In general, legal pragmatism is still the guiding philosophy of copyright expansion as an enduring way of protecting copyright.[182] In particular, the pressure of publishers and the demand of international harmonisation are also the driving forces behind the contemporary copyright expansion in duration in the UK.[183]

The worldwide attention focused on the relation between intellectual property rights and industrial growth reached a turning point in the 1990s when the transition toward the information age speeded up as the Internet and digital communications expanded.[184] Before then, the World Intellectual Property Organization (WIPO) was the principal intergovernmental organisation for the international protection of intellectual property rights since its establishment in 1967.[185] The two major international treaties of intellectual property protection – the Paris Convention and the Berne Convention – are administered by WIPO. However, WIPO's enforcing power is extremely limited.[186]

WIPO's unpromising performance compelled the US, as a key campaigner for international protection of intellectual property rights, to seek a more powerful mechanism for taking substantial actions in order to enforce the existing international treaties.[187] The General Agreement on Tariffs and Trade (GATT), established in 1947, was a ready establishment for the international protection of intellectual property rights. In 1994, after a series of laborious negotiations, the participants in the Uruguay Round of GATT eventually reached agreement on Trade-Related Aspects of Intellectual Property Rights (TRIPS) and decided to establish the World Trade Organization (WTO). In 1995, the WTO officially came into being and, consequently, GATT ended its mission and functions, and TRIPS became a cohesive part of the WTO settlement. Since then, the international protection of intellectual property rights has been directed under the framework of the WTO and WIPO. The legal foundation of TRIPS is the Berne Convention, as amended in 1967.[188] According to both TRIPS and WTO, all WTO member countries must adjust or amend their legal systems to adapt to the TRIPS requirements. Minimum but high international standards, national treatment and most-favoured-nation terms, antitrust measures, transparency and efficiency of enforcement procedures, and combination of civil and criminal remedies are accentuated in TRIPS.[189]

As 'harmonisation is seen to be a desirable objective',[190] copyright expansion in duration is harmonised among nations.[191] Under the legal regimes of TRIPS and WTO, the term of 'life of the author and fifty years after his death' is the minimum requirement of copyright protection in duration for all member states, including the US and the UK. In Europe, under the EC Term Directive, the minimum requirement for copyright duration for all members is the term of 'life plus seventy years following the death of author'.[192] In the US, to fulfil the legal requirements of TRIPS–WTO and to model the EC Term Directive, the duration of copyright protection has been extended from 'life plus fifty years' in 1978 to 'life plus seventy years' since 1998[193] under both the US 1976 Copyright Act and the US 1998 Copyright Term Extension

Act.[194] In the UK, the Copyright Designs and Patents Act of 1988, the Duration of Copyright and Rights in Performances Regulations 1995 (which implements the EU Duration Directive that endorses copyright expansion in the UK), and eventually the European Parliament and Council Directive 2006 as a reinforced version of harmonisation, reconfirmed that the copyright duration for literary, dramatic, musical, and artistic works extends to the life of the author plus 70 years.[195]

2.3 Economic justifications for copyright expansion

Two main theoretical foundations for copyright, the moral justification and the instrumental justification, have been deployed throughout its period of operation.[196] The moral justification is based on the doctrine of natural rights and focuses on the justice and fairness aspects of copyright protection. In this view, authors or creators should be awarded copyright as an exclusive privilege on their creative expressions because their personality or labour has been inherently embedded in, and instinctively constituted a natural ingredient of, their creations. Granting copyright is a natural right and a morally desirable endorsement for what authors or creators deserve.[197] Thus, 'copyright is the positive law's realisation of this self-evident, ethical precept'.[198] In contrast, the instrumental justification, anchored in the utilitarian principle, is concerned with a range of economic rights in securing copyright for rights holders and emphasises the functional mechanism of copyright for achieving certain policy goals.

The instrumental justification for copyright has been conventionally defined as an incentive argument.[199] This definition needs further examination. In history, the origin of copyright did not indicate that copyright law was designed to provide incentives for creativity or original expression.[200] Rather, British copyright law originated with publishers' monopoly and the government's censorship. The Statute of Anne, the first modern copyright law, was to some extent a continuing assurance of publishers' monopolistic power,[201] even if such power was also constrained by the legislature. Meanwhile, although the reward for authorship was specified in the Statute, the honour was more symbolic than substantial and 'the codification of authorship was merely an appeal to a straw man'.[202] In contrast, 'the publisher is the real player in the legal and commercial game'.[203]

Of course, the original orientation in copyright law cannot necessarily and fully determine copyright's function or role in the later development. However, no matter how copyright evolves, on the one hand, not all theories championing the instrumental justification make the incentive-based arguments for copyright law in a narrow sense. For instance, some economic models of copyright elaborating on the instrumental justification, such as the neoclassical model, do not necessarily formulate an incentive-oriented reasoning; at least, not in a specific or conventional sense.[204] Of course, in a general and broad sense, the neoclassical model does advise an incentive-oriented rationale for endorsing or expanding copyright in order to pursue an aggregate efficiency for society as a whole. On the other hand, in theory, the internal logic of a moral justification would not overlook the incentive factor for copyright protection. Substantiating the integrity of authorship and rewarding creators for their original activities, as a moral justification, would very likely fuel some kinds of non-commercial incentives (such as fame or adulation) to further creativities. Compared with the commercial incentives (such as pecuniary motivations) embraced in the instrumental justification, non-commercial incentives endorsed in the moral justification might also fulfil a functional purpose for promoting creativity in general and industrial creativity/growth in particular, but indirectly and implicitly. Nevertheless, these two main justifications as 'the same rhetoric' have been 'invoked to justify two centuries of copyright expansion'.[205]

Under an instrumental justification, the economic rights for copyright holders in general include their reproduction and distribution rights in exploiting their creative expressions or products. Bestowing on copyright holders these economic and monopolistic prerogatives over their creative expressions or products provides a necessary incentive to create more copyright-based products and, as a result, to enhance a society's total production or value at an optimal level.[206] In particular, when copyright expansion as an incontrovertible fact has become much broader and deeper than ever over the last two decades in the new digital environment, the instrumental justification for copyright and the copyright–creativity/growth relation should surface in certain new dimensions. This section explores these new dimensions under both the neoclassical and Schumpeterian models.

2.3.1 *The neoclassical model*

The core of the instrumental justification is to argue or validate that endorsing or expanding copyright could advance knowledge-intensive creations or enrich social production through adjusting a variety of incentives, either specific or general incentives or both, under certain endurable institutional arrangements. In other words, the instrumental justification contends that copyright law can promote original creations and should be the 'engine of creativity' through the institutional endorsement of incentives. Professor Netanel distinguished classical, neoclassical, and neoinstitutional standpoints and their various prospects as to how copyright could stimulate creative activities. However, he identified the classical view as the only one that can be classified as the incentive account.[207] This section, as above stated, explores the incentive rationale in a rather broad sense and regards the instrumental justification as an incentive-based explanation in general.

The optimist or neoclassicist perspectives that justify copyright protection and expansion for maximising productivity and efficiency, as Goldstein or Netanel explicated, should belong to the instrumental justification in a general or broad sense. Accordingly, this section adopts Netanel's categorisation but delineates the variations among the classical, neoclassical, and neoinstitutional standpoints as the instrumental justification from a slightly different angle. An examination of these variations will single out the implication of the neoclassical model and the significance of Schumpeter's model for exploring the relation between copyright expansion and the growth of the copyright industries.

1. The classical stance

Adam Smith is among those pioneering scholars who examined the role or function of copyright law from an economic approach. In his lectures, delivered at Glasgow University in 1762 and 1763, Smith made the following statement:

> The greatest part however of exclusive privileges are the creatures of the civil constitution of the country . . . Thus the inventor of a new machine or any other invention has the exclusive privilege of making the vending that invention for the space of 14 years by the law of this country, as a reward for his ingenuity, and it is probable that this is as equal as one as could be fallen upon . . .
>
> In the same manner the author of a new book has an exclusive privilege of publishing and selling his book for 14 years. Some indeed contend that the book is an entire new production of the authors and therefore ought in justice to belong to him and his heirs forever, and that no one should be allowed to print or sell it but those to whom he has given leave, by the very law of naturally reason. But it is evident that printing is no more than a speedy way of writing. Now suppose that a man had wrote a book and had lent it to another who took a copy of it, and that he afterwards sold this copy to a third; would there be here any reason to think the writer was injured. I can see none, and the same must hold equally with regard to printing. The only benefit one would have by writing a book, from the natural laws of reason, would be that he would have the first of the market and may be thereby a considerable gainer. The law has however granted him an exclusive privilege for 14 years, as an encouragement to the labours of learned men.[208]

When Smith delivered these lectures, the Statute of Anne that defined the property rights in writings was already enacted. His comments obviously reflected on the Statute. He cautiously asserted the connection between promoting creativity and protecting exclusive rights over creative works under copyright law. Professor Netanel convincingly suggests that both the Statute of Anne and Smith's reflection were based on an intuitive valuation of economic inducement invoked by copyright.[209] However, when placing Smith's statement into his whole theoretical system, it would become clear that Smith's reflection on copyright law expressed his faithfulness on the role of property rights in economic life. Smith's theoretical system consists of several key elements – the assumption of economic man, division of labour, property rights, free trade, and open market. In Smith's world, a society will maximise its total value when every rational person pursues her/his self-interest by maintaining her/his stakes in division of labour and voluntary exchanging with others in the open market under a suitable system of justice and law.[210] For Smith, 'an invisible hand' will coordinate economic activities through certain rules – laws or other institutions.[211] Nevertheless, in Smith's system, law should play a protective but passive role in defining property rights and advancing free trade.[212] Copyright law serves merely as a necessary condition for valuing the labours of creative works. Eventually, many other factors of industry or market structures (including 'law of demand and supply') would also be responsible for the valuation of creative works.

Thus, in Smith's mind, copyright law could still value the labours of creative works through protecting the 'exclusive privilege' (property rights) in writings and rewarding creative efforts.[213] According to Professor Hadfield, Smith's line of reasoning on copyright to some extent portended the role of copyright law in coping with the 'public goods' problem and 'economies of scale' under certain industry or market structures.[214] Smith offered two analogies for explicating the 'public goods' problem and the issue of 'economies of scale', respectively, whenever copyright had not been protected.

The analogy for explicating the 'public goods' problem was seen in a comparison between patent and copyright as quoted above from his Glasgow lectures. Smith argued that the same rationale lies behind both patent and copyright because both, without legal protection, could be exploited as a public good that is neither excludable nor rival. As Hadfield pointed out, 'In Smith's "injury" formulation it is precisely the "public good" nature of a literary work that disqualifies it as natural property'.[215] Following Smith's logic, protecting copyright and rewarding authors or creators, as defending patent, could overcome the 'public goods' problem in order to boost more creative products. Of course, Smith's reasoning on copyright law in his Glasgow lectures of 1762 and 1763 was original but primitive. Fourteen years later, in 1776, Smith published his *Wealth of Nations*, the paramount classic of economics, in which he furthered a justification of copyright law. To assert such justification, Smith presented an analogy between protection of copyright and operation of a joint stock company for illuminating the issue of 'economies of scale'. In other words, as Hadfield indicated, Smith underlined his concern on copyright's issue of 'economies of scale' in the context of the Joint Stock Company.[216]

In short, Adam Smith abandoned the natural law argument for copyright to some extent and ensured an economic reasoning for defending copyright law.[217] Smith's account of copyright not only explicates an economic appeal to incentive factors but also probes the economic rationale behind the incentive factors – the 'public goods' problem and the issue of 'economies of scale' – in light of property rights and industry or market structure. Nevertheless,

Smith's natural-law view of 'value' as 'the cost of production' in the long run and a function of the quantity–productivity of labour[218] still had a definite effect on his assessment of copyright. As his Glasgow lectures suggested, the importance of copyright counted on 'the real value of the work' and the inducement of the labour behind the work. It was the need to enlarge 'the real value of the work' and to entice the labour behind the work that necessitates copyright law for tackling the public goods problem and the issue of economies of scale. This stance, pursing 'the correct incentive'[219] for compensating 'the labours of learned men', did lay a classical foundation of 'incentive' for copyright justification[220] and copyright's policy directions.

2. The neoclassical stance

However, Smith's classical economics had still not been articulated in a clear and rigorous manner.[221] In particular, his account of copyright was still under-developed in many senses. Value theory as the foundation of classical economics 'was still in its infancy' in Smith's time.[222] Specifically, Smith's value theory, which assumes the universal nature of value, was not suitable for explaining the complexities of market forces, individual actions, and regulatory regimes in the process of economic development or industrial growth. At the end of the nineteenth century, classical economics gradually became outdated and neoclassical economists started to dominate the field of economics and shape the exploration of copyright issues.

'The neoclassics shifted from "value" to "utility".'[223] Utility is an abstract level of happiness or satisfaction that has been received from consuming certain products.[224] The theory of utility, especially marginal utility theory, initiated the marginal revolution in the 1870s[225] that comprised the mainstay of neoclassical economics.[226] Under the neoclassical scheme, the universality of value and labour is implausible. People are concerned with the specific utility of a product more than its general value. 'A commodity would no longer be valuable because it was costly to produce but because its services yielded utility.'[227]

Furthermore, for neoclassical economists, people as rational individuals not only adjust their behaviour on account of a cost–benefit assessment, as classical economists would assume, but also adapt their activities in view of such cost–benefit consideration at the margin. The increased utility from one more additional unit of product or service, the marginal utility of consuming a product or service rather than the labour behind a product or service as Adam Smith maintained, should be the determinant of the product or service's price from the neoclassical perspective.[228] Unlike Smith who even failed to address 'how an individual would maximise his own contribution',[229] neoclassical economists applied marginal utility theory to not only the demand side (consumption) but also the supply side (production) of the market. Under the neoclassical model, while both consumers and producers make their rational decisions on account of a cost–benefit assessment at the margin in a market of perfect competition, both should be able to maximise their interests and achieve an equilibrium that results in an ideal efficiency.[230]

Many economists, such as Stanley Jevons, Carl Menger, Leon Walras, and Alfred Marshall, contributed to the development of the marginalist school and neoclassical economics.[231] In particular, Marshall's supply–demand theory, integrating the marginalist school with some elements of classical economics, made neoclassical economics more rigorous and its analytical tools more robust.[232] In addition, Marshall delineated a fundamental criterion for appraising economic improvement and welfare maximisation. Marshall's criterion is quite simple – positive net worth. That is, in any society, if the total gains are greater than the total losses, economic progress is made and welfare maximisation is achieved, no matter who the winners or losers are and no matter who owns what.[233]

Classical economists, inspired by Adam Smith, focus on copyright's 'correct incentive', which would overcome the problem of 'public goods' through compensating the existing creators or writers for rewarding their creativity in the first place. However, Smith's view of 'correct incentive' for copyright was ambiguous.[234] Just as when viewing human nature in general, 'Smith would not have thought it sensible to treat man as a rational utility-maximiser'.[235] Accordingly, for classical economists under Smith's tradition, identifying a 'correct incentive' of copyright for fixing 'public goods' is always a tough issue while maximising rational utility is in question. In contrast, neoclassical economists, relying on marginal utility theory, clarify Smith's view of universal value and endorse a vision of relative utility – marginal utility – for envisaging the copyright issues.

Under the neoclassical system, while making their rational decisions on account of a cost-benefit assessment at the margin as indicated above, people are concerned with 'the highest marginal value'[236] rather than 'universal value'. 'Value was a function of marginal willingness to pay.'[237] In consequence, individuals or firms would maximise their total utilities whenever they could equalise their marginal values (marginal costs or benefits) across all trade transactions in the market.[238] Because people intend to consider additional or marginal values (additional or marginal costs or benefits) in trade transactions, 'the concept of value became forward- rather than backward-looking and became more concerned with potential for growth than previous commitment. The conceptual change had a remarkable impact on the legal valuation of certain property rights'.[239] Of course, in principle, 'certain property rights' include intellectual property rights. That is, from the neoclassical perspective, the legal valuation of property rights (including intellectual property rights) is an ongoing process for maximising future and potential welfare.[240]

Concerning copyright, for neoclassical economists, pursuing copyright's 'correct incentive' through compensating the existing creators and rewarding their creativity, as classical economists would endorse, is no longer a priority. Rather, neoclassical economists regard copyright law as a prospective mechanism that should effectively smooth market transactions and efficiently maximise production of creative products through realising 'full profit potential' and appreciating full values for creative works,[241] in order to encourage future creations from both existing and potential creators. Neoclassical economists attempt to deal with the efficiency issue of 'public goods' in producing and distributing creative works rather than the mere anxiety of the 'public goods' problem from the classical perspective. Consequently, neoclassical economists perceive the relation between copyright expansion and creativity as a prospective state–market interaction on account of a general incentive that would induce the creativity from potential creators or writers. In other words, for neoclassical economists, endorsing or expanding copyright not only ensures a specific incentive that would retrospectively reward existing creators or writers for their creativity as classical economists suggested, but also asserts a general incentive that would prospectively provoke the potential creators or writers in the general public to value any creative works to the full, as copyright law encourages.

Nevertheless, both classical and neoclassical economists do share some common concerns. Both sides seek to exploit the incentive factors of endorsing or expanding copyright in order to overcome market failures,[242] such as monopoly and public goods, in producing or distributing creative works. As a result, both sides agree that protecting and expanding copyright should stimulate creativity. One main aspect of their differences lies in their contentions on the level or scope of protecting or expanding copyright. For classical economists, a certain level of protection and expansion should be sufficient for exploiting the incentive factors. On the contrary, neoclassical economists presume that the incentive factors would never be efficiently exploited until full-level protection or expansion of copyright has been ensured.[243]

In the classical economics expounded by Adam Smith, economic progress or industrial growth should be a natural process along with capital accumulation and market competition. The 'public goods' problem and diseconomies of scale would be momentary and, therefore, limited copyright protection as a temporary monopoly should be able to deal with the issue of incentive. In the nineteenth century, a further observation was made that the production cost of an original creative work enduringly, rather than temporarily, surpasses its reproduction cost.[244]

When this observation was further analysed in marginal utility theory for assessing the production and distribution of creative works, the relation between incentive and the level of copyright protection or expansion becomes much clearer. For a producer or creator of creative works to maximise her/his profits, she/he should equalise her/his marginal utility[245] so that the marginal cost should be equal to the marginal benefit of a literary creative work. By equalising the marginal cost with the marginal benefit, an efficient goal would be achieved as neoclassical economists would expect. However, due to the sizeable contrast between the two (high production cost and low reproduction cost), without full-level protection or expansion of copyright, equalising marginal utility with the marginal benefit would not be able to recover the high production cost and, therefore, incentive would not be fully exploited. Of course, equalising marginal utility with the marginal benefit and exploiting full incentive are only assumed in an analytical model of neoclassical economics. In reality, the interaction between marginal utility and incentive is subject to further inspections.

3. The neoinstitutionalist stance

The neoclassical view could be perceived as a hard-line justification of copyright protection and expansion. Neoinstitutionalist economists embrace the basics of the neoclassical approach but elaborate upon an open outlook for examining the legal issues in broad socio-economic contexts. Like classical economists, the neoclassical economists in general, although recognising the complexity of market processes, still assume a complete market with a perfect competition as an economic norm; accordingly, other non-market factors, such as state intervention, are perceived as exogenous factors that would help overcome a variety of market failures for restoring the complete market process. Those non-market factors, including law or policy, should be reframed as economic or market elements for analytical purposes.[246] Ronald Coase terms this kind of analysis 'black-board economics'.[247]

The neoinstitutionalist position, under Coase's framework, disparages 'black-board economics' and stands up for the reality. From a neoinstitutionalist approach, the conception of 'market failure' may only possess an analytic meaning. In reality, due to the existence of transaction costs and other costs, many so-called non-market factors such as institutional arrangements or environments should be scrutinised as part of the complete market process.[248] Therefore, legal, political, economic, or social institutions should be integrated as endogenous factors in an inclusive model for a full investigation.[249] The conception of 'market failure' in the neoclassical model may need to be reformulated from a neoinstitutionalist perspective.

William Landes and Richard Posner can be classified as neoinstitutionalists. For a long time they collaborated on their examination of economic issues in intellectual property law. They published a series of papers on the subject. Their latest book, *The Economic Structure of Intellectual Property Law*, is a synthesis of their past studies.[250] Following the path of law and economics in general, and neoinstitutionlism in particular, Landes and Posner provided an inclusive transaction-cost-based cost–benefit assessment of legal definition and protection of intellectual property rights on the basis of the supply–demand rule under the principle of production efficiency and welfare maximisation. They examined how the costs of intellectual properties were incurred and recovered in the production and distribution processes within certain institutional arrangements or environments; what the impacts were of cost incurrence and recovery on consumers and producers of information goods under the supply–demand rule; and whether or not certain ways of cost incurrence and recovery would result in production efficiency and welfare maximisation.[251]

Under the neoinstitutionalist premise, specifically under Landes' and Posner's vision, the relation between incentive and the level of copyright protection or expansion is neither simply an issue of whether or not copyright law should provide an incentive for encouraging creative works in the first place, as classicists suggested, nor merely a question of whether the full level of copyright protection or expansion should result in efficiency or optimisation as neoclassists argued. Rather, an instrumental justification for copyright protection or expansion should be incorporated into a balance prospect. As Landes and Posner stated:

> Copyright protection – the right of the copyright's owner to prevent others from making copies – trades off the costs of limiting access to a work against the benefits of providing incentives to create the work in the first place. Striking the balance between access and incentives is the central problem in copyright law.[252]

Landes and Posner challenged conventional rationales of intellectual property law in general, and copyright law in particular, from many aspects. One of the key aspects is that their theoretical framework accentuates the concept of transaction costs and has thrown light on the substantial rationale of copyright protection or expansion. With transaction costs in mind, they stuck to the critical contention in law and economics that transaction costs necessitate legal institutions, including copyright law.[253]

Of course, Landes' and Posner's theoretical framework itself may need further scrutiny. For instance, they proposed to inspect 'the technological, cultural, legal, and economic factors'[254] that constrain the creation and exploitation of copyright but these issues have not been examined from their neoinstitutionalist perspective. Meanwhile, they attempted to make economic sense of the existing systems of copyright law in the United States as desirable institutions with incentives.[255] Their concern was whether or not the current copyright system works efficiently and effectively in maximising social welfare rather than what kinds of institutional arrangements or environments (law or regulation) of intellectual property can advance efficiency, effectiveness, and welfare maximisation the most. In other words, they were interested in the optimal outcomes that the current systems could possibly bring about, rather than the realistic course within which the institutional arrangements or environments could possibly help generate the most desirable outcomes. In brief, they focused on the result more than the process.

Moreover, although they made some efforts to explore the new issues of intellectual property law and related complexity in the information age from a new angle, Landes and Posner still passionately advanced a neoclassical and linear way of 'efficiency' thinking for defining and analysing the copyright issues in the new information age. However, they eventually depicted 'the rosy Schumpeterian picture' for illustrating a variety of issues, including the copyright issues, besieging the monopoly in some renovating industries under pressure from digital technology.[256] Their preference and focus may reflect the puzzling nature of their theories and methods in confronting these new challenges from information technology and new media.

4. Neoclassicism and neoinstitutionalism

The neoinstitutionalist perspective is a crucial improvement and amendment of neoclassical economics.[257] The key assumptions of market forces under neoclassical economics – complete rationality, information symmetry, marginal effect, perfect competition, Pareto efficiency, equilibrium, and wealth maximisation – are still sustained under the neoinstitutionalist framework.[258] What the neoinstitutionalist perspective has discerned is the institutional constraints on the functions of these market forces on account of transaction costs and property rights.[259]

Nevertheless, the neoinstitutionalist approach is not a substantial deviation from the neoclassical model. Rather, they can be consigned as the supplementary components under a larger framework of 'neoclassicism'.[260] Both exhibit the puzzling nature for exploring 'the rosy Schumpeterian picture' of copyright protection and expansion, and for investigating the new challenges to copyright protection and expansion in the information age.

2.3.2 *The Schumpeterian model*

Schumpeter's framework, in contrast to neoclassicism, is a resourceful model for exploring 'the rosy Schumpeterian picture' of copyright protection and expansion in the digital age. Of course, Schumpeter did not offer a systematic theory of intellectual property rights and he even ignored the topic, to some extent, when constructing his framework.[261] However, as one of the most prominent economists, Schumpeter did construct a unique framework that can serve as a road map for scrutinising and researching the role of copyright in developing economy and growing industry in the information age.

In the early to mid-twentieth century, Schumpeter explored the dynamic nature of modern capitalist progress. Unlike Marx and Keynes, who believed that capitalism's failure – especially the failure under the *laissez-faire* doctrine – to stimulate constant economic development could or would lead to its collapse, Schumpeter instead attributed capitalism's demise to its own success.[262] However, Schumpeter showed less interest in capitalism's final-stage than the course of its progress, in which a variety of complex and dynamic factors affected economic development and industrial growth.

In Schumpeter's system, capitalism should be studied 'as an evolutionary process'.[263] In the evolutionary process, 'the dynamic nature' of capitalism exhibits two aspects – innovation-oriented competition[264] and time-framed progress.[265] The innovation-oriented competition has transformed a variety of institutional arrangements in a destruction–creation cycle over a long time sequence, and compelled the evolutionary process as one of creative destruction

that 'is the essential fact about capitalism'.[266] This Schumpeterian dynamic –
an innovation-advancing progression of economic and industrial transformation over a long time sequence or, put simply, a process of creative destruction
with an innovation-oriented and time-framed progress of economic and industrial construction and reconstruction – is the core concept for exploring
Schumpeter's theoretical perspective and for examining the very nature of
modern capitalist economy under his vision and analytical model. To exploit
Schumpeter's model, it is necessary to review his methodological stance on
innovation-oriented competition and time-framed progress in order to investigate the forces of creative destruction and the copyright-growth interaction
under these forces.

1. Methods of dynamics

Scholars have defined Schumpeter's methodological stance in different terms
from various angles: methodological individualism,[267] methodological liberalism,[268] and methodological instrumentalism.[269] This book argues that, in
general, Schumpeter pursued methodological realism under his methodological liberalism as he gradually constructed his system. An exploration of
Schumpeter's methodological realism will provide the research on the copyright-growth relation with added vigour.

'Approaching capitalism with a worldly realism bordering on cynicism,
Schumpeter devoted his considerable rhetorical and analytical powers to
injecting Marx's theory of technical change into the marginalist framework as
a corrective to the equilibrium-fetish of neoclassical economics.'[270] On account
of methodological realism, Schumpeter's methodological scrutiny was not
only concerned with 'the testability against reality' of theoretical assumptions, but also with 'the approximation to reality'[271] of these theoretical
assumptions under a framework or model. According to Schumpeter, 'the
analytical work does not consist solely of working out formal theorems, but
also of working out a conceptual apparatus for the representation of reality,
and indeed this latter aspect comes first in importance'.[272] With a concrete
application of his methodological realism and a passionate observation on
capitalism's dynamic process, Schumpeter does offer an innovation-oriented
and time-framed dynamic analysis as a methodological foundation of his theoretical framework.

In his first book, *The Nature and Essence of Theoretical Economics*, in 1908,
Schumpeter explored his epistemological approach to theoretical construction
and verification.[273] He introduced the deductive school of instrumentalism,[274]
much earlier than Popper's groundbreaking scientific philosophy from the
1950s to 1960s,[275] and this influenced his main works afterwards, as well as
laying the methodological foundation for his later studies. Nevertheless, at
that time, the neoclassical vision of 'static system of equilibrium' rather than
methodological realism was still part of Schumpeter's methodological
stance.[276]

Three years later, in 1911, in *The Theory of Economic Development*, Schumpeter overhauled his theoretical position and methodological stance, which were launched in *The Nature and Essence of Theoretical Economics*. In this work, economic development and the driving force behind that development – innovation – became the central topic of his study. The view of the 'static system of equilibrium' was replaced with the approach of dynamics. In addition, *The Theory of Economic Development* as 'a halfway house' in Schumpeter's life-time methodological scrutiny[277] serves as a link for bonding his whole framework of methodological scrutiny and theoretical inquiry. To enhance his theoretical enquiry, Schumpeter addressed some methodological concerns in this 'halfway house'.[278]

First, according to Schumpeter, in a narrow sense, 'research method' that connects 'theory' to 'fact' should not only clarify these unanalysed and statistical facts on account of theories but also inspire 'new theoretical patterns'. This realist approach of methodology is important in Schumpeter's system but it was often overlooked. On occasion, even Schumpeter himself failed to recognise the value of research method for theoretical construction. As Simon Kuznets pointed out, Schumpeter's failure to apply a standard statistical method of time series as part of research method discounted the theoretical consistency in his main work, *Business Cycles*.[279]

Second, in Schumpeter's account, in a broad sense, some issues in 'research method' should be addressed from an epistemological approach. After his *The Theory of Economic Development* in 1911, Schumpeter continued his emphasis on 'epistemological approach', which serves as the groundwork for research method in a narrow sense. In most cases, he refused to 'set methodological assumptions once and for all our purposes' in order to explore 'a systematic regularity' and to formulate 'exact "laws"'.[280] Roncaglia emphasised this methodological stance as 'methodological liberalism'.[281] At the core of this thinking is the diversification of philosophical postulations for framing manifold explorations and explanations of the complex reality.[282] Although offering some 'paradoxical standpoints'[283] in his whole academic career, partially because of his ambition to establish a universal economic science, Schumpeter did consistently preserve his epistemological approach for his wide-ranging agenda of scrutiny. In his system, epistemological approach serves as a framework of reference for scrutinising a linkage between the breadth of economic knowledge and the complexity of economic reality. To investigate this linkage, Schumpeter was committed to diversifying his methodological scrutiny and substantive view for exploring and explaining the dynamic and complex realities of capitalism's socio-economic development. As a result, he provided deep, visionary, and realist insights for many subjects in economics, and even in social science as a whole.[284] The main weakness of this ambitious endeavour is that, when diversifying methodological scrutiny and substantive view on a large scale, the focal point of Schumpeter's scrutiny and view may be concealed, and the distinction between these two aspects – methodological scrutiny and substantive view – may not be revealed. In consequence, this is a partial reason for his failure to 'provide a road map that tells their followers and successors what to do to make a successful academic career within the school'.[285]

Nevertheless, even if 'a road map' is unavailable, reviewing Schumpeter's path of substantive view in his major studies can still uncover the clues of his realist methodological scrutiny. Indeed, the preface to the English edition of *The Theory of Economic Development* indicates that diversifying methodological scrutiny and substantive view does not prevent Schumpeter from concentrating his scrutiny and view. The focal point of his system is his innovation-oriented and time-framed dynamic analysis. Although this analysis is a methodological enquiry in his above work, reviewing his major works can find that this dynamic analysis is also a building block connecting methodological scrutiny to substantive view for his insightful investigations into various topics and subjects.

Various scholars identified the distinction between Schumpeter Mark I and Schumpeter Mark II as a Schumpeterian scheme for analysing economic development and industrial growth. Schumpeter Mark I emphasises the crucial role of small firms in promoting innovations, while Schumpeter Mark II stresses the significance of large firms in triggering innovations.[286] However, this distinction is either wrong[287] or unnecessary.[288] Schumpeter did recognise but did not signify the function of firm size on elevating innovations. In general, he was concerned with the role of innovation more than the role of firms in advancing economic development and industrial growth in the long-term process of creative destruction. In his view, creative destruction is the rule rather than the exception for economic development and industrial growth. Innovations (either technological or organisational, or both), and entrepreneurs as innovators under the sponsorship of bank credit or capital, are the motive forces behind development and growth.[289] On the whole, for Schumpeter, 'the process of economic development is generated by a succession of innovations achieved by entrepreneurs with the purchasing power supplied to them by bankers'.[290] The very essence of his theoretical framework is 'the view of a dynamic process endogenous to the economy and society'.[291]

In Schumpeter's account, dynamics exhibit two aspects – an innovation-oriented competition and a time-framed progress. Unlike classical dynamics and some of its modern versions, which focus on the time-sequenced process,[292] Schumpeter's views on dynamics grasp the very nature of economic development or industrial growth and synthesise the role of innovation and the innovation-generated process of development and growth. The concept of 'creative destruction' and related arguments were initiated from this innovation-oriented and time-framed dynamic analysis. More importantly, Schumpeter's methodological stance – methodological realism under methodological liberalism –is also crucial for exploring and explaining the complex reality of capitalist economy and society.

In his *The Theory of Economic Development*, Schumpeter declared dynamic disequilibrium rather than static equilibrium as the 'rule' of capitalist economic development and industrial growth. To comprehend the 'rule', Schumpeter propounded an embryonic form of his innovation-oriented and time-framed dynamic analysis in this work. From a standpoint of methodological realism, Schumpeter insisted that theory not only serves as the tool 'for approaching both facts and practical problems'[293] but also offers a realistic treatment of facts or phenomena. For him, 'As of economic facts in general, so we speak of economic development'.[294] Development in our sense is a distinct phenomenon, entirely foreign to what may be observed in the circular flow or in the tendency toward equilibrium. It is spontaneous and discontinuous change in the channels of the flow, disturbance of equilibrium, which forever alters and displaces the equilibrium state previously existing. Our theory of development is nothing but a treatment of this phenomenon and the processes incident to it.'[295]

Schumpeter contended that the causes of dynamic disturbance, in other words 'the mechanism of change',[296] determine the pattern of economic phenomena. Accordingly, a theory should be constructed in the first place to recognise the real causes of dynamic disturbance in order to frame an investigation into 'the effect of this disturbance and the new equilibrium'. In particular, Schumpeter focused the causes of dynamics ('the mechanism of change') on the supply side of the economy and identified two important causes of dynamic disturbance on the supply side – 'changes in technique and in productive organisation'[297]– which necessitate a theoretical recognition.

How should a theoretical recognition of these changes as the cause of dynamics ('the mechanism of change') on the supply side be offered? Schumpeter made clear that the 'static' analysis should not be the choice because it 'is not only unable to predict the consequences of discontinuous changes in the traditional way of doing things; it can neither explain the occurrence of such productive revolutions nor the phenomena which accompany them'.[298] According to him, following a 'static' approach, the core of a pure economic theory of development as implied in the traditional doctrine of capital formation lies in its concern with saving and related small-scale investing. 'In this it asserts nothing false, but it entirely overlooks much more essential things.' Thus, Schumpeter advised that 'we must take a different attitude as soon as we analyse *change*'[299] in order to recognise these 'essential things' in economic reality. Rather than staying on a 'static' path, following Schumpeter's advice, a 'dynamic' approach should be adapted to analyse these 'essential things'– the 'new combinations of productive means'[300] – as 'changes in technique and in productive organisation'. For Schumpeter, savings and supply of productive means were important but the 'new combinations' were essential for economic development.

Schumpeter defined these new combinations or changes in technique and in productive organisation on the supply side as 'innovations'.[301] Economic development 'in our sense is then defined by the carrying out of new combinations'.[302] Thus, in Schumpeter's terms, 'a theory of economic development' (as the title of Schumpeter's book) should be a realist scheme that underlines these innovations in economic reality. This realist innovation-oriented and time-framed dynamic analysis as an 'epistemological approach' is a special application of Schumpeter's methodological realism for recognising the dynamic and complex reality of economic development.

The advantage of research under methodological realism is that the balance between 'research method' and 'epistemological approach' should be expected for constructing and testing theories. Schumpeter's realist innovation-oriented and time-framed dynamic analysis as an epistemological approach facilitates a workable framework or model for exploring the dynamic and complex reality of economic activities with a specific research method from the standpoint of methodological realism. It is from the standpoint of methodological realism that Schumpeter sparked 'his aspiration to make the discipline of economics precise, objective, positivist, non-political',[303] and conceptualised the process of creative destruction as the dynamic reality of capitalism. Accordingly, in Schumpeter's account, the main aspects of economic development – such as (but not limited to) entrepreneurs' profits, money, credit, interest, and cycles – and their associations have been approached on the ground of complex and dynamic reality under his realist innovation-oriented and time-framed dynamic analysis as an epistemological approach. 'The really revolutionary change which Schumpeter proposed for the structure of economic theory was to banish some of the most important economic concepts, such as profit, entrepreneurship, and interest, from the realm of Statics and to deport them to Dynamics.'[304]

2. *Forces of creative destruction*

Under his methodological liberalism, Schumpeter made a strong effort to conceptualise the process of capitalist development in which the complex and dynamic factors shall exert their long-term effects on the economic development and industrial growth as a course of 'creative destruction'. Among these complex and dynamic factors, industry structure, competition, innovation, and entrepreneurship (introduced in Chapter 1.1) should be the powerful forces of creative destruction. In Schumpeter's scheme, a system of property rights and proprietary ownership should by no means play a crucial role in economic development and industrial growth as classical and neoclassical economists would advise. Rather, Schumpeter emphasised the forces of creative destruction and their dynamic roles in reinforcing the efficiency and effectiveness of development and growth. Following Schumpeter's reasoning, for a plausible understanding of intellectual property rights and related issues, the issue of intellectual property rights should be placed into the context of creative destruction forces – innovation, competition, industry structure, and entrepreneurship – and be inspected as one of the growth-promoting problems in the process of creative destruction rather than a resource-allocating problem. To scrutinise the whole course of creative destruction, Schumpeter analysed the four forces of the process – innovation, competition, industry structure, and entrepreneurship – and their imperative interactions.

(1)　Technological innovation

According to Schumpeter, 'The essential point to grasp is that in dealing with capitalism we are dealing with an evolutionary process . . . Capitalism, then, is by nature a form or method of economic change and not only never is but never can be stationary'.[305] What forces impel the dynamic rather than the stationary process of capitalist progress? Schumpeter asserted that innovative forces, rather than 'productive forces' as Marx has defined, should be the inherent driving forces of economic development and industrial growth in the modern economy. As he argued, 'The fundamental impulse that sets and keeps the capitalism engine in motion comes from the new consumers' goods, the new methods of production or transportation, the new markets, the new forms of industrial organisation that capitalist enterprise creates'.[306] In Schumpeter's system, 'innovation is defined changes in the methods of supplying commodities, such as introducing new goods or new methods of production; opening new markets, conquering sources of supply of raw material or manufactured goods; or carrying out a new organisation of industry, such as creating a monopoly or breaking one up'.[307] Among the wide-ranged aspects of innovations in Schumpeter's account, technology-based innovation/creativity would be one of the main sources of innovation/creativity. Unlike Smith, Marx, and many other neoclassical economists in whose systems technology or knowledge has not been recognised as a methodical factor for an integral analysis,[308] Schumpeter was among the earliest prominent economists who emphasised new technology as an essential factor of economic development and as an intrinsic analytic element in their models of economics.[309]

(2)　Dynamic competition

However, Schumpeter was not a technophile. In fact, he stressed the role of an innovative system (taking account of both technological and organisational innovations), rather than an innovative instrument, in transforming economic institutions and advancing economic progress. Moreover, according to Schumpeter, innovative forces in nature would by no means activate in a static and equilibrium manner. Rather, these forces would function in a process of 'industry mutation' that 'incessantly revolutionises the economic structure from within, incessantly destroying the old one, incessantly creating a new one. This process of Creative Destruction is the essential fact about capitalism'.[310] On account of this 'essential fact about capitalism', Schumpeter denounced a textbook-versioned concept of competition and identified a new type of competition in reality:

> The first thing to go is the traditional conception of the *modus operandi* of competition. Economists are at long last emerging from the stage in which price competition was all they saw. As soon as quality competition and sales effort are admitted into the sacred precincts of theory, the price

variable is ousted from its dominant position. However, it is still competition within a rigid pattern of invariant conditions, methods of production and forms of industrial organization in particular, that practically
monopolizes attention. But in capitalist reality as distinguished from its
textbook picture, it is not that kind of competition which counts but the
competition from the new commodity, the new technology, the new
source of supply, the new type of organization (the largest-scale unit of
control for instance) – competition which commands a decisive cost or
quality advantage and which strikes not at the margins of the profits and
the outputs of the existing firms but at their foundations and their very
lives. This kind of competition is much more effective than the other as a
bombardment is in comparison with forcing a door, and so much more
important that it becomes a matter of comparative indifference whether
competition in the ordinary sense functions more or less promptly; the
powerful lever that in the long run expands output and brings down
prices is in any case made of other stuff.

It is hardly necessary to point out that competition of the kind we now
have in mind acts not only when in being but also when it is merely an
ever-present threat. It disciplines before it attacks. The businessman feels
himself to be in a competitive situation even if he is alone in his field or
if, though not alone, he holds a position such that investigating government experts fail to see any effective competition between him and any
other firms in the same or a neighbouring field and in consequence
conclude that his talk, under examination, about his competitive sorrows
is all make-believe. In many cases, though not in all, this will in the long
run enforce behaviour very similar to the perfectly competitive pattern.[311]

This is a clear and realistic characterisation of a type of natural competition. It
is a dynamic or, named after Schumpeter, a Schumpeterian competition.
Moreover, in D'Aveni's terms, it is also a hypercompetition,[312] 'an environment in which advantages are rapidly created and erode'.[313] In such a dynamic
and hypercompetitive environment, innovation has become the keystone of
competitive advantage. Any firms that fail to innovate fail themselves. Besides
innovations, an established business should have no other strengths for
surviving and reviving. In this regard, large corporations and corresponding
industry structure should not be hostile towards innovation/creativity and
economic progress. On the contrary, for Schumpeter, large established firms
should play a necessary role in promoting innovation/creativity and economic
progress in a hypercompetitive marketplace. As he pointed out, large established corporations had 'come to be the most powerful engine of that progress
and in particular of the long-run expansion of total output not only in spite
of, but to a considerable extent through, this strategy which looks so restrictive when viewed in the individual case and from the individual point of time.
In this respect, perfect competition is not only impossible but inferior, and
has no title to being set up as a model of ideal efficiency'.[314]

(3) Concentrating industry structure

Schumpeter was the first economist who examined the interaction between competition and industry structure.[315] Of course, in Schumpeter's account, both competition and industry structure had been explored with a dynamic nature. He insisted that economic development 'is a distinct phenomenon, entirely foreign to what may be observed in the circular flow or in the tendency towards equilibrium. It is spontaneous and discontinuous change in the channels of the flow, disturbance of equilibrium, which forever alters and displaces the equilibrium state previously existing, our theory of development is nothing but a treatment of the phenomenon and the processes incident to it'.[316] In a disturbing environment of disequilibrium, economic development should 'be defined as the carrying out of new combinations' of materials and forces. One aspect of the 'new combinations' is 'the carrying out of the new organisation of any industry, like the creation of a monopoly position (for example through Schumpeter's 'trustification') or the breaking up of a monopoly position'.[317] For Schumpeter, a market of perfect competition in which producers maximise their interests in equilibrium as neoclassical economists have perceived is an exception rather than the rule.[318] Instead, a concentrating industry structure would be a desirable way of industrial organisation for economic advancement because 'big business may have had more to do with creating that (rising) standard of life than with keeping it down'.[319]

Schumpeter argued that economists and popular writers' 'fragmentary analyses' prevented them from grasping 'capitalist reality as a whole'.[320] Quite the opposite, he placed the standing of big business in perspective and endeavoured to recover the whole picture of capitalist progress, and to scrutinise the vital interaction between competition and industry structure from a new angle. The focus of the new angle is on the significance of innovative forces in economic development and industrial growth in the long-term process of creative destruction.

(4) Entrepreneurship

Schumpeter, as the 'greatest twentieth-century economist who celebrated the role of entrepreneurship',[321] has especially identified entrepreneurship as a strategic source of innovation. It is entrepreneurs who undertake diverse innovations for coping with dynamic competition under certain concentrating industry structures. No groups of people other than entrepreneurs have played the most important roles in the economic development and industrial growth in the modern age. Of course, entrepreneurs are not organised into a monolithic bloc. On the contrary, according to Schumpeter, the division between innovators and imitators inside or outside entrepreneurs should be an undeniable reality. The competition between innovators and imitators shapes the pattern of economic development and industrial growth to different extents.[322]

Nevertheless, while innovative entrepreneurs in Schumpeter's account can be regarded as 'a kind of knight'[323] and 'a businessperson who is not caught up in the circular flow of economic life',[324] imitators are not perceived as effortless apprentices. Instead, pioneer innovators, even if having secured their dominant positions and maintained their technological advances, could still be overtaken by imitators who could improve adopted innovations at more advanced levels. For Schumpeter, innovations are neutral, and the status quo for either imitators or innovators can never be stabilised. The competition between imitators and innovators, between innovators and innovators, and between imitators and imitators is innovation-oriented, time-framed,[325] unpreventable, unpredictable, unbalancing, multifarious, multilevelled, and, in one word, dynamic.[326] Under the dynamic and hypercompetitive circumstance as a main feature of the process of creative destruction, creating new technological schemes, new cost structures of production, new industry or market structures, and new ways of industrial organisation and destroying old ones should be accelerated, simultaneous, reciprocal, and 'unclear-cut'. The process of creative destruction has proceeded as a course 'whereby innovations would destroy existing technologies and methods of production only to be assaulted themselves by imitative rival products with newer, more efficient configurations'.[327] As a result, in Schumpeter's world, equilibrium is never a norm of capitalism, and dynamic disequilibrium should be the natural state of economic development and industrial growth.[328]

3. *Process of creative destruction*

Schumpeter was not the only great economist who scrutinised the process of growth and development. Compared with other scholars in the field of growth and development, Schumpeter stands out in two distinctive outlooks. First, Schumpeter expounded a micro–macro linkage in the process of economic development and industrial growth. This methodological enclosure assisted a constructive investigation into a noteworthy relation in capitalist economy – the relation, in Schumpeter's own words, 'between the structural features of capitalism as depicted by various analytic "models" and the economic performance as depicted, for the epoch of intact or relatively unfettered capitalism, by the index of total output'.[329] Second, Schumpeter's scheme of creative destruction highlights innovations (either technological or organisational innovations) as endogenous forces – firms or industries' inside propensities to exploit new ways of pursuing optimal profits for their long-run survival or success under the dynamic competition in a complex process of creative destruction – and identifies these endogenous forces as the driving forces behind economic development and industrial growth.

In brief, Schumpeter's theory of creative destruction had framed two fundamental propositions on the nature of capitalism's economic development and industrial growth – proposition of creation and proposition of destruction.[330] The proposition of creation means the creating of profitable opportunities for initiative innovators, while the proposition of destruction implies the removal of these opportunities from incumbents.[331] Schumpeter did propound 'an integrated view of how both propositions could be true'.[332] His integral effort has been embodied in his macro–micro incorporation in examining creative destruction as a process in which innovative forces (both technological and organisational innovations) obliterate existing institutional arrangements of industrial or economic systems and re-orient industrial growth or economic development in an accelerated, unstable, and inflexible way.

4. Copyright-growth under creative destruction

Schumpeter's model is not only instructive for a methodological scrutiny of the process of creative destruction in general, but also for a methodological scrutiny of the copyright-growth relation under the pressure of creative destruction in particular. In his system, legal pragmatism is a logic partner of his methodological realism. Indeed, legal forces as 'political regulation of commerce' in Schumpeter's terms[333] are parts of his early vision of economics. In his early work such as *The Theory of Economic Development*, Schumpeter still maintained, 'Always we are concerned with describing the general forms of the causal links that connect economic with non-economic data'.[334] Recent research on the printed editions of Schumpeter's works found that some pages of his *The Theory of Economic Development* have never been translated into English. These neglected pages indicate that 'Schumpeter's contribution to accounting and economics constitutes a clear justification of the dynamic entity view of the firm and provides valuable insights for a dynamic economic theory of the firm linking economics, accounting and law in an integrated approach'.[335] Schumpeter attempted to incorporate his analysis of legal forces into his realist innovation-oriented and time-framed dynamic analysis as an 'epistemological approach' for scrutinising pure economic factors or forces.

This way of reasoning was sustained in his *Business Cycles* in 1939. In this vast volume, Schumpeter reclassified economic and non-economic factors discussed in *The Theory of Economic Development* as 'some which act from within and some which act from without the economic sphere'.[336] The former are referred to as 'internal factors' and the latter as 'external factors'. For Schumpeter, 'Economic consideration can fully account for the former only; the latter must be accepted as data and all we can do about them in economic analysis is to explain their effects on economic life'.[337] From this standpoint, he had no hesitation in defining legal forces as external factors and identified the dual functions of institutions or laws – rule amendment of 'economic game' and habit adaptation of 'business behaviour'.[338] Categorising the dual functions of laws as 'external factors', Schumpeter indeed examined institutions or laws from, in Posner's terms, 'the pragmatic outlook – practical, instrumental . . . experimental'.[339] This pragmatic outlook shed light on the study of the institutional or legal role in adjusting economic activities from his realist innovation-oriented and time-framed dynamic analysis.

Capitalism, Socialism and Democracy is an agglomeration of Schumpeter's whole theoretical system. Clustering round the concept of 'creative destruction', Schumpeter epitomised a variety of both economic and non-economic factors for scrutinising the dynamic process and the dwindling end of capitalism under his realist innovation-oriented and time-framed dynamic analysis as an 'epistemological approach'. Through diagnosing the future dwindling consequence of capitalist dynamics, Schumpeter identified institutional or legal changes as a cohesive part of the dynamic progress toward a declining consequence of capitalism.[340]

As to methodological concerns, it is even more intricate to explore the complex and dynamic nature of the relation from Schumpeter's methodological realism and legal pragmatism. Under his model, the copyright-growth relation can be analysed in connection with the complex legal and policy factors (including competition policy and patent policy) of creative destruction at great length.[341] This book is endeavouring to reach a realistic and pragmatic understanding of the complex and dynamic nature of the copyright-growth relation under the forces of creative destruction. Accordingly, in this book, the roles of legal and economic factors (variables) and their interactions – particularly the role of copyright expansion in functioning and growing the firms of copyright industries under certain industry structures – are not only theoretically analysed but also empirically assessed in the context of complex and dynamic creative destruction in a long time period of over 30 years. Meanwhile, following Schumpeter's methodological realism and legal pragmatism, his own deficiency in empirical research – failure to apply standard statistical method of time series as previously addressed – should be overcome in this research.

2.4 Concluding remarks

This chapter has reviewed the historical evolution of the copyright-growth relation under the forces and process of creative destruction in the UK book publishing industry; the mechanism whereby the forces and process of creative destruction can influence the copyright-growth relation; and the legal rationale of typical statutes, court cases, and international treaties involving the copyright-growth relation. Meanwhile, in this chapter, the context of the research question is further explored through examining the neoclassical and Schumpeterian perspectives on the issues of copyright and the copyright-growth relation.

This chapter indicates that copyright expansion is an adaptive response to the pressure of creative destruction in the UK book publishing industry as a typical copyright industry and as the cradle of modern copyright law. In an ongoing process of creative destruction, copyright expansion as a legislative policy or legal force is also an intermediate factor or variable that relays the relation between the forces of creative destruction and industrial growth. The industrial players in a copyright industry under pressure from creative destruction propelled copyright expansion and tweaked the industry or market structure correspondingly.

However, the tweaked industry or market structure could be unique but not necessarily enduring under the pressure of ongoing creative destruction. Accordingly, the entrepreneurs in a copyright industry would adopt diverse competitive strategies and cope with diverse market forces for surviving, thriving, and growing under the pressure of creative destruction. The diverse market forces under some specific industry or market structure would complicate the impacts of copyright expansion as a legal force on the growth of a copyright industry in the process of creative destruction. Chapter III will address these and other related issues in the digital environment.

Notes

1 Schumpeter distinguished the term 'adaptive response' from the term 'creative response' in his article in 1947. See J. Schumpeter, 'The Creative Response in Economic History', *Journal of Economic History*, vol. 7(2), 1947, 150. However, he explored the notion of 'creative response' in his earlier works.
2 L. McKnight, P. Vaaler, and R. Katz (eds), *Creative Destruction: Business Survival Strategies in the Global Internet Economy*, The MIT Press, 2001, pp. 4–5.
3 M. Plant, *The English Book Trade: An Economic History of the Making and Sale of Books* 2nd edn, London: Allen & Unwin, 1965, pp. 117–118.
4 P. Goldstein, *Copyright's Highway: from Gutenberg to the Celestial Jukebox*, New York: Hill and Wang, 1994, pp. 37–51.
5 R. Deazley, *Rethinking Copyright: History, Theory, Language*, Edward Elgar, 2006, pp. 13–14. Plant, op. cit., pp. 117–121.
6 A. Murray, *The Regulation of Cyberspace: Control in the Online Environment*, London: Routledge-Cavendish, 2007, p. 15.
7 P. David, 'The Evolution of Intellectual Property Institutions and the Panda's Thumb', Presentation at the Meeting of the International Economic Association in Moscow, 24–28 August 1992. Online. Available <http://www.compilerpress. atfreeweb.com/Anno%20David%20Evolution%20of%20IP%20Institutions%20 199.htm> (accessed 16 December 2006), p. 17.
8 The 'conger' refers to the group of wholesale trading booksellers. Prior to 1710, many copy-owning and wholesaling congers as groups of trading booksellers under the Stationers' Company had already existed in London for a long time. See J. Feather, *A History of British Publishing* 2nd edn, London: Routledge, 2006, pp. 52–54.
9 Ibid, p. 83.
10 Plant, op. cit., pp. 200–215.
11 Ibid, pp. 222–237.
12 Deazley, op. cit., pp. 13–16. C. Seville, *Literary Copyright Reform in Early Victorian England: The Framing of the 1842 Copyright Act*, Cambridge University Press, 1999, pp. 9–16.
13 L. Lessig, *Free Culture: How Big Media Uses Technology and the Law to Lock Down and Control Creativity*, New York: The Penguin Press, 2004, pp. 89–90. Goldstein, op. cit., 1994, pp. 43–49.
14 Feather, op. cit., 2006, pp. 64–68, 78–80.
15 Goldstein, op. cit., 1994, pp. 45–48.
16 Ibid, 1994, pp. 91–92.

17 Feather, op. cit., 2006, p. 66. J. Feather, 'The Publishers and the Pirates: British Copyright Law in Theory and Practice, 1710–1775', *Publishing History*, vol. 22, 1987, 20–24.

18 P. Starr, *The Creation of the Media: Political Origins of Modern Communications*, New York: Basic Books, 2004, p. 118.

19 Feather, op. cit., 1987, 23.

20 Lessig, op. cit., 2004, pp. 93–94.

21 J. Feather, 'Publishers and Politicians: the Remaking the Law of Copyright in Britain 1775–1842 Part I: Legal Deposit and the Battle of the Library Tax', *Publishing History*, vol. 24, 1988, 49.

22 Deazley, op. cit., pp. 20–25. Feather, op. cit., Part I, 1988, 49–50.

23 J. Schumpeter, translated by R. Opie, *The Theory of Economic Development: an Inquiry into Profits, Capital, Credit, Interest, and the Business Cycle*, Harvard University Press, 1962[1911], Chapter III.

24 R. Floud and D. McCloskey (eds), *The Economic History of Britain since 1700* Volume 1: 1700–1860 2nd edn, Cambridge University Press, 1994, pp. 151–181.

25 Plant, op. cit., p. 234. J. Raven, *The Business of Books: Booksellers and the English Book Trade 1450–1850*, New Haven: Yale University Press, 2007, pp. 326–327.

26 Floud and McCloskey, op. cit., Volume 1, p. 156.

27 John Murray (1737–1793), taking bank partnership into publishing venture in the late 1760s and early 1770s, was among the earlier publishers who initiated the use of bank credit and venture capital for supporting book publishing and trading in Britain. See Feather, op. cit., 2006, p. 77.

28 Plant, op. cit., pp. 234–237.

29 Feather, op. cit., 2006, pp. 75–77.

30 Plant, op. cit., pp. 325–331.

31 Feather, op. cit., 2006, pp. 87–88.

32 Plant, op. cit., pp. 414–415.

33 Ibid, pp. 416–418.

34 Ibid, pp. 269–289.

35 Feather, op. cit., 2006, pp. 74–75.

36 Ibid, p. 83.

37 Raven, op. cit., p. 223, pp. 226–230.

38 Long before the Statute of Anne in 1710, joint wholesaling was the core for the copy-owning and wholesaling congers under the Stationers' Company. The members within the copy-owning and wholesaling congers coordinated their transactions and monopolised the wholesaling activities to protect their insiders' interests. Feather, op. cit., 2006, pp. 52–53, 80–81.

39 Ibid, p. 82.

40 J. Schumpeter, *Capitalism, Socialism and Democracy* 3rd edn, New York: Harper & Row, 1976[1942], p. 85.

41 Raven, op. cit., pp. 230–238.

42 Ibid, pp. 356–358.

43 Feather, op. cit., 2006, p. 82.

44 Ibid, p. 83.

45 Raven, op. cit., pp. 241–245.

46 T. Bresnahan and M. Trajtenberg, 'General Purpose Technologies: Engine of Growth', *Journal of Econometrics*, vol. 65, 1995, 83–108. Quoted in Helpman, op. cit., 1998, p. 3.

47 There are two fundamental views by which to perceive the relation between technology and economic development or industrial growth – endogenous and exogenous perspectives. In general, from an endogenous perspective,

technological innovation is a professional response to the commercial opportunities entrenched within economic development or industrial growth. On the contrary, an exogenous perspective regards technological progress as an endeavour motivated by a non-commercial rationale; for instance, by a scientific–technological community, irrespective of economic or industrial drive. See R. Lipsey, C. Bekar and K. Carlaw, 'What Requires Explanation?' in E. Helpman (ed), *General Purpose Technologies and Economic Growth*, The MIT Press, 1998, p. 35. R. Lipsey, K. Carlaw and C. Bekar, *Economic Transformations – General Purpose Technologies and Long-Term Economic Growth*, Oxford University Press, 2005, pp. 25–49.

48 Feather, op. cit., 2006, pp. 14–17.
49 J. Man, *The Gutenberg Revolution: the Story of a Genius and an Invention that Changed the World*, London: Review, 2002, p. 242.
50 See, for instance, Raven, op. cit., pp. 241–245.
51 Feather, op. cit., 2006, p. 71.
52 Ibid, p. 97.
53 Raven, op. cit., pp. 356–358.
54 Feather, op. cit., 2006, pp. 132–133.
55 Raven, op. cit., p. 222.
56 In this section, the legal changes in copyright are explored as a response to the process of creative destruction in publishing. For the publishing entrepreneurs, legal changes under a dynamic or Schumpeterian competition could become 'Schumpeterian law – using the law in a proactive, opportunistic, flexible, and risk-taking fashion'. Thus, entrepreneurs' responses to legal and regulatory amendments can be defined as the business reactions under the Schumpeterian competition. See V. Mayer-Schönberger, 'Schumpeterian Law: Rethinking the Role of Law in Fostering Entrepreneurship'. Online. Available <http://works.bepress.com/cgi/viewcontent.cgi? article=1001 & context= viktor_ mayer_schoenberger> (accessed on 14 March 2008), p. 29.
57 Starr, op. cit., p. 119.
58 For a general treatment of risk investment, see M. Mandel, *The Coming Internet Depression*, New York: Basic Books, 2000, pp. 21–22.
59 Feather, op. cit., 2006, p. 136.
60 D. Goyder, 'Copyright, Competition and the Media', in M. Beesley (ed), *Markets and the Media*, London: The Institute of Economic Affairs, 1996, p. 29.
61 H. MacQueen, *Copyright, Competition, and Industrial Design*, Edinburgh University Press, 1995, p. 7.
62 T. Derry and T. Williams, *A Short Story of Technology: From the Earliest Times to A.D. 1900*, Oxford University Press, 1960, pp. 320–324.
63 Feather, op. cit., 2006, pp. 88–96.
64 Raven, op. cit., p. 320.
65 Derry and Williams, op. cit., pp. 643–646.
66 Feather, op. cit., 2006, p. 99.
67 For a general but brief discussion of the interaction between technology and transaction cost reduction, see Philip Agre, 'Introduction', in P. Agre and M. Rotenberg (eds), *Technology and Privacy: The New Landscape*, The MIT Press, 1997, pp. 1–28.
68 Feather, op. cit., 2006, pp. 92–96.
69 Raven, op. cit., pp. 325–326.
70 Derry and Williams, op. cit., pp. 331–335.
71 Feather, op. cit., 2006, p. 94. Raven, op. cit., p. 370.
72 Feather, op. cit., 2006, p. 92.
73 Ibid, p. 100.
74 J. Feather, 'Publishers and Politicians: the Remaking of the Law of Copyright

in Britain 1775–1842 Part II: The Rights of Authors', *Publishing History*, vol. 25, 1988, 45.

75 Seville, op. cit., p. 18.
76 Feather, op. cit., Part I, 1988, 68–69.
77 Feather, op. cit., 2006, p. 121.
78 Seville, op. cit., pp. 100–115. Feather, op. cit., 2006, pp. 103–106, 108–121.
79 John Murray (1808–1892) was one of the 'greatest innovators' for renovating technological assumptions in the publishing industry after the 1814 Act. Murray's Family Library, established in 1829, was a good example of the use of technological innovations such as stereotyping to exploit new opportunities, while this technology of course assisted in gaining efficiency through reducing costs and prices. George Routledge (1812–1888) was another entrepreneurial publisher who remodelled technological assumptions in the field. After the 1814 Act, it was the technology of steam printing that pushed Routledge to transfer his business from remaindering to publishing. See Feather, op. cit., 2006, p. 106.
80 Seville, op. cit., p. 100.
81 Raven, op. cit., pp. 325–326. Plant, op. cit., pp. 273–281.
82 Deazley, op. cit., p. 36.
83 Seville, op. cit., pp. 16–32.
84 Feather, op. cit., Part I, 1988, p. 68.
85 Floud and McCloskey, op. cit., Volume 1, pp. 242–270.
86 Seville, op. cit., pp. 1–4.
87 Feather, op. cit., Part II, 1988, p. 46.
88 Talfourd's endeavour came up against compelling resistance. Effectively upheld by a group of eminent writers such as William Wordsworth (1770–1850), Talfourd's campaign was eventually successful. See Seville, op. cit., pp. 7–9, 149–175. Feather, op. cit., 2006, p. 114.
89 Feather, op. cit., Part II, 1988, p. 62.
90 Seville, op. cit., pp. 6–7.
91 Feather, op. cit., Part II, 1988, p. 63.
92 Feather, op. cit., 2006, p. 114. Seville, op. cit., p. 216.
93 B. Sherman and L. Bently, *The Making of Modern Intellectual Property Law: the British Experience, 1760–1911*, Cambridge University Press, 1999, pp. 126–128.
94 Nowell-Smith, op. cit., pp. 22–23.
95 D. Spar, *Ruling the Waves: Cycles of Discovery, Chaos, and Wealth from the Compass to the Internet*, New York: Harcourt Trade Publishers, 2001, p. 60.
96 Starr, op. cit., p. 114.
97 Bill Gates of the Microsoft Corporation was a contemporary example of such an organisational innovator who imitated and used others' technological knowledge.
98 Raven, op. cit., pp. 321–322.
99 Seville, op. cit., pp. 149–175, 214–218.
100 Starr, op. cit., p. 124.
101 Feather, op. cit., 2006, p. 112.
102 Ibid, p. 86.
103 Derry and Williams, op. cit., pp. 643–651.
104 Feather, op. cit., 2006, p. 103.
105 Ibid, pp. 90–91.
106 Derry and Williams, op. cit., p. 380.
107 Feather, op. cit., 2006, pp. 115–119.
108 Ibid, p. 88.
109 Starr, op. cit., p. 128. Economies of scale mean that the total average cost of a

product could be reduced in the long run as the quantity of the product increases. Stiglitz, 1997a, Chapters XI–XVII. P. Samuelson and W. Nordhaus, *Economics* 19th edn, 2010, p. 111.

110 Seville, op. cit., pp. 149–175, 214–218.
111 For a brief discussion of the innovation–market opportunity interaction in publishing, see Starr, op. cit., pp. 128–130.
112 Feather, op. cit., 2006, p. 101.
113 Ibid, pp. 100–101.
114 Raven, op. cit., pp. 342–350.
115 MacQueen, op. cit., p. 7.
116 S. Nowell-Smith, *International Copyright Law and the Publisher in the Reign of Queen Victoria*, Oxford University Press, 1968, p. 23.
117 Feather, op. cit., 2006, pp. 112–113.
118 R. Kingsford, *The Publishers Association 1896–1946*, Cambridge University Press, 1970, pp. 16–17.
119 Feather, op. cit., 2006, p. 102.
120 Ibid, p. 142.
121 Ibid, p. 112.
122 Plant, op. cit., pp. 286–289, 357–359. Feather, op. cit., 2006, p. 92.
123 Feather, op. cit., 2006, pp. 92–93.
124 Ibid, p. 95.
125 Plant, op. cit., pp. 420–425.
126 Goldstein, op. cit., 1994, pp. 181–185.
127 Feather, op. cit., 2006, p. 158.
128 Sherman and Bently, op. cit., p. 129.
129 Murray, op. cit., 2007, p. 15.
130 Feather, op. cit., 2006, p. 212.
131 Ibid, p. 217.
132 Helpman, op. cit., pp. 22–23.
133 Feather, op. cit., 2006, p. 219.
134 Ibid, pp. 222–225.
135 MacQueen, op. cit., pp. 8–9. H. MacQueen, C. Waelde, G. Laurie and A. Brown, *Contemporary Intellectual Property: Law and Policy* 2nd edn, Oxford University Press, 2011, p. 117.
136 Feather, op. cit., 2006, p. 228.
137 W. Landes and R. Posner, *The Economic Structure of Intellectual Property Law*, Harvard University Press, 2003, p. 396.
138 Meanwhile, other UK copyright industries, such as the record industry, followed almost the same course over the same period. The Copyright Act of 1911 granted UK record companies copyright over their sound recordings for 50 years from the 'date of making'. Under the 1956 Copyright Act, the 50-year term was retained but the commencement date was changed from 'the date of making' to 'the date of publishing'. Under the Copyright Act of 1988, the 50-year term remains effective but the commencement date returned to the date of making in general cases. See T. Kent, 'Sound Recording and Copyright', 2008. Online. Available <http://www.copyright. mediarights.co.uk> (accessed 30 April 2008).
139 Murray, op. cit., 2007, p. 175.
140 Ibid.
141 A. Barron, 'The Legal Properties of Films', *The Modern Law Review*, vol. 67(2), 2004, 177–208.
142 T. Wu, 'Copyright's Communications Policy', *Michigan Law Review*, vol. 103, 2004, 279.
143 Ibid, p. 285.

144 T. Wu, p. 279.
145 Murray, op. cit., 2007, p. 171.
146 L. Lessig, *Code and Other Laws of Cyberspace*, Basic Books, 1999, pp. 85–99.
147 Lessig, op. cit., 2004, p. 123.
148 Ibid, p. 123.
149 Lessig, op. cit., 2004, pp. 130–139. See also his 2001, pp. 106–107.
150 Lessig, op. cit., 2004, pp. 161–168.
151 Ibid, p. 127.
152 Ibid.
153 Ibid, p. 169.
154 Ibid, pp. 127–128.
155 A. Murray and C. Scott, 'Controlling the New Media: Hybrid Responses to New Forms of Power', *The Modern Law Review*, vol. 65(4), 2002, 491–516.
156 Ibid, 504.
157 Ibid, 505–511.
158 W. Baumol, 'Contestable Markets: An Uprising in the Theory of Industry Structure', *The American Economic Review*, vol. 72(1), 1982, pp. 1–15.
159 Murray, op. cit., 2007, pp. 22–54.
160 Ibid, p. 35.
161 Ibid, p. 37.
162 Ibid, pp. 38–39.
163 Ibid, p. 40.
164 Ibid, p. 41.
165 Schumpeter, op. cit., 1947, p. 153.
166 M. Best, *The New Competition: Institutions of Industrial Restructuring*, Polity Press, 1990, p. 124.
167 Wu, op. cit., p. 279.
168 Ibid, p. 285.
169 Murray, op. cit., 2007, pp. 40–43.
170 J. Hills and M. Michalis, 'Creative Destruction in European Internet Industries and Policies', in McKnight, Vaaler, and Katz, op. cit., 2001, p. 93.
171 Ibid, pp. 75–94.
172 Ibid, p. 94.
173 Ibid, p. 93.
174 Murray, op. cit., p. 46.
175 Ibid, p. 46.
176 Ibid, p. 15.
177 Ibid, p. 47.
178 Ibid, p. 47.
179 For an empirical assessment of the relation between copyright disputes at common law and firm performances in the UK and the US, see Y. Mazeh and M. Rogers, 'The Economic Significance and Extent of Copyright Cases: An Analysis of Large UK Firms', *Intellectual Property Quarterly*, 4th issue, 2006, 404–420. M. Baker and B. Cunningham, 'Court Decisions and Equity Markets: Estimating the Value of Copyright Protection', *Journal of Law and Economics*, vol. 2, 2006, 567–596.
180 P. Ross, 'How Long is Long Enough? Copyright Term Extensions and the Berne Convention', *Progress on Point* 13–15 June 2006. Online. Available <http:// www. pff.org> (Accessed 20 May 2009), pp. 3–4. In this book, legal pragmatism is perceived as a combination of legal realism and legal utilitarianism. For a detailed treatment of this topic, see E. Krecké, 'Economic Analysis and Legal Pragmatism', *International Review of Law and Economics*, vol. 23, 2004, 421–437. Under some circumstances, utilitarianism and pragmatism are equivalents. See, for instance, Goldstein, op. cit., 1994, pp. 179–180.

181 MacQueen, op. cit., pp. 8–17.
182 Lessig, op. cit., 2001, pp. 196–198. Ross, op. cit., pp. 3–4. MacQueen, op. cit., pp. 10–13.
183 S. Fitzpatrick, 'Prospect of Further Copyright Harmonisation?' *European Intellectual Property Review*, vol. 25(5), 2003, 215–223. HMSO, *Gowers Review of Intellectual Property*, Norwich, UK: Crown Copyright, 2006, p. 15. Y. Benkler, *The Wealth of Networks: How Social Production Transforms Markets and Freedom*, New Haven, NJ: Yale University Press, 2006, pp. 453–455. Ross, op. cit., pp. 1–3.
184 M. Ryan, *Knowledge Diplomacy: Global Competition and the Politics of Intellectual Property*, Washington, DC: Brookings Institution Press, 1998, pp. 159–171.
185 Ryan, op. cit., pp. 126–129.
186 Richards, op. cit., pp. 4–6.
187 Ryan, op. cit., pp. 131–132.
188 Idris, 2002, p. 17.
189 Ryan, op. cit., pp. 104–119. K. Maskus, *International Intellectual Property Rights and the Global Economy*, Washington, DC: Institute for International Economics, 2000. T. Cook, L. Brazell, S. Chalton and C. Smyth, *The Copyright Directive: UK Implementation*, Bristol, UK: Jordans, 2004.
190 Fitzpatrick, op. cit., p. 215.
191 Benkler, op. cit., pp. 453–455.
192 UK Copyright Designs and Patents Act of 1988, Section 12(3), W. Cornish (ed), *Cases and Materials on Intellectual Property* 5th edn, London: Sweet & Maxwell, 2006, p. 281. EC Directive Harmonising the Term of Protection of Copyright and Certain Related Rights, Article I(I). P. Goldstein, *International Copyright: Principles, Law, and Practice*, Oxford University Press, 2001, Appendix 28, p. 567.
193 Goldstein, op. cit., 2001, p. 232.
194 Ross, op. cit., pp. 1–3.
195 Bently and Sherman, op. cit., pp. 152–153. Cornish, op. cit., pp. 281–285. MacQueen, Waelde, Laurie and Brown, op. cit., pp. 117–118.
196 L. Weinreb, 'Copyright for Functional Expression', *Harvard Law Review*, vol. 111(5), 1998, 1149–1254. S. Sterk, 'Rhetoric and Reality in Copyright Law', *Michigan Law Review*, vol. 94, 1996, 1197–1249. S. Breyer, 'The Uneasy Case for Copyright: A Study of Copyright in Books, Photocopies, and Computer Programs', *Harvard Law Review*, vol. 84(2), 1970, 284–321.
197 Sterk, op. cit., 1197–1249.
198 Bently and Sherman, op. cit., p. 33.
199 Weinreb, op. cit., 1149–1254. Sterk, op. cit., 1197–1249.
200 David, op. cit., p. 14.
201 Nowell-Smith, op. cit., p. 17.
202 S. Vaidhyanathan, *Copyrights and Copywrongs: the Rise of Intellectual Property and How It Threatens Creativity*, New York University Press, 2001, p. 40.
203 Ibid.
204 N. Netanel, 'Copyright and a Democratic Civil Society', *The Yale Law Journal*, vol. 106. 1996, 283–387.
205 Sterk, op. cit., 1197.
206 Weinreb, op. cit., 1149–1254. Sterk, op. cit., 1197–1249.
207 Netanel, op. cit., 1996, 283–387.
208 A. Smith, edited by R. Meek, D. Raphael, P. Stein, *Lectures on Jurisprudence*, Indianapolis, IN: Liberty Fund, 1982[1723–1790], pp. 82–83. Overall, Gillian Hadfield offered more sufficient comments on Smith's notion of copyright, see G. Hadfield, 'The Economics of Copyright: An Historical Perspective', *ASCAP Copyright Law Symposium*, no. 38, 1992, 19–25.

209 Netanel, op. cit., 1996, 308.
210 L. Robbins, edited by S. Medema and W. Samuels, *A History of Economic Thought: The LSE Lectures*, Princeton University Press, 1998, pp. 129–131. R. Coase, *Essays on Economics and Economists*, The University of Chicago Press, 1994, pp. 87–90.
211 G. Brennan and J. Buchanan, *The Reason of Rules: Constitutional Political Economy*, Cambridge University Press, 1985, Chapter I. S. Fleischacker, *On Adam Smith's Wealth of Nations: A Philosophical Companion*, Princeton University Press, 2005, pp. 138–142.
212 A. Smith, *Wealth of Nations*, New York: Prometheus Books, 1991[1776], pp. 9–28, 471–485.
213 Hadfield, op. cit., p. 23.
214 Ibid, pp. 19–25.
215 Ibid, p. 22.
216 Smith, op. cit., 1991[1776], pp. 480–481, 483–484.
217 Hadfield, op. cit., pp. 19–25.
218 D. Bell, 'Models and Reality in Economic Discourse', in D. Bell and I. Kristol (eds), *The Crisis in Economic Theory*, New York: Basic Books, 1981, p. 49.
219 Goldstein, op. cit., 1994, p. 174.
220 Netanel, op. cit., 1996, 308.
221 Coase, op. cit., 1994, pp. 77–79.
222 Dooley, 'Value', in J. Creedy (ed), *Foundations of Economic Thought*, Basil Blackwell, 1990, p. 154.
223 P. Drucker, 'Toward the Next Economics', in Bell and Kristol, op. cit., p. 7. J. Robinson, *Economic Philosophy*, Harmondsworth, UK: Penguin, 1964, pp. 48–70.
224 G. Mankiw, *Principles of Economics* 3rd edn, Mason, OH: South-Western/Thomson Learning, 2004, p. 462.
225 L. Mainwaring, 'Marginalism and the Margin', in Creedy, op. cit., p. 93. Bell, in Bell and Kristol, op. cit., p. 49.
226 J. Robinson and J. Eatwell, *An Introduction to Modern Economics*, UK: McGraw-Hill, 1974, Book I, Chapter III. J. Oser and W. Blanchfield, *The Evolution of Economic Thought* 3rd edn, Harcourt Brace Jovanovich, 1975, p. 222.
227 Mainwaring, op. cit., p. 93.
228 Robinson and Eatwell, op. cit.
229 Bell, op. cit., p. 49.
230 Ibid, pp. 51–53.
231 Oser and Blanchfield, op. cit., p. 220. Robbins, op. cit., pp. 258–284. I. Kirzner, 'The "Austrian" Perspective on the Crisis', in Bell and Kristol, op. cit., p. 113.
232 Oser and Blanchfield, op. cit., p. 222. Robbins, op. cit., pp. 303–311. Netanel, op. cit., 1996, 311.
233 J. Robinson, *Economic Philosophy*, Harmondsworth, UK: Penguin, 1964, pp. 55–57. D. Friedman, *Law's Order: What Economics Has to Do with Law and Why It Matters*, Princeton University Press, 2000, pp. 21–25.
234 Goldstein, op. cit., 1994, pp. 173–174.
235 Coase, op. cit., 1994, p. 116.
236 H. Hovenkamp, 'The Marginalist Revolution in Legal Thought', *Vanderbilt Law Review*, vol. 46, 1993, 313.
237 Ibid, 324.
238 Ibid, 310, 321–322.
239 Ibid, 324.
240 Ibid, vol. 46, 325.
241 Netanel, op. cit., 1996, 309.

242 For a sufficient treatment of 'market failure', see J. Stiglitz, *Economics* 2nd edn, W W Norton & Company, 1997a, Chapter VII. For the implications of 'market failure' in policy analysis, see D. Weimer and A. Vining, *Policy Analysis: Concepts and Practice* 2nd edn, Upper Saddle River, NJ: Prentice-Hall, 1992, pp. 30–77. For the implications of 'market failure' in the digital environment, see N. Elkin-Koren and E. Salzberger, *Law, Economics and Cyberspace*, Cheltenham: Edward Elgar, 2004.
243 Netanel, op. cit., 1996, 309.
244 Weinreb, op. cit., 1230.
245 H. Hovenkamp, 'The Marginal Revolution in Legal Thought', *Vanderbilt Law Review*, vol. 46, 1993, 313.
246 N. Mercuro and S. Medema, *Economics and the Law: From Posner to Post-Modernism*, Princeton University Press, 2006, pp. 157–195.
247 R. Coase, *The Firm, the Market and the Law*, The University of Chicago Press, 1988, p. 19.
248 Ibid, pp. 6–31.
249 Elkin-Koren and Salzberger, op. cit., p. 8.
250 Landes and Posner, op. cit., 2003.
251 Ibid.
252 W. Landes and R. Posner, 'An Economic Analysis of Copyright Law', *Journal of Legal Studies*, vol. 18, 1989, 336.
253 Landes and Posner, op. cit., 2003.
254 Ibid, p. 37.
255 R. Towse, *Creativity, Incentive and Reward: an Economic Analysis of Copyright and Culture in the Information Age*, Cheltenham, UK: Edward Elgar, 2001, p. 10.
256 Landes and Posner, op. cit., 2003, p. 396.
257 Netanel, op. cit., 1996, 312–313. Professor Netanel at UCLA Law School expressed the same view during a conversation with the author of this book on 19 September 2006.
258 E. Furubotn and R. Richter, *Institutions and Economic Theory: the Contribution of the New Institutional Economics* 2nd edn, University of Michigan Press, 2005. In particular, Chapter X of the book offers a sufficient discussion on this topic. G. Hodgson (ed), *A Modern Reader in Institutional and Evolutionary Economics*, Cheltenham, UK: Edward Elgar, 2002, p. xiv.
259 Furubotn and Richter, op. cit., Chapter X.
260 Netanel, op. cit., 1996, 313.
261 M. Blaug, 'Why Did Schumpeter Neglect Intellectual Property Rights?' *Review of Economic Research on Copyright Issues*, vol. 2(1), 2005, 69–74.
262 Schumpeter, op. cit., 1976[1942], p. 61.
263 N. Rosenberg, *Schumpeter and the Endogeneity of Technology: Some American Perspectives*, New York: Routledge, 2000, p. 3.
264 R. D'Aveni, with R. Gunther, *Hypercompetition: Managing the Dynamics of Strategic Manoeuvring*, New York: The Free Press, 1994, pp. 365–366.
265 L. Thomas, 'The Two Faces of Competition: Dynamic Resourcefulness and the Hypercompetitive Shift', *Organization Science*, vol. 7(3), 1996, 223. J. Stiglitz, *Whither socialism?* The MIT Press, 1997b, pp. 144–146. M. Mazzucato, *Firm Size, Innovation, and Market Structure: the Evolution of Industry Concentration and Instability*, Cheltenham, UK: Edward Elgar, 2000, pp. 1–19. W. Baumol, *Economic Dynamics: an Introduction*, New York: Macmillan, 1959, pp. 1–6, 33–34. D. Kallay, *The Law and Economics of Antitrust and Intellectual Property: an Austrian Approach*, Cheltenham: Edward Elgar, 2004, pp. 40–44.
266 Schumpeter, op. cit., 1976[1942], p. 83.
267 R. Swedberg, *Joseph Schumpeter: His Life and Work*, Cambridge, UK: Polity Press, 1991, Chapter II.

268 A. Roncaglia, *The Wealth of Ideas: A History of Economic Thought*, Cambridge University Press, 2005, pp. 420–422.
269 Y. Shionoya, *The Soul of the German Historical School: Methodological Essays on Schmoller, Weber and Schumpeter*, New York: Springer-Verlag, 2005, pp. 65–72.
270 D. Foley, *Adam's Fallacy: A Guide to Economic Theology*, Belknap Press of Harvard University Press, 2006, p. 210.
271 For a brief and critical treatment of 'the approximation to reality' and 'realism', see W. Baumol, *Business Behavior, Value and Growth* Revised Edition, New York: Macmillan, 1959, pp. 4–5. W. Baumol, 'Notes on Some Dynamic Models', *Economic Journal*, vol. LVIII, 1948, pp. 506–521. D. Hausman, 'Economic Methodology in a Nutshell', *Journal of Economic Perspectives*, vol. III(2), 1989, 121.
272 Roncaglia, op.cit., p. 433.
273 Some scholars generally refer methodological issues to the very sense of 'epistemological reasoning'. See, for instance, Shionoya, op. cit. M. Blaug, *The Methodology of Economics: Or How Economists Explain* 2nd edn, 1992. R. Posner, *Overcoming Law*, 1995.
274 Shionoya, op. cit., pp. 68–75. However, Schumpeter did not deny the connection between theory and fact but approached the connection from a deductive/instrumentalist angle. He insisted that a theoretical model is built completely on assumptions and is 'a creation of our discretion' . . . 'On the one hand, our theory is in essence arbitrary, and on this are based its system, its rigor, and its exactness; on the other hand, it fits the phenomena and is conditioned by them, and this alone gives it content and significance'. Quoted in F. Machlup, 'Schumpeter's Economic Methodology', *The Review of Economics and Statistics*, vol. 33(2), 1951, p. 148.
275 K. Popper, *The Logic of Scientific Discovery*, London: Hutchinson, 1959. *Conjectures and Refutations: The Growth of Scientific Knowledge*, London: Routledge & Kegan Paul, 1963.
276 Roncaglia, op. cit., p. 422. Overall, Schumpeter's methodological individualism and instrumentalism in his 1908 work exhibited his positivist views of economic analysis. This endorsement had no conflict with his positivist views but did wander away from the reality, although Schumpeter was clear that general equilibrium theory is a grand assumption of economic phenomena and needs further verification.
277 Shionoya, op. cit., p. 147.
278 Schumpeter, op. cit., 1962[1911], pp. x–xi.
279 S. Kuznets, 'Schumpeter's Business Cycles', *The American Economic Review*, vol. 30(2), Part 1, 1940, 260.
280 Quoted in Roncaglia, op. cit., p. 420.
281 Roncaglia, op. cit., pp. 420–421.
282 Ibid, pp. 420–422.
283 E. Andersen, 'Review of R. Swedberg's "Schumpeter: A Biography"', *Journal of Economic Literature*, vol. 31, 1993, 1969–1970.
284 As noted in Section 2.4, Schumpeter was one of the earliest economists who broke new ground for public choice theory. Meanwhile, he was also one of the initiators who launched neoinstitutionalist economics and inspired modern evolutionary economics. See Swedberg, op. cit.
285 B. DeLong, 'Creative Destruction's Reconstruction: Joseph Schumpeter Revisited', *The Chronicle Review*, vol. 54(15), 7 December 2007, p. B8.
286 R. Simonetti, 'Technical Change and Firm Growth: 'Creative Destruction' in the Fortune List, 1963–87', in E. Helmstadter and M. Perlman (eds), *Behavioral Norms, Technological Progress, and Economic Dynamics: Studies in Schumpeterian Economics*, University of Michigan Press, 1996, pp. 153–154.

M. Keklik, *Schumpeter, Innovation and Growth: Long-Cycle Dynamics in the Post-WWII American Manufacturing Industries*, Hampshire, UK: Ashgate, 2003, pp. 1–7.

287 R. Langlois, 'Schumpeter and the Obsolescence', Working Paper, Department of Economics, University of Connecticut, 2002, p. 2.

288 R. Te Velde, 'Schumpeter's Theory of Economic Development Revisited', in T. Brown and J. Ulijn (eds), *Innovation, Entrepreneurship and Culture: the Interaction between Technology, Progress and Economic Growth*, Cheltenham, UK: Edward Elgar, 2004, pp. 103–104.

289 Schumpeter, op. cit., 1962[1911], Chapter III.

290 Roncaglia, op. cit., p. 416.

291 Ibid.

292 For a brief introduction of the classical dynamics and some of their modern versions, see Baumol, op. cit., 1959, pp. 3–21.

293 Schumpeter, op. cit., 1962[1911], p. xi.

294 Ibid, p. 4.

295 Ibid, p. 64.

296 Ibid, Footnote, p. 61.

297 Ibid, p. 65.

298 Ibid, pp. 62–63.

299 Ibid, p. 68.

300 Ibid, p. 66.

301 Ibid, p. 65.

302 Ibid, p. 66.

303 R. Harris, Book Review of *Prophet of Innovation: Joseph Schumpeter and Creative Destruction*. Online. Available <http://www.historycooperative.org/journals/lhr/26.3/br_23.html> (accessed 16 November 2008).

304 Machlup, op. cit., p. 150.

305 Schumpeter, op. cit., 1976[1942], p. 82.

306 Ibid, p. 83.

307 Oser and Blanchfield, op. cit., pp. 451–452.

308 J. Useem, 'Dead Thinkers' Society: Meet the New Economy's Oldest New Economist', Business 2.0, November 2001, 132–34. D. Warsh, *Knowledge and the Wealth of Nations: A Story of Economic Discovery*, W W Norton, 2006, pp. 88–139.

309 Warsh, op. cit., pp. 121–124.

310 Schumpeter, op. cit., 1976[1942], p. 83.

311 Ibid, pp. 84–85.

312 D'Aveni, with Gunther, op. cit. Quoted in Grant, op. cit., 2002, p. 93.

313 D'Aveni, with Gunther, op. cit., p. 2.

314 Schumpeter, op. cit., 1976[1942], p. 106.

315 Grant, op. cit., 2002, p. 92.

316 Schumpeter, op. cit., 1962[1911]), p. 64.

317 Ibid, p. 66.

318 Schumpeter, op. cit., 1976[1942], p. 78.

319 Ibid, p. 82.

320 Ibid.

321 W. Baumol, R. Litan and C. Schramm, *Good Capitalism, Bad Capitalism, and the Economics of Growth and Prosperity*, Yale University Press, 2007, p. 3.

322 Schumpeter, op. cit., 1962[1911].

323 R. Heilbroner, *The Worldly Philosophers: the Lives, Times, and Ideas of the Great Economic Thinkers* 6th edn, New York: Simon and Schuster, 1992, p. 297.

324 W. Lazonick, *Business Organization and the Myth of the Market Economy*, Cambridge University Press, 1991, p. 124.

325 Thomas, op. cit., p. 223. Mazzucato, op. cit., pp. 1–19.
326 Schumpeter, op. cit., 1962[1911]. See also his 1976[1942].
327 McKnight, Vaaler and Katz, op. cit., p. 3.
328 Y. Lee, *Schumpeterian Dynamics and Metropolitan-Scale Productivity*, Hampshire, UK: Ashgate, 2003, pp. 10–12.
329 Schumpeter, op. cit., 1976[1942], p. 107.
330 W. Hutton, 'Anthony Giddens and Will Hutton in Conversation', in W. Hutton and A. Giddens (eds), *Global Capitalism*, New York: The New Press, 2000, pp. 10–11.
331 C. Greenhalgh and M. Rogers, *Innovation, Intellectual Property, and Economic Growth*, Princeton University Press, 2010, pp. 121–122.
332 Ibid, p. 11.
333 Schumpeter, op. cit., 1962[1911], p. 5.
334 Ibid.
335 Y. Biondi, 'Schumpeter's Economic Theory and the Dynamic Accounting View of the Firm: Neglected Pages from *The Theory of Economic Development*', *Economy and Society*, vol. 37(4), 2008, 535.
336 J. Schumpeter, *Business Cycles: A Theoretical, Historical, and Statistical Analysis of the Capitalist Process* 2 volumes, New York: McGraw-Hill, 1939, p. 13.
337 Ibid.
338 Schumpeter, op. cit., 1939, p. 17. See also Esben Anderson, 'The Limits of Schumpeter's *Business Cycles*'. Online. Available <http://www.business.aau.dk/evolution/esapapers/esa05/businesscycles05.pdf> (accessed 12 November 2008), p. 2.
339 Posner, op. cit., 1995, p. 11.
340 Schumpeter, op. cit., 1976[1942], pp. 417–418.
341 P. Howitt, 'Growth and Development: A Schumpeterian Perspective', *Commentary*, CD Howe Institute, no. 246, April 2007, pp. 1–6. Online. Available <http://www.econ.brown.edu/fac/Peter_Howitt/> (accessed 10 August 2009).

3 Copyright in the digital age

In this chapter, the essential issues of copyright protection and expansion already addressed in Chapter 2 are further explored through reviewing the digital context of copyright protection and expansion under some specific industry or market structure from a Schumpeterian perspective. Specifically, the issues of anti-commons and antitrust behind copyright expansion will be elaborated and debates over copyright expansion will be discussed before constructing theoretical framework and conducting empirical assessment in Chapters 4 and 5.

3.1 Overview of digital copyright

As Chapter 2.1 indicates, 'Technology defined, and challenged, copyright from the very start'.[1] Digital technology is no exception. Digitalisation has posed a massive challenge or threat towards the legal protection of copyright.[2] As 'digital representation revolutionizes the characteristics of content',[3] the activities of fair dealing or fair use become the example of creative destruction. 'In this process of creative destruction, digital technology and the Internet strike at the foundation of copyright and the industries built upon copyright by eliminating the need for firms to distribute copyrighted works and for exclusive property rights to support creation.'[4] Meanwhile, digital technology has penetrated the whole economy and, as a result, all intellectual property rights, including copyright, 'are rights which are created for and exist within market contexts'.[5] Thus, how the market functions and how copyright law adapts to the digital environment have become the central issues in the copyright industries in the information age.[6] The digital challenge or threat toward copyright can be better understood when the legal protection of copyright is examined alongside developments in markets, industries, and the wider economy under the pressure of creative destruction. The issues of digital copyright are both the issues of industry or market structure of the copyright industries and issues of legal promise under unique industry or market structure in the information age.

3.1.1 *Industry structure in general*

Neoclassical economics endorses the concept of 'perfect competition'[7] and signifies a complete market with perfect competition as a typical market structure.[8] However, in reality, the market processes rarely encounter the prerequisites defined in the neoclassical model of a complete market. The model of the complete market is a model rather than an economic reality.[9] In the real world, a complete market with perfect competition is difficult to achieve, although there are many markets where the role of competition is significant enough to approach the level as defined in the model of complete market. These markets are termed as competitive markets in which many producers (firms) supply the whole market with identical products and no producers could wage market power to change market prices. In this sense, the competition between producers is intensive and nearly perfect in a competitive market. Accordingly, on some occasions, a competitive market is labelled as 'a perfectly competitive market'[10] in contrast to some other markets where competition has been often limited.

A market with limited competition may be regarded as an 'incomplete' market. There are two kinds of incomplete market – monopoly market and imperfect competition market. Imperfect competition market includes monopolistic competition and oligopoly.[11] To which category should the information market in general, and the market for copyright industries, one of which is the book publishing industry in particular, belong in the digital age? To what extent could the structure of the information market affect the cost recoveries of the production or distribution of copyright products and the copyright-growth relation in a process of creative destruction? To continue exploring these questions, an investigation into the nature of the information market should be the starting point.

3.1.2 *Industry structure of information*

In the 1970s, Coase identified the distinction between the market for goods and the market for ideas, and analysed an interesting phenomenon, which was that both US and UK intellectuals supported the government regulation in the network industry, especially in the broadcasting industry, even if in general they endorse freedom in the market for ideas.[12] However, two decades later, by the mid-1990s, when the Internet as a new network industry expanded, businesses (rather than intellectuals) and government became allies in the regulation of cyberspace.[13] The alliance shift in network regulation reveals the latest dilemma of the copyright-growth relation as a reflection of the relation between intellectual property and industrial growth in the information age.

The information market, or 'the market for ideas' in Coase's account, should be a wide-ranging concept. When introducing the term 'market for ideas', Coase meant a market of intellectual expressions that could be covered under the First Amendment of the Constitution of the United States.[14] The 'idea' in Coase's terms in this specific context is different from the one characterised in copyright law that endorses the idea–expression dichotomy. Thus, the information market is not a market of abstract ideas. Rather, it should embrace the marketplace for all knowledge-based products, which include 'information, knowledge, database, news, software, literature, arts and other forms of human creation'.[15] Copyright works are a part of information products.[16] Meanwhile, it should be noted that the information market is not a new phenomenon of the information age. The book publishing market, as one kind of information market, existed long before the modern information age. Nevertheless, the information market is growing at an accelerating rate due to the digital revolution.[17] On the one hand, digital technology has played a substantial role in creating (producing or reproducing in some contexts) and trading (distributing) information products. On the other hand, the diverse forms of digital technology themselves are among the most important information products.[18] Accordingly, an inspection of the industry or market structure of information industries and related industries in the digital age facilitates our understanding of the nature of the information market and the role of copyright protection within the market.

In *Being Digital*, Nicholas Negroponte envisaged the network nature of the information market in a digital environment. As he stated, 'The information industry will become more of a boutique business. Its marketplace is the global information highway'.[19] The network nature in this context means an industry or market where the updating information technologies are the core or necessary condition for broadening the business operation by stimulating consumers' 'joint expectations' about the size of the consumer network, and by generating economies of scale[20] in the market or industry in the digital era. The markets for telephone, email, the Internet, the Internet-related book publishing, computer hardware and software, and airline services are considered as the network market. Other related terms, such as 'network economy' or 'network business', should be understood in this context.[21] By the same token, the concept of the information market is indeed equivalent to the term 'network market'. In addition, the terms 'new economy', 'internet economy', and 'digital economy' also mainly refer to the economic circumstances under which the updating digital technologies are the core business or the necessary condition for the converging business operation in the economy.[22]

The market forces, such as pricing and cost structure,[23] in the information market in the digital era may not be any different from those in the industrial age in content, but they have played more important roles than ever in the market processes of the new economy.[24] The main features of the market forces in the information market can be identified in the following aspects: (1) complementarity, compatibility, and standards; (2) switching costs and lock-in; (3) significant economies of scale; and (4) externalities.[25] The issues of complementarity, compatibility, and standards exist in any markets.[26] In the information market, these forces have become decisive because of the nature of digitalisation.[27] Switching costs as a special part of cost structure are obviously critical in the information market. It is understandable that, once adopting an information-intensive product (such as computer software), consumers do not usually change their preferences because the costs for adaptation (such as switching MS Windows® to Apple®operating systems) are so high. High switching costs could prohibit consumers from adopting a new product and lock them into the old system (lock-in).[28] Economies of scale are significant in the information market because the sunk costs (costs that cannot be recouped) or other kinds of fixed costs of the first copy of an information product (such as computer software) are so high that the output of this product would need to be large scale (larger quantity of authorised copies) to recover these costs.[29] In the copyright industries such as the book publishing and music record/publishing industries, as technological and organisational innovations are updated, the costs of production, including the long-run average cost, will reduce in many areas with the augmentation of production scale.[30] Thus, robust economies of scale will be present in these industries.[31] Externality has not been considered in the model of the complete market. However, in the market of copyright works as an incomplete market, ignorance of externality would impede a sensible understanding of the industry or market structure and process in the copyright industries. Besides a general categorisation of positive and negative externalities, Landes and Posner also offered a special classification of two externalities – pecuniary and technological externalities[32] – which are essential for an understanding of the industry or market structure in the copyright industries.

Complementarity (along with compatibility and standards), switching costs, economies of scale, and externalities are certainly not the only market forces that could play critical roles in the information market. Many other market forces, such as price discrimination, bundling, and transaction costs (as other parts of the pricing and cost structure), also function substantially in the market processes for information products.[33] Of course, in the book publishing industry, complementarity (along with compatibility and standards) and switching costs may not play an extensive role, as in other information industries. However, because digital technology is integrating the diverse sectors of the information industries, the reproduction and distribution processes of books cannot be isolated from the other information industries. As a result, these market forces have impacted all information industries, including the publishing industry, in one way or another. In particular, these market forces have restricted the level of competition in these information industries to different extents. Accordingly, the industry or market structure of the information market, including the book publishing sector, should be non-competitive.[34] That is, the term 'non-competition' does not signify a market with no competition but indicates that the level of competition in the information market is not 'perfect' as defined under the neoclassical model. In other words, the information market is an incomplete market with an imperfect competition.

The non-competitive nature of the information market should be a critical dimension for understanding copyright and the copyright industries in the context of ongoing technological innovations and corresponding organisational innovations. Copyright – defined in Chapter 1 as a legal privilege or entitlement to own and command the expressions of information products – is indeed a legal right to reproduce and distribute these expression-formatted information products, or put simply, copyright works such as books.[35] The market forces in the information market – such as pricing, cost structure, complementarity, economies of scale, and externalities – will affect the reproduction and distribution of copyright works as information products. These market forces could play diverse roles in shaping the production and distribution processes of copyright works such as books in the information market. In particular, these forces could transform the copyright industries at an unanticipated pace under a dynamic competition that is related to imperfect competition (a key feature of an incomplete market) on the grounds of updating technological and organisational innovations. In consequence, these market forces could further complicate the production–reproduction–distribution processes of copyright works, the industry or market structure in the copyright industries, and the copyright-growth relation under the industry or market structure of imperfect competition in the process of creative destruction.

After all, 'copyright is a statutory monopoly'[36] and the structure of the copyright industries under the copyright institution will be by no means perfect competition. As digital technology has transformed and redefined the nature of monopoly in the copyright industries, this non-competitive nature of the industry or market structure in the copyright industries is one of the main features of digital copyright.

3.1.3 Schumpeterian industry structure of digital copyright

Landes and Posner's phrase, 'the rosy Schumpeterian picture', illustrates a variety of issues surrounding the monopoly in the copyright industries in the information age.[37] As digital technology has renovated the entire economy, the issues surrounding monopoly in the copyright industries are, in essence, the issues of how copyright law as a regime of monopoly adapts to the digital environment and how the market functions in the non-competitive copyright industries in the process of creative destruction. Focusing on these issues in the copyright industries, a Schumpeterian picture of digital copyright under the forces of creative destruction can be clearly drawn.

1. Digital copyright under innovation

Innovation is the primary driving force of creative destruction. In the copyright industries such as the book publishing industry, as the innovative forces (forces of either technological or organisational innovations) advance, the cost structure in the industries will experience a critical adjustment in the process of creative destruction. The marginal effect of price would not necessarily result in the market equilibrium in the copyright industries as neoclassical economists could suggest.[38] Rather, the substantial discrepancy between the initial cost of production and marginal cost of reproduction of a copyright work as a unique cost structure in the information products industries[39] can lead to various disturbing consequences for the growth of these industries. As a result, the industry or market structure in the field will transform as well. While copyright is a state-granted monopoly, the players in the copyright industries benefit from the state's legal protection. Meanwhile, as discussed above, even if the state's protection is absent, the industries can still achieve an advantageous market position through an above-marginal cost and non-competitive price, owing to strong economies of scale in these fields.[40] In addition, some other factors such as lead-time advantage[41] could also raise an above-marginal-cost and non-competitive price. In either case – with or without the state's protection – 'deadweight cost would remain'.[42] Under the circumstances, a perfect competition (price being equal to marginal cost) is unattainable. Monopoly has become a norm in the copyright industries.

In the digital age, 'Technology, however, is a double-edged sword'.[43] The innovative forces (of either technological or organisational innovations), as the main driving forces behind strong economies of scale and lead-time advantage, could also remove some or many monopolistic practices in the copyright industries through the process of creative destruction. When the copyright industries face a hypercompetitive environment under the pressure of ongoing digital innovative forces, the entrepreneurs in these industries would engage in a 'creative response' to the new environment and take innovative strategic actions to gain competitive advantages for survival.[44] In Schumpeter's terms, a creative response could be a 'Deerfoot sausage'. In the publishing industry, a popular book could serve as a creative response and make a huge difference in adjusting the cost structure in the publishing field. This is also true of a popular CD, movie or a TV series in the other copyright industries. Meanwhile, as digital technology diversifies the channels of consumption and distribution of creative works, copyright's double dimensions of reproduction rights and commercial exploitation rights become fuzzier. On the whole, innovative forces play a double-edged role for both producers and consumers of creative works at the time of digital copyright.

2. *Digital copyright under dynamic competition*

Of course, the change of the cost structure under the pressure of creative destruction in the copyright industries is complex. In Schumpeter's system, the motive behind entrepreneurs' creative response (or 'adaptive response' under certain circumstances) as one kind of innovation would be the pursuit of quasi-rent[45] in the short run. However, as the quantity of books further increases, the taste of readers (on the demand side) depreciates, and so the price of books could fall and would be close to the marginal cost over the longer period. Copyright law and economies of scale offer an innovative publisher or any other entrepreneurs the relatively certain opportunity to earn monopolistic profits in the short run. Nevertheless, no innovative publisher or any other entrepreneurs can maintain a strong market position forever. As the innovative forces continue to advance, other entrepreneurs – either innovative or imitative, or both – can also engage in creative response to a hypercompetitive environment in the process of creative destruction. The competition among entrepreneurs under the innovative encumbrance, termed as a dynamic or Schumpeterian competition,[46] could change the cost structure and, in the long run, would smooth the dynamic progression of the industry or market structure in these industries from a monopoly to competition, and in reverse.

Under the pressure of a dynamic competition, externalities can play a unique role in the market process of digital copyright works. Of course, the function of externalities in a static environment cannot be ignored. Landes and Posner looked at how externalities exert the effect on the industry or market structure in the copyright industries in a static context. Their distinction between pecuniary and technological externalities,[47] as Chapter 3.1.2 introduces, does offer a sensible approach to scrutinising the role of copyright law in the production–distribution process of creative works in terms of Marshall's standard of efficiency – the value of positive net worth. In their model, the congestion externalities in the absence of copyright protection as negative and technological externalities could downgrade the incentive of innovation or creativity and, therefore, a system of indefinite renewals for copyright protection would overcome the problem in order to reach optimality.[48] However, even if they termed the positive net worth of copyright protection as the 'dynamic benefit' of a property right and specified 'the rosy Schumpeterian picture' of copyright protection in the new economy of the digital time, it is still a deficiency for their model not to catch the complexity under a dynamic or Schumpeterian competition in the copyright industries.

Externalities play different roles in the static and dynamic contexts in the market of digital copyright works.[49] When the issue of externalities is placed into the context of a dynamic or Schumpeterian competition in the process of creative destruction, the relation between externalities and social optimality are not so clear-cut. According to Baumol, the externalities of innovation (or creativity in a broad sense), either positive or negative – or in other words, either beneficial or detrimental spillover of innovation – could enhance overall incentives of innovation and help reach social optimality.[50] He argued that the externalities associated with the process of creative destruction could exert 'a countervailing influence'[51] that counterbalances the negative effects of externalities or spillovers. He presented two aspects of such countervailing influence.

On the one hand, a full assessment of the externalities in the process of creative destruction may relax the anxiety of the standard view, endorsed by

Landes and Posner, that the beneficial spillover of an innovation to other innovators or imitators could cause an underinvestment of the creator of the innovation due to an expected disincentive. On the other hand, the counteracting between overinvestment and underinvestment would not undermine the desirable outcomes of the spillover in innovation.[52] On the whole, the externalities or spillovers of innovation in the process of creative destruction would be positive and encouraging for achieving social optimality. Accordingly, Landes and Posner's proposal for a system of indefinite renewals[53] for copyright protection may not be necessary from a standpoint of social welfare.

3. *Digital copyright under Schumpeterian industry structure*

The enduring positive and beneficial nature of externalities in innovation and economies of scale in the process of creative destruction can overhaul the industry or market structure of copyright industries to a different extent. Whenever the copyright industries have undergone a process of creative destruction, the competition between imitators and innovators, between innovators and innovators, and between imitators and imitators will be unpreventable, unpredictable, unbalancing, multifarious, multilevelled, and – in one word – dynamic. The digital–copyright-related copyright industries should be hypercompetitive. Schumpeter's realist model of innovation-oriented and time-framed dynamic analysis is more applicable to investigating the dynamics of digital–copyright-related copyright industries.

As Chapter 2.3.1 indicates, the neoclassical model assumes that full exploiting incentive and equalising marginal utility with the marginal benefit under perfect competition is necessary for achieving efficiency. Thus, neoclassicism argues that 'market pricing can direct resource allocation for the marketing and development of existing creative expression in an optimally efficient manner',[54] and 'lends unreserved support to the lengthened copyright term' as long as the existing creative works still have social values.[55] In contrast, under Landes and Posner's revised neoinstitutionalist–neoclassical model, because the balance between access and incentives is their central issue for protecting intellectual property rights, this protection should serve two goals – maximising utility and enhancing incentives.[56] For the purpose of maximising utility, the level of copyright protection seems insignificant. With minimal or no copyright protection, the loss of copyright creators or producers would possibly be balanced with the gains in imitators or consumers. Accordingly, utility maximisation may not be impaired, pecuniary externality would prevail, and technological externality would not be at issue. However, this model does not imply that a pecuniary externality would endure without copyright protection. Indeed, for Landes and Posner, diminishing copyright protection would eventually bring about the net loss of the whole value.[57] Nevertheless, under both the neoclassical and Landes and Posner models, the diverse functions of innovative forces in the copyright industries are not fully explored. For both models, the issue of technology is addressed mainly because technology widens the division between fixed and marginal costs and triggers corresponding market failure. Meanwhile, under both models, the 'time' factor is not examined[58] in light of innovation.

Schumpeter's dynamic model can, to some extent, overcome the above limitations of both the neoclassical and Landes and Posner models, and endorse a realistic way to grasp the essential feature of digital–copyright-related copyright industries. Under Schumpeter's model, the growth of digital–copyright-related copyright industries is a long-term process of creative destruction. In his terms, it is 'an endless sequence of moves and countermoves, an indefinite state of warfare between firms'.[59]

In the long-term process, the essential feature of digital–copyright-related copyright industries is that they are dynamic in nature. As digital technology, being a key innovation, creeps into the whole producing and distributing process of copyright industries, the monopolistic power of digital copyright becomes volatile over the long term. Meanwhile, in a hypercompetitive environment under the pressure of creative destruction, the value of old copyright works would rapidly decline and that of new copyright works would rise equally rapidly over the long run. In addition, the positive and beneficial externalities in innovation would initiate a creative market of innovative competition and advance a competitive entry in the copyright industries. Moreover, while perfect competition does not exist, industry concentration is a channel to make progress in the long-term process of creative destruction.[60] As a result, the state's protection of copyright would become weak, the monopolistic industry or market structure in the copyright industries become unsustainable, and the whole structure would periodically transform from one array of competition/monopoly to another under the pressure of creative destruction.

After all, industrial growth 'never can be stationary'[61] and 'perfect competition is impossible'[62] in the long-term process of creative destruction under Schumpeter's dynamic model. In this long-run process of dynamics, not only are innovative forces such as digital technology a double-edged sword, but other forces of creative destruction such as competition and concentration also play diverse and complex roles in balancing the producer–consumer and imitator–innovator interactions in the copyright industries. Under the Schumpeterian or dynamic industry structure, digital copyright – like other copyright regimes in the pre-digital age – could function in diverse and reverse directions in the long run. Accordingly, the question of whether 'copyright expansion could stimulate or restrict the growth of copyright industries as information technology advances' is a complex issue under a Schumpeterian industry structure. Of course, the role of copyright expansion in the long-term process of creative destruction is diverse but not incomprehensible. Schumpeter's dynamic model can facilitate a realistic scrutiny of the copyright-growth relation in the context of the producer–consumer and imitator–innovator interactions in the copyright industries.

3.2 Anti-commons and antitrust behind copyright expansion

The anti-commons and antitrust interaction reflects the producer–consumer and imitator–innovator interactions and complicates copyright-growth relation in the information age. Historically, the efficient result of the century-long enclosure movement provided a natural experiment for supporting the very rationale of property rights in general, and intellectual property rights in particular.[63] Meanwhile, the premise of 'tragedy of the commons' provokes a thought experiment for illustrating the inefficiency of any anti-private-property activities.[64] In both cases, 'the commons' are perceived as the barriers for optimally and sustainably utilising or creating resources – either physical or intellectual resources. In the information age, the issues concerning copyright expansion are still the issues regarding the domain in 'the commons'. To further explore the issues of copyright expansion in the information age, it is necessary to investigate the issues of 'anti-commons' and antitrust in the context of digital innovation and the corresponding Schumpeterian competition.

3.2.1 *Anti-commons and Lessig's balanced approach*

Optimists and neoclassicists strongly endorse 'enclosure-oriented' laws or policies. For them, no matter how technology evolves and how industry structure renovates, the principle of 'enclosure' should always keep up with the technological and structural changes in the copyright industries. In the digital age, under the pressure of new technology[65] and Schumpeterian competition,[66] not only has copyright expansion in both duration and scope been underway as discussed previously, but technological measures of 'enclosure' have also been reinforced at high speed.[67]

In the US, the Digital Millennium Copyright Act (DMCA) has broadly rendered illegal the circumvention of anti-copyright-piracy measures.[68] The Copyright and Related Rights Directive 2001 shares many similarities with the DMCA, both having a common root in the WIPO Copyright Treaty and Phonograms and Performances Treaty. In the UK, the Copyright and Related Rights Regulations 2003 highlight copyright protection against the circumvention of anti-piracy measures.[69] These anti-circumvention regulations broadened copyright-owners' enclosure over their rights and diversified enclosure measures against users' access to these properties. As a result, this overly broad and complex mechanism of copyright protection increased the transaction costs for clarifying these establishing or claiming rights over innovations or creativities. In consequence, the information costs (one type of transaction costs) of searching for copyright owners and acquiring their permissions are high enough to hold up any voluntary negotiations/agreements that can optimise copyrights. Accordingly, the scenario of 'anti-commons' has surfaced.[70]

Obviously, the vision of 'anti-commons' is a 'free-riding' vision of copyright monopoly. Under the optimist and neoclassical framework of copyright, the copyright institution has been designed to promote an efficient creation and optimal utilisation of expressive goods. Correspondingly, an extensive copyright enclosure is assumed to boost efficiency most. However, the stance of 'anti-commons' as a result of extensive enclosure becomes a stalemate of copyright optimisation. The reason is less complex – a 'free-riding' of copyright monopoly is not free from costs in transactions that proceed under certain copyright institution. Coase's neoinstitutionalism convincingly specifies how transaction costs affect the working of the real economic system and how the legal system is crucial for wealth maximisation whenever transaction costs are positive.[71] Nevertheless, under Coase's neoinstitutionalist framework, it is still far from clear under which conditions and what kinds of voluntary transaction institutions could emerge, and how 'anti-commons' could be overcome.[72] The core concern of 'anti-commons' is the transaction costs of voluntary negotiation/agreement regarding trade of property rights. The ineffectiveness of neoinstitutionalists', and particularly the Coase Theorem's, treatment of 'anti-commons' is to some extent attributed to the theory's original focus – the institutional arrangement of property rights in land.[73] As Stigler pointed out, some studies showed that the logic of the Coase Theorem is inclusive but its domain is partial.[74]

This could be the case when the Coase Theorem is applied to analyse the issues of 'anti-commons' and copyright efficiency in the digital age. The digital-centred new economy is more complex and dynamic than the economy of land. The issues of 'anti-commons' are more complex in a digital environment. Facing the challenge from new digital technology and the corresponding Schumpeterian industry structure, both neoclassism and neoinstitutionalism are not ready to offer a realistic agenda for exploring the mechanism of voluntary negotiation/agreement in exchanging intellectual property rights for efficient and optimal outcomes.

To retrieve such a realistic framework for examining the issues of 'anti-commons' in the information age, Lessig's balanced approach advocates an inspiring insight. He has broadly addressed a series of issues of copyright expansion, freedom (including free speech), and private property rights in the digital age in his *Code and Other Laws of Cyberspace* (1999), *The Future of Ideas* (2001), and *Free Culture* (2004). In general, what Lessig is concerned with is how to maintain the balance between copyright protection or expansion and intellectual creativity or innovation, and between freedom and control over private property rights; and, correspondingly, what types of institutional arrangements (laws or regulations) can possibly provide a platform for such balance.

Lessig has posed a strong challenge to optimists and neoclassicists for their enduring defence of copyright expansion in both duration and scope. In his view, the relation between copyright and creativity is one crucial aspect of the relation between intellectual property and intellectual creativity in the information age. However, rather than exploring the new issues of intellectual assets around property rights and focusing on the nature or direction of the relation between the two factors as both copyright optimists and pessimists do, Lessig renewed the way of thinking about the new issues and the property–creativity relation, and placed the relation between these issues into the context of American constitutionalism. He raised the sincere concern of whether or not copyright expansion affects some fundamental freedoms of property rights in creativity and innovation on the constitutional basis.[75]

Although exploration of the copyright–creativity conflict on the ground of constitutionalism is relatively recent, related issues – such as property rights versus freedom and public interest versus individual rights – have attracted a significant degree of academic attention.[76] Historically, the relation between property rights and personal liberty reflected the relation between the individual and the state.[77] Lessig observed that the Statute of Anne was more than just a copyright law. Rather, it was the government's tool to deal with the conflict between public interest and individual rights.[78] This primary but cohesive connection between copyright law and intellectual creativity as a reflection of the conflict between public interest and individual rights, underlined mainly by Lessig, affords an inquiry.

According to Lessig, a broad enclosure over property rights, as optimists and neoclassicists assert, is indeed deadlock for economic prosperity because wealth maximisation historically depends on a property system 'in which private parties can order their lives freely through contract and property'.[79] In this regard, freedom to act is the necessary condition of voluntary negotiation/agreement for wealth maximisation under certain private property institutions in the first place. Private property rights cannot be secured whenever freedom is scarce under an institution of broad enclosure. Meanwhile, 'property rights are never absolute'[80] because the inevitable conflict of interest could become an impasse for further progress whenever people exercise their freedoms to pursue their property rights with no limitations. To overcome such impasse, the state should play a balancing role in protecting people's freedoms of property rights for a common good. This balance is, therefore, 'a feature of all property' and 'an especially important feature of intellectual property'.[81]

In his *The Future of Ideas* in 2001, Lessig continued stressing the importance of transforming our way of thinking for comprehending the issues of intellectual property and the property–creativity relation in the new digital age.[82] For Lessig, the focal point for inquiry into the new issues of intellectual assets and the property–creativity relation in the digital age should be the balancing relation between freedom and control over intellectual resources. As a result, the balancing relationship between copyright and creativity has gained specific treatment in his thought-provoking works. Lessig reiterated the term 'free' by quoting the words of Richard Stallman, the founder of the Free Software Foundation: 'Free, not in the sense of free beer, but free in the sense of free speech.'[83] A free resource, according to Lessig, should have two features: '(1) one can use it without the permission of anyone else; or (2) the permission one needs is granted neutrally.'[84]

In Lessig's views, an orthodox, although legitimate, pursuit of copyright holders' interests and copyright expansion not only exerts economic/financial burden on creativity but also, more importantly, political/constitutional burden on freedom to create. Once the property–creativity relation has developed into the freedom–control interaction as copyright expansion persists, any hardliner protection of property rights would put creativity in jeopardy. As Lessig pointed out through quoting Guggenheim, 'This control creates burdens, and not just expense. 'The cost for me, Guggenheim says, "is creativity" '.[85]

Free Culture, published in 2004, is Lessig's further effort to examine the relation between freedom and control over intellectual resources in a digital environment.[86] Following the path in *The Future of Ideas*, Lessig specified a complex process of balancing the relation between copyright and creativity. He believed that copyright law was 'born righteous'; that is, copyright law was originated for the common good. Since the UK Statute of Anne, copyright law has been designed as a formal mechanism for balancing the public interest and private gain of intellectual products.[87] He observed that, at the time of the Statute of Anne, booksellers' monopolistic power constrained the spread of knowledge and, therefore, the advancement of competition among publishers, as one of the Statute's initiatives was to stimulate a culture of creativity.[88] Meanwhile, as other scholars contended, the Statute of Anne itself also reflected the very nature and fundamental principles of copyright law. These principles include (1) natural law stance, (2) labour reward, (3) creativity stimulation, and (4) social needs.[89] These principles, according to Lessig, prevailed at the early stage of copyright development, in particular, after the UK House of Lords revoked perpetual copyright and constructed the public domain following their hearing of *Donaldson v Beckett*.[90]

Overall, Lessig's balance approach is straightforward – less free expression ('speech') and more control simply mean that less or no expression of innovation or creativity would be generated in the information age. In general, the balance between access to and control over copyright as the rule rather than the exception of copyright law is proposed to create more property rights for maximising welfare for the whole society. In particular, digital technology necessitates the balanced approach to copyright protection. As Lessig put it, 'Even if the control model makes perfect sense in the world of things, the world of things is not the digital world'.[91] In the digital environment, more controls and further copyright expansion can only complicate the accessing process and accordingly construct 'anti-commons'. As a result, free culture (including free speech) has been copyrighted and copyright has been expanded to restrain speech 'without any promise of future creativity'.[92] To overcome 'anti-commons', balancing access control and curbing copyright expansion are the indispensable options in the digital age. While 'copyright law both increases speech and restricts it . . . a fairly balanced copyright law can, in principle, at least, increase more than it restricts'.[93]

Of course, enhancing free expression (speech) and curtailing copyright expansion can create the necessary conditions for dealing with the 'anti-commons' problem and promoting innovations or creativities in the information age. Meanwhile, it is clear that the 'anti-commons' problem is the issue of a general and popular enclosure, or 'closing' in Lessig's terms,[94] of content. Under an 'anti-commons' circumstance, the 'potential for strategic behaviour' by various rights holders discourages new rights creators from innovating under the shadow of increasing transaction costs in accessing.[95] Nevertheless, the 'anti-commons' problem is an essential issue of competition as copyright expansion becomes a way of seeking competitive advantage for the 'old' rights owners over the 'new' rights creators in the digital environment. Accordingly, to explore the fundamental feature of 'anti-commons' and copyright expansion in the new environment, it would better place the issues of 'anti-commons' and copyright expansion into competitive contexts in the information age.[96] In this regard, an investigation into the antitrust issue will be instructive for further examining 'anti-commons' and copyright expansion in the new competitive information market.

3.2.2 *Antitrust policy under Schumpeterian competition*

'The antitrust laws are concerned with maintaining competition in private markets.'[97] The principal view of competition that entails the conventional thinking of antitrust is the neoclassical doctrine, which cherishes the principles of perfect competition.[98] Under the neoclassical competition, the price mechanism is the only yardstick through which firms compete.[99] Following the path of neoclassical economics, the main purpose of antitrust policy is to restrain the firm's monopolistic power over output and price of specific products. However, 'Antitrust is a defensible enterprise only if it can make markets more competitive – that is, if antitrust intervention produces lower prices, larger outputs, and improved product quality'.[100] Thus, the analysis of antitrust issues shall reflect the nature of competition and competitiveness.[101] It is the point at which the Chicago School and the neoclassical doctrine that still dominates the current analysis of antitrust face new challenges. 'The analytic lenses still commonly employed today in antitrust analysis were more suitable in a world where competition was less global, where innovation was less a multinational phenomenon, where time to market was less critical, and where the successes of the pioneers and the followers were clearly separated. Changes in the global economy mean that some of "modern" antitrust is anachronistic, at least in a setting of rapid technological change.'[102] In contrast, Schumpeter's framework as 'influential theory of innovation'[103] conveys more informative messages on antitrust issues.

Schumpeter's fundamental concern is the long-term 'survival', 'growth', and 'development' of capitalist economy. In his system, the course of economic development or industrial growth is in essence a process of creative destruction as 'the gale of capitalism'. Schumpeter identified the crucial factors of the process of creative destruction – industry structure, competition, innovation, and entrepreneurship – as Chapter 1.1 introduces and analyses their imperative interactions in the course of economic development or industrial growth. For Schumpeter, innovation – especially technological innovation – is the central force of creative destruction and the driving force of capitalism.[104] The process of creative destruction is a course of dynamic competition (as Chapter 2.1 indicates) in which entrepreneurs exploit innovative forces to remodel the patterns of industry structure and to reshuffle firms' contestability in the long-term sequence of 'time'. In the long-term process, competition is innovative, innovation becomes competitive, industry structure advances over the wave from perfect competition to monopoly, and entrepreneurs are aggressive in seeking diverse opportunities of innovation – doing new things – for surviving or thriving. Competition under innovation (or 'innovative competition') is dynamic in nature. These innovation-oriented and time-framed features are the essence of a dynamic or Schumpeterian competition.[105] Fundamentally, a dynamic or Schumpeterian competition, unlike a static or routine competition in which the price mechanism plays an essential role in determining the output of a product, is a 'quality competition'.[106] As discussed in Chapter 2.3.2, this new type of competition is 'the competition from the new commodity, the new technology, the new source of supply, the new type of organization (the largest-scale unit of control for instance) – competition which commands a decisive cost or quality advantage and which strikes not at the margins of the profits and the outputs of the existing firms but at their foundations and their very lives'.[107] In other words, it is the competition for the innovative quality of firms' products in order to ensure their surviving and thriving in the long-term process of creative destruction. It 'is primarily about active, risk-taking decision makers who seek to change their parameters' and 'new ways of doing things' and is 'motivated by more than profit maximization'.[108] As quoted in Chapter 2.3.2, this dynamic or Schumpeterian competition is a hypercompetition.[109]

In Schumpeter's model, the relation between innovation and competition, especially the competition for innovation or the dynamic (Schumpeterian) competition, is a critical issue for economic development or industrial growth in the long-term process of creative destruction. Entrepreneurs under a dynamic or Schumpeterian competition are identified as the source of power that demolishes the barriers of innovation and exploits the opportunities of development or growth.[110] They are crucial risk takers who pursue firms' surviving and thriving in the course of economic development or industrial growth. In the long run, monopolistic or 'restrictive practices' in Schumpeter's term[111] as entrepreneurs' new way of business operations would be desirable.[112]

Schumpeter recognised the division between entrepreneurs' roles in maximising economic profit and in maximising social welfare.[113] In his system, the interaction between socially efficient practices and 'socially costly rent-seeking activities'[114] under a dynamic competition is an essential issue. What Schumpeter worried about was not entrepreneurs' disequilibrating function in economic development or industrial growth. Rather, the declining value of entrepreneurs in the progress of capitalism[115] was his real concern. For Schumpeter, to encourage socially efficient entrepreneurial practices, the market process as a process of creative destruction is expected to be effective for promoting competition and protecting entrepreneurs' innovative activities in the long run.

Schumpeter's views of long-run desirability of monopolistic practices and the 'effectiveness' of the market process inspired a new angle for analysing antitrust policy and the standard of 'efficiency' under a dynamic or Schumpeterian competition. In general, whether or not a market process is effective in protecting competition and promoting entrepreneurs' innovations depends on whether or not favourable opportunities would be provided for entrepreneurs rather than on whether or not a neoclassical efficiency (allocation efficiency or 'Pareto' efficiency) could be maintained in the process. According to Schumpeter, not all monopolistic practices are desirable.[116] Instead, only these restrictive practices that enhance innovations are noteworthy in the market process as a process of creative destruction. 'The impact of new things – new technologies for instance – on the existing structure of an industry considerably reduces the long-run scope and importance of practices that aim, through restricting output, at conserving established positions and at maximizing the profits accruing from them . . . Restrictive practices of this kind, as far as they are effective, acquire a new significance in the perennial gale of creative destruction, a significance which they would not have in a stationary state or in a state of slow and balanced growth.'[117]

The impact of innovations on the existing industry structure is Schumpeter's direct concern when addressing the issues of innovation-enhancing restrictive or monopolistic practices.[118] The 'new significance', according to Schumpeter, is the function of innovation-enhancing restrictive or monopolistic practices in stabilising and smoothing the industry structure in the process of creative destruction. '"Restraints of trade" of the cartel type as well as those which merely consist in tacit understandings about price competition may be effective remedies under conditions of depression. As far as they are, they may in the end produce not only steadier but also greater expansion of total output than could be secured by an entirely uncontrolled onward rush that cannot fail to be studded with catastrophes.'[119]

The stabilising function of innovation-enhancing restrictive or monopolistic practices in a process of creative destruction depends, to some extent, on the protection of property rights – particularly the protection of intellectual property rights or the property rights in innovation[120] – and related long-period contracts. In a dynamic economy, according to Schumpeter, the supply side, especially entrepreneurs, are the dominating forces for economic development or industrial growth.[121] For the entrepreneurs in a dynamic economy,

protecting intellectual property rights and related long-term contracts are
their unavoidable business strategies. As a result, innovation-enhancing
restrictive or monopolistic practices can protect 'a long-run process of expansion'.[122] Meanwhile, the smoothing function of innovation-enhancing restrictive or monopolistic practices in a process of creative destruction relies on the
aggressive actions of innovation-concentrating large corporations. As
Schumpeter put it, aggressive intrusion of large corporations 'can only in the
rarest of cases fail to improve total output in quantity or quality, both through
the new method itself – even if at no time used to full advantage – and through
the pressure it exerts on the pre-existing firms'.[123] Under the pressure of innovation, restrictive or monopolistic practices could be the strategic choices for
entrepreneurs at any point in time.

In short, innovation-enhancing restrictive or monopolistic practices stabilise and smooth the industry structure through *defensive* mechanisms (protection of intellectual properties) and *offensive* mechanisms (new methods or
pressures) respectively in the process of creative destruction. Under a stable
and smooth industry structure, entrepreneurs can expect or employ restrictive
or monopolistic practices to compete for favourable opportunities in order to
promote innovation and growth in the long run. The interaction between
competition, innovation, and growth under dynamic or Schumpeterian
competition has crept into the whole process of creative destruction.

According to Schumpeter, entrepreneurs and their firms' provocative
pursuits of innovations for surviving and thriving are vital for capitalism.
For this sake, the primary principle of economics should be 'effectiveness' of
the 'market process' in developing economy or growing industry rather than
'efficiency' of the 'market system' as classical or neoclassical economists would
endorse. In Schumpeter's account, the market process is a process of creative
destruction. In this process, entrepreneurs and their firms ('an industry' or 'an
economy' in a broad context) would seek both short-run solutions for survival
under a static competition and long-run strategies for growth under a dynamic
or Schumpeterian competition. The postulations of 'maximisation' and
'perfect competition' under the neoclassical economics reflect a partial reality
of entrepreneurs and their firms' operations or choices at most, nothing more.
In terms of methodology, 'the neoclassical proposition that "existing firms
maximise" turns into little more than the tautology that "existing firms
survive"'.[124] Thus, the endeavour of maximisation should be the effect rather
than the cause of entrepreneurs and their firms' actions. Identifying 'the effect'
as 'a doctrine of maximisation' for analysing economic behaviours shall provide
little information on economic development or industrial growth. In addition, an antitrust policy or legislation may not impact on all entrepreneurs
and their firms equally in the long run.[125] Under a long-term dynamic or
Schumpeterian competition, an antitrust legislation or policy might halt
monopolistic or restrictive practices of some entrepreneurs and their firms but
could also encourage other entrepreneurs and their firms to continue these
practices. Furthermore, in the long run, the difference between equilibrium

and disequilibrium is insignificant[126] for entrepreneurs and their firms who compete for surviving and thriving under a dynamic or Schumpeterian competition.

3.2.3 Copyright expansion and antitrust policy

Can antitrust law play an encouraging role in both promoting competition and protecting intellectual property rights (the property rights in innovation) as copyright expansion proceeds in the process of creative destruction? Perhaps Schumpeter would express reservations on this. The natures of copyright law and antitrust law signify the plausibility of Schumpeter's views on the relation between competition and innovation, and the applicability of his ideas for further exploring the relations between copyright and antitrust in general, and between copyright expansion and antitrust liability in particular.

Copyright, as indicated in Chapter 1, is designed to protect an individual's (being a legal or natural person) exclusive ownership over the reproduction or distribution of their creative or innovative expressions.[127] Such exclusive ownership confers a state-granted monopoly and market power to copyright holders in different degrees. Of course, the duration of state-granted copyright monopoly has been legally limited under most copyright regimes. However, the pursuit of copyright expansion, especially the increase in duration of copyright protection, has become the norm for decades.[128] As Chapter 2.1 explores, in the UK copyright industries, especially in the UK book publishing industry, copyright expansion is evaluated as an adaptive response to the pressure of creative destruction in the specific industrial field. Nevertheless, no matter how long the duration of copyright protection lasts, copyright protection – like the protection of other intellectual property rights – may always face the Arrow dilemma: 'in many instances in intellectual, literary, and educational life, information and entertainment are costly to produce but cheap to distribute'.[129] In consequence, either monopoly (sustaining the protection of intellectual property rights) or free-riding (withdrawing the protection of intellectual property rights) is the only policy option available consecutively and no law or policy can rectify both simultaneously.

Can antitrust law and copyright law balance to solve the Arrow dilemma? There is no easy answer. From the perspective of legislative or judicial intent, copyright law and antitrust law have been designed to cope with free-riding through state-granted monopoly,[130] and to deal with monopoly through state-promoted allocation of efficiency,[131] respectively. Thus, in theory and in policy principle, there is a conflict between the goal of copyright law and the objective of antitrust law.[132] However, this conflict should not be overemphasised.[133] Especially under the Schumpeterian competition in the new economy, the relations between copyright and antitrust in general, and between copyright expansion and antitrust liability in particular, are complex[134] and the Arrow dilemma may not be a decisive concern in the long-term process of creative destruction. Schumpeter's realist innovation-oriented and time-framed dynamic analysis offers a roadmap to approaching relations under the Arrow dilemma.

Characterising the protection of intellectual property rights as a defensive mechanism for stabilising the industry structure, Schumpeter placed the issues of protecting intellectual property rights into the perspective of economic development or industrial growth in the long-term process of creative destruction. As indicated in Chapter 2.3.2, Schumpeter emphasised both the innovation-oriented and time-framed features of a dynamic (Schumpeterian) competition, and analysed the issues of protecting intellectual property rights within the skein of these two features of dynamics. Thus, the relation between copyright expansion and antitrust liability can be accessed through analysing the dynamic or Schumpeterian competition in the process of creative destruction.

In Schumpeter's account, dynamic competition consists of a series of continuing competitive innovations (innovations under pressures) and innovative competitions (deviations from perfect competition) that transform industry structures and drive firms' contests for surviving or thriving in a long-term sequence of 'time'.[135] Under this dynamic or Schumpeterian competition, both protecting innovation and promoting competition are necessary for economic development or industrial growth. Investigating the relation between protecting innovation and promoting competition serves as a path towards the understanding of the nature of economic development or industrial growth in the long-term process of creative destruction. The relations between copyright and antitrust in general, and between copyright expansion and antitrust liability in particular, will become much clearer through exploring the long-run transformation of industry structures and advance of firms' contests under a Schumpeterian competition in the long-term process.

In general, for Schumpeter, economic development or industrial growth as a process of creative destruction is a time-framed course. The level of efficiency would depend on the range of short-term and long-term performances of the firms and effects of the firm's innovations on economic development or industrial growth in the long-term process of creative destruction. As Schumpeter observed, in the short run, the protection of intellectual property rights as a defensive mechanism stabilises the industry structure that becomes static, and an innovative firm may enjoy a temporary advantage and operate its businesses under a static competition. Efficiency may not be achieved as a whole at the industry level. In contrast, the long-term performances of each firm and long-run effects of a firm's innovations will usually expose the full scale of efficiency.[136] 'Market participants may have to tolerate short-run inefficiencies in order to gain long-run efficiencies.'[137] Meanwhile, according to Schumpeter, the process of creative destruction is also an 'organic' process.[138] Thus, both analytic and synthetic assessments would be needed for evaluating the whole picture of the performances of the firms and long-run effects of the firm's innovations on economic development or industrial growth at the firm, industry, regional, and national levels in the organic process of creative destruction.[139]

In particular, for some specific industries, such as the copyright industries, the distinction between short-term and long-term performances of the firms and the effects of the firm's innovations becomes more significant in understanding the firms' expansions and related industrial growth. In the short run, stabilising a suitable industry structure through protecting intellectual property rights may endorse some monopolistic practices for some firms. However, in the long run, encouraging some monopolistic practices may smooth the market process and transform the industry structures in an efficient pattern for long-term economic development or industrial growth. In addition, the monopolistic nature of some innovative practices may be noticeable at the industry level but would be less sizeable at the national level. Copyright expansion as a type of monopolistic practice would be efficient under dynamic competition in the long run. However, the innovation-oriented feature of the dynamic competition makes copyright expansion less desirable for long-term efficiency.

Meanwhile, antitrust policy will be also less crucial for the long-term economic development or industrial growth under dynamic competition. Indeed, 'the US and the EC - and other countries that have adopted elements of these approaches - have had competition policy regimes that over long periods of time are consistent with their attempting to maximize long-run efficiency by balancing the benefits of the short-run adverse effects of the exercise of market power on prices and output against the long-run beneficial effects of the prospect of market power on stimulating innovation and investments. That balancing effort is seen in the fact that these regimes do not prevent firms from acquiring and exercising significant market power, except in particular circumstances'.[140]

On the whole, Schumpeter believed that protecting intellectual property rights, the property rights in innovation, is an effective way for protecting innovation as the prime motive of a modern capitalist economy. In the first place, protecting intellectual property rights will offer a rational and prior justification for the investment in innovation.[141] Meanwhile, although he did not directly address the incentive and free-riding issues, Schumpeter did realise that innovations among firms are competitive. Under an innovative competition, it will be possible for some firms to resort to free-riding or imitative behaviours in order to take competitive advantages for boosting their own innovations or innovative imitations. Thus, protecting intellectual property rights will maintain an ongoing incentive for innovators and stabilise an appropriate but concentrating industry structure for encouraging both innovators and imitators to engage in innovative activities under a Schumpeterian competition. However, due to the massive and dynamic competition, a firm's innovative activities will display some features of restrictive or monopolistic practices under the pressure of dynamic competition. In this regard, protecting intellectual property rights may eventually safeguard these anticompetitive practices. The conflict between protecting innovation (through assuring intellectual property rights) and promoting competition (through enforcing antitrust policy) is unavoidable under a dynamic competition in the long-term process of creative destruction.

Therefore, no matter how we define the standing of the copyright–antitrust relation in the process of economic development or industrial growth, the conflict or tension between the two legal regimes in a general sense is undeniable.[142] Meanwhile, it is still too early to assume that some practical measures could balance or manage the conflict or tension. Schumpeter's perspective does offer a road map for placing the two legal fields into a large context of creative destruction. However, while Schumpeter's road map may direct an accessible approach to balancing the conflict as one aspect of the innovation–competition relation under the Arrow dilemma in the long-term process of creative destruction, a Schumpeterian paradox has surfaced.

In the early twentieth century, Schumpeter raised a fundamental concern of the time – 'Can capitalism survive?' To address this concern, Schumpeter attributed capitalism's future to the innovation–competition relation in the process of creative destruction and identified the innovative activities under the dynamic or Schumpeterian competition as the driving force behind capitalism's development and demise. For Schumpeter, due to the innovation under the dynamic or Schumpeterian competition, capitalism would fail to survive when it is going to thrive. This paradox is the hub of Schumpeter's empathetic observation on capitalism's fate under his model.

The Schumpeterian paradox and the Arrow dilemma, along with the Coase Theorem, are all tentative schemes for explaining the institutional features of capitalism.[143] Capitalism's property rights and market initiatives (innovation, competition, and efficiency as an evaluating benchmark of the innovation–competition relation) are presumed in one way or another in these models. The relation between institutional structure and efficiency as a reflection of the innovation–competition relation has been one of their crucial concerns. Coase believed that efficiency should result whenever an appropriate institution of property rights can be assured. Arrow argued that, at least in the information industries, efficiency is unachievable because the institution of property rights is unenforceable and the innovation–competition relation is incompatible in these fields, owing to the very nature of information. Schumpeter recognised the incompatibility between innovation and competition in general, and the conflict between intellectual property rights and the dynamic competition in particular. He was neither optimistic about an efficient market result, as Coase assumed, nor pessimistic about an efficient market process as Arrow showed. Rather, Schumpeter defined a dynamic efficiency as the result of a long-term interaction between innovation and competition in the long-term process of creative destruction. For him, efficiency should still be achievable in the long run, even if protecting intellectual property rights (property rights in innovation) and other property rights as one type of monopolistic practice would exert inefficiency in the short run.[144]

Schumpeter was 'an analytical optimist and a visionary pessimist'[145] from a methodological perspective. A vision, according to Schumpeter, is 'a sense of the way the world works', and 'a preanalytic cognitive act that supplies the raw material for the analytic effort'.[146] However, for Schumpeter, there was no clear-cut 'time order' between his vision of capitalism and his 'analytic effort' to explore capitalism. His vision surely confines his 'analytic effort'. Meanwhile, his analytic effort can in turn authenticate or adjust his vision. His realist innovation-oriented and time-framed dynamic analysis did serve as a unique methodological approach to analysing the complex reality of capitalism's market process as a process of creative destruction. This analytic approach to understanding a dynamic market process in which competitive innovation and innovative competition are the norm reveals the complex relation between innovation and competition, and the substantial meaning of the relation for capitalism's institution and evolution. It is from this analytic understanding of the complex and dynamic innovation–competition interaction and related institutional factors that Schumpeter visualised his pessimistic vision of capitalism's paradox – a living and dynamic process that would lead to a dying and static consequence.

Clearly, the Schumpeterian paradox is an exploratory construct of Schumpeter's methodological discrepancy between his visionary prospecting and his analytical reasoning on the whole-part connection of capitalism. Schumpeter's vision of capitalism is synthetic and diverse in nature. It incorporates social, economic, legal, historical, ideological, and far-sighted insights into capitalism's institution and evolution in total. On the contrary, his realist innovation-oriented and time-framed dynamic analysis is a real-world framework for assessing the complex but specific course of capitalism's economic development or industrial growth in part. 'He paid attention to vision because the ideological element inescapably intervenes in the formation of vision, and attached a great importance to the intertwinement between science and ideology. In his personal inclination, Schumpeter showed repugnance against value judgments and policy discussions and preferred to talk about the progress of science as a purely analytical apparatus.'[147] As a result, an analytical Schumpeter runs alongside an ideological Schumpeter. This methodological divergence shaped Schumpeter's paradoxical views on the state's role in pursuing antitrust policy and in preserving intellectual property rights in the context of the innovation–competition interaction.

On the one hand, Schumpeter analysed the importance of property rights for competitive innovation and valued the state's role in protecting intellectual property rights for assuring the long-term efficiency of innovative activities.[148] On the other hand, he devalued the state's function in challenging entrepreneurs and their firms' restrictions on competition. While addressing the limitation of traditional Cournot–Marshall theory of monopoly,

Schumpeter envisioned that perfect competition would be even more common than monopoly in the process of creative destruction.[149] Thus, the government's role in removing the constraints of entrepreneurial activities (mainly innovative and creative activities) may not be imperative in the long-term process of creative destruction.[150] In Schumpeter's account, the government would not achieve the goal of promoting competition through an antitrust policy or legislation in the long run. For him, 'capitalism was intrinsically dynamic and growth-oriented; he saw no need for government spending as a permanent auxiliary engine'.[151]

Of course, Schumpeter was not against the state's intervention in firms' practices but he was concerned about the very capacity of public authorities to execute rational and pro-competition regulation.[152] In his model, Schumpeter made an effort to compromise the state's role in sustaining (through protecting property rights) and smoothing (through promoting dynamic competition) capitalism's market process as a process of creative destruction. However, it is difficult to consider his efforts promising. Schumpeter was confident with capitalism's dynamic market process and its long-term efficiency. He was assertive that the dynamic competition containing some monopolistic practices would still be close to perfect competition in the long run. Were this the case, it would be unwise to argue that capitalism would not survive in due course. In this regard, the Schumpeterian paradox has been associated with some ambiguity in Schumpeter's exploration of the state's function in the capitalist market process.

Nevertheless, Schumpeter's 'synthetic vision' and 'analytic framework' are still promising, for the most part, in explaining the market process as a process of creative destruction. Even the ambiguity in Schumpeter's style can be conceived as 'stimulating' because certain levels of ambiguity in theoretical construction could help circumvent some value judgment in analysing the process of creative destruction.[153] Under Schumpeter's framework, the conflict between antitrust rights and intellectual property rights may not be resolved but can be further understood from a long-term and short-term distinction of the dynamic or Schumpeterian competition. The rationale of copyright expansion and its association with antitrust policy will become much clearer through exploring the long-term transformation of industry structures and advance of firms' contests under a dynamic or Schumpeterian competition in the long-term process of creative destruction. The industrial growth under the copyright–antitrust interaction can be explored from this unique angle under Schumpeter's model.

3.2.4 *Industrial growth under copyright–antitrust interaction*

In Schumpeter's account, in spite of his anticipation of capitalism's dwindling end and the unveiling of the Schumpeterian paradox, capitalism's evolution, development, and growth are to a large extent an irrefutable fact in the complex and dynamic process of creative destruction. Exploring the industrial growth under the copyright–antitrust interaction from Schumpeter's approach is by no means far away from the investigation into the copyright-growth relation from Schumpeter's perspective of creative destruction as discussed in Chapter 2.3.2. However, because of introducing the antitrust issue into the scenario of economic development or industrial growth under the copyright–antitrust interaction in the context of creative destruction, an exploration of other relevant but crucial issues – such as the complexity issue, the competition issue, the efficiency issue, and the entrepreneurship issue – becomes necessary for further understanding of the growth of copyright industries under the copyright–antitrust interaction from a Schumpeterian perspective.

1. Complexity issue

Antitrust policy is not encouraged in Schumpeter's model. Bringing copyright and antitrust together for analysis of the growth of the copyright industries under the model raises the complexity problem for theoretical construction and empirical assessment. The complexity and dynamics of the monopoly–innovation relation in general, of the copyright–antitrust relation in particular, and their significance for economic development or industrial growth should be clarified in the first place in order to analyse the growth issue under the copyright–antitrust interaction from Schumpeter's insights.

Noticeably, one of Schumpeter's fundamental contributions to the investigation of economic development or industrial growth is his integrating legal and economic factors or structures into a comprehensive model for analysing the process of creative destruction. Prior to Schumpeter, Smith and Ricardo already realised the importance of both economic and non-economic (law) forces for wealth building and economic development. They inspired Schumpeter to look over the role of law in economic development or industrial growth under legal pragmatism.[154] Schumpeter was one of the pioneers of public choice theory and neoinstitutionalist economics.[155] Following Schumpeter, some law and economics scholars and institutional economists even identified an indissoluble unification of legal and economic factors and 'a legal–economic nexus' in the marketplace.[156] However, Schumpeter's theory explains a complex and dynamic context of competition and development that both public-choice theory and neoinstitutionalist economics failed to explore. To inspect complexity and dynamics, Schumpeter had converged legal factors or structures with economic factors or structures for constructing his model of creative destruction. 'Convergence' does not mean that legal and economic factors or structures are integrated as a whole and cannot be analytically distinguishable in Schumpeter's framework. Rather, it does inform the concurrent effects of legal and economic factors or structures and the time-framed sequence of their impacts. Meanwhile, 'concurrence' does not imply that there would be no 'time order' between the effects of legal and economic factors or structures, even if the simultaneous effects of legal and economic factors or structures can be ascertained in some specific situations under a dynamic or Schumpeterian competition in the long-term process of creative destruction.

In a standard introduction to the role of law in economic performances, industrial activities, or any other business operations, a singular or distinct legal factor or structure (such as property law, contract law, tort law, or any other laws) would be typically identified and its role would be presumably explored from a cross-sectional angle with no consideration of 'time' factor.[157] Against this orthodox approach, Schumpeter's crucial contribution to the study of economic development or industrial growth lies not only in his integration of the role of law into his account of economic development or industrial growth, but also his explanation of dynamics of innovative forces (either technological or organisational innovations) and their complex interactions with the diverse and conflicting legal factors or structures in the course of development or growth. When inspecting legal factors or structures and their impacts on the market process, Schumpeter's focus is usually on their interactions or reciprocal impacts on the complex and dynamic course of market process.

In reality, the interactions or reciprocal impacts between or within legal and market factors or structures are the norm in the market process. Antitrust law is no exception. Under the legal structure, antitrust law does not come into force alone. 'Much of antitrust decision making is concerned with the proper allocation of regulatory power between the antitrust laws and other legal regimes, such as the intellectual property laws . . .'[158] In contrast, under the industry or market structure, competition level, price practice, contracting form, merger direction, innovation pattern, and many other market forces interact and affect the creation and implementation of antitrust law.[159] Meanwhile, how the power allocation between antitrust regime and intellectual property regime (or other regimes) affects the market process is also an important concern. Ignorance of the complexity and dynamics of the market process would not only perplex antitrust practices but also puzzle the research on the relation between antitrust and intellectual property and their impact on economic development or industrial growth. Frank Easterbrook, US Court of Appeals Judge and Professor at Chicago Law School, highlighted the confusion within the research on the relation between antitrust and innovation under Schumpeter's approach. Judge Easterbrook implied that, in part, the reason for the confusion is an unawareness of the complex context of antitrust law.[160]

Without doubt, Schumpeter explicitly identified a positive monopoly-innovation relation and implicitly queried the efficacy of antitrust policy for economic development and industrial growth.[161] He felt more confident with the market process than with the regulatory process, and preferred intellectual property rights to antitrust rights. Nevertheless, Schumpeter's assumptions and arguments are based on his observations on the complex and dynamic interaction between competition and innovation in the long-term process of creative destruction. Unlike the Chicago School economists who ignored the complexity of the market process and simplified the resulting efficiency of the process on account of perfect competition, Schumpeter focused on the complexity and dynamics of competition in the long run.[162] For him, the market power of an innovator, even if protected under the intellectual property regime, is usually relative and temporary under the complex and dynamic interaction between competition and innovation in the long run.[163] The monopoly–innovation relation and the feasibility of antitrust policy involve many other legal or economic factors and their complex interactions in the long-term process of creative destruction.

2. Competition issue

Understanding the competition issue is a key to exploring the growth of copyright industries under the copyright–antitrust interaction from a Schumpeterian perspective. The complex and dynamic competition in the process of creative destruction is an essential notion under Schumpeter's model. According to Schumpeter, the ultimate motive of industrial growth is innovation, and the innovation-oriented feature of dynamic competition is the very nature of capitalist competition. This dynamic competition in essence refers to, as previously noted, an innovation-oriented and time-framed rivalry for new ways of doing things or, in other words, a time sequence of incessant alternations between innovative competitions and competitive innovations in the process of creative destruction. In pure economic terms, the pattern of competition and the level of innovation determine the path of industrial growth in Schumpeter's framework.

On the contrary, in complex circumstances as indicated by the foregoing paragraphs, the relation between growth and dynamic competition is no longer straightforward in pure economic terms. Copyright and antitrust laws, along with related market factors, compose a specific 'legal–economic nexus' and a complex institutional structure that channel the competition–innovation–growth interaction. Could copyright and antitrust regimes as two conflicting legal structures make a difference in transforming the pattern of dynamic competition and the nature of the innovation-growth interaction? If so, how and to what extent could these two legal regimes play their roles in the course of transformation and how and to what extent could the growth of copyright industries progress or regress in the course of transformation in the long-term process of creative destruction? Addressing these questions necessitates a further reviewing of Schumpeter's perspective on the copyright–antitrust relation and the competition–innovation–growth interaction.

In Schumpeter's account, antitrust regimes play a very limited role in development or growth because, according to him, a dynamic competition is the dominant way of competition in the course of development or growth, and antitrust is less imperative for promoting competition in the long run. In contrast, copyright as one type of intellectual property right would be more valued than antitrust in Schumpeter's model because copyright regime is designed to protect the market power or interest for innovators or creators in order to provide an incentive to enhance innovation or creativity and, consequently, to smooth the progress of dynamic competition. It appears that there is a logical tension between copyright and antitrust under Schumpeter's scheme. However, a close reading of Schumpeter also reveals an inclination in his system to harmonise the conflicting rationales between antitrust and copyright laws. Eventually, although deprecating the notion of perfect competition under the neoclassical model, Schumpeter still regarded competition as the core of the process of creative destruction. A dynamic or Schumpeterian competition is still competition in nature. The only difference is that an 'innovation' factor and a 'time' factor are emphasised under a Schumpeterian competition. Meanwhile, under the Schumpeterian competition, innovative or creative practices may exhibit restrictive or monopolistic features in the short run, owing to the protection of intellectual property rights, but create a new industry structure favouring competitive activities in the long-term process of creative destruction. After all, 'the hallmark of Schumpeter's description of "capitalism as an engine of progress" is rivalry among firms in innovation'.[164]

Accordingly, in Schumpeter's system, antitrust law will not necessarily develop a hostile institutional structure toward a dynamic competition and the innovative or creative actions under the competition. Rather, antitrust policy may generate an active incentive to advance innovations or creativities under the pressure of creative destruction, while copyright law endows a passive incentive mechanism. Surely, the essential target of antitrust measure is a firm's massive market power in a specific market. When innovators' or creators' market power is still stabilising a new industry structure that continues facilitating innovation and growth, it will be possible that, as Barro was concerned, 'antitrust policy tends to penalize success and innovation and has doubtful benefits for consumers'.[165] Alternatively, when market power has been used for 'the old against the new',[166] as Lessig was concerned, antitrust law will act as a defender of innovation. The problem is the difficulty or even the infeasibility of identifying, in the long-term process of creative destruction, the point where innovators' or creators' market power might exhibit its either advancing or assaulting effect on innovations or creativities. Nonetheless, even if it is tough to determine whether or not antitrust law could reach its deliberate goal to curb firms' undesirable market power, this legal norm can still exert a deterring effect on the firms and motivate them to diversify or diffuse their innovations or creations in an efficient or effective and timely manner. As a result, antitrust law likewise bolsters innovations or creations in one way or another under a dynamic or Schumpeterian competition.

To be brief, under Schumpeter's scheme, 'it is not a matter of monopoly *versus* competition in the ordinary sense, but rather one of innovation in a process of creative destruction . . . The impact of innovation on existing firms is the competition that really counts in the Schumpeterian system'.[167] This

Schumpeterian system can serve as a framework for explaining a conflicting copyright–antitrust relation in principle and a complementary copyright–antitrust interaction in practice. In a long-term process of creative destruction, both copyright law and antitrust law construct distinctive incentive mechanisms respectively for encouraging innovations or creativities under dynamic competition. The two legal regimes constitute divergent institutional temptations that will strike an incumbent–insurgent balance and an innovator–imitator balance in the long run.

3. Efficiency issue

'A definition of economic efficiency incorporating Schumpeter's ideas has to cope with basic dynamic, rather than static, processes of an economy and with the notion of the efficiency of its creation and destruction of institutions.'[168] Schumpeter, as previously noted, grounded the concept of efficiency on the complex and dynamic process of creative destruction and considers efficiency as a long-run result of the dynamic interaction between innovation and competition in the course of economic development or industrial growth. The efficiency issue becomes a code for deciphering the effects of the competition–innovation relation on the growth of copyright industries under the copyright and antitrust structures from a Schumpeterian perspective. The Chicago School economists, like Schumpeter, also recognise the ultimate efficiency of a long-term market process under the perspective of neoclassical economics.[169] They mostly focused on static efficiencies – allocation efficiency and maximum efficiency. In contrast, what Schumpeter stressed is dynamic efficiency corresponding with the long-run progress of market processes and long-term performances of entrepreneurial firms under the dynamic competition.[170] For Schumpeter, a dynamic competition is effective in compelling firms to make a short-run innovative effort for a long-run superior effect.[171] Accordingly, dynamic efficiency in essence refers to a long-term progress of market transformation and asset maximisation through innovations under a dynamic or Schumpeterian competition. In terms of Pareto efficiency, dynamic efficiency can be defined as a progression of efficiencies that 'consist of the Pareto-optimal allocation of resources between present and future'.[172]

Is dynamic efficiency achievable or sustainable under copyright and antitrust regimes in the process of creative destruction? If so, how can dynamic efficiency be evaluated against the competition–innovation–growth interaction under the copyright and antitrust regimes? According to static equilibrium theory, static efficiency or Pareto efficiency is difficult to achieve whenever market failure, due to some factors such as (but not limited to) externalities and information asymmetry (information costs as one sort of transaction costs), is present.[173] However, cynically, a review of some literature reveals that various antitrust-style state interventions designed to overcome market failure have been held responsible for reducing static or Pareto efficiency.[174] Quite the opposite, in Schumpeter's account: dynamic efficiency is not so vulnerable to market failure and therefore will not necessarily be less achievable under state interventions.

Indeed, under a dynamic or Schumpeterian competition, protection of both antitrust rights and intellectual property rights is necessary for 'ensuring an effective competitive order' and securing a reliable process of information exchange between the demand side (individuals/consumers) and the supply side (firms/producers).[175] Meanwhile, in a long-term process of creative destruction, copyright law and antitrust law frame passive and active incentives respectively for firms to introduce and diffuse their innovations or creativities for their long-run interests. The long-run impacts of copyright and antitrust regimes on firms' long-term performances under a dynamic or Schumpeterian competition appeal to balancing the two extremes of perfect competition and full monopoly. In turn, the two legal regimes can to some extent reinforce a specific institutional environment that will strike the balance between the incumbent and insurgent firms, and between socially efficient entrepreneurial practices and 'socially costly rent-seeking activities'[176] in the long run. Taken as a whole, the effective competition order, the dual incentive mechanism, and the balancing effect under copyright and antitrust regimes can help achieve and sustain dynamic efficiency.

In the end, dynamic efficiency is a result of the competition–innovation interaction under a favourable institutional environment in the long-term process of creative destruction. Achieving and sustaining dynamic efficiency will be constructive for the industrial growth under a dynamic or Schumpeterian competition in the long-term process. However, evaluating the constructive function of dynamic efficiency in advancing growth, especially under the two legal regimes of copyright and antitrust, is a difficult task. Besides the complexity issue as previously addressed, the nature (either positive or negative) and source (either innovation or creative destruction) of externalities involving dynamic efficiency is a substantial concern. A traditional view on dynamic efficiency believes that innovation is the source of positive externalities through which the diffusion of innovation benefits consumers and competitors who bear no costs of innovation, but offers the innovator(s) less incentive to optimise future innovation(s).[177] Nevertheless, the externalities of creative destruction pervade and benefit widely. These externalities are negative ones that may balance the incentive mechanism (both passive and active incentives).[178] Even if in a general sense the institutional environment under copyright and antitrust laws can strike an incumbent–insurgent balance or a cost-efficiency balance in the long run, the externalities of creative destruction still encompass the full scale of efficiency (from static efficiency to dynamic efficiency) in the whole course (from short run to long run, or from present to future) of industrial growth.

Moreover, in the long-term process of creative destruction, adaptation to a dynamic competition and pursuit of dynamic efficiency can further remodel the nature of competition and efficiency. This remodelling can result in a hyper-competitive but still ongoing market, particularly in the copyright industries and other information industries. With the progress of hypercompetitive market, a dynamic efficiency displays four dimensions – production efficiency, innovation efficiency, access efficiency, and resource efficiency. Antitrust law may depress these types of dynamic efficiency.[179]

4. Entrepreneurship issue

The issues of complexity, efficiency, and competition relating to the growth of copyright industries under copyright and antitrust regimes in the long-term process of creative destruction are also the concerns of the entrepreneurs in the field. A review of the role of entrepreneur and entrepreneurship in the industrial growth under copyright and antitrust regimes in the long-term process may offer some clues.

In Schumpeter's model, exploring entrepreneurs and entrepreneurship is a focal point of both theoretical construction and practical consideration. Schumpeter was not only one of the great economists who stressed the importance of entrepreneurs/entrepreneurship for economic development or industrial growth but also the one who identified a dynamic role of entrepreneurs/entrepreneurship in directing development or growth.[180] This dynamic role features two essential functions of entrepreneur/entrepreneurship – innovation and progressing renovation – in the long-term process of creative destruction. In the copyright industries, these two functions will perform competently under copyright and antitrust regimes in the process.

Some dimensions of the first function, the function of innovation, are explored in Chapter 3.2.3. What is stressed here is the diversity and depth of Schumpeter's conception of entrepreneurs' innovative function. In Schumpeter's account, an entrepreneur is not merely an economic animal. Rather, 'an entrepreneur (outside any particular institutional system) was neither hedonic nor utilitarian'.[181] A social and natural environment, although not among the 'prime movers' of industrial change, still 'alters the data of economic action' and can still 'condition industrial change'.[182] Thus, entrepreneurs as the real movers of industrial change, just like other human beings, have to act as social animals under some social circumstances. 'The entrepreneur is a sociologically distinct individual separate from the capitalist and separate from the view that of a sociological type of individuals known as entrepreneurs.'[184] For Schumpeter, an entrepreneurial activity is not only a rational reaction toward the pressure of dynamic competition but also a strategic and innovative action for the firm's performance and competitive advantage. 'The entrepreneur is modelled as a specific type of economic agent who carries out innovations by setting up a firm as the organizational terrain for the new combination of productive means.'[185] In particular, Schumpeter's realist analysis focuses on the supply side of the economy, depicting a reallocation of resources and reshuffling of industry structures as a course of innovations under the pressure of dynamic competition in the long-term process of creative destruction. Entrepreneurs are the main actors in the course of innovations on the supply side of the economy.

The second function, the function of progressing renovation, refers to entrepreneurs' alternating pursuit or exploitation of innovation or imitation under a dynamic or Schumpeterian competition, over time, in the long-term process of creative destruction. Under Schumpeter's dynamic framework, a long-run course in 'time' always matters for observing entrepreneurs and their firms' activities or performances.[186] For Schumpeter, it would be meaningless to 'accept the data of the momentary situation as if there were no past or future to it'.[187] The conflict and market-power shift between the incumbent and the insurgent, and between the innovator and the imitator, are inevitable over time. The status of innovator or imitator will never be long-standing and will always be transferable among entrepreneurs and their firms over time. The interaction between innovation and imitation is the basis for further innovative actions. Under the Schumpeterian competition, any entrepreneurs – either the incumbent or the insurgent, the innovator or the imitator – entail 'a redesign of (those) complementary activities that constitute the firm's organizational capacity'[188] and a course of renovation – revising opportunities, recuperating resources, revamping economic organisations, and reforming institutional frameworks over time – in order to boost firms' performance and related industrial growth in the long-term process of creative destruction.

Under a dynamic competition, an entrepreneur is an opportunist, in a neutral sense of the word, in the long-term process of creative destruction. For an entrepreneur, neither innovation nor imitation is sacred or sinful over time. The only thing that matters is to take or refit a suitable opportunity at a right point of 'time' for securing competitive advantage through either innovation or imitation. The 'function of progressing renovation' as one kind of entrepreneur's dynamic role is the more important than the 'function of innovation'. The function of innovation as another kind of entrepreneur's dynamic role is not valuable because of the innovation itself. Instead, alongside their continuing innovations, many entrepreneurs' imitation and improvement following their innovative activities are indeed more important for enhancing their firms' performance and growth. 'The clustering of innovations' as a result of a sequence of their imitation and improvement[189] has overhauled innovations while entrepreneurs play their dynamic role of progressing renovation.

In Schumpeter's model, 'the clustering of innovations in neighbourhoods of equilibrium is relied upon to convert recovery into prosperity, and if the innovating activity were not renewed the economy would drift toward a stationary state very different from capitalist society'.[190] Because of entrepreneurs' dynamic role in the long-term process of creative destruction, a dynamic and disequilibrium state surfaces. As Peter Drucker pointed out, Schumpeter 'postulated that dynamic disequilibrium brought on by the innovating entrepreneur, rather than equilibrium and optimization, is the "norm" of a healthy economy and the central reality for economic theory and economic practice'.[191]

Certainly, entrepreneurs and entrepreneurship do not function in a vacuum. Entrepreneurs face the pressure of dynamic competition and corresponding institutional constraints from inside and outside the firms under certain legal structures. In Schumpeter's account, 'the interaction between institutional forms and entrepreneurial activity'[192] is a crucial subject for exploring economic development and industrial growth in theory.[193] In practice, Schumpeter had identified the 'shaping' influence of institutional forms and the 'bursting' influence of entrepreneurial activity on development and growth.[194] Entrepreneurs' ways to tackle 'the interaction between institutional forms and entrepreneurial activity' under certain legal structures determine the firms' performances and growths. Investigating 'the interaction between institutional forms and entrepreneurial activity' in a context of dynamic competition under copyright and antitrust regimes is a necessary step for examining the growth of copyright industries.

While addressing the institutional issues, Schumpeter emphasised these institutional factors at both micro (inside the firm, such as the corporation) and macro (outside the firm, such as copyright and antitrust laws) levels.[195] As Chapter 2.2.1 indicated, 'the interaction between institutional forms and entrepreneurial activity', as Schumpeter referred to it, exhibits a reciprocal impact between the 'shaping' influence of institutional forms and the 'bursting' influence of entrepreneurial activity at both levels under a dynamic competition in the long-term process of creative destruction. The 'shaping' influence of institutional forms on development and growth relies on entrepreneurs' adaptation to these institutional forms at both (macro and micro) levels. Of course, entrepreneurs' adaptation to a dynamic economy is not a simple adjustment to existing institutional frameworks at all. Rather, it is a creative or adaptive response under certain circumstances, in Schumpeter's terms.[196] Copyright expansion, as noted in Chapter 2.1, is one such type of adaptive response because, as previously indicated, protecting intellectual property rights and related long-term contracts are necessary business strategies for entrepreneurs under a dynamic or Schumpeterian competition. In this sense, a Schumpeterian entrepreneurship is an institutional leadership.[197]

In the meantime, the 'shaping' influence of institutional frameworks on economic development and industrial growth under the dynamic competition is also dynamic in the long run. An institutional dynamic refers to an unintended, complex, and joint creative effect of certain institutional structures on entrepreneurs' capacities and entrepreneurship over time in the long-term process of creative destruction. When analysing a specific institutional framework or arrangement, such as the way of corporation inside a firm, copyright law, antitrust law, or any related particular institutional framework or arrangement, the desired effect of this institutional framework or arrangement alone will be clear. However, while some institutional frameworks or arrangements at both micro and macro levels function jointly, the overall effect in the long run will be unpredictable and complex over time. The copyright–antitrust relation can result in such an institutional dynamic in the long term. According to Wu, the task of copyright law in essence is to adjust the 'competition among rival disseminators'[198] for information products. Coincidentally, the mission of antitrust law is to sustain the competition among rivals. Under the

Schumpeterian competition in the long-term process of creative destruction, these two legal structures can reinforce each other's power in strengthening competition. Correspondingly, the two legal regimes and the institutional arrangement inside the firms under the Schumpeterian competition can create a complex, constructive, and conductive institutional framework that encourages entrepreneurs to play their dynamic role (the function of innovation and the function of progressive renovation) in exploiting diverse opportunities for development and growth in the long run. An institutional dynamic gives structure to an organised way of constraining industrial dynamics in the long-term process of creative destruction.

Interestingly, several decades after Schumpeter's investigation into the issue of entrepreneurs and entrepreneurship in his dynamic model, the static model on the issue still stands out and raises more complex concerns. Coase's static model on entrepreneurs and entrepreneurship is a good example. Under Coase's framework of neoinstitutionalism, an entrepreneur is perceived as a coordinator for directing the firm's allocation of resources on account of the managing (organising) costs inside the firm and responds to the price mechanism in consideration of the marketing costs outside the firm.[199] As discussed in Chapter 2.3.1, Coase made a methodical effort to explain why a firm is necessary for economic activities and to identify the role of institutions in adjusting market transactions either within the firm or among the firms (in the market). The problem is that the Coase Theorem of the firm fails to account for the firms' development and growth. Although some newly developed theories of the firm, such as the perspective of 'core competence', attempt to expound the organisational growth of firms, these approaches are still incapable of explaining 'the uneven, erratic performances of firms over time'.[200] In contrast, a Schumpeterian perspective on the dynamic role of entrepreneur and entrepreneurship in economic development and industrial growth can provide an endurable framework for exploring the firms' erratic performances over time in the long-term process of creative destruction.

In brief, 'Disequilibrium conditions create high-return, high-growth opportunities . . . Disequilibrium situations usually depend on radical changes in technology, but sometimes entrepreneurs can create disequilibrium by seeing sociological opportunities to change human habits'.[201] In the information industries in general, and copyright industries in particular, diverse entrepreneurs compete and different groups of entrepreneurs will benefit with either copyright law or antitrust law, or both. Entrepreneurs are real players who play a dynamic role in growing industry and developing economy under a dynamic or Schumpeterian competition and copyright-antirust regimes in the long-term process of creative destruction.

3.3 Debates over copyright expansion in the digital age

Historically in the UK book publishing industry, as Chapter 2.1 shows, whenever a new technology changed the way of reproduction and distribution of books as a type of copyright goods, the industry or market structure of book publishing correspondingly transformed and, sooner or later, copyright expansion followed. Copyright protection facing the challenge of digital technology has followed the same path. Under the pressure of both digitalisation and globalisation in the information age, copyright expansion in either duration or scope has prevailed in the UK and the US, and indeed all over the world, under WTO and WIPO. However, no matter what driving forces may compel copyright expansion in the digital age, the battles and related debates over copyright expansion are still far from over. In particular, some legal battles provoked or reinforced these debates.

The development of UK copyright law indicates that the balance between private rights and public interests is a critical concern of copyright protection.[202] Whenever new technologies impel copyright expansion,[203] they also create opportunities to balance access and control over copyright.[204] The debates over copyright expansion in the digital age are in essence the deliberations on how to balance access and control over copyright in light of digital technology under certain industry or market structures. In brief, the access–control relation of copyright in general, and the copyright expansion and growth of copyright industries in particular, are the main concerns whenever facing technological innovations and related organisational innovations.

3.3.1 *Debate over copyright expansion in the United States*

In the US, the case of *Sony v Universal City Studios* in the period from 1976 to 1984 was the first legal battle on the access and control over copyright under new technology. The critical facts of *Sony* were not intricate. Since the 1970s, recording devices such as VCRs had spread widely in the US. Many consumers used these new devices to copy movies or other video programmes for their viewing at a later time ('time-shifting') in their homes. Worried about their potential or actual commercial losses, some corporations (such as Universal City Studios and Walt Disney Productions) sued Sony, the producer of Betamax VCRs, for its liability for users' free duplication of video programmes. Finally, in 1984, the US Supreme Court ruled in favour of Sony and relieved them of legal liability for contributory infringement in the pre-digital age.[205]

The term of 'pre-digital' is used here because, at the time of the *Sony* case, digital technology was not widely employed to reproduce or distribute copyright works, and the *Sony* case itself was not involved in this new technology. However, the principles of the ruling in this case are applicable to similar legal issues regarding copyright expansion in the digital age. Indeed, this landmark ruling set a precedent for future legal actions in the application of high technologies in the copyright industries in the digital age. In judging *Sony*, the US Supreme Court adopted a philosophy of legal pragmatism.

On the one hand, the Court was unenthusiastic about expanding copyright into the private domain of consumers' homes.[206] However, as the number of American households who possessed VCRs was rising, the Court could not ignore the reality.[207] Facing this reality, the Court did not rule against a rising population and a booming business. Rather, it decided that 'time-shifting was fair use'.[208] On the other hand, it was very unlikely that the US Supreme Court would deny the fact that the private copying and 'time-shifting' did and would exert a sizeable impact on the copyright industries. To cope with this reality, the Court did not directly grant Sony an exempted fair use – to exempt it from copyright infringement – as the US District Judge did in 1979.[209] Instead, the Court created a presumption of fair use on the basis of a cost–benefit assessment between the infringing use and 'substantial non-infringing use' of VCRs.[210]

This pragmatic legal reasoning upheld the principle of fair use under the challenge of new technology but did leave room for future adjustment or amendment. Nevertheless, no matter how the Justices of the US Supreme Court reasoned the case, the most significant message of *Sony* is that copyright expansion to tackle new technology is discouraged, and fair use is sustained under the pressure of the cultural industries. For the information technology industries such as the consumer electronic industry, the *Sony* decision may be seen as a 'Magna Carta' moment.[211] Unfortunately, 16 years later, this 'Magna Carta' for the information technology industries played no active role in the case of *A&M Records Inc v Napster Inc*.

The legal dispute over Napster in the late 1990s was a milestone legal case in the US in the new information age. Napster, established in 1999, was an online service provider that enabled Internet users to download music files from other online terminals: a peer-to-peer free distribution channel, serviced through specific software.[212] In the same year, the Recording Industry Association of America (RIAA) filed a lawsuit against Napster for its liability of contributory infringement. To contest the charge, the defence attorneys for Napster applied the *Sony* defence to argue their case.[213] As they contended, following *Sony*, Napster should not be liable for contributory infringement because Napster, like Sony, provided individual consumers with a type of device – a peer-to-peer distribution channel just like VCRs – that allowed them to make 'personal non-commercial copies of music'.[214] Thus, individual consumers' use of peer-to-peer distribution channel fitted the category of 'substantial non-infringing use' defined in *Sony*.[215]

In two hearings in 2000 and 2001, in the case of *A&M Records Inc v Napster Inc*, Napster lost its battle to the RIAA, first in the US District Court and then in the US Court of Appeals for the Ninth Circuit in San Francisco.[216] Interestingly, in the case of *Metro-Goldwyn-Mayer Studios Inc v Grokster Ltd* in 2004, the same US Court of Appeals that ruled against Napster, dismissed the charges against Grokster with contributory infringement because the Court believed that Grokster, unlike Napster, did not direct Internet users to duplicate copyrighted materials in a central server.[217] In 2005, the US Supreme Court granted a hearing of the *Grokster* appeal and overturned the 2004 decision of the US Court of Appeals for the Ninth Circuit. As a result, the copyright industries eventually won the battle in *Grokster*.[218]

In 1999, the same year when Napster was challenged, the US Copyright Term Extension Act (the CTEA), expanding the duration of copyright protection from life plus 50 years in 1978 to life plus 70 years, was challenged in the case of *Eldred v Ashcroft*. Lessig's balanced approach to intellectual property rights was his guiding philosophy as he acted as attorney for the petitioner, Eric Eldred. On Eldred's behalf, in the US Federal District Court of Washington DC in 1999, Lessig challenged the constitutionality of the CTEA. Before the district court, he presented two central arguments: (1) extending existing copyright terms violated the Constitution's Copyright Clause of 'limited times', (2) extending existing copyright terms for another 20 years violated the First Amendment.[219] The federal district court dismissed Lessig's claim. Although succeeding in bringing the case into the Court of Appeals of Washington DC, and eventually the US Supreme Court, Eldred and Lessig lost the legal battle in 2003.[220] However, the case *Eldred v Ashcroft* has influenced debates over the access–control relation of copyright in general, and the relation between copyright expansion and growth of copyright industries in particular.

The case of *Authors Guild v Google* in 2005 is probably the most notable legal case on the access–control relation of copyright in the US and 'the most important fair use case of the twenty-first century'.[221] In September of the same year in which the US Supreme Court ruled against *Grokster*, the Association of American Publishers and various writers filed a class action lawsuit against Google for its copyright infringement in the Google Books scheme, which was designed to digitalise the full texts of books for users' access.[222] In October 2005, five other major publishers filed a similar lawsuit against Google.[223] In 2008, both sides reached a settlement waiting on judicial authorisation. This settlement was a $120-million deal for settling down the above two lawsuits against Google. If the Court approved the deal, Google would be authorised to make the full or part texts of out-of-print book available in varying ways unless the copyright holders make specific requests on the availability.[224] In September 2009, the US Department of Justice issued a Statement of Interest against the approval of the Google Books settlement. Responding to the statement of the Department of Justice, lawyers for the plaintiffs and Google revised the proposed settlement and filed the Amended Settlement Agreement (the ASA) to the US District Court of the Southern District of New York in November 2009 for approval.[225] In March 2011, the Court issued a ruling that rejected the ASA because it 'is not fair, adequate, and reasonable'.[226]

The US federal judges' fluctuating stances in *Sony*, *Napster*, *Eldred*, *Grokster*, and *Google* reflects how legal pragmatism can still direct legal policies towards the new issues on access and control over copyright in the context of technological innovation. Of course, while case laws played crucial roles in setting up public policies on the access–control relation of copyright in the US, statutory laws are also the main sources for defining the access–control relation of copyright in general, and the copyright expansion in duration in particular.

In 2002, 17 economists had issued an amicus brief endorsing the petitioners in *Eldred v Ashcroft*.[227] More interestingly, among these 17 economists were some leading supply-side economists, in particular those Nobel laureates in economics – George Akerlof, Kenneth Arrow, James Buchanan, Ronald Coase, and Milton Friedman. Unlike Lessig, these economists not only questioned the constitutionality of the CTEA but also doubted the economic rationale behind the Act. They regarded the process of copyright expansion under the CTEA as a process of 'rent seeking' without enhancing incentives for creativities.[228] Specifically, they believe that retroactive extension of copyright term for existing copyright works makes no economic sense and prospective extension for future (new) works has insignificant incentive effect.[229] Their opposition to copyright expansion implies that over-protection of copyright is against economic rationality.

Of course, these leading economists' perspective on copyright expansion is not beyond question. The issue of 'rent seeking' behind the CTEA is an essential constitutional concern[230] in the relation between access and control over copyright in general, and between copyright expansion and growth of copyright industries in particular. The question is whether or not 'rent seeking' is the real issue behind the CTEA. According to Scott Martin, an assertion of 'rent seeking' might be a kind of 'myth of public domain' because those who made this assertion might ignore the fact that, under the CTEA, some public service institutions such as libraries and archives can still enjoy sizeable exceptions from the expanded copyright protection, and publishers can still make profits after their copyright works enter the public domain.[231] Thus, the 'rent seeking' behind the CTEA, as these 17 economists alleged, may be exaggerated. Meanwhile, Liebowitz and Margolis question these economists' views on retroactive and prospective extensions of copyright term for existing and future copyright works respectively. According to Liebowitz and Margolis, these economists doubt the effect of retroactive extension for existing copyright works just because of the monopoly deadweight losses from retroactive extension. However, in Liebowitz and Margolis's view, the monopoly deadweight losses are only one of many concerns on the efficient management of existing creative works. Besides deadweight losses, offensive derivative use of existing copyright works and network effects are also serious concerns regarding the efficient management of existing creative works. To overcome derivative misuse and to enhance positive network effects, copyright term extension for existing copyright works may be necessary for the efficient use of these existing works.[232]

The incentive of prospective extension of copyright term for future (new) copyright works seems less deniable and more controversial. The 17 economists who supported the petitioners in *Eldred* insist that the incentive of prospective extension, particularly in the form of additional royalties from term extensions, is too trivial to boost new creative works. On the contrary, Liebowitz and Margolis suggest that these economists might ignore the elasticity of supply of creative works. While this elasticity of supply exists, a small increase in royalty payment due to copyright term extension may provoke a significant growth of new creative works. It is only for the small proportion of creative works that possess the large share of market values that the incentive of prospective extension for these works is weak,[233] because the elasticity of supplying the small portion is lower.

Indeed, the issue of incentives for creativities under the CTEA is a more fundamental concern for the relation between access and control over copyright in general, and between copyright expansion and growth of copyright industries in particular. Nevertheless, whether or not this term extension of copyright under the CTEA can trigger incentives for creativity of new works or growth of copyright industries is an empirical rather than a theoretical issue. A normative inquiry into the constitutionality of the statute cannot account for the empirical issue. Rather, an empirical investigation is more appropriate. Landes and Posner conducted an empirical research on the incentive effects of copyright extensions under several statutes and international laws in the US. Under their neoclassical model of copyright, they examined the impacts of the expected copyright duration, the 1962 Amendment of Copyright Act, the 1972 Extension of Copyright Act, the 1976 Copyright Act, the 1988 Berne Convention Ratification, and the 1998 CTEA on the creativity and growth in the US book publishing industry for the period 1910–2000. Their testing results show that, except for the 1976 Copyright Act, other 'statutory changes' in the US copyright law, including the CTEA, have not exerted significant effects on the copyright registrations (which are an indicator of the creativity and growth of US book publishing industry) in the period of 1910–2000.[234]

Of course, Landes and Posner's empirical research, like any other empirical studies, may pose some methodological concerns. First, the number of cases (around 90 only) is lower while nine explanatory (independent) variables are included in their multi-regression analysis. This low number of cases raises serious concern on the strength of their results. Second, besides legal factors (several US statutes of copyright), many other social and economic factors that may have impacts on the growth of the US book publishing industry are not incorporated in their analysis. Encompassing legal factors alone cannot draw the whole picture of creativity and growth in the US book publishing industry. Third, the elasticity of supply of creative works is still an issue if all copyright registrations are taken into consideration in Landes and Posner's empirical assessment. Because of the market value concentration of creative works, the incentives under the CTEA may only induce a small part of all 'copyright registrations'.

3.3.2 *Debate over copyright expansion in Europe*

In Europe, the debate over copyright expansion in duration is not a new issue.[235] What makes the debate over the expansion of copyright in contemporary Europe more contentious is the process of harmonisation and digitalisation in the European Union. The debate in Europe over copyright expansion in duration also focuses on the relation between access and control over copyright in general, and between copyright expansion and growth of copyright industries in particular. In particular, the extension of copyright term for sound recordings in light of harmonisation and digitalisation gains more attention. Of course, the debate over the copyright term extension for sound recordings can still address some general concerns on copyright protection and expansion.

In 2005, James Purnell, the then UK Minister for Broadcasting, Creative Industries and Tourism, proposed to extend the copyright term for sound recordings from the current 50 years to 90 years. His reasoning was that the record industry needed financial resources for cherishing more new talent.[236] In February 2008, Charlie McCreevy, the EU Internal Market Commissioner, announced his policy proposal of the European Copyright Term Extension Directive to extend the European copyright term for sound recordings from 50 to 95 years.[237] McCreevy's message provoked strong reactions and opposition. After his announcement, within one and a half years, a series of individual or joint letters or statements from various European scholars and practitioners were issued to the European Commission for repealing McCreevy's policy initiative.

On 18 February 2008, right after McCreevy announced his policy initiative, Martin Kretschmer, Professor and Director of the Centre for Intellectual Property Policy and Management at the University of Bournemouth, UK, first published a letter to the *Financial Times*, 'Copyright Extension Will Benefit Few', to challenge McCreevy's policy recommendation.[238] In April 2008, David Newbery, Professor of Economics at University of Cambridge, was joined by 32 scholars and practitioners in writing a 'Joint Letter Regarding Term Extension for Phonograms' to José-Manuel Barroso, President of the European Commission. Among the signatories to this letter, two professors – Sir James Mirrlees and Kenneth Arrow – are Nobel Laureates in economics.[239] In June 2008, on behalf of 51 scholars and practitioners, Martin Kretschmer issued an open letter and a joint academic statement to Barroso. Their joint academic statement offers a concise but comprehensive empirical assessment on the effects of the proposed copyright term extension.[240] On 21 July 2008, Lionel Bently and Martin Kretschmer, joined by 17 scholars, published a letter in *The Times*, 'Copyright Extension is the Enemy of Innovation', which reinforced the arguments in Kretschmer's letter to the *Financial Times* on 18 February 2008.[241] On 11 March 2009, just before the European Parliament was scheduled to vote on the proposed European Copyright Term Extension Directive on 23 March 2009, 100 scholars and practitioners issued an open letter to make a last-minute appeal for the proposed Directive to be withdrawn.[242]

In spite of some differences in style and emphasis, all of these letters or statements shared the common cause in questioning the public policy justification, the economic rationale, and the empirical foundation for the proposed

Term Extension Directive. Among these letters or statements, the joint academic statement to Barroso in June 2008 systematically analyses the empirical evidence of the artists' earnings effect, the supply effect, the price effect, and the trade argument of the proposed Directive, and offers the policy alternatives for protecting European artists' copyright. It is sensible to regard the following answers to the four effects in the June 2008 joint statement as a summary of the arguments of these opposing letters or statements.

> Answer 1: We have seen no evidence that living artists as a whole would benefit decisively from an extension of exclusive rights held by record companies. The benefits will fall to those who need it least: already wealthy performers, and their estates and record companies. In fact, in as much as innovative musicians are users of existing recordings, their artistry will be hindered, not enabled, by extension.

> Answer 2: An exclusive term of protection of 50 years should be more than sufficient to cover the investment horizon of record producers. Any retrospective protection is in effect a windfall that will negatively affect access to, and exploitation of the back catalogues of recorded music. The evidence is clear: As the recordings of the 1950s and 1960s come to the end of their current 50-year term, they will become *more* available, not less.

> Answer 3: Exclusive rights are unlikely to be cost-free. For sound recordings, copyright is provided so that record companies invest from a prospect of higher returns during the protected period. While the empirical evidence is missing, it is simply preposterous to claim both, that term extension does not make any difference to consumer prices, and that record companies need term extension to boost their revenues.

> Answer 4: In terms of comparative advantage, the shorter term gives Europe an edge in innovation. Regarding the balance of payments, reliable empirical evidence is difficult to obtain. In any case, the effects of term reduction should be as thoroughly investigated as the proposed extension.[243]

The main sources for repealing the proposed Term Extension Directive are the Cambridge Study for the Gowers Review – *Review of the Economic Evidence Relating to an Extension of the Term of Copyright in Sound Recordings* of the Centre for Intellectual Property and Information Law at University of Cambridge – and the Institute for Information Law (IViR) Report at the University of Amsterdam, both from 2006. The Cambridge Study indicates that retrospective term extension will have no effect on creating new works and the effect of prospective term extension on creativity is insignificant (1 per cent or less). Meanwhile, copyright term extension will incur more costs to consumers than the benefits to the record industry and will exert a negative effect on balance of trade.[244] The IViR Report conducts an empirical analysis on the economic effects of copyright term extension on creativity and growth in the record industry. According to the Report, inspecting the length of time for recouping the investment is an adequate way to explore copyright term extension. Based on available data, it is estimated that 50 years are sufficient enough for the record industry to recover their investments. Thus, a term extension from 50 to 90 years is unnecessary.[245] In addition, as time passes, the majority of sound recordings will have less and less market value, with only a small number of long-term bestsellers still making their profits. From a public welfare perspective, copyright term extension can constrain people from exploiting the majority of non-popular but still valuable sound recordings, and will accordingly reduce public welfare. For popular works, copyright term extension can only help draw market value from substantial promotion rather than quality improvement. Moreover, as copyright term extends, digitalisation can help consolidate monopoly and an extension beyond 50 years will create more unnecessary deadweight costs.[246]

The opposition against copyright expansion and questioning the justifications of copyright term extension for sound recordings are forcefully strong in Europe. Meanwhile, the proponents of copyright term extension also made efforts to raise their voices. In 2006, the same year as the Cambridge Study and the IViR Report were published, the British Phonographic Industry (BPI), as the major trade association of the UK record industry, contracted PricewaterhouseCoopers LLP (PwC) to prepare a report of empirical assessment on the impacts of copyright term extension for the UK record industry, *The Impact of Copyright Extension for Sound Recordings in the UK*, for the Gowers Review. Specifically, the report examines the financial impacts, market impacts, private costs, and social costs of copyright term extension. According to the report, to assess the impacts of copyright term extension, it is needed to measure the effect of no extension of copyright term beyond the current duration of 50 years (in 2006) on the UK record industry.[247]

The report estimates that extending copyright term for 10 years would increase revenues for the UK record industry from £2.2 to £34.9 million in present value terms, and for 50 years would increase the revenues from £8.3 to £162.8 million in present value terms.[248] For market impacts, the report concentrates on the price and availability of recordings. The statistical analysis in the report shows that the impact of copyright term extension on the average price of popular recordings would not be statistically significant and, for the average price of classic recordings, the impact is inconclusive.[249] Due to limited data, it is difficult to estimate whether or not extending copyright term could boost the availability of recordings.[250] In addition, the report has not discovered convincing evidence for supporting the claimed private and social costs of extending copyright term.[251] Overall, the report indicates that the benefits of extending copyright term are larger than the costs of extension.

Png and Wang's empirical analysis in 2006 partially supports the empirical assessment of PricewaterhouseCoopers LLP. On the basis of the data from

19 OECD (Organisation for Economic Co-operation and Development) countries that extended the duration of copyright, Png and Wang estimate that the extension of copyright duration did exert a positively significant impact on movie production.[252] To some degree, Liebowitz's empirical study in 2007 upholds the assessments of both Png and Wang and PricewaterhouseCoopers LLP. According to Liebowitz, extending copyright term would create a very substantial proportion of revenues of sound recordings in the first 50 years of extension in present value terms. 'This means that sales of records more than 50 years after their original production are still a reasonable component of revenues and can therefore be expected to impact the behaviour of record companies and their production of new recordings.'[253] However, in 2009, Png and Wang's new research based on data from 23 OECD countries nearly reversed their analysis in 2006 and indicated no significant impact of copyright expansion on movie production.[254]

The European Parliament, facing fervent opposition from various scholars and practitioners, postponed the vote on the proposed European Copyright Term Extension Directive scheduled for 23 March 2009.[255] Over a month later, on 12 May 2009, the Parliament resumed the vote. The Directive was passed in a revised version, extending the copyright term for sound recordings from the current 50 years to 70 years, rather than 90 years originally proposed. On the same day, the British Phonographic Industry (BPI), the Association of Independent Music (AIM), the Musician's Union, and the PPL (the music licensing company that undertakes collective rights management) issued a joint statement applauding the Directive.[256]

3.4 Concluding remarks

This chapter examines the digital context and related issues of copyright expansion protection and expansion under some specific industry or market structure from a Schumpeterian perspective. The issues of anti-commons and antitrust behind copyright expansion, and debates over the justifications for copyright expansion, are discussed before constructing theoretical framework and conducting empirical assessment in Chapters 4 and 5. Considering the similarity of the industry structure between the UK book publishing and record industries,[257] considering the issues in the record industry is informative for the investigation of the issues in the book publishing industry.

Eventually, the question of whether copyright expansion could stimulate or restrict the growth of copyright industries as information technology advances is an empirical issue. To conduct an empirical assessment, a theoretical inquiry is necessary. This will be the task of next chapter.

Notes

1 P. Goldstein, *Intellectual Property: the Tough New Realities That Could Make or Break Your Business*, New York: Portfolio, 2007, p. 70.

2 L. Lessig, *Code and Other Laws of Cyberspace*, Basic Books, 1999, pp. 124–125.
3 R. Ku, 'The Creative Destruction of Copyright: Napster and the New Economics of Digital Technology', *University of Chicago Law Review*, vol. 69, 2002, 270.
4 Ibid, 269.
5 P. Drahos, *A Philosophy of Intellectual Property*, Aldershot, UK: Dartmouth, 1996, p. 119.
6 R. Towse, *Creativity, Incentive and Reward: an Economic Analysis of Copyright and Culture in the Information Age*, Cheltenham, UK: Edward Elgar, 2001, p. 1.
7 G. Hodgson, *Economics and Institutions: A Manifesto for a Modern Institutional Economics*, Cambridge, UK: Polity Press, 1988, p. 187.
8 Adam Smith, the framer of modern economics, initiated his primitive 'analytical system' of complete market in which a competition-dominated market as 'an invisible hand' has been assumed to co-ordinate producers (firms) and consumers (individuals) in an efficient way. See Smith, op. cit., 1991[1776]. R. Coase, *Essays on Economics and Economists*, The University of Chicago Press, 1994, p. 83. J. Case, *Competition: The Birth of a New Science*, New York: Hill and Wang, 2007, pp. 193–204. J. Stiglitz, *Economics* 2nd edn, W. W. Norton & Company, 1997a, Chapters VIII-XIII.
9 For a sufficient treatment of the discrepancy between the model of complete market and economic reality, see Stiglitz, 1997a, Chapter VII.
10 G. Mankiw, *Principles of Economics* 3rd edn, Mason, OH: South-Western/ Thomson Learning, 2004, p. 290.
11 In an incomplete market, such as monopoly, oligopoly, or monopolistic competition, competition either does not exist or has been contained in different degrees (Stiglitz, 1997a, Chapter XV). The market for the book publishing or music record/publishing industry as one area of the information market signifies a monopolistic competition market.
12 R. Coase, 'The Market for Goods and the Market for Ideas', *American Economic Review*, vol. 64, 1974, 384–391.
13 L. Lessig, *The Future of Ideas: the Fate of the Commons in a Connected World*, New York: Vintage Books, 2001, pp. 104–110. See also Lessig 1999.
14 Coase, op. cit., 1974.
15 S. Choi and A. Whinston, *The Internet Economy: Technology and Practice*, Austin, TX: SmartEcon Publishing, 2000, p.165.
16 R. Cooter and T. Ulen, *Law and Economics* 4th edn, Boston, MA: Addison-Wesley, 2004, p. 120, pp. 132–133.
17 M. Castells, *The Rising of the Network Society* 2nd edn, Malden, MA: Blackwell Publishing, 2000, pp. 78–100.
18 D. Quah, 'Digital Goods and the New Economy', in D. Jones (ed), *New Economy Handbook*, Academic Press, 2003, pp. 289–321.
19 N. Negroponte, *Being Digital*, New York: Vintage Books, 1995, p. 85.
20 O. Shy, *The Economics of Network Industries*, Cambridge University Press, 2001, pp. 3–6.
21 Shy, op. cit., 2001, pp. 1–10.
22 Castells, op. cit., 2000, pp. 77–162. D. Evans and R. Schmalensee, 'Some Economic Aspects of Antitrust Analysis in Dynamically Competitive Industries', Cambridge, MA: National Bureau of Economic Research, 2001, pp. 7–15. R. Alcaly, *The New Economy*, Farrar, Straus and Giroux, 2003. B. Kogut (ed), *The Global Digital Economy*, The MIT Press, 2003.
23 'Pricing' and 'cost' are two distinct market forces. As Loretta Anania and Richard Solomon pointed out, 'In the real world, pricing has little to do with cost, since entrepreneurs will charge whatever price they can get away with. Pricing decisions by management typically precede cost–benefit analysis . . .' (L. Anania and R. Solomon, 'Flat – The Minimalist Price', in L. McKnight and

J. Bailey (eds), *Internet Economics*, The MIT Press, 1998, p. 91.) Varian specified 'cost structure' as an array of fixed costs, marginal costs, switching costs, transaction costs, and related pricing practices such as price discrimination and bundling. (H. Varian, 'High-Technology Industries and Market Structure', in The Federal Reserve Bank of Kansas City, *Economic Policy for the Information Economy*, The Federal Reserve Bank of Kansas City, 2001, pp. 65–101. G. Moore, *Living on the Fault Line: Managing for Shareholder Value in the Age of the Internet*, 2000, pp. 92–138.) A high fixed cost and a low marginal cost as an acknowledged facet of the cost structure of information products have been recognised in exploring the cost issues of copyright works. (R. Towse, 'Economics and Copyright Reform: Aspects of the EC Directive', *Telematics and Informatics*, vol. 22, 2005, 11–24.)

24 Varian, op. cit., pp. 65–101.

25 Externalities, or 'network externalities' as they are sometimes called, refer to economic activities that have affected others for better or worse but have not paid those others or have not been compensated by those others for their consequences (Samuelson and Nordhaus, op. cit., pp. 35–37). While economies of scale surface, network externalities or effects may enhance the economic welfares for both producers and consumers (Varian, op. cit., pp. 81–85).

26 Complementarity means that consumers will demand a series of products whenever she or he purchases one of these products. For instance, if one were to purchase a stapler, one would naturally buy staples (complementarity) suitable for that particular stapler (compatibility), and one would also expect to get the same kind of staples made to the same standards in many other countries, wherever one took the stapler, such as overseas for a conference (standards). Shy, op. cit., 2001, pp. 1–10.

27 Ibid.

28 Shy, op. cit., 2001, pp. 1–10. N. Le, 'Microsoft Europe and Switching Costs', Presentation at Annual Congress of the Society for Economic Research on Copyright Issues in Turin, Italy, 8–9 July 2004, pp. 21–30.

29 Shy, op. cit., 2001, p. 5.

30 W. Landes and R. Posner, *The Economic Structure of Intellectual Property Law*, Harvard University Press, 2003, pp. 48–50.

31 Economies of scale imply the prospect that copyright holders may still recover their costs and secure their benefits in the absence of copyright protection. However, also due to strong economies of scale, a natural monopoly will be expected in the field. If this were the case, a state intervention would be desirable (Shy, op. cit., 2001, pp. 5–8). Whenever strong economies of scale prevail in certain markets, such as the markets of creative products, these markets will become incomplete markets with an imperfect competition and a natural monopoly (Shy, op. cit., 2001, p. 5).

32 Landes and Posner, op. cit., p. 20, pp. 224–226.

33 Choi and Whinston, op. cit., pp. 165–198. Moore, op. cit., pp. 92–138. Varian, op. cit., pp. 65–101.

34 Shy, op. cit., 2001, p. 6. Varian, op. cit., pp. 65–101.

35 Landes and Posner used the term 'expressive works' to specify copyright-based information products. See Landes and Posner, op. cit., 2003, p. 37.

36 Towse, op. cit., 2001, p. 169.

37 Landes and Posner, op. cit., 2003, p. 396.

38 Hodgson, op. cit., p. 187.

39 R. Towse, 'Copyright and Economics', in S. Frith and L. Marshall (eds), *Music and Copyright* 2nd edn, UK: Edinburgh University Press, 2004, p. 60.

40 Landes and Posner, op. cit., 2003, pp. 48–53.

41 Goldstein introduced Breyer's notion of 'lead-time advantage' in his *Copyright's Highway: from Gutenberg to the Celestial Jukebox*, New York: Hill and Wang, 1994, pp. 22–23. See also S. Breyer, 'The Uneasy Case for Copyright: A Study of Copyright in Books, Photocopies, and Computer Programs', *Harvard Law Review*, vol. 84(2), 1970, 281–351.

42 W. Gordon, 'Introduction', in W. Gordon and R. Watt (eds), *The Economics of Copyright: Developments in Research and Analysis*, Cheltenham, UK: Edward Elgar, 2003, xvii.

43 Ku, op. cit., p. 274.

44 The present argument is based on Grant's analysis of Schumpeter's notion of dynamic competition. See Grant, op. cit., 2002, pp. 92–95, 304–313.

45 T. Shen, 'Schumpeterian Competition and Social Welfare', in E. Helmstadter and M. Perlman (eds), *Behavioral Norms, Technological Progress, and Economic Dynamics: Studies in Schumpeterian Economics*, University of Michigan Press, 1996, p. 51. Quasi-rent is a special form of economic rent that, unlike an ordinary payment to a landlord, signifies monopolists' economic profits while denying the entrance of competitors into the field (Stiglitz, 1997a, Chapter XII). For example, a publisher who issued a popular novel could raise the price far above the marginal cost of production and make enormous economic 'rent' in a short period.

46 Shen, op. cit., p. 51. See also D. Mowery and N. Rosenberg, *Technology and the Pursuit of Economic Growth*, Cambridge University Press, 1989, p. 106.

47 Landes and Posner's distinction between pecuniary and technological externalities concerns the cost and benefit trade-off between the outcomes of right protections, including copyright protection, and the net worth of these outcomes. A technological externality refers to the net loss of the overall value as the results of certain individual, policy, or legal actions. A pecuniary externality, on the contrary, indicates a transfer of values due to these actions with no alteration of the total worth (Landes and Posner, op. cit., 2003, pp. 20, 224). In contrast, the distinction between positive and negative externalities considers whether a society could gain or lose from a rights or interest-related action whenever the individual or firm that took the action did not take the gain or loss into account based on a cost–benefit assessment (Stiglitz, 1997a, Chapter XXI. Samuelson and Nordhaus, op. cit., pp. 272–280).

48 Landes and Posner, op. cit., 2003, pp. 228–234.

49 Hakfoort, op. cit., pp. 70–73.

50 W. Baumol, 'Innovation and Creative Destruction', in L. McKnight, P. Vaaler and R. Katz (eds), *Creative Destruction: Business Survival Strategies in the Global Internet Economy*, The MIT Press, 2001, pp. 21–38.

51 Ibid, p. 23.

52 Ibid, pp. 21–28.

53 Landes and Posner, op. cit., 2003, pp. 210–249.

54 Netanel, op. cit., 1996, pp. 286–287.

55 Ibid, pp. 367–368.

56 Landes and Posner, op. cit., 2003, p. 222.

57 Ibid, pp. 224–226.

58 Hakfoort, op. cit., pp. 68–72.

59 Schumpeter, op. cit., 1976[1942], p. 79.

60 Ibid, pp. 93–97.

61 Ibid, p. 82.

62 Ibid, p. 106.

63 Landes and Posner, op. cit., 2003, pp. 11–16.

64 Towse, op. cit., 2004, p. 59.

65 Goldstein, op. cit., 2007, p. 71

66 Ku, op. cit., pp. 268–269.
67 Litman, op. cit., 2002, p. 131. J. Boyle, *The Public Domain: Enclosing the Commons of the Mind*, Yale University Press, 2008, pp. 42–53.
68 P. Samuelson, 'Intellectual Property and the Digital Economy: Why the Anti-Circumvention Regulations Need to be Revised?' Berkeley Technology Law Journal, vol. 14, 1999, 519–566.
69 P. Tang, 'Digital Copyright and the "New" Controversy: Is the Law Moulding Technology and Innovation?' *Research Policy*, vol. 34, 2005, 862. H. MacQueen, C. Waelde, G. Laurie and A. Brown, *Contemporary Intellectual Property: Law and Policy* 2nd edn, Oxford University Press, 2011, p. 262.
70 Lessig, op. cit., 2001, pp. 214–215. Towse, op. cit., 2004, pp. 59–60.
71 Coase, op. cit., 1994, pp. 3–14.
72 R. Merges, 'Intellectual Property Rights and the New Institutional Economics', *Vanderbilt Law Review*, vol. 53(6), 2000, 1865–1866.
73 Friedman, op. cit., 2000, p. 44.
74 G. Stigler, 'Two Notes on the Coase Theorem', *Yale Law Journal*, vol. 99, 1989, 632.
75 Lessig, op. cit., 2001, pp. 103–119; 2004, pp. 116–173.
76 Kallay, op. cit.
77 R. Epstein, 'The "Necessary" History of Property and Liberty', Chapman Law Review, vol. 6(1), 2003, 1–29. Epstein also refers to M. Kramer *et al*, *A Debate Over Rights: Philosophical Inquiries*, 1998. See also D. Seipp, 'The Concept of Property in the Early Common Law', Law and History Review, vol. 12(1), 1994, 29–91.
78 Lessig, op. cit., 2004, pp. 85–92.
79 Lessig, op. cit., 1999, pp. 130–131.
80 Ibid, p. 131.
81 Ibid.
82 Ibid, pp. 3–16.
83 Ibid, p. 12.
84 Ibid.
85 Lessig, op. cit., 2001, p. 4.
86 Ibid, pp. 1–13, 147–173.
87 Ibid, pp. 85–94. See also Goldstein, op. cit., 1994. Drahos, op. cit. G. Davies, *Copyright and Public Interest* 2nd edn, London: Sweet & Maxwell, 2002.
88 Lessig, op. cit., 2004, pp. 85–89.
89 Davies, op. cit., p. 13.
90 Lessig, op. cit., 2004, pp. 92–93.
91 Lessig, op. cit., 2001, p. 115.
92 Ibid, pp. 197–198.
93 Ibid, p. 197.
94 Ibid, p. 217.
95 Ibid, p. 215.
96 Ibid, pp. 214–217.
97 H. Hovenkamp, *The Antitrust Enterprise: Principle and Execution*, Harvard University Press, 2005, p. 13.
98 L. Burlamaqui, 'How Should Competition Policies and Intellectual Property Issues Interact in a Globalised World? A Schumpeterian Perspective', Presentation at the Seminar 'Contributions to the Development Agenda on Intellectual Property Rights', United Nations University, Maastricht, Netherlands, 23–24 September 2005. Online. Available <http://hum.ttu.ee/wp/paper6.pdf> (accessed 26 March 2011).
99 T. Jorde and D. Teece (eds), *Antitrust, Innovation, and Competitiveness*, Oxford University Press, 1992, p. 5. Kallay, op. cit., pp. 90–91.

100 Hovenkamp, op. cit., 2005, p. 39.
101 R. Bork, *The Antitrust Paradox: A Policy at War with Itself*, New York: Maxwell Macmillan International, 1993, p. 7.
102 Jorde and Teece, op. cit., p. 233.
103 Landes and Posner, op. cit., 2003, p. 379.
104 Schumpeter, op. cit., 1976[1942], pp. 82–83. See also his *Business Cycles: A Theoretical, Historical, and Statistical Analysis of the Capitalist Process* 2 volumes, New York: McGraw-Hill, 1939, p. 104.
105 Schumpeter, op. cit., 1976[1942], pp. 82–97.
106 Ibid, p. 84.
107 Ibid.
108 J. Ellig and D. Lin, 'A Taxonomy of Dynamic Competition Theories', in J. Ellig (ed), *Dynamic Competition and Public Policy: Technology, Innovation, and Antitrust Issues*, Harvard University Press, 2001, p. 18. Kallay, op. cit., pp. 40–44.
109 D'Aveni, with Gunther, op. cit., 1994, quoted in Grant, 2002, p. 93.
110 Schumpeter, 1976[1942], pp. 81–106.
111 Ibid, p. 87.
112 Ellig, op. cit., pp. 18–19.
113 Schumpeter, op. cit., 1976[1942], p. 74.
114 Landes and Posner, op. cit., 2003, p. 378.
115 M. Ricketts, *Economics of Business Enterprise: an Introduction to Economic Organization and the Theory of the Firm* 3rd edn, Edward Elgar, 2002, p. 68. Of course, Schumpeter's prediction on innovative entrepreneurs and their roles in economic development is less robust in the history of capitalist economy after World War II. As Thurow pointed out, 'Joseph Schumpeter thought that capitalism would die out because it would be undercut by the bureaucratization of invention and innovation and by the intellectual scribblers who would point to the noble goals of other systems such as socialism . . . Historically, he was wrong about R&D, identified the wrong scribblers, and is looking ever more right about family'. L. Throw, *The Future of Capitalism: How Today's Economic Forces Shape Tomorrow's World*, New York: Penguin, 1996, p. 317.
116 R. Clemence and F. Doody, *The Schumpeterian System*, New York: A M Kelley, 1966, p. 63.
117 Schumpeter, op. cit., p. 87.
118 Schumpeter, op. cit., 1976[1942], p. 89.
119 Ibid, p. 88.
120 Grant, op. cit., 2002, p. 336.
121 Schumpeter, op. cit., 1962[1911], Chapter II, p. 64.
122 Schumpeter, op. cit., 1976[1942], pp. 77–80, 102–103. Ellig, op. cit., p. 88.
123 Schumpeter, op. cit., 1976[1942], p. 89.
124 Hodgson, op. cit., p. 77.
125 Ricketts, op. cit., p. 506.
126 Schumpeter, op. cit., 1976[1942], pp. 77–80, 102–103. Ellig, op. cit., p. 17.
127 Goldstein, op. cit., 1994, pp. 3–36. Grant, op. cit., 2002, pp. 336–337. Litman, op. cit., 2002, p. 131.
128 Lessig, op. cit., 2004, pp. 130–139. See also his 2001, pp. 106–107. H. MacQueen, *Copyright, Competition, and Industrial Design*, Edinburgh University Press, 1995, pp. 8–9. Netanel, op. cit., 1996, 298. B. Sherman and L. Bently, *The Making of Modern Intellectual Property Law: the British Experience, 1760–1911*, Cambridge University Press, 1999, p. 152. T. Dreier, 'Regulating Competition by Way of Copyright Limitations and Exceptions', in P. Torremans (ed), *Copyright Law: A Handbook of Contemporary Research*, Cheltenham, UK: Edward Elgar, 2007, pp. 232–242.

129 Goldstein, op. cit., 1994, p. 177.

130 Ibid, pp. 37–77.

131 N. Mercuro and S. Medema, *Economics and the Law: From Posner to Post-Modernism*, Princeton University Press, 2006, pp. 144–155.

132 Kallay, op. cit., pp. 8–10. D. Goyder, 'Copyright, Competition and the Media', in M. Beesley (ed), *Markets and the Media*, London: The Institute of Economic Affairs, 1996, pp. 43–47. G. Ramello, 'Copyright and Antitrust Issues', in W. Gordon and R. Watt (eds), *The Economics of Copyright: Developments in Research and Analysis*, Edward Elgar, 2003, pp. 118–124. Hovenkamp, op. cit., 2005, p. 255.

133 Hovenkamp, op. cit., 2005, pp. 254–256.

134 Landes and Posner, op. cit., 2003, pp. 386–402. M. Einhorn, *Media, Technology and Copyright: Integrating Law and Economics*, Cheltenham, UK: Edward Elgar, 2004, pp. 141–149.

135 For a further discussion of the analytic elements of the dynamic or Schumpeterian competition, see Ellig and Lin, op. cit., pp. 16–21.

136 Schumpeter, op. cit., 1976[1942], p. 83.

137 Ellig and Lin, op. cit., p. 19.

138 Schumpeter, op. cit., 1976[1942], p. 83.

139 Ibid, p. 83.

140 D. Evans, 'Why Different Jurisdictions Do Not (and Should Not) Adopt the Same Antitrust Rules', *Chicago Journal of International Law*, vol. 46(1), 2009–2010, 168.

141 Schumpeter, op. cit., 1976[1942], p. 88.

142 Kallay, op. cit., pp. 8–10. Goyder, op. cit., pp. 43–44. Ramello, op. cit., pp. 118–124. Hovenkamp, op. cit., 2005, p. 255.

143 R. Clemence and F. Doody offered a brief explanation of the institutional nature of Schumpeter's model. Clemence and Doody, op. cit., pp. 33–35. See also Schumpeter, op. cit., 1976[1942], pp. 72–76.

144 Schumpeter, op. cit., 1976[1942], pp. 87–106. Einhorn, op. cit., p. 5.

145 Heilbroner, op. cit., 1993, p. 126.

146 Quoted in T. McCraw, 'Alfred Chandler: His Vision and Achievement', *Business History Review*, vol. 82(2), 2008, p. 214.

147 Y. Shionoya, *The Soul of the German Historical School: Methodological Essays on Schmoller, Weber and Schumpeter*, New York: Springer-Verlag, 2005, p. 133.

148 Schumpeter, op. cit., 1976[1942], pp. 87–90.

149 Ibid, p. 85, pp. 99–100.

150 Ibid, pp. 107–108.

151 Heilbroner, op. cit., 1992, pp. 291–292.

152 Schumpeter, op. cit., 1976[1942], p. 91.

153 Baumol, op. cit., 2001, p. 21.

154 Schumpeter, op. cit., 1962[1911], Footnote, pp. 59–60.

155 Samuelson and Nordhaus, op. cit., pp. 308–309.

156 Mercuro and Medema, op. cit., pp. 236–239. O. Pavlve, 'Dynamic Analysis of an Institutional Conflict: Copyright Owners against Online File Sharing', *Journal of Economic Issues*, vol. XXXIX(3), 2005, p. 636.

157 Cooter and Ulen, op. cit. S. Shavell, *Foundations of Economic Analysis of Law*, Harvard University Press, 2004. N. Georgakopoulos, *Principles and Methods of Law and Economics*, Cambridge University Press, 2005.

158 Hovenkamp, op. cit., 2005, p. 13.

159 O. Williamson, 'Antitrust Lenses and the Uses of Transaction Cost Economics Reasoning', in Jorde and Teece, op. cit., pp. 137–164.

160 F. Easterbrook, 'Ignorance and Antitrust', in Jorde and Teece, op. cit., pp. 119–136.

161 Schumpeter, op. cit., 1976[1942], pp. 87–110.
162 Ibid, pp. 83–86.
163 Ibid, pp. 102–103.
164 Jorde and Teece, op. cit., p. 185.
165 R. Barro, *Nothing is Sacred: Economic Ideas for the New Millennium*, The MIT Press, 2002, xviii.
166 Lessig, op. cit., 2001, p. 199.
167 Clemence and Doody, op. cit., p. 63.
168 E. Zajac, *Political Economy of Fairness*, The MIT Press, 1995, p. 21.
169 Hovenkamp, op. cit., 2005, pp. 32–35.
170 D'Aveni, with Gunther, op. cit., pp. 364–367. Zajac, op. cit., pp. 11–22.
171 Schumpeter, op. cit., 1976[1942], pp. 82–85.
172 W. Baumol and J. Ordover, 'Antitrust: Source of Dynamic and Static Inefficiencies?' in Jorde and Teece, op. cit., p. 83.
173 B. Carlsson and S. Jacobsson, 'Technological Systems and Industrial Dynamics: Implications for Firms and Governments', in Helmstadter and Perlman, op. cit., pp. 265–266. D. Weimer and A. Vining, *Policy Analysis: Concepts and Practice* 2nd edn, Upper Saddle River, NJ: Prentice-Hall, 1992, pp. 30–77.
174 J. Jayaratne and P. Strahan, 'Entry Restrictions, Industry Evolution, and Dynamic Efficiency: Evidence from Commercial Banking', *Journal of Law and Economics*, vol. 41(1), 1998, 239.
175 Kallay, op. cit., pp. 104–106.
176 The phrase is quoted in Landes and Posner, op. cit., 2003, p. 378.
177 Baumol, op. cit., 2001, p. 23. Baumol and Ordover, in Jorde and Teece, op. cit., pp. 83–84.
178 Baumol, op. cit., 2001, pp. 27–28.
179 D'Aveni, with Gunther, op. cit., pp. 364–367.
180 T. McCraw, *Prophet of Innovation: Joseph Schumpeter and Creative Destruction*, Harvard University Press, 2007, pp. 69–75, p. 496. See also R. Arena and P. Romani, 'Schumpeter and Entrepreneurship', in R. Arena and C. Dangel (eds), *Contribution of Joseph Schumpeter to Economics: Economic Development and Institutional Change*, London: Routledge, 2002, pp. 167–183.
181 B. McDaniel, 'A Contemporary View of Joseph A. Schumpeter's Theory of the Entrepreneur', *Journal of Economic Issues* Vol. XXXIX(2), 2005, p. 488.
182 Schumpeter, op. cit., 1976[1942], p. 82.
183 McDaniel, op. cit., p. 488.
184 Clemence and Doody, op. cit., p. 41.
185 A. Ebner, 'Institutions, Entrepreneurship, and the Rationale of Government: An Outline of the Schumpeterian Theory of the State', *Journal of Economic Behavior & Organization*, vol. 59, 2006, 503.
186 Schumpeter, op. cit., 1976[1942], pp. 83–84.
187 Ibid, p. 84.
188 N. Foss and V. Mahnke (eds), *Competence, Governance, and Entrepreneurship: Advances in Economic Strategy Research*, Oxford University Press, 2000, p. 158.
189 For a sufficient treatment of 'the clustering of innovations', see Clemence and Doody, op. cit., pp. 51–57.
190 Ibid, pp. 51–57.
191 P. Drucker, *Innovation and Entrepreneurship*, New York: HarperBusiness, 1985, p. 27.
192 J. Schumpeter, 'The Creative Response in Economic History', *Journal of Economic History*, vol. 7(2), 1947, p. 153.
193 Ibid, pp. 149–159.
194 Ibid, p. 153.
195 Ibid, pp. 149–159.

196 J. Schumpeter, *Journal of Economic History*, p. 150.
197 Ebner, op. cit., p. 503.
198 T. Wu, 'Copyright's Communications Policy', *Michigan Law Review*, vol. 103, 2004, 279.
199 Coase, op. cit., 1988, pp. 33–55.
200 Foss and Mahnke, op. cit., pp. 180–181.
201 L. Thurow, *Building Wealth: The New Rules for Individuals, Companies, and Nations in a Knowledge-Based Economy*, New York: HarperBusiness, 1999, p. 33.
202 MacQueen, op. cit., pp. 15–17.
203 Ibid, pp. 8–9.
204 Lessig, op. cit., 2004, p. 172.
205 Goldstein, op. cit., 1994, pp. 144–158.
206 Goldstein, op. cit., 2007, p. 81.
207 Ibid, p. 83.
208 R. Boucher, 'The Future of Intellectual Property in the Information Age', in A. Thierer and W. Crews (eds), *Copy Fights: the Future of Intellectual Property in the Information Age*, Washington DC: Cato Institute, 2002, p. 98.
209 Goldstein, op. cit., 2007, p. 82.
210 Goldstein, op. cit., 1994, p. 156.
211 J. Reichman, G. Dinwoodie and P. Samuelson, 'A Reverse Notice and Takedown Regime to Enable Public Interest Uses of Technologically Protected Copyrighted Works', *Berkeley Technology Law Journal*, vol. 22, 2007, 998.
212 Lessig, op. cit., 2001, pp. 130–132. D. Post, 'His Napster's Voice', in Thierer and Crews, op. cit., pp. 107–124.
213 Reichman, Dinwoodie and Samuelson, op. cit., pp. 1013–1015.
214 Litman, op. cit., 2001, p. 159.
215 Post, op. cit., p. 110.
216 Goldstein, op. cit., 2007, pp. 158–159.
217 'Appeals Court Ruling Favors File-Sharing: Judge Cites Software's Legitimate Uses', *Washington Post*, 20 August 2004. Online. Available <http://www.washingtonpost.com/wp-dyn/articles/A17326–2004Aug19.html> (accessed 10 April 2005).
218 Goldstein, op. cit., 2007, p. 159.
219 Lessig, op. cit., 2004, p. 228.
220 Ibid, pp. 228–241.
221 P. Samuelson, 'Legally Speaking: The Dead Souls of the Google Booksearch Settlement', 2009. Online. Available <http://radar.oreilly.com/2009/04/legally-speaking-the-dead-soul.html> (accessed 10 March 2011).
222 MacQueen, Waelde, Laurie and Brown, op. cit., p. 239.
223 P. Samuelson, 'Google Book Search and the Future of Books in Cyberspace', 2010. Online. Available <http://www.ischool.berkeley.edu/ pam> (accessed 10 March 2011), p. 5.
224 Ibid, p. 6.
225 Ibid, pp. 6–8.
226 05 Civ. 8136 (DC) Document 971 (SDNY 2011).
227 S. Liebowitz and S. Margolis, 'Seventeen Economists Weigh in on Copyright: the Role of Theory, Empirics, and Network Effects', AEI-Brookings Joint Centre for Regulatory Studies, 2004, p. 1.
228 Lessig, op. cit., 2004, p. 232.
229 Liebowitz and Margolis, op. cit., pp. 2–3.
230 P. Schwartz and W. Treanor, '*Eldred* and *Lochner*: Copyright Term Extension and Intellectual Property as Constitutional Property', *The Yale Law Journal*, vol. 112, 2004, 2342–2344.

231 S. Martin, 'The Mythology of the Public Domain: Exploring the Myths Behind Attacks on the Duration of Copyright Protection', *Loyola of Los Angeles Law Review*, vol. 36, 2002, 277–279.
232 Liebowitz and Margolis, op. cit., pp. 4–9.
233 Ibid, pp. 12–24.
234 Landes and Posner, op. cit., 2003, pp. 244–249.
235 As earlier as in the 1930s, Sir Arnold Plant, Sir Ernest Cassel Professor at London School of Economics, was not only the one, as Coase pointed out, 'who opened up the subject' of economic analysis of copyright in book publishing, but also the one who used historical data to examine the economic issues in the development of UK copyright laws. See Coase, op. cit., 1994, p. 182. Sir Arnold's specific goal was to examine the role of copyright protection in the creativity and growth of the UK book publishing industry under certain industry or market structures. Although copyright expansion in duration was not his main concern, Plant did address the effect of copyright term extension on the creation of new works. For Plant, copyright term extension can raise the profits for successful books but may not increase the output of new creations. A. Plant, 'The Economic Aspects of Copyright in Books', *Economica*, May 1934, 182, 191.
236 A. Porter, 'Plan to Extend Copyright on Pop Classics', *The Sunday Times*, 5 June 2005. Online. Available <http://www.timesonline.co.uk/tol/news/uk/article530132.ece> (accessed 10 March 2011).
237 D. Cronin, 'Proposed EU Copyright Term Extension Faces Vocal Opposition in Parliament', Intellectual Property Watch, 27 January 2009. Online. Available <http://www.ip-watch.org/weblog/2009/01/27/eu-copyright-term-extension-meets-vocal-opposition-in-parliament/> (accessed 10 March 2011).
238 Online. Available <http://www.ft.com/cms/s/0/f8f81e30-ddc2–11dc-ad7e-0000779fd2ac.html#axzz1IWVQ73Oi> (accessed 10 March 2011).
239 Online. Available <http://www.cippm.org.uk/pdfs/A%20Joint%20Letter%20Regarding%20Term%20Extension%20for%20Phonograms.pdf> (accessed 10 March 2011).
240 M. Kretschmer *et al*, 'Creativity Stifled? A Joint Academic Statement on the Proposed Copyright Term Extension for Sound Recordings', *European Intellectual Property Review*, vol. 30(9), 2008, 341–347.
241 M. Kretschmer *et al*, 'Copyright Extension is the Enemy of Innovation', *The Times*, 21 July 2008. Online. Available <http://www.timesonline.co.uk/tol/comment/letters/article4374115.ece> (accessed 10 March 2011).
242 Online. Available <http://www.cippm.org.uk/downloads/Press%20Release%20Copyright%20Extension.pdf> (accessed 10 March 2011).
243 Kretschmer *et al*, op. cit., 2008, pp. 341–347.
244 CIPIL, *Review of the Economic Evidence Relating to an Extension of the Term of Copyright in Sound Recordings*, Centre for Intellectual Property and Information Law, University of Cambridge, 2006, pp. 49–51.
245 IIL, *The IViR Report*, Institute for Information Law, University of Amsterdam, 2006, pp. 112–113.
246 Ibid, pp. 114–119.
247 PwC, *The Impact of Copyright Extension for Sound Recordings in the UK: A Report for the Gowers Review of Intellectual Property prepared by PwC on Behalf of the BPI*, PricewaterhouseCoopers LLP, 2006, p. 13.
248 Ibid, p. 32.
249 Ibid, p. 49.
250 Ibid, p. 51.
251 Ibid, pp. 51–55.
252 I. Png and Q. Wang, 'Copyright Duration and the Supply of Creative Work', 2006, p. 15.

253 S. Liebowitz, 'What are the Consequences of the European Union Extending Copyright Length for Sound Recordings?' 2007, p. 22.

254 Png and Wang, 'Copyright Law and the Supply of Creative Work: Evidence from the Movies', 2009, p. 3.

255 The information is based on the news report 'Extension of Copyright Term Postponed in the European Parliament'. Online. Available <http://www.metamorphosis.org.mk/en/news/world/1466-ep-go-odlozi-prodolzuvanjeto-na-periodot-na-vaznost-na-avtorskite-prava> (accessed 10 March 2011).

256 The information is based on the news report 'European Parliament Pass Copyright Extension in the UK up to 70 Years'. Online. Available <http://www.generator.org.uk/blog/european-parliament-pass-copyright-extension-uk-70-years> (accessed 10 March 2011).

257 MacQueen, op. cit., p. 15.

4 Theoretical framework

This chapter develops the theoretical framework that is applied to explore the relation between copyright expansion and the growth of the UK book publishing industry. Principally, this chapter explains why a Schumpeterian perspective, especially Schumpeter's framework of creative destruction, provides insights for investigating the relation between copyright expansion and the growth of the UK book publishing industry as a typical copyright industry, and as the cradle of modern copyright law.

4.1 Law and economic development

In principle, the relation between copyright expansion and industrial growth can be seen as the relation between law and economic development in general, and between intellectual property rights and economic development in particular. Frequently, the relation between intellectual property rights and economic development has been examined at either the national or the international level (or both).[1] In contrast, the relation between copyright (protection or expansion) and industrial growth has been investigated at either the firm or the industry level (or both).[2] However, no matter at which level, the problems and issues concerning the interactions among legal institutions, industrial growth, and economic development do overlap. Thus, a concise appraisal of the two relations at either the national or international level can further an understanding of the relation between copyright expansion and industrial growth at the firm or the industry level in the UK book publishing industry.

Converging at either the national or international level, 'economic development' is certainly 'the big picture'.[3] Smith, Marx, and Schumpeter are all among the prominent figures who explored 'the big picture' and the role of legal institutions in it. In Smith's mind, law should play a passive but protective role in defining property rights and advancing free trade.[4] For Marx, law is a functional device of capitalist private ownership and property rights.[5] In spite of the differences in their underlying principles, both Smith's and Marx's theories do suggest that the nature of law would be clearly grasped in the context of economic systems and the role of law in economic development should be undeniable.[6] As one of the pioneers who laid the foundation for public choice theory,[7] Schumpeter not only identified the role of intellectual property law in industrial growth but also underscored the impact of legal rules, especially those in financial systems, on entrepreneurship and economic development.[8] Of course, the focal point of these three pioneers was on Western jurisdictions.

According to Dam, research on 'the big picture' of economic development has focused more recently on the developing world. It was both neoinstitutional economics and the new economic conditions in the developing world after World War II that necessitated a new direction in examining the relation between law and economic development. To elucidate this new direction, he identified three stages of economic development thinking. At the first stage, immediately after the War, as more former colonies acquired their independence, economic development became the primary issue faced by these new nations. Following the path of the classical economics, many policy makers and advocates, both domestically and internationally, convinced themselves that the traditional factors of production – capital, labour, and land – were the bottleneck of economic development. Accordingly, introducing economic aid programmes and instituting financial agencies, such as the World Bank, became the main policy options for boosting economic growth in the developing world. Meanwhile, when endorsing these factor-empowerment measures – such as economic aid and direct investments – these developing countries also adopted import-substitution policies, restricted international trade, and subsidised their developing industries. However, these policies did not work well initially and encountered severe setbacks such as inflation and economic isolation. To overcome these problems, at the second stage, the developing nations embraced neoclassical economics as their key insight for making their developmental policies. As a result, a series of free-market-oriented policies at both microeconomic and macroeconomic levels – such as opening domestic markets, revoking price control, promoting competition, and reforming industry structure – were either advocated or implemented. In the 1990s, state-owned enterprises were privatised and financial and labour markets were restructured. More recently, the third stage has been initiated. The role of institutions, especially legal institutions, in economic development became an essential concern at this stage, and the neoinstitutional economics started to dominate the third stage of economic development thinking.[9] The main research topics under neoinstitutionalism at this stage – such as the issues of property rights and financial institutions – are still within the realm of Smith, Marx, and Schumpeter. The significant contribution of the neoinstitutionalism-directed research is their elaboration of the microeconomic basis of legal institutions regarding economic development and their efforts to consolidate methodological strengths.

The underlying principle behind TRIPS (Trade-Related Aspects of Intellectual Property Rights) is neoclassical economics. As addressed in

Chapter 2.3.1, from a standpoint of neoclassical economics, legal protection of intellectual property rights should effectively smooth market transactions and efficiently maximise production of creative products through appreciating the full value of creative works[10] in order to encourage future creations from both existing and potential creators. For neoclassical economists, the ample disparity between a high production cost and a low reproduction cost in producing intellectual property goods could cause a serious problem of disincentive. In terms of business operation and industrial growth, this is 'the appreciability problem' that troubled the advocates of TRIPS.[11] For 'rights-based' promoters, the goals of protecting intellectual property rights is clear – protecting private property rights, promoting public welfare, encouraging innovation or creativity, and strengthening competitiveness.[12] Yet, as Grossman and Lai put it, intellectual property rights 'remain a highly contentious issue in international relations, because many developing countries believe that TRIPs was forced upon them by their economically more powerful trading partners and that this move toward harmonisation of patent and other IPR policies serves the interests of the North at the expense of their own'.[13]

The division between the developing countries of the South and the wealthier, developed countries of the North over the cross-border protection of intellectual property rights raises the issue of the efficacy of the ever-increasing international protection of intellectual property rights in advancing economic development at either the national or the international level. Susan Sell questioned the assumed role of TRIPS as a global regime of intellectual property rights in promoting the economic development in the developing countries. She argued that TRIPS expanded the scope of global protection of intellectual property rights and squeezed the available opportunities for the developing world to modernise their economies through the same course as the West followed in the past. In addition, at least in the short run, a stronger global protection of intellectual property rights, as introduced by TRIPS, can only facilitate a transfer of resources from the developing countries to the developed countries.[14] Grossman and Lai analysed the contextual factors that may affect the function of the TRIPS regime in economic development. In particular, they identified economic openness as an important factor. Their research indicates that, when taking account of the factor of economic openness, a regime of protecting intellectual property rights would not play an active role in economic development as neoclassical economists would expect.[15]

Grossman and Lai's research, along with other studies on the relation between intellectual property rights and economic development on the international stage,[16] has raised concern about how to analyse the interaction between legal institutions and economic development in the context of industry or market structure and market forces at either the national or the international level. Stryszowski further addressed this concern in his research on the relation between intellectual property rights and economic development under the forces of globalisation from Schumpeter's standpoint of creative destruction. Following Schumpeter's stance and its reformulations by other scholars, Stryszowski constructed a Schumpeterian multi-region model categorising a South–North boundary, formalising a series of factors – such as industry structure, consumption, production, research and development, spillover of innovation, and relevant stock market – which could affect the relation between intellectual property rights and economic development across the South–North boundary. Under this model, when these control variables were held constant, Stryszowski's assessment showed that the correlation between 'the quality of intellectual property rights' and 'the distance to the frontier' is negative. That is, a strong regime of intellectual property rights might drive down the distance between the developing and developed countries under the forces of globalisation.[17]

Of course, the above estimate, in Stryszowski own words, is not 'a definitive econometric demonstration' and, therefore, 'a more in-depth empirical analysis of this issue is a worthwhile subject of future research'.[18] The merit of Stryszowski's research alongside Grossman and Lai's analysis is that they inspired a positive and multifaceted approach to investigating the macro-level issues on the relation between intellectual property rights and economic development under a variety of market forces that would reinforce the process of creative destruction. At the micro-level within national borders, the market forces that affect the macro-level relation between intellectual property rights and economic development would still play roles in the growth of the innovation–creativity-based industries (including copyright industries). Furthermore, growth at the firm and industry levels is a necessary condition for the economic development at the national and international levels.

Moreover, in terms of methodology, the effects of legal protection of intellectual property rights on the innovation–creativity-based industries (including copyright industries) at the firm and industry levels are readily discernible for further analysis. When concentrating on the copyright industries at the firm and industry levels, it is practical for the present book to distinguish both the micro-level and macro-level market forces under a particular industry or market structure, and to specify the impacts of these forces on the interaction between copyright expansion and industrial growth in a process of creative destruction. Once a certain term of copyright expansion has been legislated for, a legal institution is established. This institution, like other legal institutions, will create an environment of 'stability and predictability' for business operations.[19] A stable and predictable environment provides a staunch mechanism for the entrepreneurs in the industry, innovators or imitators, authors or publishers, to grow their commerce and pursue their profits.[20] Meanwhile, under the pressure of creative destruction, the function of legal institutions stipulating copyright expansion will be constrained by the market forces under certain industry or market structures. When placing it in the context of market forces and industry or market structure in a process of creative destruction, the question of whether 'copyright expansion could stimulate or restrict the growth of copyright industries as information technology advances' will be explored in a constructive way.

4.2 Copyright expansion and the Schumpeterian firm

Unlike Marx or Keynes, whose theories mainly focus on the macro factors of economic development, Schumpeter concentrated his framework on the micro issues[21] of industry structure, competition, innovation, and entrepreneurship at the firm and industry levels in the long-term process of creative destruction. Of course, both Marx and Schumpeter shared a dynamic view on capitalism as a process.[22] The process of creative destruction as an evolutionary process 'is a reflection of certain dynamic forces that Schumpeter, along with Marx, believed are inherent in the incentive structure, the pursuit of profits, and the competitive institutions that lie at the basis of capitalism'.[23] Thus, in Schumpeter's system, the function and operation of firms is one of the essential issues with regard to the economic development and industrial growth in a long-term evolutionary and dynamic process of creative destruction.

In Schumpeter's account, a firm is an institute of innovation resting on the strength of entrepreneur/enterprise and corresponding entrepreneurship under a dynamic competition – the competition for survival and revival by means of successive innovations and/or creative response in a process of creative destruction. Because equilibrium is, for the most part, unachievable under capitalism, a firm (according to Schumpeter) would not simply pursue a balancing return between increasing and diminishing returns on account of the marginal consideration (an assessment of marginal costs and benefits) through the price mechanism, as Marshall suggested, or predictably maximise its interests once reinforcing desirable institutional arrangements for minimising transaction costs, as Coase implied. Rather, in Schumpeter's world, a firm will and should consolidate its organisational capacities and competitive advantage for its changing interests and future values through innovation and 'creative response'[24] towards dynamic environments and disequilibrium opportunities.

While it becomes clear that both growing existing firms and creating new ones will provide economic stability,[25] Schumpeter identified two facets of creating and growing firms: (1) the internal motives, the innovations, and innovative entrepreneurs inside the firm, and (2) the external pressures, the dynamic environments, and disequilibrium opportunities outside the firm.[26] It should be obvious for Schumpeter that a process of creative destruction not only involves the firm but also the industry in which the firm locates. Accordingly, under a dynamic competition, entrepreneurial style, innovation in systems, production schemes, industry structure, and the way of industrial organisation are key factors for both growing existing firms and creating new ones in a process of creative destruction. Of course, the regulatory framework, the firm's competitive strategy, and technological assumptions or possibilities are also critical factors that are strongly related to these key factors for creating and growing firms in the process.[27] Meanwhile, Schumpeter recognised that the variety of monopolistic practices (including monopolistic competition, oligopoly, and monopoly) of firms in the process of creative destruction should be examined from a new standpoint.

On the one hand, perfect competition as an opposing force to monopolistic practices is either unsustainable or undesirable for a firm's survival in the process of creative destruction. As Schumpeter noted, 'The introduction of new methods of production and new commodities is hardly conceivable with perfect – and perfectly prompt – competition from the start . . . Perfect competition is and always has been temporarily suspended whenever anything new is being introduced.'[28] 'The firm of the type that is compatible with perfect competition is in many cases inferior in internal, especially techno-logical, efficiency.'[29] On the other hand, monopolistic practices, such as intel-lectual property protection (amongst which Schumpeter particularly mentioned patent protection) are not necessarily undesirable for the industrial growth in a process of creative destruction. Schumpeter placed these monopo-listic practices into a multipart and long-term context in the process, and inspected them under such wider circumstances. He argued that 'the net effect' of these practices 'is a question of the circumstances and of the way in which and the degree to which industry regulates itself in each individual case'.[30] In the short run, the forces of creative destruction can make many firms monopolistic. In the long run, however, also under the pressure of crea-tive destruction – specifically the pressure of dynamic competition between imitators and innovators – monopolistic firms have been forced to adapt their monopolistic behaviours and to do 'the work of the competitive mechanism'.[31] As a consequence, 'monopoly prices are not necessarily higher or monopoly outputs smaller than competitive prices and outputs would be at the levels of productive and organisational efficiency'.[32] In the meantime, according to Schumpeter, owning intellectual property such as a patent as a competitive power does not necessarily bestow a monopolistic position. In the long run, the duration of patent should be less important because the permanent demand schedule for a new device or commodity under the regime of patent 'has been established before the patent expired'.[33]

In contrast to the duration of patent, the duration of copyright may play a different role in creating and growing firms in the process of creative destruc-tion. However, Schumpeter's view on the duration of patent is still informa-tive for understanding the meaning of copyright expansion for the function and operation of an innovative firm. Eventually, the duration of protection is more crucial for a firm under a static competition than under a dynamic competition. Under a dynamic competition, creating and protecting new copyright as a new property right will be more urgent than extending existing property rights for an innovative firm and its entrepreneurs. Copyright expan-sion may help retain a firm's short-term profit gain but do little to consolidate the firm's competitive advantage and strengthen its entrepreneurship in the long run.

4.3 Copyright expansion and Schumpeterian growth

In Schumpeter's analysis, market forces and industry or market structure do not work independently. Instead, entrepreneurs play an active role in coping with the market forces and industry or market structure under the pressure of creative destruction. As discussed in Chapter 2.3.2, Schumpeter considered an innovative entrepreneur to be 'a kind of knight'[34] for business operations, and the interaction between institutional forms and entrepreneurial activity as a driving force for industrial growth. For him, entrepreneurs are expected to tackle the conflict between incentive motive and strategic action under a dynamic competition for their business operations and, ultimately, for industrial growth.

4.3.1 A Schumpeterian model of copyright-growth relation

In the copyright industries, copyright law establishes a regulatory platform for the business operations and growth of these industries under a dynamic competition. However, a regulatory platform is not more than a necessary condition for the operations and growth of these industries. Although 'the ability to effectively protect one's intellectual creations through the legal system and not through one's sheer power in the market provides entrepreneurs an important incentive to innovate',[35] as Mayer-Schönberger put it, entrepreneurs should eventually pursue profit, achieve growth, and even take advantage of legal protection through their entrepreneurial performances. In the case of copyright law, no matter how long the copyright duration has been extended by the state, under the pressure of creative destruction no entrepreneurs would wait until the law-granted copyright term expires before engaging in any business actions. As Lessig pointed out, 'Innovators don't simply sit on their hands until a guaranteed return is offered; real capitalists invest and innovate with the understanding that competitors will be free to take their ideas and use them against the innovators.'[36]

Copyright law as a legal institution can function as a leveller, as a protector, and as an enforcer for entrepreneurs.[37] Meanwhile, market institutions remain in play. As new innovative forces such as digitalisation come to the fore, many prominent cyber lawyers and cyber scientists have particularly scrutinised 'the role the market plays in encouraging human creativity and the production of intellectual products within the digital environment'.[38] This scrutiny requires that, when taking into account the role of copyright law in adjusting the market forces and related industry or market structure in the other copyright industries, the concern shall be on how to analyse the complex and dynamic interaction among copyright expansion, industrial growth, market forces, and industry or market structure in a process of creative destruction.

The first concern is how market forces could complicate the relation between copyright expansion and industrial growth under the pressure of creative destruction. As indicated in Chapter 3.1, cost structure, economies of scale, and externalities could function diversely in shaping the production and distribution of copyright works such as books in the information market as an incomplete market. If this is the case, entrepreneurial activities rather than copyright expansion might function well in promoting industrial growth at the firm and industry levels. For the neoclassical economists, 'the collective of the firm has been considered as an empty point in an infinite space of demand and supply'.[39] Accordingly, a firm in the copyright industries would automatically respond to the incentives related to copyright expansion. In the neoinstitutionalist sphere, a firm in the copyright industries is no longer an empty point but an entity that takes transaction costs seriously in the course of production and distribution of a copyright work or, in short, in the market process. Due to the existence of transaction costs, an initial legal arrangement of copyright should be crucial for the final efficiency.[40] However, copyright expansion is hardly critical from a neoinstitutionalist approach. In addition, neoinstitutionalism offers no scheme for a firm that experiences the process from the initial legal arrangement to the final efficiency; that is, the market process of a copyright work.

Nevertheless, for a Schumpeterian entrepreneur, how to exploit the process from the initial legal arrangement to the final efficiency is vital for her/his firm. Under the pressure of creative destruction, entrepreneurs and their firms will take strategic actions on account of these market forces alongside legal arrangements. The initial legal arrangement may not be decisive for exploiting the process. When the cost structure with a substantial fixed cost and diminutive marginal cost of a copyright work prevailed, 'a lead-time advantage' rather than a legal arrangement for the copyright owner would be significant.[41] As economies of scale and network externalities surfaced, firms possessing copyright works would seize the opportunities, no matter what form the legal arrangement would take. The cost advantage, the return with economies of scale, and the benefit from network externalities shall be realised through entrepreneurs' competitive strategies in the market process.[42] Indeed, in the information market, some firms may adopt non-exclusive strategies for their successful returns or growths.[43] Under the circumstances, copyright expansion may not function smoothly as copyright optimists/neoclassicists would suggest.

Second, while examining the relation between copyright expansion and industrial growth in a process of creative destruction, furthering an investigation into entrepreneurs' competitive strategies or creative responses (or 'adaptive response' under certain circumstances) under certain industry or market structures can help explore the question of whether 'copyright expansion could stimulate or restrict the growth of copyright industries as information technology advances'. For this consideration, comparing two legislative policies that will in general have impacts on the industry or market structure of the copyright industries – copyright expansion and antitrust policy[44] – and corresponding entrepreneurial strategies will clarify the impacts of the industry or market structure on the relation between copyright expansion and industrial growth. If copyright expansion may not function well in fostering industrial growth, would an antitrust policy as an antithesis of copyright expansion[45] be desirable for industrial growth under the pressure of creative destruction?

The answer is not simple either. Surely, on the one hand, copyright law creates an industry or market structure of monopoly or oligopoly.[46] However, the copyright-endorsed monopoly 'stood apart from institutional or industry-wide monopolies'.[47] In the copyright industries such as the book publishing industry, just as in other information industries, a dynamic or Schumpeterian competition still dominates the market process with the advance and application of technological and organisational innovations. The copyright owners still need to confront substantial competitive forces.[48] To survive and thrive, unlike in a neoclassical scenario where firms stumble on random fluctuations and optimise responses to prices,[49] in Schumpeter's vision, the firms and their entrepreneurs on either the imitation or innovation side should take creative responses (or adaptive response under certain circumstances) to the market uncertainties for achieving their market power and competitive advantage. Under the circumstances, competition and concentration will become two cohesive aspects of the industry or market structure in the copyright industries,[50] although with different meanings from the neoclassical economics. The dynamic competition is unquestionably imperfect but not necessarily undesirable. The industrial concentration under a dynamic competition may further encourage innovation, creativity, and industrial growth under certain conditions. Thus, antitrust law or measures may obstruct the opportunity for entrepreneurial innovations[51] and accordingly curb industrial growth.

On the other hand, a copyright system also 'values innovation and protection equally'.[52] In certain periods of the process of creative destruction, when a start-up firm possesses creative and innovative capabilities but faces temporary performance setbacks, copyright expansion could serve as a protector for the firm's growth, although not necessarily for industrial growth on the whole in a specific industrial field. For an established firm, copyright expansion would serve only as a leveller and could possibly hold back the industrial growth on the whole in the industrial field.

Third, the social and economic efficiency of copyright expansion at the level above a specific industry is still a legitimate concern. Within a specific copyright industry, the relation between copyright expansion and industrial growth under certain industry or market structures may take different patterns in different periods of a process of creative destruction. However, especially at the level above a specific industry, as Lessig put it, 'Intellectual property is both an input and an output in the creative process; increasing the "cost" of intellectual property thus increases both the cost production and the incentives to produce'.[53] In a broad sense, even for most economists, the duration limit of copyright is justifiable from many angles of the cost structure of copyright works, and from the original rationale of copyright protection.[54] Accordingly, copyright expansion may not make economic sense for expected economic efficiency. As Posner stated, 'An expansion of copyright protection might . . . reduce the output of literature . . . by increasing the royalty expense of writers'.[55]

4.3.2 Creative destruction of copyright-growth relation

Economic efficiency, for Schumpeter, is 'gauged by the production of new innovations, rather than by the micro-economic consideration of aggregate social welfare at any one moment'.[56] Schumpeter did not deprecate the process of rationalisation, as classical and neoclassical economists endorse. Rather, he identified the process of creative construction as a dynamic process of innovative rationalisation over a long time sequence. Technological innovation, dynamic competition, and concentrating industry structure consist of the main forces of the long-term process of creative destruction. As the transformation from a mechanised economy to a software-based economy was happening in the twentieth century, as Paul Romer asserted,[57] technological innovation and technology-promoted organisational innovation are elevating a restructuring of the socio-economic systems in the information age.[58] Classical and neoclassical standard economic theories that have left no methodical spaces for technology and related transformations encounter tremendous difficulty in explaining the new events and trends in the digital age. In this context, Schumpeter's theory has displayed its strengths for examining the fundamental changes of knowledge accumulation and economic development or industrial growth in the new digital economy.[59] In fact, Peter Drucker realised the applicability of Schumpeter's views to exploring the complexity of the industry structures in the post-capitalist, knowledge-based society of the early 1990s.[60] In the new millennium, Manuel Castells applauded Schumpeter's view of 'creative destruction' as the 'spirit of informationalism', which analogises Max Weber's vision of the 'spirit of capitalism'.[61]

Schumpeter's views on intellectual property, particularly on patents, in the context of creative destruction are still informative for our understanding of copyright expansion in general, and the expansion in the digital age in particular. In Schumpeter's account, while a firm's role is 'one of strategic agent seeking to overcome constraints',[62] securing or protecting intellectual property rights in advance is one of the diverse monopolistic practices for a firm's survival and industrial growth in the process of creative destruction. Schumpeter emphasised the forces of creative destruction – such as technological innovation, dynamic competition, and concentrating industry structure – and stressed how these forces have shaped the circumstances or contexts in which diverse monopolistic practices (including protection of intellectual property) could play certain roles in advancing the firm's changing interests and industrial growth. In the digital age, as the Internet has become one of the dynamic forces of creative destruction,[63] 'copyright issues move to centre stage in the policy arena with the advent of digital technology and the capacity of the Internet to move audio, video, text and numeric data from point to point in a short amount of time'.[64] Accordingly, the copyright regime has become one of the main targets for the forces of creative destruction.[65] Facing the unpredictability, uncertainty, and insecurity caused by technological innovation, dynamic competition, and concentrating industry structure in the digital environment, copyright expansion should be deliberated not only to protect the intellectual expressions from harmful duplication but, more importantly, to function as a mechanism of competitive advantage[66] and risk aversion for copyright owners in growing copyright industries in the uneasy time.[67] In the US, *MGM Studios Inc vs Grokster Ltd* in 2005 indicates that copyright expansion signals the expectations of copyright industries and judicial branches facing the process of creative destruction.[68] In Europe, one of the strategic rationales of *The Directive on the Harmonisation of Certain Aspects of Copyright and Related Rights in the Information Society* in 2001[69] is to cope with the challenges from new information technology and the high-technology-based institutional transformations through extending copyright and related rights.[70] As Timothy Wu stated in Lawrence Lessig's blog, the *Grokster* opinion presents 'words that could have been penned by Schumpeter'.[71]

Professor Wu also proposes a regulation/competition view on copyright law when exploring copyright's communications policy.[72] Wu's view reflects a Schumpeterian perspective in many aspects, and can be incorporated into Schumpeter's theory for investigating the relation between copyright expansion and industrial creativity/growth under a dynamic or Schumpeterian competition in the process of creative destruction.

First, Schumpeter placed the issues of intellectual property in the context of dynamic competition and considered protecting intellectual property (such as patent) a strategic manoeuvre for industrial growth rather than an incentive reflection.[73] Schumpeter seemed to envision Wu's position in a certain way. Wu reveals the insufficiency of classical or neoclassical economists' perspectives on copyright law, expressed mainly in author-centre and incentive-based utilitarian or economic theories of copyright, in inspecting the role of copyright law in the era of accelerating technological changes.[74] Both could agree that their anxieties focused on classical or neoclassical economists' approaches to the issues of intellectual property at the time of innovation.

Second, Schumpeter examined the relation between the process of creative destruction and the firm's creative response to the process. In Schumpeter's system, creative destruction and creative response (or adaptive response under certain circumstances) should be two sides of the same coin of economic development and industrial growth.[75] From a historical perspective, Schumpeter identified creative response as an entrepreneurial function of 'the doing of new things or the doing of things that are already being done in a new way (innovation)'[76] for reacting to the change in opportunity and conditions. Without a doubt, a creative response is, in essence, a type of organisational innovation undertaken by entrepreneurs as a cohesive part of the process of creative destruction. Even within the same industrial field, an entrepreneur's organisational innovations in one firm as a creative response to the pressure of creative destruction on account of the innovative forces (forces of either technological or organisational innovations) from the other firms could reformulate a new pressure of creative destruction for these firms. In other words, a creative response from one firm could create a new pressure of creative destruction for another firm in the same process of creative destruction within the same industry. For instance, in the US Internet industry, the entrepreneurial organisational innovations of Google as a creative response to the existing pressure of creative destruction engendered a new pressure of creative destruction for Microsoft. As a creative response, Microsoft started to take a substantial step to purchase Yahoo in 2008.[77] In 2009, Microsoft and Yahoo reached an agreement that they should be partners in their search and advertising businesses.[78]

When observing that the efficiency-oriented market forces and related institutions can no longer function well under a dynamic competition, Schumpeter accordingly created a 'space for a more general theory of regulation'[79] – a survey on a kind of government involvement that can direct the conflict between incentive motive and strategic action under the dynamic competition. Wu seemed to occupy the same 'space' but through a more specific theory of regulation – his regulation/competition view on copyright law.

Wu believes that copyright law can serve as a regulatory regime for tackling the conflicts between efficiency and innovation, and between incentive motive and strategic action at the time of innovation. The role of copyright law, according to Wu, is to regulate the 'competition among rival disseminators',[80] or more specifically, 'to manage competition among natural rivals in the world of packaged information'.[81] Disseminators usually refer to the firms in creative and information industries in Wu's account. Wu elaborates on the complexity of the conflict between incumbent and new disseminators, and the difficulty of their copyright relations. In his account, the competition in the copyright industries would become more dynamic as the disseminators become more diverse, the information from these disseminators and their performances become more asymmetric, and the technology of dissemination becomes more advanced. Meanwhile, as the competition becomes more dynamic, the contest for favourable copyright policy would become more intensive. In consequence, copyright enforcement would be more problematic, and copyright conflict would be more sobering. As Wu puts it, 'Copyright enforcement can be costly and challenging. The knowledge that government action may be of unpredictable effectiveness increases the uncertainty that leads to copyright conflicts'.[82] Obviously, Wu presents a Schumpeterian vision of copyright enforcement and conflict in the context of dynamic competition among information disseminators in the copyright industries.

Third, when addressing the link between the competition among disseminators and their copyright actions, Wu indeed recognises the dynamic interactions between industry structure, copyright enforcement, and the growth of copyright industries at the time of innovation. Copyright has been regarded as a government-granted monopoly.[83] The level of government intervention in copyright enforcement reflects the mode of the industry structure and the method of industrial organisation in the copyright industries on the one hand, and transforms the mode on the other hand. According to Wu, facing the advance of technological innovations, the role of copyright law in directing competition and allocating resources has been diversified. As a result, the mode of the industry structure and the method of industrial organisation have become unbalancing in the copyright, creative, or information industries. Correspondingly, the operation of the firms and the growth of creative/information industries have experienced a significant transformation with the adjustment of copyright's communications policy.[84] In Wu's own words, his account of the interactions among the mode of the industry structure and the method of industrial organisation in the copyright, creative, or information industries, the operation of the firms, the growth of the whole industries, and copyright's communications policy could be 'penned by Schumpeter'.

Wu's provocative appraisal of 'Schumpeter's pen' makes a strong case for appreciating the applicability of the Schumpeterian growth model in investigating the copyright-growth relation under the forces of creative destruction in the UK copyright industries. Of course, one critical way to appraise the applicability of this model is to conduct empirical research on the copyright-growth relation under the model or related framework.

Schumpeter's theory and method can provide an enlightening and realistic framework and model for investigating the dynamic relation between copyright expansion and the growth of copyright industries in the process of creative destruction. Wu's theme of copyright's communications policy in many senses specifies Schumpeter's vision and concretises the copyright-growth relation in the process, even if Wu does not often mention Schumpeter. Following Schumpeter's path and Wu's account, three forces of creative destruction – technological innovation, dynamic competition, and concentrating industry structure – are assumed to exert effects on the relation between copyright expansion and the growth of copyright industries. Accordingly, two central arguments are made in this book, taking account of the three forces of creative destruction: 1. Copyright expansion as a type of monopoly will exert effects on the growth of the copyright industries in the process of creative destruction; 2. The forces of creative destruction will impinge on the pattern of the copyright-growth relation.

The empirical assessment in the next chapter will provide some clues for examining the complex and dynamic nature of the copyright-growth relation and its mechanism under the forces of creative destruction from Schumpeter's methodological realism and legal pragmatism.

Notes

1 D. Gould and W. Gruben, 'The Role of Intellectual Property Rights in Economic Growth', *Journal of Development Economics*, vol. 48, 1996, pp. 323–350.

K. Idris, *Intellectual Property: A Power Tool for Economic Growth* WIPO Publication No. 888, Geneva: World Intellectual Property Organization, 2002.

2 R. Towse, *Creativity, Incentive and Reward: an Economic Analysis of Copyright and Culture in the Information Age*, Cheltenham, UK: Edward Elgar, 2001. R. Towse (ed), *Copyright in the Cultural Industries*, Edward Elgar, 2002.

3 K. Dam, *The Law-Growth Nexus: the Rule of Law and Economic Development*, Washington, DC: Brookings Institution Press, 2006, p. 9.

4 A. Smith, *Wealth of Nations*, New York: Prometheus Books, 1991[1776].

5 R. Tucker, *The Marx-Engels Reader*, W. W. Norton & Company, 1972. P. Phillips, *Marx and Engels on Law and Laws*, Totowa: Barnes and Noble Books, 1980.

6 For a brief discussion of Smith and Marx's enquiry into the role of legal institutions in economic development, see D. North and R. Thomas, 'Conclusion', *The Rise of the Western World: A New Economic History*, Cambridge University Press, 1973.

7 P. Samuelson and W. Nordhaus, *Economics* 19th edn, 2010, p. 309.

8 V. Mayer-Schönberger, 'Schumpeterian Law: Rethinking the Role of Law in Fostering Entrepreneurship'. Online. Available <http://works.bepress.com/cgi/viewcontent.cgi?article=1001&context=vikt or _mayer_schoenberger> (accessed 14 March 2008), p. 29.

9 Dam, op. cit., pp. 1–6.

10 N. Netanel, 'Copyright and a Democratic Civil Society', *The Yale Law Journal*, vol. 106, 1996, p. 309.

11 M. Ryan, *Knowledge Diplomacy: Global Competition and the Politics of Intellectual Property*, Washington, DC: Brookings Institution Press, 1998, p. 5.

12 Ibid, pp. 6–19.

13 G. Grossman and E. Lai, 'International Protection of Intellectual Property', *The American Economic Review*, vol. 94(5), 2004, p. 1635.

14 S. Sell, *Private Power, Public Law: the Globalisation of Intellectual Property Rights*, Cambridge University Press, 2003, pp. 9–10.

15 Grossman and Lai, op. cit., pp. 1635–1636.

16 Gould and Gruben, op. cit., pp. 323–350. Idris, op. cit. K. Maskus, *International Intellectual Property Rights and the Global Economy*, Washington, DC: Institute for International Economics, 2000. K. Maskus, op. cit., 2004.

17 P. Stryszowski, 'Intellectual Property Rights, Globalisation and Growth', *Global Economy Journal*, vol. 6(4), 2006, pp.1–31.

18 Ibid, p. 25.

19 A. Stone, B. Levy and R. Paredes, 'Public Institutions and Private Transactions', in L. Alston, T. Eggertsson, and D. North (eds), *Empirical Studies in Institutional Change*, Cambridge University Press, 1996, p. 101.

20 S. Shane, *A General Theory of Entrepreneurship: the Individual-Opportunity Nexus*, Cheltenham, UK: Edward Elgar, 2003, p. 155.

21 For a brief treatment of Schumpeter's shift from the macro issue to the micro issue, see W. Baumol, 'Innovation and Creative Destruction', in L. McKnight, P. Vaaler and R. Katz (eds), *Creative Destruction: Business Survival Strategies in the Global Internet Economy*, The MIT Press, 2001, pp. 21–38.

22 W. Baumol, *Economic Dynamics*, 1959, pp. 23–36.

23 Nathan Rosenberg, *Schumpeter and the Endogeneity of Technology: Some American Perspectives*, New York: Routledge, 2000, p. 9.

24 J. Schumpeter, *Journal of Economic History*, vol. 7(2), 1947, 149–159.

25 A. Gabor, *The Capitalist Philosophers: the Geniuses of Modern Business – Their Lives, Times, and Ideas*, New York: Crown Business, 2000, p. 327.

26 J. Schumpeter, *Capitalism, Socialism and Democracy* 3rd edn, New York: Harper & Row, 1976[1942]. See also his *The Theory of Economic Development*, Harvard University Press, 1962[1911].

27 McKnight, Vaaler and Katz, op. cit., pp. 4–5.
28 Schumpeter, op. cit., 1976[1942], p. 105.
29 Ibid, p. 106.
30 Ibid, p. 91.
31 Ibid, p. 101.
32 Ibid.
33 Ibid, p. 102.
34 R. Heilbroner, *The Worldly Philosophers: the Lives, Times, and Ideas of the Great Economic Thinkers* 6th edn, New York: Simon and Schuster, 1992, p. 297.
35 Mayer-Schönberger, op. cit., p. 12.
36 L. Lessig, *The Future of Ideas: the Fate of the Commons in a Connected World*, New York: Vintage Books, 2001, p. 71.
37 Mayer-Schönberger, op. cit., pp. 6–15.
38 A. Murray, *The Regulation of Cyberspace: Control in the Online Environment*, London: Routledge-Cavendish, 2007, p. 168.
39 R. Te Velde, 'Schumpeter's Theory of Economic Development Revisited', in T. Brown and J. Ulijn (eds), *Innovation, Entrepreneurship and Culture: the Interaction between Technology, Progress and Economic Growth*, Cheltenham, UK: Edward Elgar, 2004, p. 104.
40 R. Watt, *Copyright and Economic Theory: Friends or Foes?* Cheltenham, UK: Edward Elgar, 2000, pp. 16–17.
41 S. Breyer, 'The Uneasy Case for Copyright: A Study of Copyright in Books, Photocopies, and Computer Programs', *Harvard Law Review*, vol. 84(2), 1970, 281–351.
42 J. Hakfoort, 'Copyright in the Digital Age: the Economic Rationale Re-Examined', in Towse (ed), 2002, p. 80.
43 Y. Benkler, *The Wealth of Networks: How Social Production Transforms Markets and Freedom*, New Haven, NJ: Yale University Press, 2006, pp. 41–48.
44 G. Ramello, 'Copyright and Antitrust Issues', in W. Gordon and R. Watt (eds), *The Economics of Copyright: Developments in Research and Analysis*, Cheltenham, UK: Edward Elgar, 2003, pp. 118–124.
45 W. Landes and R. Posner, *The Economic Structure of Intellectual Property Law*, Harvard University Press, 2003, pp. 372–375. Ramello, op. cit., pp. 118–147.
46 M. O'Hare, 'Copyright: When is Monopoly efficient?' *Journal of Policy Analysis and Management*, vol. 4(3), 1985, 407–418. Ramello, op. cit., pp. 118–147.
47 Goldstein, 1994, p. 173.
48 D. Kallay, *The Law and Economics of Antitrust and Intellectual Property: an Austrian Approach*, Cheltenham: Edward Elgar, 2004, p. 7.
49 J. Mathews, 'A Resource-Based View of Schumpeterian Economic Dynamics', *Journal of Evolutionary Economics*, vol. 106, 2002, p. 13.
50 N. Netanel, 'Copyright and "Market Power" in the Marketplace of Ideas', in F. Leveque and H. Shelanski (eds), *Antitrust, Patents and Copyright: EU and US Perspectives*, Cheltenham, UK: Edward Elgar Publishing, 2005, p. 154.
51 M. Katz and H. Shelanski, '"Schumpeterian" Competition and Antitrust Policy in High-Tech Markets', *Competition*, vol. 14, 2005, pp. 4–5. L. Thurow, 'Needed: A New System of Intellectual Property Rights', *Harvard Business Review*, September-October 1997, p. 98.
52 Murray, op. cit., 2007, p. 169.
53 Lessig, op. cit., 2001, p. 203.
54 Landes and Posner, op. cit., 2003, p. 213. R. Towse, 'Copyright and Economics', in S. Frith and L. Marshall (eds), *Music and Copyright* 2nd edn, UK: Edinburgh University Press, 2004, p. 61.
55 Quoted in Lessig, op. cit., 2001, p. 203.

56 M. Einhorn, *Media, Technology and Copyright: Integrating Law and Economics*, Cheltenham, UK: Edward Elgar, 2004, p. 5.

57 Quoted in R. Grant, *Contemporary Strategy Analysis: Concepts, Techniques, Applications* 4th edn, Malden, MA: Blackwell Publishers, 2002, pp. 93–94.

58 M. Castells, *The Rising of the Network Society* 2nd edn, Malden, MA: Blackwell Publishing, 2000, Chapters II, III, & IV. See also J. Davidson and W. Rees-Mogg, *The Sovereign Individual: Mastering the Transition to the Information Age*, New York: Touchstone, 1997, pp. 153–195.

59 J. Useem, 'Dead Thinkers' Society: Meet the New Economy's Oldest New Economist', *Business 2.0*, November 2001, 132–134.

60 P. Drucker, *Post-Capitalist Society*, New York: HarperBusiness, 1993, pp. 57–59.

61 Castells, op. cit., 2000, p. 215. Interestingly, since the financial crisis in 2008, *The Economist* has launched a business column 'Schumpeter' in order to explore some critical issues concerning the innovation or renovation during economic downturns from a Schumpeterian perspective. See, for instance, *The Economist*, 26 September – 2 October 2009, p. 82, 3 – 9 October 2009, p. 82, and 10 – 16 October 2009, p. 70.

62 M. Best, *The New Competition: Institutions of Industrial Restructuring*, Polity Press, 1990, p. 124.

63 McKnight, Vaaler and Katz, op. cit.

64 Einhorn, op. cit., p. 6.

65 R. Ku, 'The Creative Destruction of Copyright: Napster and the New Economics of Digital Technology', *University of Chicago Law Review*, vol. 69, 2002, pp. 263–322.

66 Grant, op. cit., 2002.

67 James Gibson proposes that copyright users' risk aversion and corresponding licence securing, conceptualised as a practice of 'doctrinal feedback', could play a role in expanding copyright from an unusual down-to-up way. See his 'Risk Aversion and Rights Accretion in Intellectual Property Law', *The Yale Law Journal*, vol. 116, 2007, 886–933. In this research, copyright holders' risk aversion will be considered as a responding factor for copyright expansion.

68 R. Spinello and H. Tavani (eds), *Intellectual Property Rights in a Networked World: Theory and Practice*, Hershey, PA: Information Science Publishing, 2005, pp. 44–48. See also Editorials, '*MGM vs Grokster*: A Chance to Foster Innovation – and Fight Piracy', *Business Week*, 4 April 2005, 158. J. Krim, 'Court Weighs File Sharing: Technology Advances vs. Copyrights in Grokster Case', *Washington Post*, 30 March 2005.

69 T. Cook, L. Brazell, S. Chalton and C. Smyth, *The Copyright Directive: UK Implementation*, Bristol, UK: Jordans, 2004, pp. 113–131.

70 Cook, Brazell, Chalton and Smyth, op. cit.

71 Online. Available <http://ipcentral.info/blog/archives/2004_08_01_index.shtml> (accessed 6 September 2006).

72 T. Wu, 'Copyright's Communications Policy', *Michigan Law Review*, vol. 103, 2004, pp. 278–366.

73 Schumpeter, op. cit., 1976[1942].

74 Wu, op. cit., pp. 278–280.

75 Some scholars emphasised the differentiations between these two sides correctly but, to some extent, unnecessarily. See E. Helmstadter and M. Perlman, 'Introduction', in E. Helmstadter and M. Perlman (eds), *Behavioral Norms, Technological Progress, and Economic Dynamics: Studies in Schumpeterian Economics*, University of Michigan Press, 1996, pp. 1–6.

76 Schumpeter, op. cit., 1947, p. 151.

77 J. Greene, 'Will Yahoo! Feel the Love?' *Business Week*, 18 February 2008, pp. 26–28.

134 *Theoretical framework*

78 'A Deal between Microsoft and Yahoo! Bingoo!' *The Economists*, 1 August 2009, p. 57.
79 Best, op. cit., p. 124.
80 Wu, op. cit., p. 279.
81 Ibid, p. 285.
82 Ibid, p. 296.
83 G. Mankiw, *Principles of Economics* 3rd edn, Mason, OH: South-Western/ Thomson Learning, 2004, p. 316.
84 Wu, op. cit., Section II.

5 Empirical research on UK book publishing

This chapter conducts empirical quantitative research into the extent to which the forces of creative destruction can affect the relation (interaction or correlation) between copyright expansion and industrial growth in the UK book publishing industry, at both the firm and industry levels, in the 30-year period from 1976 to 2006. Correspondingly, the relation (interaction or correlation) between copyright expansion and the growth of the UK book publishing industry, and the role of copyright expansion in growing the UK book publishing industry, are estimated over the same period. First, a concise account of the UK book publishing industry over the period is offered. Then, the methodological issues concerning the proposed empirical assessment, such as unit of analysis, sample, measurement, hypothesis construction, and econometric procedures, are addressed. With the methodological issues informing the research, the empirical assessment is conducted and corresponding results are presented.

5.1 Overview of the industry

The UK book publishing industry over the period from 1976 to 2006 experienced the most significant transformations in the history of this field. Among many driving forces behind the transformations, technological innovations are one of the most noteworthy.

5.1.1 Technological innovation

As Chapter 2.1.4 indicates, the application of general-purpose technologies in the UK information industries has overhauled the wider fields in general. In particular, computer and digital technology had profound effects on the UK book publishing industry between 1976 and 2006. In the 1970s, the first computerised typesetting system was introduced within the publishing industry. The late 1980s then witnessed word-processing systems and desktop publishing packages as more advanced computerising innovations shaped the new pattern of the entire UK publishing world.[1] Since 1995, the Internet has furthered the changes in the renewed UK publishing field.[2] Overall, since the late 1970s, the application of computer and digital technology in the UK book publishing industry has brought about many innovations, from the author–publisher relation, the finance–stock arrangement, the production–distribution process, to the new market development.[3] As technological innovations have advanced, the process of competition and the industry structure in the book industry have undergone rapid transformations over the decades.

5.1.2 *Dynamic competition*

In the 1970s, in spite of the observable impact of new technologies such as computerised typesetting, photocopying, and microforms on UK book publishing,[4] these new technologies seemed neither to consolidate monopolistic powers for some firms nor to facilitate the entry to or exit from the UK publishing industry of other firms. The UK market was still competitive.[5] Nevertheless, the competition was far from perfect. However, by the end of the decade, the process of competition in the field started to change. One signal of this change was that, in the late 1970s and early 1980s, the UK book publishing industry largely relied on economies of scale.[6] This change implied that the UK book publishing market could no longer maintain a competitive equilibrium.[7] Although economies of scale did not bestow advantages to the established firms over the entrepreneurial firms, the entrepreneurial firms were still under pressure to join the established firms to survive.[8]

The 1980s was a crucial period for the UK book publishing industry. From the beginning of that decade, recession struck the British economy and the book publishing industry as well. However, the recession did not prevent diverse industrial groups from plunging into the publishing market – quite the opposite.[9] Diverse forces energised the field. In the meantime, computer and digital technology changed the course of the whole book industry.[10] Competition became much more fierce.[11] However, under the Net Book Agreement, price competition in the sector was stifled to some extent. As a result, non-price competition such as advertising, promoting, and free services replaced price competition to varying degrees in the 1980s. Under non-price competition, innovation was restrained and consumers' interests were not served.[12]

Nevertheless, the UK book industry in the 1980s might still be classified as a contestable market.[13] Under this market, due to the minimised costs of firms' entry and exit, a competitive outcome may still be expected even if a natural monopoly surfaced.[14] Of course, a natural monopoly almost never became an issue in the book industry. Even the level and scope of contestability in the UK book publishing market in the 1980s was still uncertain.[15] What can be assured in this decade was that, under the expanding competition nationwide,[16] a competitive climate was sustained in book publishing.[17] At the end of the decade, there were around 13,000 organisations involving the field.[18] On the whole, the 1980s was 'largely a decade of transition from fragmentation and old-fashioned approaches to consolidation and rationalisation'.[19]

Digitalisation and globalisation gradually created massive opportunities for the UK book publishing industry in the 1990s.[20] The free-market crusade in the 1980s[21] and the powerful initiations of chain booksellers in the early 1990s eventually demolished the Net Book Agreement in 1995, which had been in force for nearly a century.[22] For the first time in the century-old British book publishing industry, price competition became reality. Meanwhile, concurrently, the Internet started to widely infiltrate the book publishing sector when the Net Book Agreement came to an end. 'The advent of sophisticated, and affordable, publishing technology has enabled new participants to enter the publishing market extremely easily.'[23] Above all, from the mid-1980s to the new century, 'wholly new technology made a radical difference to the very fundamentals of the publishing of the publishing industry'.[24] As a result, more price competition and other innovations have made the process of competition more complex in the publishing field since the 1980s. As Table 5.1 shows, compared with the 1970s, the scores of dynamic index, which measure the dynamic competition, have become lower and more unpredictable since the 1980s. This trend may reflect the complex and dynamic impact of technological innovations on the competition within the industry. As the application of technological innovations became routine, a dynamic competition – the competition for new things – is still unpredictable[25] but the overall level of the dynamic competition may be lower.

5.1.3 *Concentrating industry structure*

The industry structure of UK book publishing in the late 1970s still highlighted a high level of competition[26] and a high level of concentration. This picture has not changed drastically since the early 1980s. As Table 5.1 indicates, in the late 1970s, the concentration ratio of top 10 firms in book publishing was around 57 per cent. In contrast, the ratio of the top 10 was around 50 per cent in the early 1980s.[27] The industry structure indeed remained oligopolistic[28] and concentrated under a contestable market.[29] Although the driving forces behind the concentrated industry structure were complex, the merger and acquisition movement in the UK book publishing industry has evidently played a vital role in advancing concentration.

Of course, mergers and acquisitions in the UK book publishing industry started before the 1970s.[30] In the 1970s, economies of scale already played a sizeable role in the book publishing industry and larger firms visibly dominated the field.[31] In the 1980s, technological change and globalisation further conveyed to the British publishing industry a clear message that only by doing things in a business-like way could they survive in the global market. This commercial urgency compelled the industry to plunge into merger and acquisition in the worldwide context.[32] In consequence, most British independent publishing houses could no longer be sustained and international publishers dominated the concentrating process.[33] With the advance of technological change and globalisation, the 1980s saw an acceleration of concentration in the

Table 5.1 UK book publishing dynamic index and concentration ratio (1976–2006)

Years	Dynamic competition (Dynamic Index – Overall Average Standard Error/ Year Mean %)[a]	Concentrating industrial structure (Concentration Ratio – Top 10 Sales Total/Industry Sales Total %)[b]
1976–77	45	57
1977–78	47	56
1978–79	40	59
1979–80	38	54
1980–81	34	51
1981–82	30	44
1982–83	27	47
1983–84	24	49
1984–85	21	19
1985–86	17	42
1986–87	13	44
1987–88	19	72
1988–89	24	51
1989–90	22	51
1990–91	22	51
1991–92	20	55
1992–93	19	55
1993–94	18	50
1994–95	16	52
1995–96	16	41
1996–97	15	44
1997–98	21	45
1998–99	20	46
1999–00	19	35
2000–01	17	40
2001–02	16	54
2002–03	17	58
2003–04	17	58
2004–05	16	56
2005–06	15	49
2006–07	15	49

a. Dynamic Index (Overall Average Standard Error/Year Mean %) is computed under Formula 2 of Appendix A.
b. The Concentration Ratios (Top 10 Sales Total/Industry Sales Total %) in 2005–06 and 2006–07 are estimated with SPSS Procedure of 'Mean Missing Replacement' because the data of concentration in these two years are not available in ICC Information Group, *Business Ratio Report–Book Publishers* 30th edn, London, UK: ICC Business Publications Ltd, 2008. Meanwhile, the analysis in this research is conducted under 'a Revised Distributed Lag Model' as defined in Formula 4 of Appendix A, the Concentration Ratio in 2006–07 is no longer reckoned for the analysis for the period of 1976–2006 under the model.

British publishing industry. This trend continued in the 1990s and into the new century.[34]

In general, during the period from 1976 to 2006, the application of technological innovations in the UK book publishing industry was diverse. The dynamic competition was complex but sustained. A concentrating industry structure continued and was consolidated. The three forces of creative destruction – technological innovation, dynamic competition, and concentrating industry structure – restructured and restricted the industry to varying degrees. Meanwhile, the book publishing industry eventually became a typical copyright industry. The copyright expansion in the Copyright, Designs and Patents Act 1988 and the Duration of Copyright and Rights in Performances Regulations 1995 reflected the changes in the sector under the forces of creative destruction and reinforced the institutional arrangement for the growth of the industry.

5.2 Methodological issues

5.2.1 Operational model

To examine the impact of the forces of creative destruction on the relation (interaction or correlation) between copyright expansion and industrial growth at the firm and industry levels in the UK book publishing industry, a theoretical framework from Schumpeter's perspective of creative destruction has been established in Chapter 4. To conduct the research for assessing the role of copyright expansion in the growth of copyright industries under the pressure of creative destruction, an operational model is constructed under the established framework.[35] The model is displayed in Figure 5.1.

This model reflects Schumpeter's theory of creative destruction and specifies the forces of creative destruction (technological innovation, dynamic competition, and concentrating industry structure) and the effects they would exert on the relation (interaction or correlation) between copyright expansion and growth in copyright industries. The links between the factors in this model

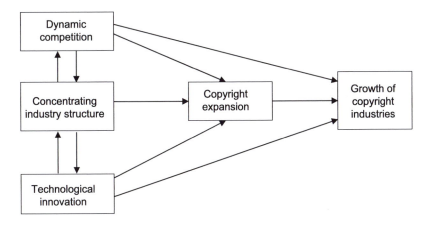

Figure 5.1 Operational model of research question.

illustrate the two arguments drawn from the Schumpeterian perspective: 1. Copyright expansion as a type of monopoly exerts effects on the growth of the copyright industries in the process of creative destruction; 2. The forces of creative destruction impinge on the pattern of the copyright-growth relation.

The following research hypotheses under the operational model are developed and tested.

> Hypothesis 1: The correlation between copyright expansion and the growth of the UK book publishing industry at the firm and industry levels is insignificant, non-controlling for (excluding) the factors of creative destruction in the model.

> Hypothesis 2: The correlation between copyright expansion and the growth of the UK book publishing industry is insignificant at the firm and industry levels, controlling for (including) the factors of creative destruction in the model.

> Hypothesis 3: The correlation between dynamic competition and the growth of the UK book publishing industry is significant, controlling for (including) the factor of copyright expansion in the model.

> Hypothesis 4: The correlation between industrial concentration and the growth of the UK book publishing industry is significant, controlling for (including) the factor of copyright expansion in the model.

> Hypothesis 5: The correlation between technological innovation and the growth of the UK book publishing industry is significant, controlling for (including) the factor of copyright expansion in the model.

The primary unit of analysis in this research is 'the firm' within the UK book publishing industry. The exploration of the firm as a basic unit of analysis in copyright studies has been carried out recently.[36] However, 'the firm' in this research should be examined as both a classic profit maximiser and a unique Schumpeterian institute of creativity or innovation. The firms in the UK book publishing industry as a typical copyright industry are assumed to be creative information disseminators that function and operate to achieve competitive advantage under a series of copyright laws in the process of creative destruction. As both a classic profit maximiser and a unique Schumpeterian institute of creativity or innovation, the firms are assumed to secure necessary information on the legal changes of copyright protection for their own interests and needs. The growth of these firms comprises and represents the growth of the industries in which these firms locate.

5.2.2 *Data collection and sample*

The empirical quantitative study in this book is designed as a non-reactive, quasi-experimental research in natural settings or as a non-reactive quasi-natural experimental research that uses econometric archival data from certain agencies or institutions.[37] Specifically, the data used in this book were collected and compiled from the industrial datasets of the UK book publishing industry for the period from 1976 to 2006. Key Note's publications of business data were the primary source for data collection. Key Note has published *Business Ratio Reports* of ICC Information Group, 'over 148 titles evaluating each UK industry sector'[38] every year for the last 30 years. As stated in its official introduction, the comprehensive business data in each industry sector, including the book publishing, music record/publishing, and other copyright industries, have been compared, contrasted, and analysed in corresponding *Business Ratio Reports* of ICC Information Group.[39]

In addition, the British Library of Political and Economic Science maintains the financial database 'Orbis', which includes full searching facilities and global standard report format for in-depth international searches and analysis.[40] Although covering financial information for the last 10 years only, it is an important additional source for reference in this study. Moreover, the datasets of the professional associations of the UK book publishing industry serve as supplemental sources for data collection. The Publishers' Association's *UK Book Publishing Industry Statistics Yearbook* covers UK book publishing firms' volume, revenue, and value sales (home and export) under the Publishers' Association's Statistical Collection Scheme (PASCS).

The data were collected at both the firm and industry levels. Due to the patchiness of data, obtaining a random sample or building up a representative sample at both levels is unrealistic. On account of the available industrial statistics, the sample in this book consists of two sets of data. Specifically, two sets of time series data and pooled/panel data are constructed – one set at the firm level, the other at the industry level – for conducting time series analysis and pooled/panel data analysis on the copyright-growth relation in the UK book publishing industry as a typical copyright industry under the operational model seen in Figure 5.1.

At the industry level, the records of annual aggregate ratios of industrial performance (sales growth ratio, profits margin ratio, profit growth ratio, and return on capital ratio) in the UK book publishing industry from 1976 to 2006 were compiled from *Business Ratio Reports*. Meanwhile, the sales (gross turnover) records of 327 UK book publishing firms[41] were also compiled for constructing a 'dynamism score' in order to measure dynamic competition as the level of competition in the UK book publishing industry. The data of the top 10 companies' market shares were collected from *Business Ratio Reports* for measuring 'concentrating industry structure' as the level of concentration in the industry.

At the firm level, a set of 15 book publishing firms whose financial records and reports were covered in *Business Ratio Reports* and Orbis for the period from 1976 to 2006 were drawn from the industry.[42] These 15 firms are: A & C Black Plc, B T Batsford Ltd, Blackwell Science Ltd, Constable & Co Ltd, David & Charles (Holdings) Plc, Faber & Faber (Publishers) Ltd, Frederick

Warne & Co Ltd, Hodder & Stoughton Holdings Ltd, Ian Allan Ltd, Ladybird Books Ltd, Marshall Cavendish Ltd, Mills & Boon Ltd, Penguin Books Ltd, Thames & Hudson Ltd, and Wiley & Sons Ltd.

Of course, no matter how many sources can be exploited for data collection, inconsistency and deficiency are always common with secondary data for a period of 30 years. Due to the scarcity of data in the UK book publishing industry, data availability and reliability are the primary considerations for selecting these firms and compiling their records in this research. These firms were included in the sample for this study mainly because their full industrial records were available for the full 30-year period in question.

5.2.3 Measurement of variables

To measure the variables under the operational model as displayed in Figure 5.1, diverse measuring schemes were adopted from existing law and economics literature.

1. Dependent and independent variables

The three forces of creative destruction (dynamic competition, concentrating industry structure, and technological innovation) that are assumed to influence the copyright-growth relation with regard to these firms and their corresponding industry are measured, or operationally assessed, in terms of the level of competition, the level of industrial concentration, and the stage of technological innovation. Copyright expansion is measured as 'the year of legal intervention' with regard to the Copyright, Designs and Patents Act 1988, the Duration of Copyright and Rights in Performances Regulations 1995, and TRIPS (Trade-Related Aspects of Intellectual Property Rights) in 1996, which have amended or extended the scope or duration of copyright in the different time periods. The growth of copyright industries is measured by the growth rates of the firms' profits and sales at the firm level and the annual aggregate ratios of industrial performance (sales growth ratio, profits margin ratio, profit growth ratio, and return on capital ratio) at the industry level in the UK book publishing industry. The level of competition, the level of industrial concentration, the stage of technological innovation, and copyright expansion are the independent or explanatory variables. The growth rates of the firms' profits at the firm level, and the annual aggregate ratios of industrial performance at the industry level, are the dependent or response variables.[43]

2. Measurement procedure of variables

The level of competition, the level of industrial concentration, and the stage of technological innovation, as measures of the three forces of creative destruction (dynamic competition, concentrating industry structure, and technological innovation), are either firm-specific or industry-specific indicators.

Specifically, the stage of technological innovation is a firm-specific indicator while both the level of competition and the level of industrial concentration are industry-specific indicators. The stage of technological innovation is denoted as 'the time when technological innovations as intervention events had been adopted in the operating and functioning processes of the UK book publishing industry' in the period from 1976 to 2006. The level of competition is estimated in a competition index that can be constructed through a review of Mazzucato, Thomas, Li and Xu, and Vaaler and McNamara's schemes.[44] The level of industrial concentration can be assessed in reference to Blair and Davis's methods.[45] Of course, their schemes or methods are modified to quantify the attributes of the UK book publishing industry.

(1) Measures of competition

Li and Xu's study, focusing on the telecommunications sector, measures the level of competition under a classic scheme of measuring competition through counting the number of telecommunicating operators in both fixed and mobile lines.[46] However, this classic scheme is not adequate for quantifying the level of competition within a competitive or relatively competitive industrial sector. Thomas made an evident and theoretical distinction between the static competition and the dynamic or Schumpeterian competition.[47] Nevertheless, his measurement of competition counts on the concentration ratio and fails to account for the evident distinction between the two types of competition.

In this research, following Mazzucato's suggestion that Schumpeterian dynamic theories 'require dynamic indices of competition to replace static indices which focus on the level of concentration at one period of time',[48] 'instability index' as a dynamic index is constructed as 'competition index' for measuring the level of competition. Mazzucato presented an instability index developed by Hymer and Pashigian in 1962, and revealed how this instability index 'captures the important aspect of competition'.[49] In their index, the level of competition is measured by the totality of the absolute values of the market-share differences of firms at different points in time for all firms in a group or an industrial sector.[50] However, the concern is that their measurement focuses on the level of concentration and could face difficulty in distinguishing competition from concentration. To address this concern and construct 'a dynamic index of competition' under Schumpeter's framework as illustrated in Figure 5.1, Vaaler and McNamara's study offers an informative reference.

In reviewing the dynamism in a variety of industrial fields, Vaaler and McNamara demonstrated the plausibility of using 'performance instability' (such as swings in profitability, sales, and market share) rather than market share alone for measuring the dynamic features of competition in the technology-intensive industries.[51] In addition, following research done by others, they calculated a dynamism score for measuring the level of dynamic competition in those industrial sectors. To compute such a score, they first run a simple regression analysis of the correlations between industry sales and years in a five-year panel as variables. Then they divided the standard error derived from the regression analysis by the average (mean) value of industry sales for a specific sector, and use the quotient as a dynamism score for the industry in each year of four five-year periods.[52]

In this book, performance instability is noteworthy for revealing the dynamic aspects of competition exhibited in the UK book publishing industry as an information sector,[53] and for constructing an instability index as 'a dynamic index of competition'. Specifically, Vaaler and McNamara's formula of 'dynamism score' is adopted with a slightly different computing procedure for calculating a time-serial dynamism score for the period from 1976 to 2006, which will serve as a dynamic index of competition for measuring the level of competition in the UK book publishing industry. The sales (gross turnover)[54] of UK book publishing firms as recorded in *Business Ratio Reports* from 1976 to 2006 are counted for computing purposes as the time-serial 'dynamism score'. The sales of each firm in a specific year as a dependent or response variable are regressed using time as an independent variable in a simple regression analysis. The correlation coefficient and standard error are reported, and the time-serial dynamism score is calculated. To some extent, a performance instability index is a proxy for a dynamic index of competition. Caution is needed in constructing a performance instability index as a dynamic index of competition for measuring the level of competition in the book publishing sector.

(2) Measures of concentration

The measurement of the level of concentration in this book will resort to Blair's definition of concentration, which weighs up 'the share of the output accounted for by the 4 (or 8) largest firms' in an industrial sector,[55] with some adjustments. The major adjustment is that the top 10 firms rather than four or eight are listed, and the share of sales as the output is counted. In other words, the percentage of the sales of the top 10 firms in the whole industrial sector will serve as the measure of the level of concentration in this sector. The value of sales is always one of the main indicators of a firm's financial operation. Using the captivation of sales in the top firms to measure the level of concentration in the sector can provide a more informative and distinctive picture of the concentration issues.

(3) Measures of technological innovation

While measuring the stage of technological innovation, Vaaler's application of 'event study methods'[56] is revealing because it informs an analytical scheme for evaluating how an institutional change of creative destruction as an intervention event could affect the firm's performance. Vaaler conducted an analysis of variance (ANOVA) for quantifying the impact of an intervention event. In this book, following Vaaler's treatment, technological innovations – just as copyright expansion is measured through indicating 'Year of Legal Intervention' with regard to a variety of laws – are taken into account as intervention events at different stages and are measured with 'Year of Technological Intervention' corresponding to different years when a related technological innovation emerged. The Box–Jenkins models of time series analysis are applied to assess the impact of technological innovations as intervention events on the industrial growth of the UK book publishing industry, at both the industry and firm levels, at different stages in the period from 1976 to 2006.

This uncommon measure of the stage of technological innovation indicates that, under the pressure of creative destruction, technological opportunity created by specific technological innovations at different stages indeed affects the operation and growth of certain industries.[57] Once a new technology has emerged, entrepreneurs under a dynamic competition should seize the opportunity for exploitation. Seizing this opportunity is more crucial than the amount of technology investment for firm growth and business operations. As to the concern about what types of technological innovations are measured, although the meaning of technology could be wide-ranging from a Schumpeterian perspective,[58] this book focuses on digital technology. In line with John Feather's breakdown,[59] 'digital technology in 1985' and 'the Internet in 1990' are identified as the UK book publishing industry's two stages of technological innovation between 1976 and 2006. Because these innovations are strongly associated, and even identical to some extent, Year 1985 of Technological Intervention and Year 1990 of Technological Intervention are combined as one factor and 'Year 1995' is defined as a 'code year' in order to construct a dummy variable for measuring the stages of technological innovation for the UK book publishing industry.

(4) Measures of copyright expansion and growth

Overall, under the operational model depicted in Figure 5.1, the focus of empirical assessment is on the impacts of creative destruction on the relation (interaction or correlation) between copyright expansion and the growth of copyright industries in the UK. To carry on the empirical assessment, dynamic competition, concentrating industrial structure, technological innovation, copyright expansion (as the independent or explanatory variables), and the growth of the firms' profits at the firm level, and the industrial performance at the industry level in the UK book publishing industry (as the dependent or response variables) have been measured through a series of empirical indicators.

The Copyright, Designs and Patents Act of 1988 (in the UK), the Duration of Copyright and Rights in Performances Regulations 1995, which implements the EU Duration Directive that endorses copyright expansion in the UK, and TRIPS in 1996 are analysed as the variables of UK copyright expansion for the UK book publishing industry as a typical copyright industry. Considering that the duration range of copyright expansions under these laws is not wide, the Copyright, Designs and Patents Act 1988 is identified as the sole variable of UK copyright expansion. Copyright expansion in duration under the 1988 Act is assumed to subject entrepreneurs and their firms to the governance of regulatory rules by means of standard setting, information gathering, and behaviour modification. This mechanism, as defined by Murray and Scott,[60] translates legal and regulatory arrangements into entrepreneurial strategies, and the firm's activities are presumed to function in a process of creative destruction. On account of these measurements, the effects of each independent variable and all independent variables as a whole on the dependent or response variable – the growth of copyright industries – are estimated and analysed.

5.2.4 Econometric model

While the theoretical framework in this book has been established to explain the copyright-growth relation in the process of creative destruction, and the operational model as illustrated in Figure 5.1 has been constructed to direct the research on the copyright-growth relation under the forces of creative destruction, appropriate econometric models are needed for conducting the research in order to assess the role of copyright expansion in growing the UK copyright industries, specifically the UK book publishing industry, under these forces.

Building a suitable econometric model requires two essential considerations – the type of data collected and the purpose of the research illustrated in the operational model. The data collected for this research are classified as *time series data* and *pooled/panel data* (based on time series data). Corresponding to the time period of data collection, the time series data consist of weekly, monthly, quarterly, and annual data. The data in this book are annual time series data at both industry and firm levels in the UK book publishing industry. On account of the nature of time series data, the purpose of the research, and the operational model in Figure 5.1, the Box–Jenkins models of time series analysis and pooled/panel data analysis are the principal choices for the empirical data analyses on the impacts of creative destruction on the relation (interaction or correlation) between copyright expansion and the growth of the UK book publishing industry.

The Box–Jenkins models of time series analysis belong to one crucial type of diverse time series analytical models. In general, there are two fundamental time series analytical models – regression models and the Box–Jenkins models.[61] Auto-regressive integrated moving average (ARIMA) models, intervention models, and transfer function models are among the main types of Box–Jenkins models.[62] Importantly, considering that many econometric models are constructed for the purpose of analytical estimating or forecasting rather than for the purpose of causal reasoning, the forecasting scheme under the Box–Jenkins models can provide 'a highly efficient technique for forecasting in situations where the inherent pattern in an underlying series is very complex and difficult to discern'.[63] The time series data that are collected and analysed for this book fit with this type of series: the Box–Jenkins models – ARIMA models, intervention models, and transfer function models – are accordingly the primary analytical models for empirical assessments in this research as a non-reactive, quasi-natural experimental research. Under the Box–Jenkins models, to assess the role of copyright expansion (stipulated in the Copyright, Designs and Patents Act 1988 as the independent 'intervention variable/experimental treatment' in this non-reactive, quasi-natural experimental research), the Year of 1988 is identified as the year of intervention/treatment, and the growth data of two UK copyright industries in the pre-test period (i.e. before 1988) and the post-test period (i.e. after 1988) are classified and analysed.

No matter how diverse the time series models, a typical time series model formalises two fundamental components – the deterministic component (the 'explained' component in the model) and the stochastic component (the 'unexplained' component, the 'error term' of the time series, or the 'serial error term' in the model).[64] As the crucial type of time series models, the Box–Jenkins models of time series analysis are no exception with regard to dealing with these two fundamental components. In particular, reflecting the general practical purpose of the Box–Jenkins models of time series analysis, in an intervention model, the two special components in a Box-Jenkins model are commonly termed as the 'intervention' component and the 'noise' component respectively.[65] Figure 5.2 displays the structure of a typical time series.

The main practical purpose of an intervention time series model as the primary analytical model for this research is to assess the impact of an intervention of policy, law, programme, or event on the outcome of a certain 'target' through evaluating or estimating the changes or variations in time series data.[66] The outcome of a certain target is the objective that such a policy,

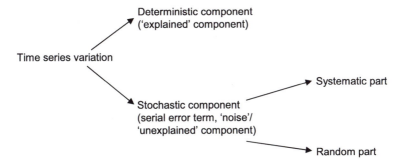

Figure 5.2 Compositions of a typical time series model.

law, programme, or event was designed or assumed to change. Thus, the impact of an intervention is assessed as the deterministic (explained) component in the model. With a unique advantage, an intervention time series model can readily illustrate the core of most time series analyses – how to dissect the structure of the noise or stochastic (unexplained) component, especially its systematic part, in order to comprehend the impacts of the intervention or deterministic (explained) component.

In this book, it is straightforward to distinguish between the two fundamental components of a time series model for explaining the changes or variations in the growth of UK copyright industries as the dependent or response variable. The deterministic (explained) component indicates that, as the theoretical framework identifies and the operational model specifies, certain factors such as the independent or explanatory variables – the Copyright, Designs and Patents Act 1988 that endorses copyright expansion, and all three forces of creative destruction (dynamic competition measured by the level of competition, concentrating industry structure measured by the level of industrial concentration, and technological innovation measured by the stage of technological innovation) – determine the changes or variations in the growth of UK copyright industries.

Meanwhile, the noise or stochastic (unexplained) component shows that these factors identified as the independent or explanatory variables cannot fully account for the changes or variations in the growth of UK copyright industries. Instead, some unidentified factors may also contribute to these changes or variations. Among these unidentified factors, those time-associated (or time-dependent) factors still affect the changes or variations in the growth of UK copyright industries in a systematic way (the systematic part of the noise or stochastic component), even if the independent or explanatory variables cannot explain this 'systematic way'. The rest of these unidentified factors influence the changes or variations in a random way (the random part of the noise or stochastic component).

In other words, the role of copyright expansion as a law/policy intervention in growing the UK copyright industries, and the impact of creative destruction on the role of that law/policy intervention, are the main concerns. Explicitly, the main concerns are whether or not the changes or variations in the growth of copyright industries, as measured by our time series data, reflect the changes or variations in the law of copyright expansion, and whether or not the three forces of creative destruction exert certain effects on the relation (interaction or correlation) between the changes or variations in the growth of copyright industries and in the law of copyright expansion. To give an example, if a UK book publishing firm's growth slowed down or speeded up after the Copyright, Designs and Patents Act was enacted in 1988, it should be examined whether or not the changes or variations in the firm's growth after 1988 were a response to the law of copyright expansion stipulated in the Act. If so – that is, if the relation (interaction or correlation) between the changes in the firm's growth and the changes in the law of copyright expansion was confirmed – it would need to be further examined as to whether or not the three forces of creative destruction played a role in the interaction between the changes in the firm's growth and the changes in the law of copyright expansion. Formula 3 in Appendix A formalises these two components in the intervention time series model for this research.

To carry on the above inquiry, the copyright-growth relation (interaction or correlation), or in terms of empirical assessment, the impact of copyright expansion as a law/policy intervention under the Copyright, Designs and Patents Act 1988 on the growth of the UK book publishing industry, is first estimated and analysed before assessing the impact of the three forces of creative destruction on this relation. Under the operational model in Figure 5.1, it is theorised and hypothesised that the the growth of the UK book publishing industry in a specific year, for instance in 1990, should be the function of the independent or explanatory variables – the Copyright, Designs and Patents Act 1988 that endorses copyright expansion and all three forces of creative destruction (dynamic competition, concentrating industry structure, and technological innovation) – in that year. However, because of the nature of time series data, an essential concern with an intervention time series analysis should be the issue of 'serial correlation' or 'autocorrelation' – the correlations between the neighbouring error terms (or 'residuals' as estimates of the 'true' error terms) over one or more time periods.[67] In other words, the 'noise' or stochastic ('unexplained') component needs serious attention. Once the noise or stochastic (unexplained) component has been analysed, the impact of the 1988 Act and the effects of the three forces of creative destruction as the other independent or explanatory variables (the deterministic or explained component) can be assessed. In short, the noise or stochastic (unexplained) component should be inspected first before exploring the deterministic (explained) component. This is the universal route for any time series analyses. The Box–Jenkins models in general, and intervention models in particular, will follow this path.

Why does serial correlation or autocorrelation, as the core element of the systematic part in the noise or stochastic component, matter? The main concern is that a failure to resolve the problem of serial correlation or autocorrelation would distort the outcome of a standard or regular regression analysis of the relations between the independent or explanatory and dependent or response variables with time series data. In principle, to conduct a standard regression analysis (an 'ordinary least squares' [OLS] regression analysis) involving multiple and partial correlation analyses with time series data, the assumption of no autocorrelation or serial correlation in the error terms should be satisfied.[68] Otherwise, the final results of these analyses would either overestimate or underestimate the real impact of a law/policy intervention, the law of copyright expansion, which is of interest in this book.

Why could autocorrelation or serial correlation as the core element of the systematic part in the noise or stochastic component of a time series surface? The reasons are complex. The most identifiable causes are secular trend, cyclical effect, seasonal effect in a time series, and random effect that is unexplained by these three causes.[69] Nevertheless, no matter what factors could engender autocorrelation or serial correlation, their existence-discounts the merit of a standard regression analysis of the relation (interaction or correlation) between the independent (explanatory) and dependent (response) variables in a time series.[70] The Box–Jenkins models as proposed econometric models for this research shall take existing or potential autocorrelation or serial correlation into account in order to direct a robust data analysis.

Are the time series data in this research vulnerable to serial correlation or autocorrelation when used to examine the impact of copyright expansion as a law/policy intervention on the growth of copyright industries under the pressure of creative destruction? It is necessary to further specify the Box–Jenkins models of time series analysis in order to detect serial correlation or autocorrelation and to discern the impact of copyright expansion under the pressure of creative destruction as the deterministic (explained) component in the model. At the initial stage of the empirical assessment in this study, before specifying and applying the Box–Jenkins models of time series analysis, regression models of time series analysis can serve as an early test tool for detecting the pattern of data, especially the pattern of possible serial correlation or autocorrelation, whenever the data are collected over time. Thus, a standard regression analysis of time series with the Durbin–Watson test is first run to check whether serial correlation or autocorrelation exist in the time series of the growth of copyright industries as the dependent or response variable.

As discussed in Chapter 5.2.3, the growth of copyright industries is measured by the growth rates of the UK book publishing industry at both firm and industry levels. Because the measure of the growth of copyright industries at the industry level consists of a series of ratios rather than the growth rates of profits, the Durbin–Watson test may not be applicable. Accordingly, a Durbin–Watson test for serial correlation or autocorrelation on the data of annual profits over 30 years (1976–2006) in the UK book publishing industry is conducted at the firm level. At this level, the annual profit rates of 15 UK book publishing firms as the measure of the growth of copyright industries at the firm level are examined. To enhance the power of the Durbin–Watson test and related econometric estimation, pooled and panel regular regression analysis, or OLS regression analysis of pooled and panel data,[71] is applied for running the test and estimation on the pooled and panel data of the annual profits of the 15 UK book publishing firms over 30 years (1976–2006).

To conduct a Durbin–Watson test and related econometric estimation, a pooled or panel time series matrix for the annual profit data of the 15 UK book publishing firms under consideration should be constructed. Clearly, in the data set of 30 years, annual profits over those 30 years are time series data, while annual profits of these firms and other variables in a specific year are cross-sectional data. While there are different formulas for arranging the two types of data in a pooled or panel time series matrix, the standard procedure is to assemble the cross-sectional data first in rows and then place the time series data in columns.[72] Table 1 in Appendix B presents the pooled or panel time series matrix for both time series and cross-sectional data of the 15 UK book publishing firms over the 30-year period (1976–2006). Bearing in mind the lagged effects of some independent variables, mainly the two forces of creative destruction – dynamic competition and concentrating industry structure – the dataset will include the records of these two variables in 1976. Accordingly, the covered period of the pooled or panel time series matrix is 31 years. To analyse these lagged effects, the pooled or panel standard regression analysis in this research is specified as a revised distributed lag model for conducting a Durbin–Watson test and related econometric estimation.[73]

5.2.5 Model specification and construction

Overall, this book examines the extent to which the factors in the deterministic component as the independent or explanatory variables – the UK's Copyright, Designs and Patents Act 1988, which endorses copyright expansion, and all three forces of creative destruction – can affect the changes or variations in the time series of the growth rates of UK book publishing industry (i.e. a representative sector of the UK copyright industries) as the dependent or response variable.

However, the presence of a serial correlation or autocorrelation, as stated above, would disturb or puzzle a standard or regular regression analysis of the relation (interaction or correlation) between the growth of these firms and the law of copyright expansion – the Copyright, Designs and Patents Act 1988 – as the intervention variable (one type of the independent or explanatory variable) in the intervention or deterministic (explained) component in this (or any other) time series data. To deal with the issue of serial correlation or autocorrelation and other issues related to time series data in this research, it is necessary to further inspect the levels and patterns of the detected serial correlation or autocorrelation and other features of time series data in the noise or stochastic (unexplained) component in order to conduct a robust data analysis. For this purpose, after running a standard or regular regression analysis with the Durbin–Watson test for the time series data on the annual profits of the 15 UK book publishing firms over 30 years (as Table 5.2 reports), two main types of the Box–Jenkins models – auto-regressive integrated moving average (ARIMA) models[74] and intervention models – are applied to assess the noise or stochastic (unexplained) component and the intervention or deterministic (explained) component in the 30-year time series data, respectively, at the firm level. On account of the analyses under these two Box–Jenkins models, pooled and panel data analyses are conducted to assess the same datasets at both the firm and industry levels.

Table 5.2 Durbin–Watson test for 15 UK publishing firms' annual profits (1976–2006)

Dependent Variable: Y = Annual Profits of Set of 15 UK Book Publishing Firms

Method: Pooled Least Squares
Sample: 1976–2006
Cross-sections included: 15
Included observations: 31

Total pool (balanced) observations: 465

Variable	Coefficient	Std. Error	t-Statistic	Prob.
C	10552.73	19572.52	0.539160	0.5900
X_TIME[a]	–107.9818	388.9528	–0.277622	0.7814

R-squared	0.000166	Mean dependent var		5205.746
F-statistic	0.077074	Durbin-Watson stat[b]		2.035475
Prob (F-statistic)	0.781427			

Dependent Variable: Y = Annual Profits of Set of 15 UK Book Publishing Firms

Method: Panel Least Squares
Sample: 1976–2006
Periods included: 31
Cross-sections included: 15

Total panel (balanced) observations: 465

Variable	Coefficient	Std. Error	t-Statistic	Prob.
C	–4339.387	7134.543	–0.608222	0.5433
X_TIME	579.5439	390.2906	1.484904	0.1382

R-squared	0.004740	Mean dependent var		4914.622
F-statistic	2.204939	Durbin-Watson stat		2.065479
Prob (F-statistic)	0.138250			

a. This Eviews printout reports a standard regression analysis with the Durbin–Watson tests for the time series data on the annual profits of the 15 book publishing firms over 30 years. This standard analysis detects the correlation between the annual profits and time (or – in technical terms – this standard analysis 'regresses the annual profits on a 30-year time series as a predictor') for the set of 15 book publishing firms.
b. The pooled pair Durbin–Watson statistics – 2.035475 – and panel pair Durbin–Watson statistics – 2.065479 – for the set of 15 book publishing firms in each pair are important indicators. These scores suggest that there is no evidence that serial correlation or autocorrelation is present in the pooled or panel time series profits with the set of 15 book publishing firms over 30 years. However, it is possible that there may be evidence that serial correlation or autocorrelation in the time series profit with each individual book publishing firm over 30 years.

1. Assessment of stochastic component

In general, **ARIMA** models are built for assessing the pattern, explaining the change, and forecasting the trend of diverse time series data.[75] In this research, suitable **ARIMA** models are constructed for inspecting the noise or stochastic component of the time series data of annual profits of these 15 UK book publishing firms. A specific ARIMA model has inscribed three structural factors in the systematic part of the noise or stochastic component in a time series – auto-regressive order (symbolised by p), stationarity (symbolised by d, which indicates the order of differencing for achieving stationarity), and moving average order (symbolised by q). These three factors depict the link between the random part of the noise or stochastic component (also termed as 'white noise' or 'random shock') and the time series.[76] A typical ARIMA modelling process runs through three stages – identification, estimation, and diagnosis – for identifying and constructing appropriate ARIMA (p, d, q) models.[77]

(1) IDENTIFICATION

The goal at the stage of identification is, through empirical procedures,[78] to decode the systematic part of the noise or stochastic component in any observed and empirical time series data in order to advise some tentative ARIMA (p, d, q) models for analysing these observed and empirical time series data. For this goal, it is essential to detect the levels and patterns of autocorrelation functions (ACFs) and partial autocorrelation functions (PACFs) as the core element of the noise or stochastic (unexplained) component in these observed and empirical time series data. Because annual time series data with less or no seasonal variations are employed in this research, some non-seasonal ARIMA (p, d, q) models are identified and constructed for the data analysis in this book. Before conducting this test, the general pattern of the time series profit data of these 15 UK book publishing firms over 30 years (1976–2006) is checked.

As Figure 5.3 shows, after the Copyright, Designs and Patents Act 1988, for most of these 15 UK book publishing firms, the general growth of annual profits was noticeable but still gradual until 2000. This path of growth indicates that the impact of the 1988 Act initially appears moderate or weak on most firms but becomes stronger on some firms in due course. To conduct a test of ACFs and PACFs with this complex and overall variety of intervention impact, the test shall cover the whole time series data[79] on the annual profits for all 15 firms over 30 years (1976–2006).

Table 5.3 details the levels and patterns of ACFs and PACFs in the original time series data of 15 book publishing firms' annual profits. Figures 5.4–5.18 present the test results that specify the levels and patterns of ACFs and PACFs in the original time series data of all 15 firms' annual profits. Overall, the detected levels and patterns of ACFs and PACFs from all 15 firms' original time series data in Tables 5.3 and Figures 5.4–5.18 serve as the crucial graphs and statistics for revealing the stationarity (d) of all 15 firms' time series before inspecting their white noise process, auto-regressive order (p), and moving average order (q).

As these graphs and statistics indicate, the ACFs in the original time series data of 10 firms among the 15 book publishing firms – Faber & Faber Ltd, Ian

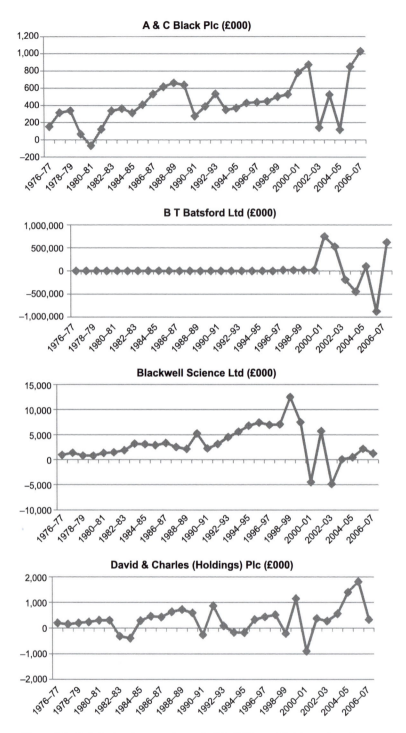

Figure 5.3 Original time series of 15 UK publishing firms' annual profits (1976–2006).

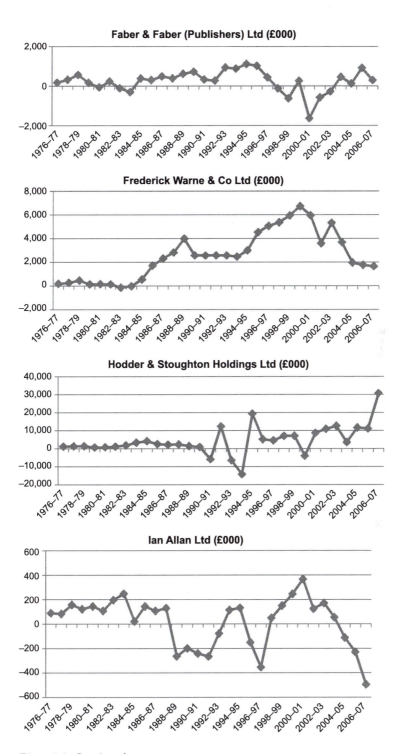

Figure 5.3 Continued

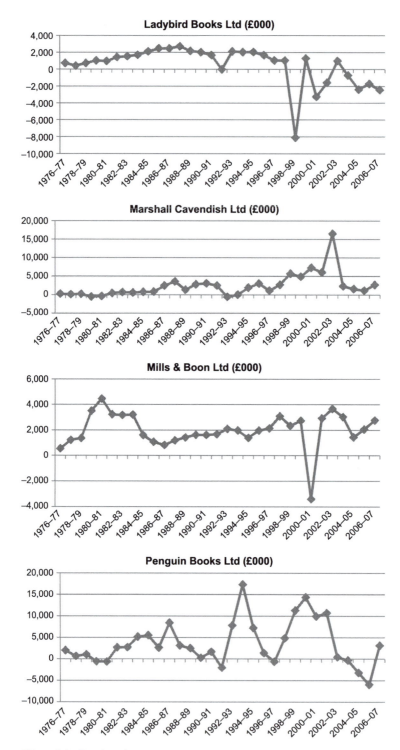

Figure 5.3 Continued

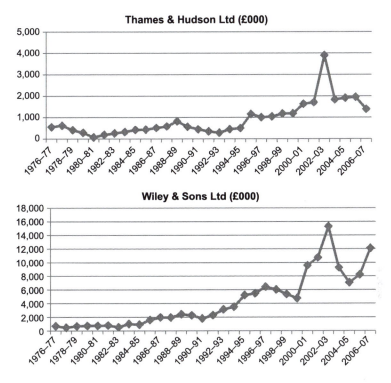

Figure 5.3 Continued

Allan Ltd, Marshall Cavendish Ltd, Penguin Books Ltd, B T Batsford Ltd, Blackwell Science Ltd, David & Charles Plc, Hodder & Stoughton Holdings Ltd, Ladybird Books Ltd, and Mills & Boon Ltd – do appear to be cutting off or dying down fairly quickly. This fashion suggests that these 10 firms' original time series are stationary. Thus, there is no need to difference their original time series data. In contrast, as these lag graphs also show, the ACFs of original time series from the other five firms – A & C Black Plc, Constable & Co Ltd, Frederick Warne & Co Ltd, Thames & Hudson Ltd, and Wiley & Sons Ltd – do not appear to be cutting off or dying down quickly. Rather, they seem to be decaying slowly or not decaying at all. This implies that these five firms' time series are not stationary. As a result, it is necessary to differentiate and transform the original time series data of these five firms. Based on the same lag graphs in Figures 5.4–5.18, first differencing (differencing once) is advised for transforming these non-stationary original data. Table 5.4 and Figures 5.19–5.23 present the SPSS (Statistical Package for the Social Sciences) outputs for the first difference of these five firms' original time series data over 30 years.

On account of the statistics in Tables 5.3–5.4 and lag graphs in Figures 5.4–5.23, along with the identification criteria in Table 5.5, the white

Table 5.3 ACFs & PACFs of 15 UK publishing firms' original time series (1976–2006)

Firm	Lag	Partial Autocorrelation (PACF)		Autocorrelation (ACF)		Box–Ljung Statistic		
		Partial Autocorrelation	Std. Error	Autocorrelation	Std. Error[a]	Value	Df	Sig.[b]
A & C	1	.458	.180	.458	.171	7.145	1	.008
Black Plc	2	.094	.180	.284	.168	9.982	2	.007
	3	.103	.180	.241	.165	12.112	3	.007
	4	.072	.180	.215	.162	13.866	4	.008
	5	.328	.180	.404	.159	20.274	5	.001
	6	−.071	.180	.255	.156	22.933	6	.001
	7	−.082	.180	.121	.153	23.556	7	.001
	8	−.032	.180	.088	.150	23.900	8	.002
B T	1	−.180	.180	−.180	.171	1.103	1	.294
Batsford	2	.023	.180	.055	.168	1.210	2	.546
Ltd	3	−.162	.180	−.170	.165	2.271	3	.518
	4	−.305	.180	−.229	.162	4.255	4	.373
	5	−.283	.180	−.147	.159	5.105	5	.403
	6	.076	.180	.188	.156	6.550	6	.364
	7	−.047	.180	−.005	.153	6.551	7	.477
	8	−.214	.180	−.002	.150	6.551	8	.586
Blackwell	1	.324	.180	.324	.171	3.585	1	.058
Science	2	.331	.180	.401	.168	9.267	2	.010
Ltd	3	.079	.180	.257	.165	11.683	3	.009
	4	−.220	.180	.026	.162	11.710	4	.020
	5	−.205	.180	−.073	.159	11.922	5	.036
	6	.009	.180	−.081	.156	12.192	6	.058
	7	.030	.180	−.143	.153	13.064	7	.071
	8	−.072	.180	−.174	.150	14.417	8	.072
Constable	1	.513	.180	.513	.171	8.984	1	.003
& Co Ltd	2	.310	.180	.492	.168	17.515	2	.000
	3	.107	.180	.404	.165	23.491	3	.000
	4	−.089	.180	.260	.162	26.053	4	.000
	5	−.296	.180	.034	.159	26.098	5	.000
	6	−.059	.180	.005	.156	26.099	6	.000
	7	.097	.180	−.024	.153	26.122	7	.000
	8	.110	.180	−.049	.150	26.231	8	.001
David &	1	.199	.180	.199	.171	1.356	1	.244
Charles	2	.173	.180	.206	.168	2.856	2	.240
Plc	3	−.099	.180	−.024	.165	2.877	3	.411
	4	−.096	.180	−.073	.162	3.080	4	.545
	5	−.109	.180	−.154	.159	4.008	5	.548
	6	.229	.180	.131	.156	4.715	6	.581
	7	−.050	.180	−.030	.153	4.752	7	.690
	8	.083	.180	.152	.150	5.782	8	.672
Faber &	1	.432	.180	.432	.171	6.368	1	.012
Faber Ltd	2	.252	.180	.392	.168	11.786	2	.003
	3	−.247	.180	.048	.165	11.869	3	.008
	4	−.165	.180	−.076	.162	12.088	4	.017
	5	−.401	.180	−.430	.159	19.364	5	.002

	6	.047	.180	−.301	.156	23.077	6	.001
	7	.136	.180	−.288	.153	26.610	7	.000
	8	−.208	.180	−.263	.150	29.679	8	.000
Frederick	1	.891	.180	.891	.171	27.084	1	.000
Warne &	2	−.037	.180	.787	.168	48.912	2	.000
Co Ltd	3	−.003	.180	.693	.165	66.481	3	.000
	4	−.320	.180	.546	.162	77.759	4	.000
	5	−.155	.180	.389	.159	83.708	5	.000
	6	−.022	.180	.257	.156	86.404	6	.000
	7	.207	.180	.169	.153	87.627	7	.000
	8	−.045	.180	.077	.150	87.891	8	.000
Hodder &	1	.188	.180	.188	.171	1.205	1	.272
Stoughton	2	.122	.180	.153	.168	2.029	2	.363
Holdings	3	.184	.180	.223	.165	3.847	3	.279
Ltd	4	.173	.180	.240	.162	6.021	4	.198
	5	−.024	.180	.079	.159	6.267	5	.281
	6	.109	.180	.183	.156	7.641	6	.266
	7	−.127	.180	.001	.153	7.641	7	.365
	8	−.014	.180	.044	.150	7.727	8	.461
Ian Allan	1	.523	.180	.523	.171	9.335	1	.002
Ltd	2	−.158	.180	.159	.168	10.225	2	.006
	3	−.172	.180	−.109	.165	10.656	3	.014
	4	−.121	.180	−.245	.162	12.924	4	.012
	5	.013	.180	−.201	.159	14.507	5	.013
	6	−.281	.180	−.291	.156	17.965	6	.006
	7	.051	.180	−.185	.153	19.426	7	.007
	8	−.114	.180	−.131	.150	20.189	8	.010
Ladybird	1	.149	.180	.149	.171	.755	1	.385
Books Ltd	2	.341	.180	.356	.168	5.216	2	.074
	3	.166	.180	.229	.165	7.130	3	.068
	4	−.161	.180	.014	.162	7.138	4	.129
	5	−.003	.180	.122	.159	7.725	5	.172
	6	.242	.180	.194	.156	9.271	6	.159
	7	.153	.180	.155	.153	10.301	7	.172
	8	−.096	.180	.117	.150	10.912	8	.207
Marshall	1	.441	.180	.441	.171	6.623	1	.010
Cavendish	2	.230	.180	.380	.168	11.714	2	.003
Ltd	3	−.019	.180	.216	.165	13.422	3	.004
	4	.134	.180	.258	.162	15.953	4	.003
	5	−.143	.180	.061	.159	16.101	5	.007
	6	−.131	.180	−.024	.156	16.125	6	.013
	7	.110	.180	.025	.153	16.152	7	.024
	8	−.031	.180	−.009	.150	16.155	8	.040
Mills &	1	.100	.180	.100	.171	.341	1	.559
Boon Ltd	2	−.066	.180	−.056	.168	.451	2	.798
	3	−.073	.180	−.084	.165	.711	3	.871
	4	.198	.180	.182	.162	1.960	4	.743
	5	.008	.180	.058	.159	2.092	5	.836
	6	−.025	.180	−.028	.156	2.123	6	.908
	7	.128	.180	.078	.153	2.384	7	.936
	8	.007	.180	.062	.150	2.553	8	.959

(*Continued overleaf*)

Table 5.3 Continued

Firm	Lag	Partial Autocorrelation (PACF)		Autocorrelation (ACF)		Box–Ljung Statistic		
		Partial Autocorrelation	Std. Error	Autocorrelation	Std. Error[a]	Value	Df	Sig[b]
Penguin	1	.574	.180	.574	.171	11.230	1	.001
Books Ltd	2	−.276	.180	.144	.168	11.964	2	.003
	3	−.165	.180	−.155	.165	12.838	3	.005
	4	−.063	.180	−.261	.162	15.418	4	.004
	5	.181	.180	−.096	.159	15.778	5	.008
	6	−.044	.180	.037	.156	15.835	6	.015
	7	.021	.180	.112	.153	16.372	7	.022
	8	−.005	.180	.098	.150	16.797	8	.032
Thames &	1	.753	.180	.753	.171	19.319	1	.000
Hudson	2	.284	.180	.690	.168	36.099	2	.000
Ltd	3	.000	.180	.585	.165	48.611	3	.000
	4	−.136	.180	.457	.162	56.526	4	.000
	5	−.203	.180	.304	.159	60.153	5	.000
	6	.015	.180	.225	.156	62.226	6	.000
	7	.126	.180	.176	.153	63.540	7	.000
	8	−.099	.180	.068	.150	63.746	8	.000
Wiley &	1	.798	.180	.798	.171	21.722	1	.000
Sons Ltd	2	.108	.180	.676	.168	37.856	2	.000
	3	.105	.180	.605	.165	51.248	3	.000
	4	.179	.180	.594	.162	64.617	4	.000
	5	−.304	.180	.446	.159	72.454	5	.000
	6	−.003	.180	.352	.156	77.513	6	.000
	7	−.236	.180	.215	.153	79.486	7	.000
	8	.056	.180	.168	.150	80.738	8	.000

a. The underlying process assumed is independence (white noise).
b. Based on the asymptotic chi-square approximation.

noise process, auto-regressive orders (p), and moving average orders (q) for the 15 book publishing firms' time series data can be detected. Among the 10 firms whose original time series data are stationary, six of them – B T Batsford Ltd, Blackwell Science Ltd, David & Charles Plc, Hodder & Stoughton Holdings Ltd, Ladybird Books Ltd, and Mills & Boon Ltd – have original time series that are a white noise process.[80] Accordingly, it will be unnecessary to further dissect the three structural factors (or filters) in the systematic part of the noise or stochastic component – autoregressive order (p), stationarity (d), and moving average order (q) – for these six book publishing firms' original time series. An ARIMA (0, 0, 0) model is directly identified for estimating all of the six firms' original data over 30 years. Besides these six firms, the other four firms – Faber & Faber Ltd, Ian Allan Ltd, Marshall Cavendish Ltd, and Penguin Books Ltd – comprising the 10 book publishing firms with stationary time series, their time series are, of course, stationary but not a white noise

Table 5.4 First-Order Differencing ACFs & PACFs of five book publishing firms' time series data (1976–2006)

Firm	Lag	Partial Autocorrelation (PACF)		Autocorrelation (ACF)		Box-Ljung Statistic		
		Partial Autocorrelation	Std. Error	Autocorrelation	Std. Error[a]	Value	Df	Sig.[b]
A & C	1	−.401	.183	−.401	.174	5.317	1	.021
Black Plc	2	.047	.183	.200	.171	6.689	2	.035
	3	−.181	.183	−.247	.168	8.849	3	.031
	4	−.340	.183	−.115	.165	9.339	4	.053
	5	−.029	.183	.111	.161	9.814	5	.081
	6	.081	.183	.030	.158	9.850	6	.131
	7	−.142	.183	−.028	.155	9.882	7	.195
	8	−.121	.183	−.006	.151	9.884	8	.273
	9	.170	.183	.071	.148	10.114	9	.341
	10	−.008	.183	−.073	.144	10.371	10	.409
	11	−.143	.183	.031	.141	10.419	11	.493
	12	.105	.183	.015	.137	10.430	12	.578
	13	.088	.183	−.035	.133	10.501	13	.653
	14	.019	.183	.113	.129	11.272	14	.665
	15	−.052	.183	−.107	.125	12.008	15	.678
	16	−.089	.183	−.062	.121	12.269	16	.725
	17	−.056	.183	−.008	.116	12.274	17	.783
	18	.017	.183	.040	.112	12.400	18	.826
	19	−.057	.183	.016	.107	12.422	19	.867
	20	−.133	.183	−.011	.102	12.434	20	.900
	21	−.040	.183	−.039	.097	12.593	21	.922
	22	.030	.183	.008	.091	12.601	22	.944
	23	−.038	.183	.047	.085	12.900	23	.954
	24	.031	.183	.034	.079	13.085	24	.965
	25	.096	.183	−.012	.072	13.110	25	.975
	26	−.051	.183	−.051	.065	13.737	26	.976
	27	−.076	.183	−.024	.056	13.921	27	.982
	28	.044	.183	.001	.046	13.922	28	.988
Constable	1	−.542	.183	−.542	.174	9.728	1	.002
& Co Ltd	2	−.312	.183	.073	.171	9.913	2	.007
	3	−.035	.183	.094	.168	10.230	3	.017
	4	−.027	.183	−.091	.165	10.536	4	.032
	5	−.057	.183	.007	.161	10.538	5	.061
	6	−.073	.183	.000	.158	10.538	6	.104
	7	−.053	.183	−.005	.155	10.539	7	.160
	8	−.035	.183	−.001	.151	10.539	8	.229
	9	−.027	.183	−.001	.148	10.539	9	.309
	10	−.026	.183	−.001	.144	10.539	10	.395
	11	−.026	.183	−.002	.141	10.539	11	.483
	12	−.025	.183	−.002	.137	10.540	12	.569
	13	−.025	.183	−.002	.133	10.540	13	.649
	14	−.025	.183	−.002	.129	10.540	14	.722
	15	−.026	.183	−.002	.125	10.540	15	.784
	16	−.027	.183	−.002	.121	10.541	16	.837

(Continued overleaf)

Table 5.4 Continued

Firm	Lag	Partial Autocorrelation (PACF)		Autocorrelation (ACF)		Box-Ljung Statistic		
		Partial Autocorrelation	Std. Error	Autocorrelation	Std. Error[a]	Value	Df	Sig.b
	17	−.029	.183	−.003	.116	10.541	17	.879
	18	−.031	.183	−.003	.112	10.542	18	.913
	19	−.033	.183	−.003	.107	10.543	19	.938
	20	−.035	.183	−.003	.102	10.544	20	.957
	21	−.038	.183	−.003	.097	10.545	21	.971
	22	−.041	.183	−.003	.091	10.546	22	.981
	23	−.042	.183	−.003	.085	10.547	23	.987
	24	−.043	.183	−.003	.079	10.549	24	.992
	25	−.045	.183	−.003	.072	10.550	25	.995
	26	−.031	.183	.007	.065	10.562	26	.997
	27	−.022	.183	.000	.056	10.562	27	.998
	28	−.019	.183	.001	.046	10.562	28	.999
Frederick	1	−.025	.183	−.025	.174	.021	1	.884
Warne & Co	2	−.062	.183	−.062	.171	.152	2	.927
Ltd	3	.323	.183	.325	.168	3.905	3	.272
	4	.081	.183	.065	.165	4.060	4	.398
	5	−.165	.183	−.186	.161	5.395	5	.370
	6	−.411	.183	−.248	.158	7.852	6	.249
	7	−.086	.183	.028	.155	7.885	7	.343
	8	.043	.183	−.082	.151	8.180	8	.416
	9	.171	.183	−.146	.148	9.161	9	.423
	10	.045	.183	−.006	.144	9.163	10	.517
	11	−.004	.183	.095	.141	9.620	11	.565
	12	.005	.183	.098	.137	10.127	12	.605
	13	−.251	.183	−.164	.133	11.655	13	.556
	14	−.026	.183	.104	.129	12.306	14	.582
	15	−.140	.183	−.018	.125	12.327	15	.654
	16	.006	.183	−.150	.121	13.861	16	.609
	17	.037	.183	−.042	.116	13.994	17	.668
	18	.024	.183	−.064	.112	14.318	18	.708
	19	−.093	.183	−.061	.107	14.642	19	.745
	20	−.058	.183	−.044	.102	14.826	20	.786
	21	−.077	.183	.013	.097	14.845	21	.831
	22	−.010	.183	.031	.091	14.958	22	.864
	23	−.024	.183	−.001	.085	14.958	23	.896
	24	−.033	.183	.022	.079	15.034	24	.920
	25	−.022	.183	.011	.072	15.057	25	.940
	26	−.056	.183	.004	.065	15.061	26	.956
	27	.057	.183	.004	.056	15.067	27	.968
	28	−.002	.183	.000	.046	15.067	28	.978
Thames &	1	−.463	.183	−.463	.174	7.088	1	.008
Hudson Ltd	2	−.161	.183	.088	.171	7.351	2	.025
	3	.032	.183	.052	.168	7.448	3	.059
	4	−.084	.183	−.119	.165	7.972	4	.093
	5	−.125	.183	−.002	.161	7.972	5	.158
	6	−.168	.183	−.063	.158	8.130	6	.229

	7	.095	.183	.159	.155	9.185	7	.240
	8	−.002	.183	−.122	.151	9.832	8	.277
	9	−.070	.183	.019	.148	9.849	9	.363
	10	−.130	.183	−.030	.144	9.891	10	.450
	11	−.106	.183	−.040	.141	9.973	11	.533
	12	−.070	.183	.004	.137	9.975	12	.618
	13	−.079	.183	−.025	.133	10.009	13	.693
	14	−.031	.183	.070	.129	10.299	14	.740
	15	−.023	.183	−.027	.125	10.347	15	.797
	16	−.040	.183	.004	.121	10.348	16	.848
	17	−.044	.183	.001	.116	10.348	17	.888
	18	−.024	.183	−.002	.112	10.348	18	.920
	19	−.028	.183	−.004	.107	10.350	19	.944
	20	−.042	.183	−.006	.102	10.353	20	.961
	21	−.073	.183	.001	.097	10.353	21	.974
	22	−.098	.183	−.030	.091	10.458	22	.982
	23	−.078	.183	.007	.085	10.465	23	.988
	24	−.062	.183	−.005	.079	10.469	24	.992
	25	−.039	.183	.014	.072	10.507	25	.995
	26	−.032	.183	.008	.065	10.523	26	.997
	27	−.032	.183	.004	.056	10.528	27	.998
	28	−.033	.183	.005	.046	10.542	28	.999
Wiley & Sons Ltd	1	−.037	.183	−.037	.174	.045	1	.833
	2	−.164	.183	−.162	.171	.944	2	.624
	3	−.561	.183	−.532	.168	11.013	3	.012
	4	−.026	.183	.105	.165	11.422	4	.022
	5	−.090	.183	.119	.161	11.969	5	.035
	6	.005	.183	.279	.158	15.071	6	.020
	7	.064	.183	−.055	.155	15.197	7	.034
	8	.164	.183	.016	.151	15.207	8	.055
	9	.205	.183	−.062	.148	15.384	9	.081
	10	.076	.183	−.008	.144	15.387	10	.119
	11	.121	.183	−.025	.141	15.418	11	.164
	12	.017	.183	−.001	.137	15.418	12	.219
	13	−.060	.183	.006	.133	15.420	13	.282
	14	−.055	.183	.036	.129	15.499	14	.345
	15	−.140	.183	−.008	.125	15.504	15	.416
	16	−.144	.183	−.028	.121	15.559	16	.484
	17	−.089	.183	−.006	.116	15.561	17	.555
	18	−.139	.183	−.033	.112	15.651	18	.617
	19	−.095	.183	−.010	.107	15.660	19	.680
	20	−.057	.183	−.017	.102	15.687	20	.736
	21	−.046	.183	.002	.097	15.688	21	.787
	22	−.028	.183	−.015	.091	15.716	22	.830
	23	−.030	.183	−.019	.085	15.763	23	.865
	24	.019	.183	−.011	.079	15.783	24	.896
	25	−.002	.183	−.007	.072	15.792	25	.921
	26	.050	.183	.018	.065	15.867	26	.939
	27	.060	.183	−.007	.056	15.884	27	.955
	28	.031	.183	−.019	.046	16.053	28	.965

a. The underlying process assumed is independence (white noise).
b. Based on the asymptotic chi-square approximation.

Table 5.5 Properties of ACF & PACF for ARIMA models[83]

Model	ACF	PACF
$(1, d, 0)$	Exponential or oscillatory decay.	$\phi_{kk} = 0$ for $k > 1$.
$(2, d, 0)$	Exponential or sine wave decay.	$\phi_{kk} = 0$ for $k > 2$.
$(p, d, 0)$	Exponential and/or sine wave decay.	$\phi_{kk} = 0$ for $k > p$.
$(0, d, 1)$	$\rho_k = 0$ for $k > 1$.	Dominated by damped exponential.
$(0, d, 2)$	$\rho_k = 0$ for $k > 2$.	Dominated by damped exponential or sine wave.
$(0, d, q)$	$\rho_k = 0$ for $k > q$.	Dominated by linear combination of damped exponentials and/or sine waves.
$(1, d, 1)$	Tail off. Exponential decay from lag 1.	Tail off. Dominated by exponential decay from lag 1.
(p, d, q)	Tail off after $q - p$ lags. Exponential and/or sine wave decay after $q - p$ lags.	Tail off after $q - p$ lags. Dominated by damped exponentials and/or sine waves after $q - p$ lags.

p — autoregressive order
d — order of differencing (times of applying a difference equation) for stationarity
q — moving average order
k — number of lags (1, 2, 3,...) in the time series
ρ — parameter autocorrelation
ϕ — correlation coefficient of autoregressive function.

process. The auto-regressive order (p) and/or moving average order (q) of their time series should be detected through reviewing the lag graphs of ACFs and PACFs illustrated in Figures 5.9, 5.12, 5.14, and 5.16. As these figures show, in general, the lag graphs of ACFs in these four series appear to be dying down in the shape of a sine wave (such as Faber & Faber Ltd, Ian Allan Ltd, and Penguin Books Ltd) or dying down fairly quickly (such as Marshall Cavendish Ltd). The lag graphs of PACFs cut off after lag 1. This pattern of ACFs and PACFs points towards a first-order auto-regressive model. Correspondingly, an ARIMA (1, 0, 0) model is identified for estimating these four time series.

The model identification for the time series of the remaining five book publishing firms with non-stationary original time series – A & C Black Plc, Constable & Co Ltd, Frederick Warne & Co Ltd, Thames & Hudson Ltd, and Wiley & Sons Ltd – is slightly complex. The statistics and graphs of first-differencing-transformed time series of these five firms in Table 5.4 and Figures 5.19–5.23 suggest that, after first differencing, all five firms' time series become stationary to some extent. However, the lag graphs in Figures 5.19–5.23 show an intricate picture for identifying a tentative ARIMA model. Referring to the identification criteria in Table 5.5, it shall be considered that a first-order auto-regressive process (p) may exist in the first-order-differenced time series of A & C Black Plc. In the first-order-differenced time series of Constable & Co Ltd and Thames & Hudson Ltd, a moving average process is noticeable. Accordingly, a tentative ARIMA (1, 1, 0) model is identified for estimating A & C Black Plc's original time series, while a tentative ARIMA (0, 1, 1) model is identified for the original time series

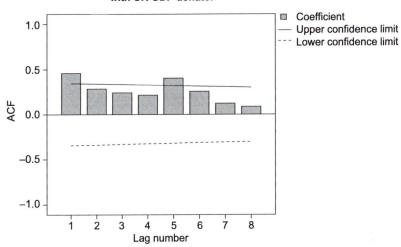

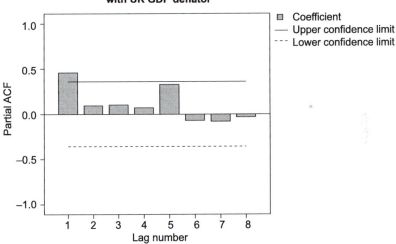

Figure 5.4 AFC & PAFC correlograms of A & C Black original annual profits with UK GDP deflator.

**Pre-tax profit (£000) of BT Batsford Ltd (ProfitBatsfd)
MEAN missing replace with UK GDP deflator**

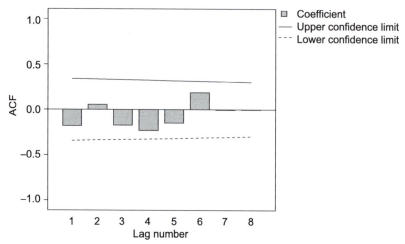

**Pre-tax profit (£000) of BT Batsford Ltd (ProfitBatsfd)
MEAN missing replace with UK GDP deflator**

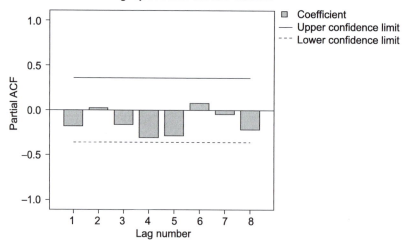

Figure 5.5 AFC & PAFC correlograms of B T Batsford original annual profits data
with missing data mean replacement & UK GDP deflator.

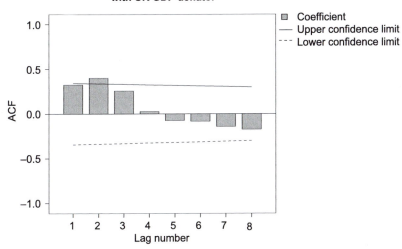

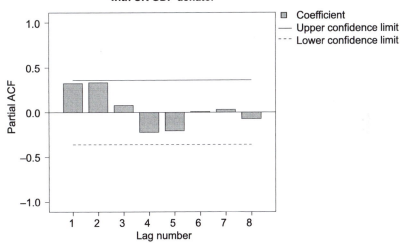

Figure 5.6 AFC & PAFC correlograms of Blackwell Science original annual profits
data with UK GDP deflator.

Pre-tax profit (£000) of Constable & Co Ltd (ProfitConsta)
MEAN missing replace with UK GDP deflator

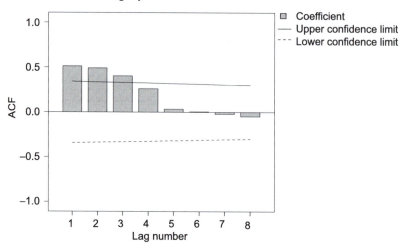

Pre-tax profit (£000) of Constable & Co Ltd (ProfitConsta)
MEAN missing replace with UK GDP deflator

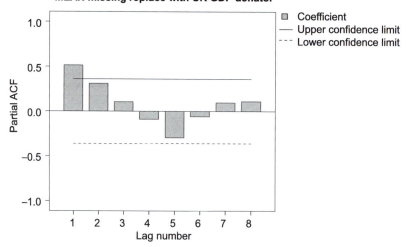

Figure 5.7 AFC & PAFC correlograms of Constable & Co original annual profits data with missing data mean replacement & UK GDP deflator.

**Pre-tax profit (£000) of David & Charles Holdings Plc
(ProfitDaid) MEAN missing replace with UK GDP deflator**

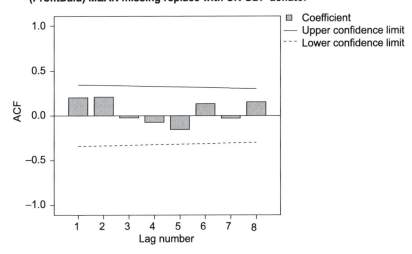

**Pre-tax profit (£000) of David & Charles Holdings Plc
(ProfitDaid) MEAN missing replace with UK GDP deflator**

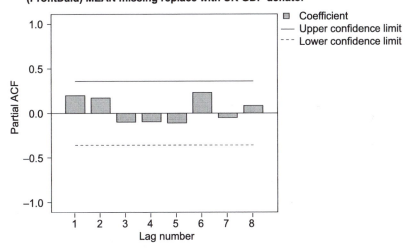

Figure 5.8 AFC & PAFC correlograms of David & Charles original annual profits
data with missing data mean replacement & UK GDP deflator.

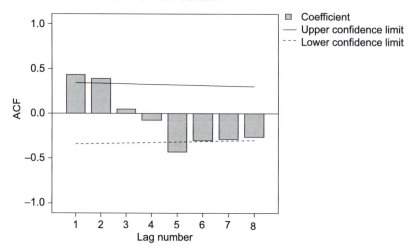

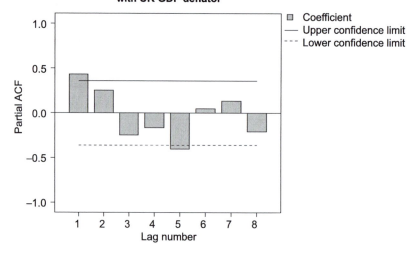

Figure 5.9 AFC & PAFC correlograms of Faber & Faber original annual profits data with UK GDP deflator.

**Pre-tax profit (£000) of Frederick Warne & Co Ltd
(ProfitFred) MEAN missing replace with UK GDP deflator**

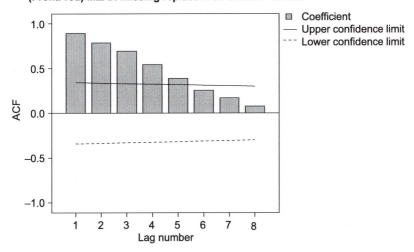

**Pre-tax profit (£000) of Frederick Warne & Co Ltd
(ProfitFred) MEAN missing replace with UK GDP deflator**

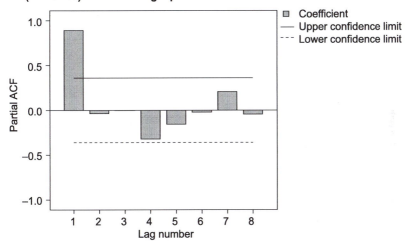

Figure 5.10 AFC & PAFC correlograms of Frederick Warne & Co original annual
profits data with missing mean replacement& UK GDP deflator.

**Pre-tax profit (£000) of Hodder & Stoughton Holdings Ltd
(ProfitHodder) MEAN missing replace with UK GDP deflator**

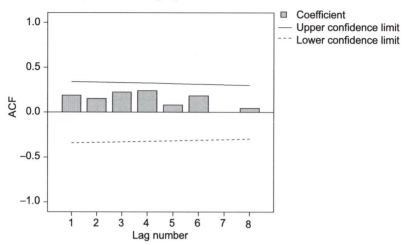

**Pre-tax profit (£000) of Hodder & Stoughton Holdings Ltd
(ProfitHodder) MEAN missing replace with UK GDP deflator**

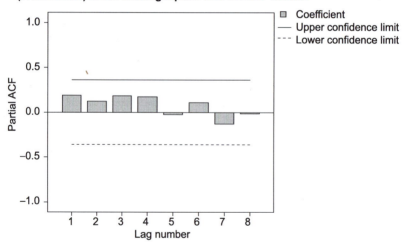

Figure 5.11 AFC & PAFC correlograms of Hodder & Stoughton Holdings original
annual profits data with missing mean replacement & UK GDP deflator.

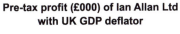

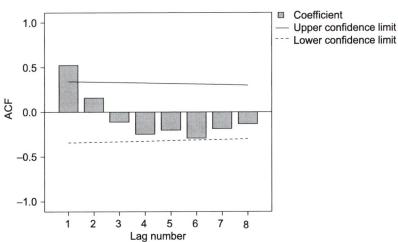

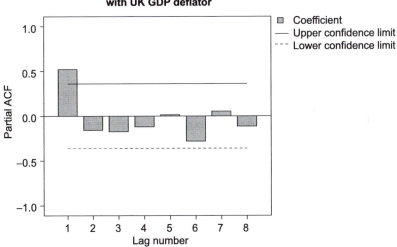

Figure 5.12 AFC & PAFC correlograms of Ian Allan original annual profits data with UK GDP deflator.

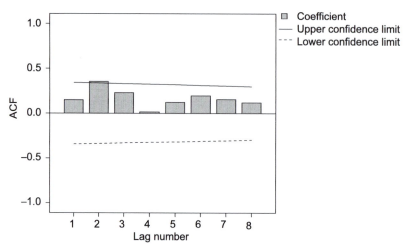

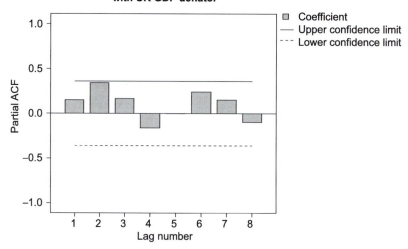

Figure 5.13 AFC & PAFC correlograms of Ladybird Books original annual profits data with UK GDP deflator.

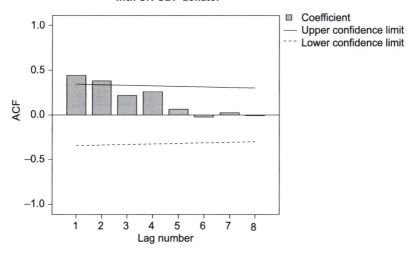

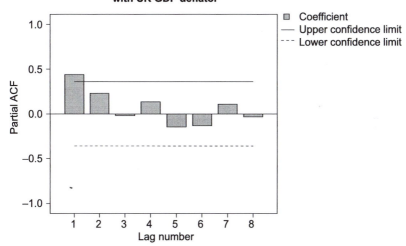

Figure 5.14 AFC & PAFC correlograms of Marshall Cavendish original annual
profits data with UK GDP deflator.

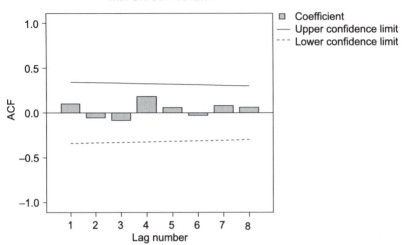

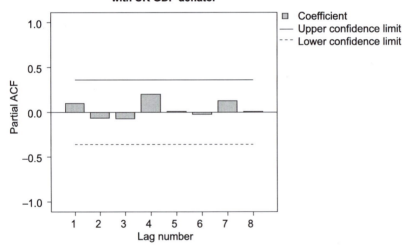

Figure 5.15 AFC & PAFC correlograms of Mills & Boon original annual profits data with UK GDP deflator.

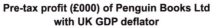

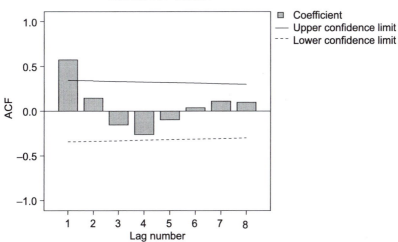

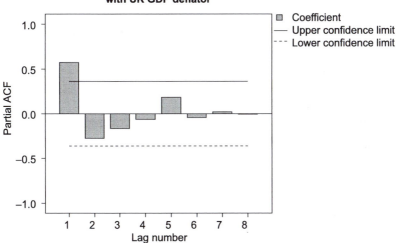

Figure 5.16 AFC & PAFC correlograms of Penguin Books original annual profits data with UK GDP deflator.

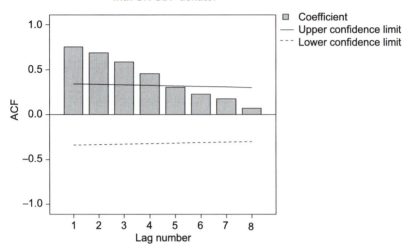

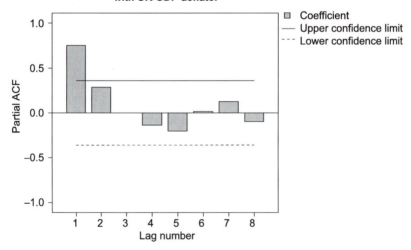

Figure 5.17 AFC & PAFC correlograms of Thames & Hudson original annual profits data with UK GDP deflator.

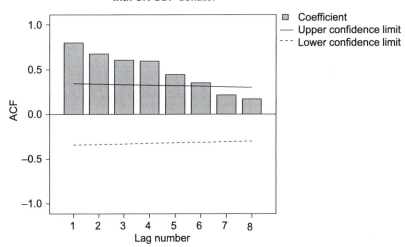

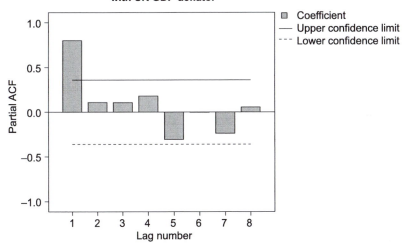

Figure 5.18 AFC & PAFC correlograms of Wiley & Sons original annual profits data with UK GDP deflator.

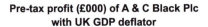

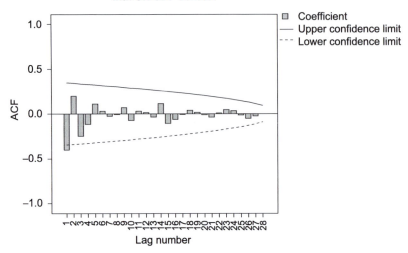

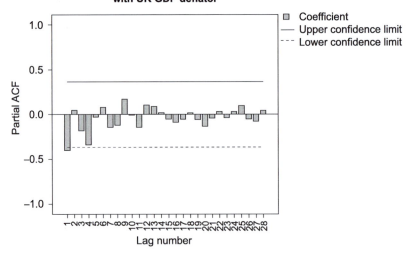

Figure 5.19 First-order differencing AFC & PAFC correlograms of pre-tax profit
(£'000) of A & C Black Plc with UK GDP deflator.

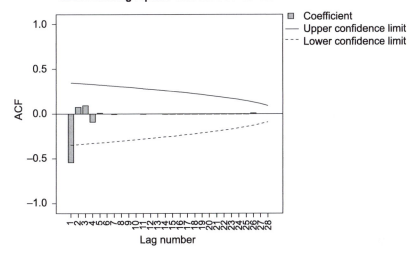

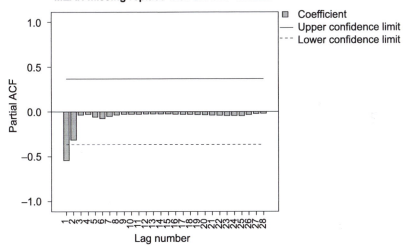

Figure 5.20 First-order differencing AFC & PAFC correlograms of pre-tax profit (£'000) of Constable & Co Ltd MEAN missing replace with UK GDP deflator.

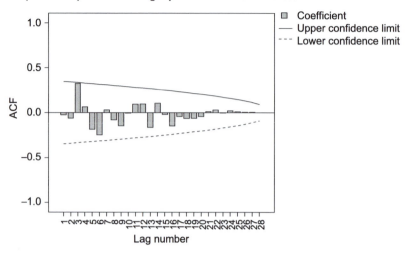

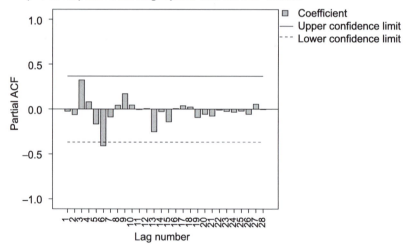

Figure 5.21 First-order differencing AFC & PAFC correlograms of pre-tax profit (£'000) of Frederick Warne & Co Ltd MEAN missing replace with UK GDP deflator.

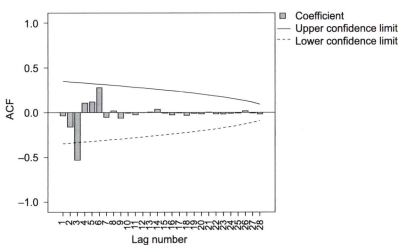

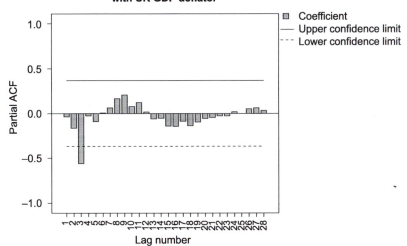

Figure 5.22 First-order differencing AFC & PAFC correlograms of pre-tax profit (£'000) of Thames & Hudson Ltd with UK GDP deflator.

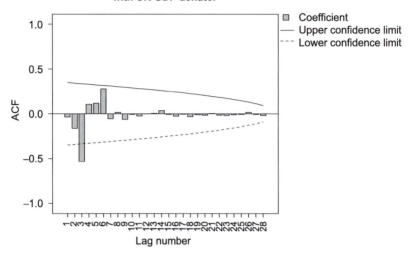

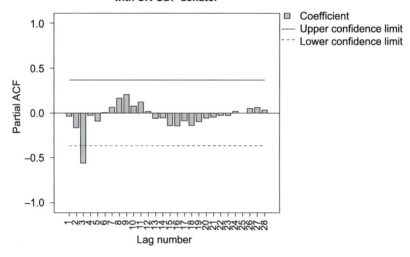

Figure 5.23 First-order differencing AFC & PAFC correlograms of pre-tax profit (£'000) of Wiley & Sons Ltd with UK GDP deflator.

of Constable & Co Ltd and Thames & Hudson Ltd. Inspecting the first-order-differenced time series of Frederick Warne & Co Ltd and Wiley & Sons Ltd reveals that a further differencing is likely to be necessary for the two firms' time series. Tables 5.6 and Figures 5.24–5.25 present the test results of the levels and patterns of ACFs and PACFs in the second-order-differenced time series for Frederick Warne & Co Ltd and Wiley & Sons Ltd.

The lag graphs in Figures 5.24–5.25 show that a first-order auto-regressive process may surface in Wiley & Sons Ltd's time series and a second-order auto-regressive process may occur in Frederick Warne & Co Ltd's time series. Thus, a tentative ARIMA (1, 2, 0) model and an ARIMA (2, 2, 0) model are identi-fied for estimating the original time series for Wiley & Sons Ltd and Frederick Warne & Co Ltd respectively. In total, Table 5.7 displays identified but tentative ARIMA (p, d, q) models for all 15 book publishing firms.[81]

(2) ESTIMATION

The goal at the stage of estimation is to assess the correlation coefficients of auto-regressive functions (ϕ) and/or the correlation coefficients of moving averages (θ) in these tentative ARIMA (p, d, q) models that were identified at the stage of identification. If these identified but still tentative ARIMA (p, d, q) models are acceptable, two requirements must be met. First, the ϕ and θ values must stand within the bounds of stationarity and invertibility. What are these bounds of stationarity and invertibility? For the first order ARIMA models – ARIMA (1, 0, 0) model or ARIMA (0, 0, 1) model – each of the ϕ and θ values should not be equal to or above +1. For the second or higher order ARIMA models – for instance, the ARIMA (2, 0, 0) or ARIMA (0, 0, 2) models – the sum of ϕ or

Table 5.6 Second-order differencing ACFs & PACFs of two book publishing firms' time series data (1976–2006)

Firm	Lag	Partial autocorrelation (PACF)		Autocorrelation (ACF)		Box–Ljung statistic		
		Partial Autocorrelation	Std. Error	Autocorrelation	Std. Error[a]	Value	Df	Sig.[b]
Frederick	1	−.483	.186	−.483	.176	7.485	1	.006
Warne &	2	−.581	.186	−.212	.173	8.983	2	.011
Co Ltd	3	−.248	.186	.316	.170	12.439	3	.006
	4	.024	.186	.008	.167	12.441	4	.014
	5	.212	.186	−.107	.163	12.870	5	.025
	6	−.179	.186	−.159	.160	13.862	6	.031
	7	−.270	.186	.194	.156	15.402	7	.031
	8	−.323	.186	−.023	.153	15.424	8	.051
	9	−.151	.186	−.101	.149	15.885	9	.069
	10	−.070	.186	.020	.145	15.904	10	.102
	11	−.073	.186	.051	.141	16.035	11	.140

(Continued overleaf)

Table 5.6 Continued

Firm	Lag	Partial autocorrelation (PACF)		Autocorrelation (ACF)		Box–Ljung statistic		
		Partial Autocorrelation	Std. Error	Autocorrelation	Std. Error[a]	Value	Df	Sig.[b]
	12	.165	.186	.125	.138	16.856	12	.155
	13	−.091	.186	−.260	.133	20.652	13	.080
	14	.012	.186	.191	.129	22.842	14	.063
	15	−.129	.186	.004	.125	22.843	15	.088
	16	−.136	.186	−.116	.120	23.779	16	.094
	17	−.096	.186	.060	.116	24.047	17	.118
	18	.026	.186	−.006	.111	24.049	18	.153
	19	−.015	.186	−.009	.105	24.057	19	.194
	20	−.011	.186	−.020	.100	24.096	20	.238
	21	−.089	.186	.021	.094	24.144	21	.286
	22	−.073	.186	.023	.088	24.212	22	.336
	23	−.057	.186	−.029	.082	24.338	23	.385
	24	−.061	.186	.015	.075	24.379	24	.440
	25	−.015	.186	.001	.067	24.379	25	.498
	26	−.120	.186	−.006	.058	24.389	26	.554
	27	−.054	.186	.001	.047	24.389	27	.609
Wiley & Sons Ltd	1	−.416	.186	−.416	.176	5.552	1	.018
	2	.034	.186	.201	.173	6.900	2	.032
	3	−.431	.186	−.451	.170	13.923	3	.003
	4	−.323	.186	.108	.167	14.342	4	.006
	5	−.091	.186	−.006	.163	14.343	5	.014
	6	−.020	.186	.188	.160	15.721	6	.015
	7	−.169	.186	−.110	.156	16.213	7	.023
	8	.003	.186	.079	.153	16.482	8	.036
	9	.098	.186	−.077	.149	16.746	9	.053
	10	−.046	.186	.011	.145	16.751	10	.080
	11	.006	.186	−.009	.141	16.755	11	.115
	12	.013	.186	−.017	.138	16.771	12	.158
	13	−.043	.186	.008	.133	16.774	13	.210
	14	−.010	.186	.032	.129	16.834	14	.265
	15	−.002	.186	−.008	.125	16.838	15	.329
	16	−.049	.186	−.011	.120	16.847	16	.396
	17	.028	.186	.024	.116	16.890	17	.462
	18	.002	.186	−.039	.111	17.013	18	.522
	19	−.031	.186	.022	.105	17.056	19	.586
	20	−.005	.186	−.023	.100	17.107	20	.646
	21	−.005	.186	.012	.094	17.122	21	.704
	22	−.034	.186	−.002	.088	17.123	22	.757
	23	−.038	.186	.001	.082	17.123	23	.803
	24	−.007	.186	−.001	.075	17.123	24	.843
	25	−.038	.186	−.005	.067	17.128	25	.877
	26	−.042	.186	−.006	.058	17.140	26	.905
	27	−.025	.186	−.004	.047	17.146	27	.927

a. The underlying process assumed is independence (white noise).
b. Based on the asymptotic chi-square approximation.

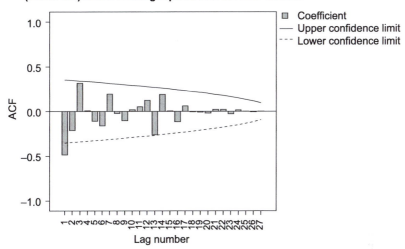

**Pre-tax profit (£000) of Frederick Warne & Co Ltd
(ProfitFred) MEAN missing replace with UK GDP deflator**

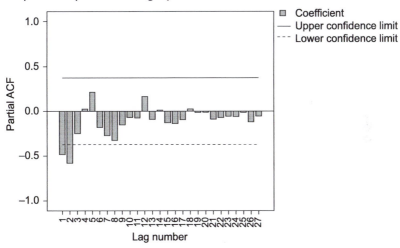

**Pre-tax profit (£000) of Frederick Warne & Co Ltd
(ProfitFred) MEAN missing replace with UK GDP deflator**

Figure 5.24 Second-order differencing AFC & PAFC correlograms of pre-tax profit
(£'000) of Frederick Warne & Co Ltd MEAN missing replace with UK
GDP deflator.

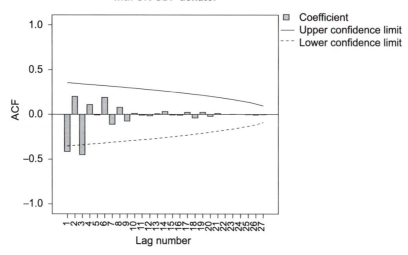

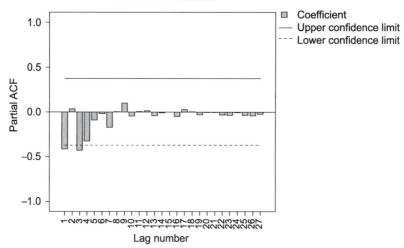

Figure 5.25 Second-order differencing AFC & PAFC correlograms of pre-tax profit (£'000) of Wiley & Sons Ltd with UK GDP deflator.

Table 5.7 Identified tentative ARIMA models for 15 book publishing firms

Firm	ARIMA Model
A & C Black Plc	(1, 1, 0)
B T Batsford Ltd	(0, 0, 0)
Blackwell Science Ltd	(0, 0, 0)
Constable & Co Ltd	(0, 1, 1)
David & Charles Plc	(0, 0, 0)
Faber & Faber Ltd	(1, 0, 0)
Frederick Warne & Co Ltd	(2, 2, 0)
Hodder & Stoughton Ltd	(0, 0, 0)
Ian Allan Ltd	(1, 0, 0)
Ladybird Books Ltd	(0, 0, 0)
Marshall Cavendish Ltd	(1, 0, 0)
Mills & Boon Ltd	(0, 0, 0)
Penguin Books Ltd	(1, 0, 0)
Thames & Hudson Ltd	(0, 1, 1)
Wiley & Sons Ltd	(1, 2, 0)

θ values ($\phi1 + \phi2$ or $\theta1 + \theta2$) should not be equal to or above $+1$. Likewise with the absolute values of $\phi2$ or $\theta2$ ($|\phi2|$ or $|\theta2|$). Second, the estimated ϕ and θ values (so-called 'parameter estimates') should be statistically significant.[82]

Among the 15 book publishing firms' original time series, those from six firms – B T Batsford Ltd, Blackwell Science Ltd, David & Charles Plc, Hodder & Stoughton Holdings Ltd, Ladybird Books Ltd, and Mills & Boon Ltd – have already been identified as the series in a white noise process. Thus, no further estimation is needed for the series data of these six book publishing firms. Instead, the identified ARIMA models for the original time series of the other nine book publishing firms (Constable & Co Ltd, Thames & Hudson Ltd, A & C Black Plc, Wiley & Sons Ltd, Frederick Warne & Co Ltd, Faber & Faber Ltd, Ian Allan Ltd, Marshall Cavendish Ltd, Penguin Books Ltd) are estimated. Table 5.8 presents the estimating results for these identified models. These results indicate that, on the whole, the requirements as stated above are met when running the ARIMA models for these nine firms' original time series.

First, as Table 5.8 shows, among all of these identified ARIMA models, two first-order moving average models – MA(1) – are identified for the original time series of Constable & Co Ltd and Thames & Hudson Ltd. The values of the correlation coefficients of moving average functions (θ) in the two MA(1) models (in the junction of the column of 'Estimate' with the row of 'MA Lag 1' in Table 5.8) are .634 and .587 respectively. Meanwhile, six first-order auto-regressive models – AR(1) – are identified for the original time series of A & C Black Plc, Faber & Faber Ltd, Ian Allan Ltd, Marshall Cavendish Ltd, Penguin Books Ltd, and Wiley & Sons Ltd. The values of the correlation coefficients of auto-regressive functions (ϕ) in the six AR(1) models are: $-.396$, .421, .737, .434, .561, and $-.420$ respectively (in the junction of the

Table 5.8 Estimation of identified **ARIMA** models for nine 'no white process' book publishing firms

Firm	Data transformation	ARIMA Model	Estimate	SE	T	Sig.
Constable & Co Ltd	No Transformation	(0, 1, 1) Constant	7459.457	5681.541	1.313	.200
		Difference	1			
		MA Lag 1	.634	.151	4.209	.000
Thames & Hudson Ltd	No Transformation	(0, 1, 1) Constant	62.688	40.069	1.565	.129
		Difference	1			
		MA Lag 1	.587	.165	3.564	.001
A & C Black Plc	No Transformation	(1, 1, 0) Constant	33.988	28.698	1.184	.246
		AR Lag 1	-.396	.175	-2.268	.031
Faber & Faber Ltd	No Transformation	(1, 0, 0) Constant	156.218	132.018	1.183	.246
		AR Lag 1	.421	.168	2.512	.018
Ian Allan Ltd	No Transformation	(1, 0, 0) Constant	-42.255	89.612	-0.472	.641
		AR Lag 1	.737	.175	4.219	.000
Marshall Cavendish Ltd	No Transformation	(1, 0, 0) Constant	2031.716	889.064	2.285	.030
		AR Lag 1	.434	.166	2.608	.014
Penguin Books Ltd	No Transformation	(1, 0, 0) Constant	2626.231	1481.487	1.773	.087
		AR Lag 1	.561	.152	3.704	.001
Wiley & Sons Ltd	No Transformation	(1, 2, 0) Constant	123.433	317.41	.389	.700
		AR Lag 1	-.420	.178	-2.358	.026
		Difference	2			
Frederick Warne & Co Ltd	No Transformation	(2, 2, 0) Constant	-18.939	68.031	-.278	.783
		AR Lag 1	-.766	.158	-4.856	.000
		Lag 2	-.595	.163	-3.647	.001
		Difference	2			

column of 'Estimate' with the row of 'AR Lag 1'). All of these correlation coefficient values are lower than +1. A second-order auto-regressive model – AR(2) – is identified for the original time series of Frederick Warne & Co Ltd. The values of the two correlation coefficients of auto-regressive functions (ϕ) are –.766 and –.595 respectively (in the junction of the column of 'Estimate' with the rows of 'AR Lag 1' and 'AR Lag 2'). The sum of the two values ($\phi 1 + \phi 2$) is not equal to or above +1. Likewise with the absolute value of

$\phi2$ (–.595 of 'AR Lag 2'). Second, in Table 5.8, the estimated 'T' values corresponding with ϕ and θ values (in the junction of the column of 'T' and 'Sig' with the rows of 'MA Lags' and 'AR Lags') are all statistically significant (an absolute value of 'T' above '1.96' is a rule of thumb for indicating statistical significance). Thus, all of these identified ARIMA models for the nine book publishing firms are acceptable for analysing their original time series.

(3) DIAGNOSIS

The goal at the stage of diagnosis is to inspect whether or not these acceptable ARIMA (p, d, q) models as assessed at the stage of estimation are appropriate for analysing the original time series of these nine firms' annual profits. At the stage of identification, an ARIMA (0, 0, 0) model has been identified for analysing the original time series of six book publishing firms (B T Batsford Ltd, Blackwell Science Ltd, David & Charles Plc, Hodder & Stoughton Holdings Ltd, Ladybird Books Ltd, and Mills & Boon Ltd) because their time series data have exhibited a white noise process. In the meantime, diverse ARIMA models have also been identified for assessing the time series data for the other nine book publishing firms. At the stage of estimation, these models have been assessed as acceptable models. Finally, at the stage of diagnosis, the concern should be on whether or not these acceptable ARIMA models can appropriately control for the stochastic (unexplained) components of the time series of the nine firms. To address this concern, the Box–Ljung statistics of the stochastic (unexplained) components under these estimated acceptable ARIMA models should be inspected for diagnosing the appropriateness of these models.

Table 5.9 and Figures 5.26–5.30 display the results of diagnosis. Table 5.9 indicates that the levels of significance at all 27 lags (in the fifth column of the table) for the Box–Ljung statistics – or Q statistics – of the stochastic (unexplained) component (the serial error term) in the time series of nine book publishing firms' annual profits are above .05. This means that the Box–Ljung statistics at all first 27 lags are not significant at .05 levels. Meanwhile, in Figures 5.26–5.30, almost all coefficients of AFC and PAFC rank within both Lower Confidence Limit and Upper Confidence Limit. Of course, the peaks of AFC and PAFC coefficients of Faber & Faber Ltd's time series at Lag 5 (in Figure 5.28) reach beyond Upper Confidence Limit. The peaks of AFC and PAFC coefficients of Wiley & Sons' time series at Lag 3 (in Figure 5.29) also reach beyond Upper Confidence Limit. However, these outliers should not affect the whole picture. On the whole, the insignificance of the Box–Ljung statistics and minor coefficients of almost all autocorrelations reveal that, under these identified and estimated ARIMA models, the stochastic (unexplained) component of the time series of nine firms' annual profits in the period of 1976–2006 becomes random. In econometric terms, these time series have become a white noise process. Accordingly, these identified and

Table 5.9 Diagnosis of identified ARIMA models for nine 'no white process' book publishing firms

Firm	ARIMA Model	Ljung–Box Q		
		Statistics	DF	Sig.
Constable & Co Ltd	(0, 1, 1)	1.780	17	1.000
Thames & Hudson Ltd	(0, 1, 1)	4.630	17	.999
A & C Black Plc	(0, 1, 1)	9.699	17	.916
Faber & Faber Ltd	(1, 0, 0)	16.136	17	.514
Ian Allan Ltd	(1, 0, 0)	14.057	17	.663
Marshall Cavendish Ltd	(1, 0, 0)	6.450	17	.990
Penguin Books Ltd	(1, 0, 0)	13.335	17	.713
Wiley & Sons Ltd	(1, 2, 0)	12.454	17	.772
Frederick Warne & Co Ltd	(2, 2, 0)	17.870	16	.332

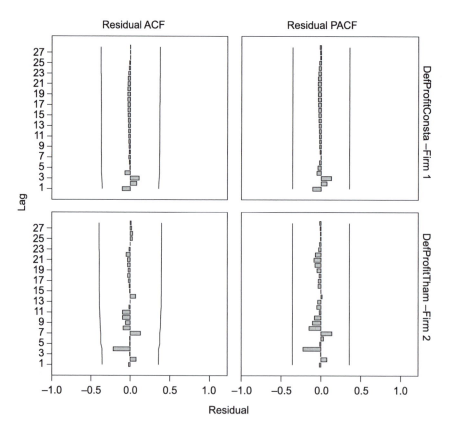

Figure 5.26 Diagnosis of AFC & PAFC correlograms for Constable & Co Ltd (Firm 1) & Thames & Hudson Ltd (Firm 2).

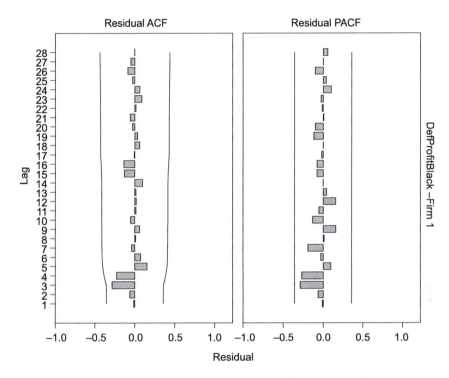

Figure 5.27 Diagnosis of AFC & PAFC correlograms for A & C Black Plc.

estimated **ARIMA** models are appropriate models for analysing the nine firms' time series.

2. *Assessment of deterministic component*

Once the appropriateness of these diverse **ARIMA** (*p*, *d*, *q*) models for formalising the noise or stochastic (unexplained) components of the time series for all these 15 UK book publishing firms is confirmed through the identification, estimation, and diagnosis stages, intervention models for formalising the deterministic (explained) components will be added to these identified, estimated, and diagnosed **ARIMA** models in order to analyse the impact of the Copyright, Designs and Patents Act 1988 and the forces of creative destruction – dynamic competition, concentrating industry struc-ture, and technological innovation – as the deterministic (explained) com-ponent on the growth of these 15 UK book publishing firms' annual profits over 30 years.

As previously indicated, the main purpose of an intervention model is to assess the impact of an intervention of policy, law, or programme as the

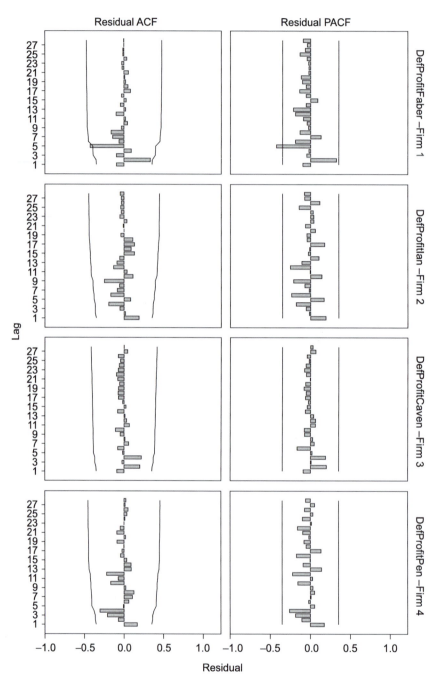

Figure 5.28 Diagnosis of AFC & PAFC correlograms for Faber & Faber Ltd (Firm 1), Ian Allan Ltd (Firm 2), Marshall Cavendish Ltd (Firm 3), and Penguin Books Ltd (Firm 4).

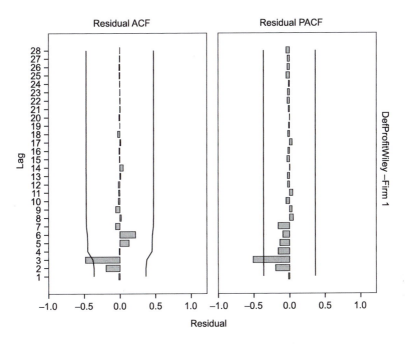

Figure 5.29 Diagnosis of AFC & PAFC correlograms for Wiley & Sons Ltd.

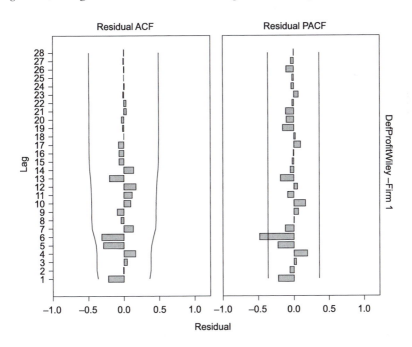

Figure 5.30 Diagnosis of AFC & PAFC correlograms for Frederick Warne & Co Ltd.

independent or explanatory variable on a certain target that such policy, law, or programme was designed or assumed to change through estimating the changes or variations of the target across both space and time. In this research, the intervention is the Copyright, Designs and Patents Act 1988 while the target is the growth of these 15 firms measured by the time series of their annual profits. To estimate the impact of the Copyright, Designs and Patents Act 1988 as an intervention of the independent or explanatory variable (the deterministic or explained component) on the time series of these 15 firms' annual profits, it is necessary to adapt a specific intervention model from three main intervention models: (1) an abrupt and constant change in the time series, (2) a gradual and constant change in the time series, and (3) an abrupt and temporary change in the time series.[84]

As in the process of identification, estimation, and diagnosis for assessing the appropriateness of these ARIMA (p, d, q) models (as indicated in Tables 5.7–5.9) for the noise or stochastic (unexplained) components, a trial-and-error process for evaluating the suitability of an intervention model (the deterministic or explained component) is also necessary. In general, if no clear clues to the intervention pattern were available, the researcher would first try the third model – the model for an abrupt and temporary change in the time series – before choosing a suitable one.[85] However, in this research, to estimate the sole effect of the 1988 Act before conducting pooled and panel data analysis, it is assumed that the effect of the Act on the profit growth of these 15 firms is a gradual process and the first model is tried – the model for 'an abrupt and constant change in the time series'. This first model of intervention is added to these identified, estimated and diagnosed ARIMA models and, accordingly, certain joint models of the first model of intervention and diverse ARIMA models are constructed for analysing both the deterministic components and the stochastic components in the time series of these 15 firms' annual profits at the firm level. The joint models formalise the compositions of a typical time series model, as depicted in Figure 5.2.

5.3 Assessment findings and analysis

The operational model that is defined under Schumpeter's theoretical framework in Chapter 5.2.1 offers five hypotheses. These hypotheses predict that copyright expansion under the Copyright, Designs and Patents Act of 1988 will have an insignificant effect on the growth of the UK book publishing industry, and that the forces of creative destruction – dynamic competition, concentrating industry structure, and technological innovation – will promote growth when controlling for the impact of copyright expansion. Applying the intervention models and pooled/panel models, these hypotheses are tested against the collected data in the UK book publishing industry at both firm and industry levels. Through hypothesis testing, the impact of copyright expansion as a law/policy intervention under the 1988 Act on the growth of UK book publishing industry and the impact of the forces of creative destruction on the copyright-growth relation are inferred and analysed at firm and industry levels.

5.3.1 Empirical assessment and findings at firm level

Table 5.10 presents the estimates of the effect of the Copyright, Designs and Patents Act 1988 that endorses copyright expansion on the profit growth of these 15 firms under the ARIMA models and the first model of intervention (the model for an abrupt and constant change in the time series). As Table 1 of Appendix B shows, the annual profits of these 15 firms have been adjusted by the UK GDP Deflator to control for inflation.[86]

The estimates in Table 5.10 demonstrate that the intervention effect of the 1988 Act that endorses copyright expansion on profit growth appears statistically significant for five firms – Blackwell Science Ltd, Hodder & Stoughton Ltd, Marshall Cavendish Ltd, Mills & Boon Ltd, and Thames & Hudson Ltd – among all 15 book publishing firms. For the other 10 book publishing firms, the 1988 Act seems less effective for promoting their profit growth.

Of course, these estimates assess the sole effect of the Act on the profit growth of these 15 firms under the joint models of the first model of intervention (the model for an abrupt and constant change in the time series) and diverse ARIMA models. For the overall purpose of this research, the impact of creative destruction on the copyright-growth relation should be assessed and, accordingly, three more independent variables – dynamic competition (measured by Dynamic Index), concentrating industry structure (measured by Industrial Concentration Ratio in UK Book Publishing Industry), and technological innovation as three forces of creative destruction defined in the operational model of Figure 5.1 – are added to these joint models for assessment.

However, there are only 30 or 31 observations (30 or 31 years) in each firm's annual time series data. This length of time series is insufficient to estimate the effects of four independent variables on the profit growth of each individual firm separately. To overcome this problem, a pooled time series analysis and a panel data analysis, as introduced in Chapter 5.2.4, are conducted under the joint models of the ARIMA models and the first model of intervention. Because diverse ARIMA models have been already identified, estimated, and diagnosed (as Tables 5.7–5.9 show) for analysing the 15 firms' time series, building pooled or panel time series metrics for certain firms should take account of these identified ARIMA models. To run a vigorous pooled time series analysis or panel data analysis, the data are pooled or panelled for those firms' time series that fit with the same ARIMA model. Obviously, among all 15 firms, two groups of firms are ready for pooling or panelling. One book publishing group includes six firms – B T Batsford Ltd, Blackwell Science Ltd, David & Charles Plc, Hodder & Stoughton Holdings Ltd, Ladybird Books Ltd,

Table 5.10 Intervention estimates of UK's 1988 Copyright Act for 15 book publishing firms

Firm	Data transformation	ARIMA Model		Estimate	SE	T	Sig.
B T Batsford Ltd	No transformation	(0, 0, 0)	Constant	99.318	77096.274	.001	.999
			Copyright Act 1988	24994.286	101176.110	.247	.807
Blackwell Science Ltd	No transformation	(0, 0, 0)	Constant	913.350	825.965	1.106	.278
			Copyright Act 1988	2259.305	1083.942	2.084	.046
David & Charles Plc	No transformation	(0, 0, 0)	Constant	116.885	136.717	.855	.400
			Copyright Act 1988	250.477	179.418	1.396	.173
Hodder & Stoughton Ltd	No transformation	(0, 0, 0)	Constant	845.334	2061.862	.410	.685
			Copyright Act 1988	5365.689	2705.854	1.983	.057
Ladybird Books Ltd	No transformation	(0, 0, 0)	Constant	735.768	507.273	1.450	.158
			Copyright Act 1988	-1112.750	665.711	-1.672	.105
Mills & Boon Ltd	No transformation	(0, 0, 0)	Constant	847.215	316.240	2.679	.012
			Copyright Act 1988	883.125	415.012	2.128	.042
Constable & Co Ltd	No transformation	(0, 1, 1)	Constant	-2864.476	6676.159	-.429	.671
			Difference	1			
		MA	Lag 1	.784	.135	5.794	.000
			Copyright Act 1988	16267.093	9198.510	1.768	.088
Thames & Hudson Ltd	No transformation	(0, 1, 1)	Constant	-1.595	26.881	-.059	.953
			Difference	1			
		MA	Lag 1	.978	.399	2.450	.021
			Copyright Act 1988	117.266	39.108	2.999	.006
Faber & Faber Ltd	No transformation	(1, 0, 0)	Constant	102.692	197.000	.521	.606
		AR	Lag 1	.418	.171	2.443	.021
			Copyright Act 1988	92.735	251.226	.369	.715
Ian Allan Ltd	No transformation	(1, 0, 0)	Constant	-10.583	108.014	-.098	.923
		AR	Lag 1	.713	.181	3.944	.000
			Copyright Act 1988	-49.080	113.349	-.433	.668

Company	Transformation	Model	Parameter				
Marshall Cavendish Ltd	No transformation	(1, 0, 0)	Constant	478.691	1051.564	.455	.652
		AR	Lag 1	.295	.180	1.636	.113
			Copyright Act 1988	2705.691	1361.311	1.988	.057
Penguin Books Ltd	No transformation	(1, 0, 0)	Constant	1726.302	2008.304	.860	.397
		AR	Lag 1	.528	.159	3.323	.002
			Copyright Act 1988	1575.855	2501.329	.630	.534
Wiley & Sons Ltd	No transformation	(1, 2, 0)	Constant	17.088	531.070	.032	.975
		AR	Lag 1	-.421	.181	-2.321	.028
			Difference	2			
			Copyright Act 1988	170.581	676.868	.252	.803
Frederick Warne & Co Ltd	No transformation	(2, 2, 0)	Constant	26.434	115.205	.229	.820
		AR	Lag 1	-.769	.160	-4.796	.000
			Lag 2	-.601	.166	-3.616	.001
			Difference	2			
			Copyright Act 1988	-72.397	147.404	-.491	.628

and Mills & Boon Ltd – under the ARIMA (0, 0, 0) model. Another group consists of four firms – Faber & Faber Ltd, Ian Allan Ltd, Marshall Cavendish Ltd, and Penguin Books Ltd – under the ARIMA (1, 0, 0) model.

The time series data of two groups are pooled and panelled, and a corresponding time series analysis of pooled and panel data is conducted for each group under a joint model of the ARIMA (0, 0, 0) model (for the group of six book publishing firms) or ARIMA (1, 0, 0) model (for the group of four book publishing firms), and the first model of intervention (the model for an abrupt and constant change in the time series). Considering the effects of two forces of creative destruction as two independent variables – dynamic competition and concentrating industry structure – may be lagged, the data of these two variables are transformed, and the two variables are designed and measured as the lagged level of competition and the lagged level of industrial concentration in a joint model for each group.

One of the main advantages of pooled time series or panel data analysis is to avoid heterogeneity bias caused by ignoring the spatial and temporal effects of the omitted independent or explanatory variables in the proposed model (the operational model as depicted in Figure 5.1). Specifically, a pooled or panel model is designed to control the effects of variables that are excluded (mismeasured or unobserved) in the proposed model but are still associated with the independent or explanatory variables included in the model through estimating the cross-sectional and time dimensions of the effects of these excluded variables.[87] There are three basic models for estimating pooled time series data or panel data – the constant coefficients (ordinary regression or common constant) model, the fixed coefficients (fixed effects) model, and the random coefficients (random effects) model.[88] The fixed coefficients model is also called the least squares dummy variable (LSDV) model, the within-group model, or the covariance model. The random coefficients model is also called the variance components model or the error components model[89] and can be further analysed as the one-way or two-way random effects (error components) model.[90] Although some specification tests are proposed, model selection is still an uneasy choice for analysing panel data.[91] In this research, all three models are applied for a comparison of assessments. It has been one of the significant theoretical concerns in the econometrics of panel data to explore the issues of autocorrelation or serial correlation under a specific model of panel data such as an error components model.[92] In this research, because the noise or stochastic structure of two groups of panel data – ARIMA (0, 0, 0) and ARIMA (1, 0, 0) – have been already identified, the issues of autocorrelation or serial correlation and the role of the 1988 Copyright, Designs and Patents Act are explored under an ARIMA-intervention joint model with the estimations of specific panel data models. First, the constant coefficients model is applied and the pooled and panel ordinary least squares (OLS) estimations under the constant coefficients model are conducted for assessing the two groups of pooled and panel data. Then, the fixed coefficients model and the random coefficients model are employed with both the OLS and the feasible generalised least squares (FGLS) or estimated generalised least squares (EGLS) estimations for analysing the two sets of pooled and panel data.

Tables 5.11–5.12 present the OLS estimating results of these two book publishing groups in the ARIMA (0, 0, 0) and ARIMA (1, 0, 0) models, respectively, under the constant coefficients model of panel data. The OLS estimating results in Tables 5.11–5.12 demonstrate a mixed picture. In general, the UK's Copyright, Designs and Patents Act 1988, which endorses copyright expansion, and all three forces of creative destruction – dynamic competition, concentrating industry structure, and technological innovation – as the four independent variables, do not exhibit a statistically significant effect on the original time series of these 10 firms in the two book publishing groups. However, after taking natural log transformation of the original time series for all 10 firms, the 1988 Act that endorses copyright expansion as an independent variable does show statistical significance in influencing the transformed time series for the 10 firms. Meanwhile, as indicated in Table 5.12, dynamic competition and technological innovation exhibit statistical significance in affecting the transformed time series for the group of four firms but not for the group of six firms. Overall, on account of these estimates of panel data under two specific joint models, the 1988 Act appears statistically significant in affecting the transformed time series of these 10 firms in the two groups. Among the three forces of creative destruction as the independent or explanatory variables, dynamic competition and technological innovation appear statistically significant in one way or another in affecting the transformed time series of these four firms in Table 5.12.

Table 5.11 Estimates of whole model for six book publishing firms (1976–2006)

Independent Variables	(1)	(2)	(3)	(4)
Competition	646.623	–0.044	646.624	646.624
	(0.35)	(–1.64)	(0.35)	(0.35)
Concentration	–802.852	–0.005	–802.853	–802.852
	(–0.74)	(–0.31)	(–0.74)	(–0.74)
Technological Innovation	5310.943	0.232	5310.943	5310.943
	(0.26)	(0.4)	(0.27)	(0.27)
UK Copyright Act of 1988	13329.91	1.4*	13329.91	13329.91
	(0.36)	(3.65)	(0.37)	(0.37)
Durbin–Watson	2.245139	0.222137	2.245139	2.245139
R^2	0.004226	0.430104	0.004226	0.004226
Number of Observations	186	84	186	186

Column 1 – Pooled OLS Estimates on Pre-Tax Profits (£'000) with UK GDP Deflator.

Column 2 – Pooled OLS Estimates on Natural Log of Pre-Tax Profits (£'000) with UK GDP Deflator.

Column 3 – Panel OLS Estimates on Pre-Tax Profits (£'000) with UK GDP Deflator.

Column 4 – Panel OLS Estimates on Natural Log of Pre-Tax Profits (£'000) with UK GDP Deflator.

t-statistics are displayed in parentheses.

* Statistically significant at the 5% level.

Table 5.12 Estimates of whole model for four book publishing firms (1976–2006)

Independent Variables	(1)	(2)	(3)	(4)
Competition	−16.494	0.08*	16.837	16.837
	(−0.25)	(2.55)	(0.28)	(0.28)
Concentration	1.908	0.032	−34.053	−34.053
	(0.05)	(1.43)	(−0.98)	(−0.98)
Technological Innovation	842.962	0.8	582.542	582.542
	(1.29)	(1.76)	(0.91)	(0.91)
UK Copyright Act of 1988	679.119	3.322*	1355.129	1355.129
	(0.56)	(4.74)	(1.15)	(1.15)
Durbin–Watson	0.779159	0.215838	0.873025	0.873025
R^2	0.057624	0.357013	0.060420	0.060420
Number of Observations	120	95	124	124

Column 1 – Pooled OLS Estimates on Pre-Tax Profits (£'000) with UK GDP Deflator.
Column 2 – Pooled OLS Estimates on Natural Log of Pre-Tax Profits (£'000) with UK GDP Deflator.
Column 3 – Panel OLS Estimates on Pre-Tax Profits (£'000) with UK GDP Deflator.
Column 4 – Panel OLS Estimates on Natural Log of Pre-Tax Profits (£'000) with UK GDP Deflator.
t-statistics are displayed in parentheses.
* Statistically significant at the 5% level.

The OLS estimator is unbiased and consistent, even if less efficient, in assessing the pooled time-independent time series data or panel data, such as the panel data of the group of six book publishing firms under the ARIMA (0, 0, 0) model. However, to assess the pooled or panel data in connection with autocorrelation or serial correlation, such as the panel data of the group of four book publishing firms under the ARIMA (1, 0, 0) model, the OLS estimator is biased due to the existence of the first-order auto-correlation or first-order moving average.[93] To overcome this bias, the pooled and panel FGLS estimation under the ARIMA (1, 0, 0) model is needed. Tables 5.13–5.14 report this pooled and panel FGLS or EGLS and the seemingly unrelated regressions (SUR) of the FGLS (SUR FGLS or EGLS) estimating results for these two groups in the two specific models – ARIMA (0, 0, 0) and ARIMA (1, 0, 0) respectively – under the random coefficients (or random effects) model of panel data.[94] Similarly, as the OLS estimates suggest, the FGLS and SUR FGLS estimates indicate that the 1988 Act and all three forces of creative destruction, as the four independent variables, do not demonstrate a statistically significant effect on the original time series of these 10 book publishing firms in the two groups. However, unlike the OLS estimates, after taking natural log transformation of the original time series for all 10 firms, among the four independent variables only two variables of creative destruction – dynamic competition and technological

Table 5.13 EGLS estimates of whole model for six book publishing firms (1976–2006)

Independent Variables	(1)	(2)	(3)	(4)
Competition	646.624	−0.045*	646.624	646.624
	(0.6)	(−2.29)	(0.33)	(0.33)
Concentration	−802.853	−0.005	−802.853	−802.853
	(−0.94)	(−0.43)	(−0.71)	(−0.71)
Technological Innovation	5310.943	1.4*	5310.943	5310.943
	(0.25)	(5.1)	(0.25)	(0.25)
UK Copyright Act of 1988	13329.91	0.232	13329.91	13329.91
	(0.7)	(0.56)	(0.35)	(0.35)
Durbin–Watson	2.243055**	0.434368**	2.243055**	0.003802**
R^2	0.003802**	0.596083**	0.003802**	2.243055**
Number of Observations	186	84	186	186

Column 1 – Pooled EGLS Estimates on Pre-Tax Profits (£'000) with UK GDP Deflator.
Column 2 – Pooled EGLS Estimates on Natural Log of Pre-Tax Profits (£'000) with UK GDP Deflator.
Column 3 – Panel EGLS Estimates on Pre-Tax Profits (£'000) with UK GDP Deflator.
Column 4 – Panel EGLS Estimates on Natural Log of Pre-Tax Profits (£'000) with UK GDP Deflator.
t-statistics are displayed in parentheses.
* Statistically significant at the 5% level.
** Weighted statistics.

innovation – show statistical significance in influencing the transformed time series for all 10 firms.

5.3.2 Empirical assessment and findings at industry level

The empirical assessments at the industry level are conducted in a slightly different way from the estimating/evaluating procedures at the firm level. At the industry level, the values of four industrial performance ratios – sales growth ratio, pre-tax margins ratio, pre-tax return ratio, and return on capital ratio – as the measures of industrial growth are compiled for analysis. These four industrial performance ratios are the aggregate data of growth ratios at the industry level. Due to this common nature, it is not needed to estimate the intervention effect of the 1988 Act that endorses copyright expansion on each individual ratio under the joint models or first model of intervention, and ARIMA models as the analyses at the firm level. Instead, these four industrial performance ratios are ready for pooling and panelling. Accordingly, pooled and panel data analyses are proper choices for analysing the UK book publishing industry at the industry level.

Table 5.15 reports the pooled and panel estimating results of OLS, FGLS or EGLS, and the SUR FGLS or EGLS for these four industrial performance ratios as the aggregate data of growth ratios at the industry level under the constant coefficients model and the random coefficients model. All of these

Table 5.14 EGLS estimates of whole model for four book publishing firms (1976–2006)

Independent Variables	(1)	(2)	(3)	(4)	(5)	(6)
Competition	-9.28	-0.091*	16.837	-5.721	16.837	-5.721
	(-0.49)	(-3.03)	(0.3)	(-0.26)	(0.3)	(-0.26)
Concentration	-0.039	0.022	-34.053	-5.206	-34.053	-5.206
	(-0.008)	(1.38)	(-1.04)	(-0.72)	(-1.04)	(-0.72)
Technological Innovation	-13.78	1.578*	582.542	-87.399	582.542	-87.399
	(-0.07)	(2.85)	(0.97)	(-0.33)	(0.97)	(-0.33)
UK Copyright Act of 1988	92.337	-0.313	1355.129	233.909	1355.129	233.91
	(0.36)	(-0.43)	(1.23)	(0.64)	(1.23)	(0.64)
Durbin–Watson	2.11511**	0.968612**	1.047563**	2.108382**	1.047563**	2.108382**
R^2	0.442827**	0.856722**	0.216015**	0.397719**	0.216015**	0.397719**
Number of Observations	116	40	124	120	124	120

Column 1 – Pooled EGLS (Cross-section SUR) Estimates on Pre-Tax Profits (£'000) with UK GDP Deflator.
Column 2 – Pooled EGLS (Period random effects) Estimates on Natural Log of Pre-Tax Profits (£'000) with UK GDP Deflator.
Column 3 – Panel EGLS (Period random effects) Estimates on Pre-Tax Profits (£'000) with UK GDP Deflator.
Column 4 – Panel EGLS (Cross-section SUR) Estimates on Pre-Tax Profits (£'000) with UK GDP Deflator.
Column 5 – Panel EGLS (Period random effects) Estimates on Natural Log of Pre-Tax Profits (£'000) with UK GDP Deflator.
Column 6 – Panel EGLS (Cross-section SUR) Estimates on Natural Log of Pre-Tax Profits (£'000) with UK GDP Deflator.
t-statistics are displayed in parentheses.
* Statistically significant at the 5% level.
** Weighted statistics.

Table 5.15 Estimates of UK book publishing industry performance (1976–2006)

Independent Variables	(1)	(2)	(3)	(4)
Competition	-0.11	-0.11	-0.11	-0.11
	(-0.5)	(-0.52)	(-0.5)	(-0.52)
Concentration	-0.053	-0.053	-0.053	-0.053
	(-0.41)	(-0.42)	(-0.41)	(-0.42)
Technological Innovation	-1.784	-1.784	-1.784	-1.784
	(-0.75)	(-0.77)	(-0.75)	(-0.77)
Copyright Act of 1988	-3.155	-3.155	-3.155	-3.155
	(-0.72)	(-0.75)	(-0.72)	(-0.75)
Durbin–Watson	1.417003	1.698619**	1.417003	1.698619**
R²	0.020214	0.198430**	0.020214	0.198430**
Number of Observations	124	124	124	124

Column 1 – Pooled OLS Estimates on UK Book Publishing Industry Ratios (%).

Column 2 – Pooled EGLS Estimates on UK Book Publishing Industry Ratios (%).

Column 3 – Panel OLS Estimates on UK Book Publishing Industry Ratios (%).

Column 4 – Panel EGLS Estimates on UK Book Publishing Industry Ratios (%).

t-statistics are displayed in parentheses.

* Statistically significant at the 5% level.

** Weighted statistics.

estimating results indicate that the 1988 Act that endorses copyright expansion and all three forces of creative destruction (dynamic competition, concentrating industry structure, and technological innovation) as the four independent variables do not show any statistical significance in influencing the time series of these four industrial performance ratios as the aggregate data of growth ratios in the UK book publishing industry at the industry level.

5.3.3   Inference and analysis of empirical findings

Evidently, the results of empirical assessments at both the firm and industry levels are, to some extent, consistent with the predictions of the five hypotheses under Schumpeter's theoretical framework. Reviewing these consistencies and accordingly testing these hypotheses can infer the pattern of copyright-growth relation and the impact of creative destruction on the pattern. Corresponding analysis of the pattern and the impact is conducted as reviewing and testing proceed.

At the firm level, while only considering of the effect of copyright expansion under the Copyright, Designs and Patents Act 1988 without inspecting the impact of creative destruction in the model, the connection between the Act and the profit growth of these 15 UK book publishing firms over 30 years is weak. Hypothesis 1 is partially confirmed. This weak connection infers that copyright expansion may not play a significant role in promoting the growth of the UK book publishing industry. Of course, the growth data from 15 firms might not necessarily depict the whole picture of the UK book publishing industry. However, a complete data set of 15 main firms that have survived for 30 years can still show a fair picture of the industry. In addition, these firms are more likely to be the active forces behind copyright expansion under the 1988 Act. As opposed to expectations, these assessment results show that the effect of copyright expansion under the 1988 Act on the growth of the UK book publishing industry is very limited.

While the effect of copyright expansion on growth is minimal and has no control over the impact of creative destruction, controlling for this impact in the model creates different patterns of the copyright-growth relation with original and natural-log-transformed time series data of the 10 UK book publishing firms in two groups over 30 years. For the original data of the 10 firms, the connection between the 1988 Act and the profit growth of these 10 firms over 30 years is insubstantial. The forces of creative destruction make no difference to the pattern of copyright-growth relation. On the contrary, for the natural-log-transformed time series data of these 10 firms over 30 years, the copyright-growth connection appears notable. Hypothesis 2 is partially confirmed with the growth data of the 10 book publishing firms.

The notable connection between the 1988 Act and the profit growth of these 10 firms, controlling for the impact of creative destruction in the model, perhaps suggests that the impact of creative destruction on the copyright-growth relation in the UK book publishing industry over 30 years, at the firm level, should not be ignored. In particular, among the three forces of creative destruction (dynamic competition, concentrating industry structure, and technological innovation), two of them – dynamic competition and technological innovation – appear to be positively related to the profit growth of these 10 firms over 30 years under consideration. These positive relations may partially confirm Hypothesis 3 and Hypothesis 5, but leave Hypothesis 4 unverified.

At the industry level, the connection between the 1988 Act (that endorses copyright expansion) and the growth of the UK book publishing industry, while controlling for the impact of creative destruction in the model, is insignificant. This pattern of copyright-growth relation possibly implies that copyright expansion may not play a role in advancing the growth of the UK book publishing industry as a whole, under the pressure of creative destruction. Meanwhile, among the three forces of creative destruction, none of them appears either positively or negatively related to the aggregate growth of the UK book publishing industry at the industry level over 30 years. Therefore, Hypotheses 1 and 2 are sustained but Hypotheses 3, 4 and 5 are unverified. These testing outcomes infer that, at the industry level, copyright expansion and the forces of creative destruction exhibit no effects on the aggregate growth of the UK book publishing industry over 30 years.

Overall, all the results from empirical assessments indicate that the impact of the forces of creative destruction on the relation between copyright expansion and the growth of UK book publishing industry is moderate at the firm level and negligible at the industry level in the 30-year period from 1976 to 2006. These assessments infer that the UK book publishing industry, although the recipient of the extended copyright protection mainly under the 1988 Act, did not demonstrate the growth that was strongly related to the extended protection within that period. The relation (correlation or interaction) between copyright expansion and the growth of the UK book publishing industry was weak during that period. Copyright expansion did not appear to significantly respond to the pressure of creative destruction or to extensively promote industrial growth under these pressures in the period when a Schumpeterian growth cycle is supposed to be present.

5.3.4 Limitations of empirical assessment

The empirical assessment in this research makes an effort to overcome the limitations of Schumpeter's own empirical research into growth and development,[95] and to test the authenticity of Schumpeter's theory for explaining the copyright-growth relation in the dynamic process of creative destruction in the UK book publishing industry as a typical copyright industry and the cradle of modern copyright law.

The Box–Jenkins models and panel models as models of longitudinal analysis can be applied to assess the causal relationships between variables in experimental, quasi-experimental, or non-experimental research under certain theoretical frameworks.[96] However, in this book, the term 'causal relationship' has rarely appeared when assessing the relations between these variables under Schumpeter's framework. This intentional 'ignorance' certainly does not mean that a causal inference cannot be drawn from the empirical assessment on the impact of the forces of creative destruction on the relation between copyright expansion and the growth of the UK book publishing industry in this study. Rather, a joint venture of both the Box–Jenkins and panel models can strengthen an investigation into the causal relationships in this empirical research as a non-reactive, quasi-natural-experimental research.

To confirm a causal relationship between a pair of variables (typically, one is the independent variable as the cause and the other the dependent variable as the effect), it is necessary to ascertain: (1) the correlation between the pair, (2) time order of cause preceding effect in the pair, and (3) controlling for the other variables affecting the pair and blurring their correlation.[97] These three necessary conditions must be met for making a causal inference. Among these three conditions, the first one – the correlation – is the most significant. Only after a correlation can be verified against empirical data can the causal time order and controlling for the other variables for clarifying the causal relationship be put on the agenda for further inquiry. Otherwise, if no correlation is confirmed, there would be no need to proceed in making a causal inference.

In this book, the relation between copyright expansion and the growth of UK copyright industries is the primary concern for theoretical inquiry and empirical assessment. The correlation – an empirical indication of the relation – between copyright expansion and the growth of the UK book publishing industry, as discussed in Chapters 5.3.2 and 5.3.3, has been partially verified. This weak correlation might trigger some essential concerns on the statistical conclusion validity of the causal relationship in this study.

In experimental or quasi-experimental research, the main threats to statistical conclusion validity may come from low statistical power, assumption violations, reliability of measures, error-rate problem, reliability of treatment implementation, random irrelevances in experimental setting, and random heterogeneity of respondents.[98] Of course, not all of these threats would surface in each experimental or quasi-experimental research project. In this study, because it is designed as non-reactive, quasi-natural-experimental research (as indicated in Chapter 5.2.2), the data collected at both firm and industry levels for empirical assessment can be identified as passive observational data.[99] For a statistical inference from non-reactive, quasi-natural-experimental research assessing passive observational data, many research-subject-reaction-related threats – in which the reactions of individual persons as research subjects to the independent variable as an intervention factor in an experiment or quasi-experiment would affect the 'statistical conclusion' – might not appear. Reliability of treatment implementation, random irrelevances in experimental settings, and random heterogeneity of respondents are among these research-subject-reaction-related threats that may not surface to impinge on the statistical conclusion in this research.

Meanwhile, error-rate problems are not addressed in this research because ANOVA and multiple comparisons of mean differences where error-rate problems might rise are not the main techniques for the empirical assessment. Reliability of measures is an issue but not a critical one in this research. The measures of all variables – both the independent and dependent variables – in this study are adopted from existing researches and their reliabilities were already evaluated to different degrees. Assumption violations of statistical tests should be the essential concerns in any empirical quantitative studies. In this research, the longitudinal analysis under the Box–Jenkins models and panel models are designed to overcome the violations of crucial assumptions to a considerable extent. Thus, the threat of assumption violations to statistical conclusion validity in this research is minimal.

Perhaps, the critical threat to statistical conclusion validity in this study is low statistical power. The level of significance (α level) is set at .05 for all hypothesis tests in this research. However, because of the incompleteness of available data, the sample size is relatively small in this study. With a lower α level and small sample size, it will be more likely to confirm a null hypothesis of the copyright-growth relation (no correlation between copyright expansion and the growth of the UK book publishing industry) when this hypothesis of no correlation may indeed be invalid.[100] Accordingly, it is less possible to sufficiently address the issue of statistical power on account of the available data in the empirical assessment of this research.

Nevertheless, while statistical conclusion validity is not strong due to the threat of low statistical power, the existence of a correlation is more important than the level of the correlation for a causal inference. Thus, it is still plausible to proceed to infer a possible or potential causal relationship between copyright expansion under the 1988 Copyright, Designs and Patents Act and the growth of the UK book publishing industry.

5.4 Concluding remarks

Some progress has been made in managing historical or time series data in order to investigate the function of copyright law. This research explores both methodological aspects and theoretical positions. The analysis in this research focuses on the econometric estimates solely on the basis of the time series of the firms in the UK book publishing industry over a 30-year period (1976–2006). Meanwhile, statistical significance should be distinguished from practical significance whenever engaging in any econometric analyses. It is the researchers who determine the level of significance and a series of rules of estimation for pursuing a valid and reliable assessment.

However, no matter how valid and reliable an econometric estimate could be, the information that an estimate could provide is always a message of probability rather than certainty. A scientific researcher could tell the entrepreneurs of these

15 firms what the chances were that the 1988 Act could increase the annual profits for their firms. The chances may be low or high in terms of statistical significance. But for these or other entrepreneurs, especially for Schumpeterian entrepreneurs, any chance is large enough to pursue. Moreover, from a Schumpeterian perspective, 'the creation of imaginative new products, markets, production strategies and organisational structures is the key to the competitiveness and dynamism of an economy. Nurturing the capacity for generating innovative ideas, and for being individually and institutionally receptive to these ideas when created, therefore becomes central to the success of an economy or firm; and understanding the institutional requirements of different innovation strategies becomes correspondingly central to economic and policy analysis'.[101] An economic and legal analysis of UK copyright Acts should follow the same logic. This issue and other related issues are addressed in the following chapter.

Notes

1   J. Feather, *A History of British Publishing* 2nd edn, London: Routledge, 2006, pp. 216–217.
2   Feather, op. cit., 2006, p. 218.
3   Feather, op. cit., 2006, pp. 216–219. P. Curwen, *The UK Publishing Industry*, Oxford: Pergamon Press, 1981, pp. 53–59. M. Field, *The Publishing Industry – Growth Prospects Fade?* London: Comedia, 1986, pp. 42–43.
4   Curwen, op. cit., pp. 53–56.
5   Ibid, pp. 16–18.
6   ICC Information Group, *Business Ratio Report - Book Publishers* 4th edn, London, UK: ICC Business Publications Ltd, 1981, Sector Analysis Commentary, p. 1.
7   O. Shy, *The Economics of Network Industries*, Cambridge University Press, 2001, p. 5.
8   Curwen, op. cit., p. 17.
9   ICC Information Group, *Business Ratio Report - Book Publishers* 6th edn, 1983, Sector Analysis Commentary, p. 1.
10 Feather, op. cit., 2006, p. 217.
11 ICC Information Group, *Business Ratio Report - Book Publishers* 8th edn, 1985, Sector Analysis Commentary, p. 3.
12 W. Allan and P. Curwen, *Competition and Choice in the Publishing Industry*, London: Institute of Economic Affairs, 1991, pp. 22–23.
13 Allan and Curwen, op. cit., pp. 26–27.
14 W. Baumol, 'Contestable Markets: An Uprising in the Theory of Industry Structure', *The American Economic Review*, vol. 72(1), 1982, pp. 1–15. E. Zajac, *Political Economy of Fairness*, The MIT Press, 1995, pp. 32–33.
15 Allan and Curwen, 1991, p. 27.
16 R. Floud and D. McCloskey (eds), *The Economic History of Britain since 1700* Volume 3: 1939–1992 2nd edn, Cambridge University Press, 1994, pp. 184–185.
17 Feather, op. cit., 2006, p. 220.
18 ICC Information Group, *Business Ratio Report - Book Publishers* 13th edn, 1990, Sector Analysis Commentary, p. 10.
19 Ibid, p. 16.
20 Commission of the European Communities, Directorate-General for Enterprise, *Competitiveness of the European Union publishing Industries: Final Report*, Luxembourg: Office for Official Publications of the European Communities, 2000, p. 105.
21 Feather, op. cit., 2006, p. 220.

22 Feather, op. cit., 2006, p. 226. ICC Information Group, *Business Ratio Report - Book Publishers* 20th edn, 1997, Industry Comment, p. 365.

23 ICC Information Group, 20th edn, 1997, Industry Comment, p. 364.

24 Feather, op. cit., 2006, p. 212.

25 W. Baumol, *The Free-Market Innovation Machine: Analysing the Growth Miracle of Capitalism*, Princeton University Press, 2002, p. 11.

26 Curwen, op. cit., p. 22.

27 The concentration ratios in the late 1970s and early 1980s are estimated on account of the sales data of the top 10 companies in the two periods that were recorded in several issues of ICC Information Group's *Business Ratio Report - Book Publishers* from 3rd edn in 1980 to 11th edn in 1988.

28 Allan and Curwen, op. cit., p. 30.

29 Ibid, pp. 26–27.

30 E. Bellaigue, *British Book Publishing as a Business since the 1960s*, The British Library, 2004, p. 3.

31 ICC Information Group, *Business Ratio Report – Book Publishers* 4th edn, 1981, Sector Analysis Commentary, pp. 1–6.

32 Feather, op. cit., 2006, pp. 222–225.

33 ICC Information Group, *Business Ratio Report – Book Publishers* 13th edn, 1990, Sector Analysis Commentary, pp. 15–16.

34 Bellaigue, op. cit., pp. 3–5.

35 Considering that it functions constantly along with the three forces of creative destruction (technological innovation, dynamic competition, and concentrating industry structure), entrepreneurship is included in these forces as a non-independent constant rather than an independent variable.

36 See, for example, C. Fisk, 'Assembly Line Creativity: The Transformation of Innovation within Corporations, 1875–1930', Paper Presented at London School of Economics, 7 December 2006.

37 For a systematic treatment of 'non-reactive research', see R. Lee, *Unobtrusive Methods in Social Research*, Philadelphia, PA: Open University Press, 2000. For a succinct but sufficient treatment of the distinctions among experiment, quasi-experiment, and natural experiment, see W. Shadish, T. Cook and D. Campbell, *Experimental and Quasi-Experimental Designs for Generalized Causal Inference*, Boston, MA: Houghton Mifflin, 2002, pp. 12–18.

38 The complete information on Key Note Ltd is available at http://www.keynote.co.uk (accessed 10 June 2008).

39 This official introduction is available at http://www.keynote.co.uk/GlobalFrame.htm (accessed 10 June 2008).

40 The database is available under referring word 'ORBIS' in 'Data Library' at http://lsedatalibrary.blogspot.com/search/label/Orbis. This dataset can also be accessed at https://orbis.bvdep.com/version-201054/cgi/template.dll?checkathens=1&kick=1&product=13&user=LIUJ4%40lse.ac.uk&pw=wAxEKTWaQew3jos1xp%2bJ%2bQ%3d%3d (accessed 10 May 2010).

41 Table 2 in Appendix B provides the list of these 327 UK book publishing firms.

42 Table 1 in Appendix B presents the time series matrix of annual profits for the set of 15 UK book publishing firms.

43 For a discussion of the plausibility of using profitability as a workable measure of firm growth, see Y. Mazeh and M. Rogers, 'The Economic Significance and Extent of Copyright Cases: An Analysis of Large UK Firms', *Intellectual Property Quarterly*, 4th issue, 2006, pp. 404–420. M. Baker and B. Cunningham, 'Court Decisions and Equity Markets: Estimating the Value of Copyright Protection', *Journal of Law and Economics*, vol. 2, 2006, pp. 567–596.

44 M. Mazzucato, *Firm Size, Innovation, and Market Structure: the Evolution of Industry Concentration and Instability*, Cheltenham, UK: Edward Elgar, 2000.

L. Thomas, 'The Two Faces of Competition: Dynamic Resourcefulness and the Hypercompetitive Shift', *Organization Science*, vol. 7(3), 1996, pp. 221–242. W. Li and L. Xu, 'The Impact of Privatization and Competition in the Telecommunications Sector around the World', *Journal of Law and Economics*, vol. XLVII, 2004, pp. 395–430. P. Vaaler and G. McNamara, 'Are Technology-Intensive Industries More Dynamically Competitive? No and Yes'. Online. Available <http://www.business.uiuc.edu/Working_Papers/papers/06–0124. pdf.2006> (accessed 10 June 2008).

45 J. Blair, *Economic Concentration: Structure, Behavior and Public Policy*, New York: Harcourt Brace Jovanovich, 1972, pp. 3–24. P. Davis, 'The Effect of Local Competition on Admission Prices in the U.S. Motion Picture Exhibition Market', *Journal of Law and Economics*, vol. XLVIII, 2005, pp. 677–708.

46 Li and Xu, op. cit., p. 402.

47 Thomas, op. cit., pp. 221–242.

48 Mazzucato, op. cit., pp. 13–14.

49 Mazzucato, op. cit., p. 14.

50 Hymer and Pashigian's formula is presented in Formula 1 of Appendix A. See Mazzucato, op. cit., p. 14, 30.

51 Vaaler and McNamara, op. cit., pp. 5–11. Vaaler and McNamara's formula is presented in Formula 2 of Appendix A.

52 Vaaler and McNamara, op. cit., p. 23.

53 A. Carter, 'Production Workers, Metainvestment, and the Pace of Change', in Helmstadter and Perlman, op. cit., pp. 190–191.

54 According to the definition from *Business Ratio Report* 1981, 'sales' as gross turnover 'will include turnover from overseas activities, and will normally include exports and inter-group sales'. ICC Information Group, *Business Ratio Report – Book Publishers* 4th edn, 1981, DEF IB79.

55 Blair, op. cit., p. 7.

56 P. Vaaler, 'Creating and Destroying Shareholder Value across Borders', in L. McKnight, P. Vaaler and R. Katz (eds), *Creative Destruction: Business Survival Strategies in the Global Internet Economy*, The MIT Press, 2001, pp. 145–166.

57 M. Kamien, 'Market Structure and Innovation Revisited', *Japan and World Economy*, vol. 1, 1989, p. 336.

58 L. Béjar, 'The Evolutionary Approach to Technological Change: A Framework for Microeconomic Analysis', in K. Nielsen and B. Johnson (eds), *Institutions and Economic Change: New Perspectives on Markets, Firms and Technology*, Northampton, NA: Edward Elgar, 1998, p. 60. P. Krugman has also explored the concept of 'technology' 'in the broad sense'. See endnote 36 of Chapter I.

59 Feather, op. cit., 2006, pp. 215–219.

60 A. Murray and C. Scott, 'Controlling the New Media: Hybrid Responses to New Forms of Power', *The Modern Law Review*, vol. 65(4), 2002, 491–516.

61 C. Ostrom, *Time Series Analysis: Regression Techniques*, Newberry Park, CA: Sage Publications, 1990, p. 6. B. Bowerman, R. O'Connell and A. Koehler, *Forecasting, Time Series, and Regression: an Applied Approach* 4th edn, Belmont, CA: Thomson Brooks/Cole, 2005, pp. 21–24.

62 In essence, intervention models under the Box–Jenkins methods are the special cases of transfer function models. Some scholars emphasise the distinguishable aspects of these two models. G. Box, G. Jenkins and G. Reinsel, *Time Series Analysis: Forecasting and Control* 4th edn, New York: John Wiley, 2008, p. 529. D. McDowall, R. McCleary and E. Meidinger, *Interrupted Time Series Analysis*, Newbury Park, CA: Sage Publications, 1990, pp. 10–15.

63 W. Mendenhall, J. Reinmuth, R. Beaver and D. Duhan, *Statistics for Management and Economics* 5th edn, Boston, MA: Duxbury Press, 1986, p. 675.

64 For a brief treatment of the compositions in a typical time series model, see T. Cook and D. Campbell, *Quasi-Experimentation: Design & Analysis Issues for Field Settings*, Boston, MA: Houghton Mifflin, 1979, pp. 235–236.

65 McDowall, McCleary and Meidinger, op. cit., pp. 64–66. For a detailed discussion of the two fundamental components in a time series in general, and the two special components in a time series under the Box–Jenkins models in particular, see Formula 3 in Appendix A.

66 W. Dunn, *Public Policy Analysis: An Introduction* 2nd edn, Upper Saddle River, NJ: Prentice-Hall, 2004, p. 376. Cook and Campbell, op. cit., p. 207. McDowall, McCleary and Meidinger, op. cit., p. 5.

67 Ostrom, op. cit., p. 9. W. Mendenhall and T. Sincich, *A Second Course in Statistics: Regression Analysis* 5th edn, Upper Saddle River, NJ: Prentice Hall, 1996, p. 522.

68 For a brief but sufficient treatment of this topic, see L. Schroeder, D. Sjoquis and P. Stephan, *Understanding Regression Analysis: an Introductory Guide*, Newbury Park, CA: Sage Publications, 1986, pp. 72–75. For a detailed discussion, see Ostrom, op. cit., pp. 9–29.

69 Mendenhall and Sincich, op. cit., p. 518. McDowall, McCleary and Meidinger, op. cit., pp. 13–14.

70 McDowall, McCleary and Meidinger, op. cit., p. 14.

71 'Pooling is the simple combining of cross-sectional and time-series data without adjustment.' (M. Baddeley and D. Barrowclough, *Running Regressions: A Practical Guide to Quantitative Research in Economics, Finance and Development Studies*, p. 254.) This standard or regular regression analysis on the 'pool' or 'mixture' set of time series and cross-section data is also termed as a 'pooled time series analysis'. (L. Sayrs, *Pooled Time Series Analysis*, Newbury Park, CA: Sage, 1989, p. 7.) While time series data are the data collected at repeated points in time, cross-section data refer to the data 'gathered at essentially one point in time'. (Singleton, Straits and Straits, op. cit., p. 254.) As a regression analysis on the mixing data of time series and cross-section, a pooled time series analysis or a panel data analysis provides the main advantage of examining the changes or variations across various units of specific factors or variables in a study in both space and time. This is particularly true when the sample size is not so large and the time series is not so lengthy in a research, a pooled or panel regression analysis of time series is a suitable choice for data analysis. (Sayrs, op. cit., p. 7.) In this research, this pooled or panel regression analysis of time series is employed for conducting the initial Durbin–Watson test and related econometric estimation.

72 Sayrs, op. cit., pp. 10–11.

73 For a brief treatment of distributed lag models, see Ostrom, op. cit., pp. 58–60. The revising procedures of a distributed lag model are explained in Formula 4 of Appendix A.

74 Some textbooks or academic works suggest that 50 observations (time points) would be sufficient for a time series analysis. See, for example, Cook and Campbell, op. cit., p. 228. However, the rule of thumb for the number of observations is not rigid. For instance, The Institute for Forecasting Education (IFE), a US-based worldwide agency of consulting services on business forecasting, advises that 20 observations (time points) for annual data should be satisfactory for conducting a time series analysis under the ARIMA models of Box and Jenkins. See IFE, 'Ten Forecasting Tips & Caveats'. Online. Available <http://www.Forecastingeducation.com/tentips.htm> (accessed 16 October 2009). See also T. Mills, *Time Series Techniques for Economists*, Cambridge University Press, 1990, pp. 132–134.

75 Mills, op. cit., pp. 61–62.

76 McDowall, McCleary and Meidinger, op. cit., p. 16.
77 For a sufficient treatment of the three-stage process for constructing the time series models, see Cook and Campbell, op. cit., pp. 235–252. McDowall, McCleary and Meidinger, op. cit., pp. 15–64.
78 McDowall, McCleary and Meidinger, op. cit., p. 17.
79 McDowall, McCleary and Meidinger, op. cit., p. 86.
80 The Box–Ljung statistics can serve as a tentative technique for detecting a white noise process for a time series. Table 5.3 reports the results of the Box–Ljung test. As Table 5.3 shows, all of the Box–Ljung statistics, or 'Q statistics', for six firms – B T Batsford Ltd, Blackwell Science Ltd, David & Charles (Holdings) Plc, Hodder & Stoughton Holdings Ltd, Ladybird Books Ltd, and Mills & Boon Ltd – in the eighth column of the table are higher than .05 and thus are not significant at .05 levels. The insignificance of the Box–Ljung statistics implies that the noiseor stochastic (unexplained) component of these six publishing firms' time series data of annual profits in the period of 1976–2006 is random. In econometric terms, the time series raw data of these six firms are white noise process. A white noise process is one type of stationary process. On the contrary, all of the Box–Ljung statistics for the other nine publishing firms – A & C Black Plc, Constable & Co Ltd, Faber & Faber (Publishers) Ltd, Frederick Warne & Co Ltd, Ian Allan Ltd, Marshall Cavendish Ltd, Penguin Books Ltd, Thames & Hudson Ltd, and Wiley & Sons Ltd – in the eighth column of Table 5.3 are lower than .05 and thus are significant at .05 levels. The significance of the Box–Ljung statistics indicates that the noise or stochastic (unexplained) component of these nine firms' time series data of annual profits in the period of 1976–2006 is not random. In econometric terms, the time series raw data of these nine publishing firms are 'no white noise process'. See Cook and Campbell, op. cit., p. 244.
81 These models are formalised in Formula 6 of Appendix A.
82 Cook and Campbell, op. cit., p. 251.
83 This table is directly adopted from Mills, op. cit., p. 130.
84 Cook and Campbell, op. cit., p. 262.
85 Cook and Campbell, op. cit., p. 269.
86 For some details on the UK GDP Deflator, see http://www.measuringworth.org/ukgdp (accessed 6 January 2010). For a brief discussion of price adjustment of time series data, see *The Economist Numbers Guide: the Essentials of Business Numeracy* 5th edn, London: Profile Books, 2003, p. 90.
87 C. Hsiao, *Analysis of Panel Data* 2nd edn, Cambridge University Press, 2003, pp. 5–9.
88 Diverse terms are employed to describe these differences models. See, for instance, L. Mátyás and P. Sevestre (eds), *The Econometrics of Panel Data: A Handbook of the Theory with Applications* 2nd rev, The Netherlands: Kluwer Academic Publishers, 1996, pp. 26–32. See also Sayrs, op. cit., pp. 10–16. D. Asteriou and S. Hall, *Applied Econometrics: A Modern Approach using EViews and Microfit*, New York: Palgrave Macmillan, 2007, pp. 345–348.
89 Hsiao, op. cit., pp. 33–34. Sayrs, op. cit., p. 6.
90 B. Baltagi, *Econometric Analysis of Panel Data* 3rd edn, Chichester, UK: John Wiley, 2008, pp. 13–55.
91 Ibid, pp. 21–22.
92 B. Baltagi and B. Raj, 'A Survey of Recent Theoretical Developments in the Econometrics of Panel Data', *Empirical Econometrics*, vol. 17, 1992, 91.
93 Hsiao, op. cit., pp. 73–74.
94 For a formula of a pooled feasible or estimated generalised least squares (FGLS or EGLS) and SUR GLS estimations in an ARIMA model under the random coefficients (or random effects) model of panel data, see Formula 8 of Appendix A.

95 S. Kuznets, 'Schumpeter's Business Cycles', *The American Economic Review*, vol. 30(2), Part 1, 1940, 260. R. Swedberg, *Joseph Schumpeter: His Life and Work*, Cambridge, UK: Polity Press, 1991, Chapter VI.
96 Cook and Campbell, op. cit., pp. 1–36. S. Menard, *Longitudinal Research* 2nd edn, Thousand Oaks, CA: Sage Publications, 2002, pp. 15–23, p. 81, Note 2.
97 Ibid.
98 Cook and Campbell, op. cit., pp. 42–44.
99 For a concise treatment of passive observation, see Cook and Campbell, 1979, op. cit., pp. 295–298.
100 Ibid, p. 42.
101 R. Bronk, *The Romantic Economist: Imagination in Economics*, Cambridge University Press, 2009, p. 208.

6 Policy implications of empirical research

The empirical research in Chapter 5 demonstrates the impact of the forces of creative destruction on the copyright-growth relation in the UK book publishing industry at the firm and industry levels in the 30-year period from 1976 to 2006. Among the three forces of creative destruction, two of them in particular (dynamic competition and technological innovation) exhibited greater effects on the copyright-growth relation in the industry. However, overall, the relation revealed in the research appears more complex and less conclusive than copyright optimists/neoclassicists and pessimists/minimalists would expect. This complexity and uncertainty brings about some policy concerns, not only with copyright's cultural policy but also with copyright's entrepreneurship policy in the process of creative destruction. Reflecting upon the empirical findings of Chapter 5, this chapter addresses the policy implications of the research in tackling the complexity and uncertainty of the copyright-growth relation under a dynamic or Schumpeterian competition in the process of creative destruction.

6.1 Implications of copyright's cultural policy

Underproduction is the common problem of the copyright industries.[1] Indeed, as early as the 1930s, in his endeavour to examine copyright law from the perspective of economics, Sir Arnold Plant raised his concern about the problem of underproduction in creative production when there is no copyright protection.[2] In the 1960s, in revealing the Arrow dilemma of information production, Kenneth Arrow addressed the cohesive connection between underproduction and underutilisation in protecting intellectual property rights because information is both the input and output for producing creative or innovative works.[3] Considering the dual nature of information in creation or innovation, copyright's cultural policy should target both underproduction and underutilisation issues. Surely the essential concern of copyright protection is with incentive to create.[4] However, on the whole, as Landes and Posner point out, 'Striking the correct balance between access and incentives is the central problem in copyright law'.[5] The main concern of copyright's cultural policy should be on how to boost individual creativity[6] and advance industrial growth[7] in the copyright industries on account of the access–incentive relation under copyright law.

6.1.1 *Policy implications from the nature of information*

Does copyright expansion in duration serve the goal of copyright's cultural policy? The research in Chapter 5 indicates that this may not be the case. Only at the firm level is the growth effect somewhat noticeable, although even then not significant. At both the firm and industry levels, copyright expansion did not show a significant growth effect on the UK book publishing industry in the 30-year period under consideration. Thus, even in the best interests of British book publishers, and in consideration of financial impacts, extending the copyright term as endorsed in the EU Copyright Term Extension Directive 2009 may not be a sensible policy direction.

In the copyright industries in general, under the pressure of creative destruction, a Schumpeterian competition rather than perfect competition prevails in the process of creativity and growth. Because of information asymmetry and the dual nature of information as both input and output in creation or innovation, the Schumpeterian competition becomes more complex in the process of creation or innovation. When the British Phonographic Industry (BPI) contracted PricewaterhouseCoopers to evaluate the impact of copyright expansion on the record industry as a typical copyright industry, they solely focused on the expected legal change to the copyright term but accounted for the current structural and technological factors – such as level of competition, level of concentration, and stage of technological innovation – as the constants for anticipating the impacts of copyright expansion in the future decades. The future dynamic changes of competition, concentration, and technological innovation in the UK record industry were not modelled into their assessment framework. Accordingly, the impact evaluation may be partial and ambiguous. The empirical assessment in this book implies that, without considering the complexity and uncertainty of creativity and growth in the copyright industries in the information age, initiating a rigid policy of copyright expansion would be a biased option.

The most predictable policy bias of copyright expansion is probably the anti-commons orientation of the policy. Undeniably, the European tradition of respecting authors' natural rights has provoked the appeal for the long-term copyright on account of author's life, and the author-life-based long-term copyright became the yardstick of international copyright harmonisation.[8] In the meantime, demanding new exceptions to copyright protection in the digital age is also an area of international consensus under WIPO (World Intellectual Property Organization). The fair dealing or fair-use doctrine is a guiding principle for exploiting digital copyright.[9] Unfortunately, the policies of copyright expansion at the moment, such as the one endorsed in the EU Copyright Term Extension Directive 2009, can readily broaden the anti-commons space. In consequence, this type of expansion policy can only ameliorate digital protection of authors' natural rights as a minimum, but can annihilate digital fair dealing or fair use as a maximum in the information economy. Authors' natural rights can still survive in the public domain but fair dealing or fair use cannot survive in the digital age under a stiff, anti-commons-oriented policy of copyright expansion.

As a result of such a copyright policy, to avoid the possible liability or litigation due to some fair dealing or fair-use activities, authors or publishers as copyright users would take 'necessary' risk-averse measures in the process of creativity or industrial growth.[10] However, these necessary measures may not be necessary in the first place under a reasonable copyright regime. It is an anti-commons-oriented copyright policy that generates extra transaction costs for authors or publishers in the book publishing industry in particular, and in the copyright industries (the author–publisher distinction in a broad sense)[11] in general. One of the apparent consequences of higher transaction costs in the copyright industries is the lower incentive to use information as the input for fostering creativity and growth as the output of information. Accordingly, in the long run, underutilisation of information leads to underproduction of information. Ironically, the incentive for creativity and growth that copyright expansion is supposed to enhance is indeed diminished under a stiff policy of copyright expansion.

6.1.2 *Policy implications from the nature of copyright industries*

In the UK book publishing industry, the core of copyright consists of the reproduction and distribution rights under the Copyright, Designs and Patents Act 1988.[12] The research in Chapter 5 shows that the copyright expansion endorsed in the 1988 Act does not exert a significant financial impact on the reproduction and distribution of the industry in terms of financial ratios. The empirical results may imply that copyright expansion did not cope with the underutilisation/underproduction interaction in the reproduction and distribution of information as both input and output in the industry. This implication can be a reflection of copyright's cultural policy regarding copyright expansion on account of the general nature of all copyright industries.

Whether or not copyright expansion in duration can trigger incentive for creativity or growth of the copyright industries is indubitably controversial.[13] When considering the general nature of the copyright industries, the debate *per se* would be more complex and uncertain. The copyright industries are the information industries. The creative products are made of both information (idea) and expression. To advance the growth of the copyright industries, a variety of creativities including (but not limited to) artistic creativity, scientific creativity, and economic creativity are needed.[14] Within or among these creativities, the borderline between information (idea) and expression is vague. This vague distinction is a general feature of the copyright industries in terms of reproducing and distributing creative works. This feature may partially explain why, as Litman pointed out, although it is designed to protect expression rather than information, copyright has often been applied to protect information (idea).[15] As information technology – mainly digital technology – advances, the vague borderline and the twofold role of copyright will further intensify under the pressure of creative destruction in the copyright industries. Under this circumstance, copyright expansion will not only generate policy ambiguity but also stifle free expression and free contracts in these industries. As a result, the processes of creativity and growth will slow down.

Copyright's cultural policy should recognise that diverse and complex ideas (information) and expressions and their blurred distinction highlight more than ever the copyright industries in the information age. The special cost structure of creative works in these industries, 'a high ratio of fixed to marginal costs',[16] is to a greater extent accredited to the diversity and complexity of ideas (information) and expressions in the new economy under the pressure of creative destruction. The copyright of a creative good can be protected and the high fixed cost of the good can be recouped only if, among the attributes of the diverse and complex ideas (information) and expressions related to the good, 'protected attributes that are easy to recognize and define make it easier for observers to cognize the boundaries of the good'.[17] However, the information costs to 'make it easier for observers to cognize the boundaries of the good' are high.[18] Copyright expansion in the new digital environment would make the information costs much higher. In consequence, in light of the very nature of copyright industries in the digital age, copyright expansion is a costly policy option for coping with the Arrow dilemma for propping up creativity and innovation.

In the long run, underutilisation is a cradle of underproduction in the copyright industries. The *laissez faire* of the diversity of ideas and expressions (free speech) is more cost-effective than the 'defining' of the attributes of ideas and expressions (copyright) for boosting creativity and innovation. In particular, when the information costs (one type of transaction costs) for clarifying the vague borderline between information (idea) and expression are high, due to the market failure from high transaction costs, fair dealing or fair use as copyright's free speech should be a cost-efficient option[19] for copyright's cultural policy. In this regard, copyright's cultural policy may embrace a free contract approach under the Coase Theorem for a cost-efficient option. Under the Coase Theorem, as Section 3.2 discusses, an efficient output can result as long as equal owners of property rights can reach free contracts while transaction costs are minimal.[20] Thus, copyright law as 'a tax on readers'[21] like Pigovian tax may not be necessary for an efficient utilisation of creative works as long as copyright's free speech can be assured.

6.2 Implications of copyright's entrepreneurship policy

Copyright's cultural policy concerns the overall orientation of governmental actions on the creativity and growth in the copyright industries under certain institutional arrangements of copyright. In contrast, copyright's entrepreneurship policy involves a specific orientation of governmental actions on the firm and growth in the copyright industries under certain institutional arrangements of copyright.[22] In the process of creativity and growth of the copyright industries, publishers play a crucial role in mediating creators (authors or artists), consumers, and other producers.[23] For the copyright industries in particular, in the new information age, it is creative entrepreneurs who direct the firms and transform information into products.[24] In this regard, publishers and entrepreneurs for the copyright industries would be the same group of people.[25]

The empirical research on the copyright-growth relation under Schumpeter's theoretical framework in Chapter 5 indicates the nature and level of the relation under the forces of creative destruction in the UK book publishing industry as a typical copyright industry. To conduct such research on account of an econometric analysis, the level of significance and a series of rules of estimation have been determined for pursuing a valid and reliable assessment. However, no matter how robust an econometric estimate, the information that an estimate could provide is always a message of probability rather than certainty. Complexity and uncertainty are the indisputable rule in the process of creative destruction. How to take on the specific message of probability is a matter of practical reflection or moral and political judgment beyond a scientific concern for the rule of probability. Facing complexity and uncertainty in the copyright industries, creative entrepreneurs – especially these dynamic or Schumpeterian entrepreneurs – play a decisive and dynamic role in industrial growth under certain legal frameworks of intellectual property rights. Specifically, in Schumpeter's account, entrepreneurs serve as both opportunity adaptor and resource enhancer for economic development and industrial growth in a dynamic process of creative destruction. The function of legal rules is to smooth the course of opportunity adapting and resource enhancing. Entrepreneurs are creative and active players in applying legal rules for promoting the growth of the copyright industries in the process. Thus, copyright's entrepreneurship policy should shape a constructive structure and course in order to reinforce entrepreneurs' role in opportunity adapting and resource enhancing under certain copyright arrangements for the creativity and growth of the copyright industries.

6.2.1 Policy implications for adapting opportunities

Although the research in Chapter 5 indicates a moderate copyright-growth correlation under the forces of creative destruction at the firm level only, the impacts of copyright protection and expansion on the copyright industries will turn out to be more practically substantial when addressing entrepreneurs' role in adapting opportunities for growing the industries from a Schumpeterian perspective. However, under Schumpeter's framework, the duration expansion of protection for intellectual property rights does not make a significant difference for the dynamic or Schumpeterian entrepreneurs.

In Schumpeter's dynamic system, entrepreneurs are an active force that reforms the institutional framework and economic organisation for boosting economic performance. It is entrepreneurs who push through credit and banking systems for innovative advances that further economic development and industrial growth. From his realist innovation-oriented and time-framed dynamic analysis, Schumpeter identified three aspects of entrepreneurs' decisive and dynamic role in an economic system of dynamic disequilibrium. First, an entrepreneurial function is to reform or revolutionise the pattern of production through revealing or reorganising the possibility, environment, and resources for 'new things'. These new things include new products or methods. Second, entrepreneurial disequilibrating activity is 'responsible for cycles of prosperity and depression'.[26] Third, entrepreneurs will overcome resistance to, and create new conditions or opportunities for, 'getting things done'.[27] To be brief, in Schumpeter's terms, an entrepreneurial opportunity refers to 'a situation in which a person can create a new mean-ends framework for recombining resources that the entrepreneur believes will yield a profit'.[28] Dynamic entrepreneurs will not only respond to existing opportunities that legal rules warrant but also adapt the available opportunities and create new opportunities under the pressure of creative destruction.

What should copyright's entrepreneurship policy function be for these dynamic entrepreneurs' course of 'opportunity adapting'? On the one hand, the dynamic entrepreneurs are the driving forces behind the reforming of existing copyright policy under certain institutional frameworks (including legal rules). On the other hand, institutional frameworks (including legal rules) can serve as a leveller, as a protector, and as an enforcer for entrepreneurs,[29] as Chapter 4.3.1 addressed, and can provide a scheme for fostering entrepreneurial opportunity adaptations. Indeed, there are three sources for the dynamic entrepreneurial opportunities – technological changes, political and regulatory changes, and social and demographic changes.[30] Political and regulatory changes are institutional changes that nurture entrepreneurial opportunity adaptations.

In the copyright industries, copyright's entrepreneurship policy should provide a framework for entrepreneurs who adapt opportunities and tackle the issues in the copyright-growth relation under the pressure of creative destruction. Copyright expansion may not bestow such a framework for entrepreneurs due to the features of entrepreneurs' opportunities. In Schumpeter's system, entrepreneurial opportunities exhibit several features – disequilibrating, new information, innovativeness, creativity, and rareness.[31] Meanwhile, these micro-level features of entrepreneurial opportunities become more observable at the macro level. Schumpeter believed that, at the macro level, the capitalist process strikes its own institutional framework – 'property' and 'free contracting'.[32] Thus, entrepreneurial opportunities will be more uncertain and more tentative as the dynamic process of creative destruction proceeds. No matter how crucial institutions (including legal rules) are for economic performance, as neoinstitutionalism suggests, their importance for entrepreneurs will diminish under a dynamic or Schumpeterian competition. Entrepreneurs should explore their own ways of opportunity adaptation in light of the features of entrepreneurs' opportunities. In this environment, law is a constant rather than a variable.[33]

Under these circumstances, long-term copyright expansion will create an environment that pressures entrepreneurs to pursue short-term strategies for exploiting favourable opportunities in a process of creative destruction. The reason is straightforward – a long-term expansion of copyright as the measure of risk aversion and right accretion[34] would ensure various certainties for all entrepreneurs in the field. The promise of an opportunity from copyright expansion for all entrepreneurs would arouse a sense of insecurity for many of them in the short term because anyone could use the same legal force of copyright expansion to promote their competitive advantages through innovation and creativity.

It is interesting to realise that a long-term copyright expansion could stimulate some short-term strategic actions for some entrepreneurs and their firms due to their reasonable expectations of dynamic competition among themselves. In consequence, disequilibrating entrepreneurial opportunities become more diverse, and new information becomes more asymmetrical among entrepreneurs and their firms. The dynamics of firms' entry, exit, expansion, and concentration[35] will become more disequilibrating. Short-term and immediate static actions will become crucial for the survival and revival of entrepreneurs and their firms. Copyright's entrepreneurship policy should recognise the short-term effect of copyright expansion and encourage entrepreneurs' opportunity adaptations in the long run.

6.2.2 *Policy implications for resource enhancing*

The above analysis of entrepreneurs' roles in opportunity adapting for industrial growth furthers the understanding of the copyright-growth relation in the copyright industries. By the same token, considering that 'the empirical evidence supports the proposition that adequate capitalisation is important to the exploitation of entrepreneurial opportunities',[36] an examination of the entrepreneurs' role in both opportunity adapting and resource enhancing from a Schumpeterian perspective will inform a more comprehensible grasp of the copyright-growth relation, and entail a more inclusive implication to copyright's entrepreneurship policy in the copyright industries.

Copyright, from entrepreneurs' strategic view, is a property right in innovation.[37] This dual quality of copyright – right and innovation – indeed complicates copyright's entrepreneurship policy on the copyright-growth relation in the copyright industries. Under a dynamic or Schumpeterian competition, entrepreneurs and their firms should not only cope with the dynamic competition through adapting opportunities for a favourable market position, but should also be concerned with the innovative quality of their products. In this regard, copyright's entrepreneurship policy should consider the impact of copyright expansion on entrepreneurs' role in resource enhancing. In contemporary business studies in particular, research on 'the firm's resources as the foundation for firm strategy' has revived from 'old theories of profit and competition associated with the writings of David Ricardo, Joseph Schumpeter, and Edith Penrose'.[38] It will thus be more promising to investigate the entrepreneurs' role in resource enhancing in order to construct a full picture for revisiting copyright's entrepreneurship policy on the copyright-growth relation in the copyright industries.

As Chapters 2.3.2 and 3.1 indicated, Schumpeter emphasised the forces of creative destruction – technological innovation, dynamic competition, concentrating industry structure, and entrepreneurship – and stressed how these forces could function in various ways to enhance a firm's changing interests and industrial growth. Schumpeter's theory of profit and competition, and his view on entrepreneurs' role in resource enhancing, are developed from his realist innovation-oriented and time-framed dynamic analysis. In Schumpeter's account, entrepreneurial profit should be the core of his theory of profit and competition. Entrepreneurs and their firms pursue their above-marginal-cost profits through a dynamic or Schumpeterian competition – the 'competition which commands a decisive cost or quality advantage and which strikes not at the margins of the profits and the outputs of the existing firms but at their foundations and their very lives',[39] according to Schumpeter's definition. 'Their foundations and their very lives' entail the firms' internal resources or instinctive capacities.

In the copyright industries, both entrepreneurial strategic actions on account of firms' resources or capacities and legal protection are crucial for a firm's surviving and thriving in a process of creative destruction because of copyright's dual quality of right and innovation. In Schumpeter's system, as indicated in Chapter 2.1, the creative destruction of institutional arrangements (including legal or regulatory rules) is part of the whole process of creative destruction. In a methodological sense, Schumpeter framed the issues of a firm's resources, business strategy, and legal or regulatory policy in terms of their long-run and short-run impacts on economic development and industrial growth in a dynamic process of creative destruction.[40] To explore these issues in the process, according to Schumpeter, 'traditional theory' and 'old propositions about perfect competition' and free trade 'cannot be held with the old confidence'.[41] Instead, Schumpeter advised that 'dynamic analysis' as 'the analysis of sequences in time'[42] is needed to approach these issues. Dynamic analysis is, in fact, another term of Schumpeter's realist innovation-oriented and time-framed dynamic analysis. Under this approach, legal or regulatory policy as an institutional arrangement would not serve well as a protector of (property) rights in the long term because innovative forces will make some (property) rights out of date. In the short term, legal protection may solve some problems in the dynamic process. However, entrepreneurs should always exploit the quality of innovation for enhancing firms' resources or capacities over the long term. The method of resource enhancing can shed new light on the implication of copyright's entrepreneurship policy to the growth of copyright industries.

6.3 Concluding remarks

Schumpeter was both a 'thesis' and an 'antithesis' of capitalism. For Schumpeter, capitalism's development is irreversible but its destiny is finite. Anthony Giddens agreed with Schumpeter and consented that 'capitalism does thrive upon innovation and the capacity to leave the past behind'.[43] Meanwhile, Giddens also recognised capitalism's 'constructive qualities' but with the need of regulation.[44] Schumpeter's realist innovation-oriented and time-framed dynamic analysis as an epistemological approach paves the way to approaching the growth issues of copyright industries under a dynamic or Schumpeterian competition. Under Schumpeter's dynamic model, copyright law should be the key regulation for sustaining and smoothing capitalism's constructive qualities of growth in the information industries in general, and copyright industries in particular, under dynamic competition in the long-term process of creative destruction.

Notes

1 Bernard Casey, Rachael Dunlop and Sara Selwood, *Culture as commodity? The Economics of the Arts and Built Heritage in the UK* (London: Policy Studies Institute, 1996), pp. 5–6.
2 A. Plant, 'The Economic Aspects of Copyright in Books', *Economica*, May 1934, 177.
3 K. Arrow, 'Economic Welfare and the Allocation of Resources for Invention', in *The Rate and Direction of Inventive Activity: Economic and Social Factors*, Princeton University Press, 1962, pp. 616–619.
4 P. Heald, 'Property Rights and the Efficient Exploitation of Copyrighted Works: An Empirical Analysis of Public Domain and Copyrighted Fiction Bestsellers', *Minnesota Law Review*, vol. 92, 2008, p. 1031.
5 W. Landes and R. Posner, 'An Economic Analysis of Copyright Law', *Journal of Legal Studies*, vol. 18, 1989, 326.
6 R. Towse, 'Copyright Policy, Cultural Policy and Support for Artists', in W. Gordon and R. Watt (eds), *The Economics of Copyright: Developments in Research and Analysis*, Cheltenham, UK: Edward Elgar, 2003, p. 76.
7 C. Handke, 'Copyright and Digital Copying Technology', in C. Eisenberg, R. Gerlach and C. Handke (eds), *Cultural Industries: The British Experience in International Perspective*, Berlin: Centre for British Studies at Humboldt University, 2006, pp. 71–72.
8 N. Netanel, 'Copyright and a Democratic Civil Society', *The Yale Law Journal*, vol. 106, 1996, 366–367.
9 P. Ganley, 'Digital Copyright and New Creative Dynamics', *International Journal of Law and Information Technology*, vol. 12(3), 2004, 312–313.
10 J. Gibson, 'Risk Aversion and Rights Accretion in Intellectual Property Law', *The Yale Law Journal*, vol. 116, 2007, 900.

11 R. Towse, *Creativity, Incentive and Reward: an Economic Analysis of Copyright and Culture in the Information Age*, Cheltenham, UK: Edward Elgar, 2001, p. 191.

12 H. Jones and C. Benson, *Publishing Law* 3rd edn, London: Routledge, 2006, p. 13.

13 S. Martin, 'The Mythology of the Public Domain: Exploring the Myths Behind Attacks on the Duration of Copyright Protection', *Loyola of Los Angeles Law Review*, vol. 36, 2002, 272–274.

14 UNCTAD and UNDP, *The Creative Economy Report 2008*, United Nations, 2008, pp. 9–10.

15 J. Litman, 'Copyright and Information Policy', *Law and Contemporary Problems*, vol. 55(2), 1992, 185.

16 W. Landes and R. Posner, *The Economic Structure of Intellectual Property Law*, Harvard University Press, 2003, p. 23.

17 C. Long, 'Information Costs in Patent and Copyright', *Virginia Law Review*, vol. 90(2), 2004, 477.

18 Ibid, 508–516.

19 Towse, op. cit., 2001, pp. 13–14.

20 For a brief discussion of applying the Coase Theorem to economic analysis of copyright, see R. Towse, 'Copyright and Economics', in S. Frith and L. Marshall (eds), *Music and Copyright* 2nd edn, UK: Edinburgh University Press, 2004, pp. 61–62.

21 Quoted in S. Breyer, 'The Uneasy Case for Copyright: A Study of Copyright in Books, Photocopies, and Computer Programs', *Harvard Law Review*, vol. 84(2), 1970, 281.

22 For a general treatment of entrepreneurship policy, see A. Lundström and L. Stevenson, *Entrepreneurship Policy: Theory and Practice*, Springer, 2010.

23 Ganley, op. cit., pp. 299–300.

24 UNCTAD and UNDP, op. cit., pp. 16–17.

25 Towse, op. cit., 2001, p. 195.

26 M. Ricketts, *Economics of Business Enterprise: an Introduction to Economic Organization and the Theory of the Firm* 3rd edn, Edward Elgar, 2002, p. 66.

27 J. Schumpeter, *Capitalism, Socialism and Democracy* 3rd edn, New York: Harper & Row, 1976[1942], p. 132.

28 S. Shane, *A General Theory of Entrepreneurship: the Individual-Opportunity Nexus*, Cheltenham, UK: Edward Elgar, 2003, p. 18.

29 V. Mayer-Schönberger, 'Schumpeterian Law: Rethinking the Role of Law in Fostering Entrepreneurship'. Online. Available <http://works.bepress.com/cgi/viewcontent.cgi?article=1001&context=viktor_mayer_schoenberger> (accessed on 14 March 2008), pp. 6–15.

30 Shane, op. cit., pp. 20–23.

31 Ibid, pp. 20–21.

32 Schumpeter, op. cit., 1976[1942], p. 141.

33 Andrew Murray, my doctorial supervisor at London School of Economics, made his comment that 'law is a constant rather than a variable' during a conversation with the author of this book on 17 November 2009.

34 J. Gibson, 'Risk Aversion and Rights Accretion in Intellectual Property Law', *The Yale Law Journal*, vol. 116, 2007, 886–933.

35 Y. Lee, *Schumpeterian Dynamics and Metropolitan-Scale Productivity*, Hampshire, UK: Ashgate, 2003, p. 11.

36 Shane, op. cit., p. 162.

37 R. Grant, *Contemporary Strategy Analysis: Concepts, Techniques, Applications* 4th edn, Malden, MA: Blackwell Publishers, 2002, p. 336.

38 R. Grant, 'The Resource-Based Theory of Competitive Advantage: Implications for Strategy Formulation', in H. Costin (ed), *Readings in Strategy and Strategic Planning*, Orlando, FL: Harcourt Brace, 1998, pp. 291–309.

39 Schumpeter, op. cit., 1976[1942], p. 84.
40 Ibid, pp. 87–106.
41 Ibid, p. 103.
42 Ibid.
43 W. Hutton, 'Anthony Giddens and Will Hutton in Conversation', in W. Hutton and A. Giddens (eds), *Global Capitalism*, New York: The New Press, 2000, p. 10.
44 Ibid, pp. 10–11.

7 Conclusions

'Does copyright expansion stimulate or restrict the growth of copyright industries as information technology advances?' In theory, the relation between copyright expansion and the growth of UK copyright industries as the primary concern of this book can be viewed under diverse perspectives. However, in reality, for some copyright optimists or neoclassicists, creators or holders, and their supporters in legislative bodies, this relation is not an issue worth discussing in the first place. In their minds, a positive relation between copyright expansion and the growth of copyright industries is a rational assumption. In the UK, the duration of copyright protection has been extended four times since the Statute of Anne in 1710 from just 28 years (maximum) to life plus 70 years, potentially a protected period in excess of 140 years (a potential five-fold increase).

The reality of copyright expansion complicates the investigation into its role in growing the copyright industries as the focal point of the book. After the Introduction in Chapter 1, Chapter 2 explores the historical background and legal–economic contexts of the relation between copyright expansion and the growth of copyright industries as the primary concern of this book from a Schumpeterian perspective. What was explored in Chapter 2 lays the foundation for further discussion of the primary concern and focal point of this book, and for further articulation of the central theme of the book – the copyright-growth relation in the UK copyright industries under the forces of creative destruction.

An exploration of the historical background and legal–economic contexts of the copyright-growth relation indeed raises concerns about the interactions between entrepreneurs' pursuit of short-term profit and long-term growth promotion, between entrepreneurs' private benefit and public responsibility, and between entrepreneurs' innovation and imitation in the UK copyright industries. Creativity and innovation at both the firm and industry levels need not only be an expectation or incentive from protection of property but also an encouragement from protection of freedom. The economic justifications of copyright emphasise the aspects of expectation or incentive concerning the copyright-growth relation from protection of property rather than from protection of freedom. In contrast, Lessig's balance justification of copyright (as discussed in Chapter 3) is a theoretical endeavour to delineate the interaction between copyright, creativity, innovation, growth, incentive, competition, and freedom under diverse institutions – from legal institutions to market institutions – in the information age.

In Lessig's views, a key interaction in the US copyright industries is the relationship between the West Coast Code and East Coast Code in the digital age. In his account, the West Coast Code refers to 'the instructions imbedded in the software and hardware that make cyberspace work',[1] and which are created by the forces of innovation and creativity across the US western coast areas where Silicon Valley is the hub. On the contrary, the East Coast Code symbolises the legislations or regulations of the status quo that direct the orientation of Washington DC. To encourage creativity and innovation, both codes should maintain a checking and balancing interaction. However, according to Lessig, as the West Coast Code (in creativity and innovation) becomes commercial, both codes gradually converge and the checking and balancing interaction cannot be sustained.[2] When all codes become part of the law for protecting property rights in creativity and innovation, the 'old' creativity and innovation would override the 'new' creativity and innovation.[3] As a result, creativity and innovation vanish. In other words, creativity and innovation would not be achieved if the balance between the West and East Coast Codes cannot be struck.

In spite of some substantial differences among optimists/neoclassicists and pessimists/minimalists on copyright, as explored in Chapter 2, both perspectives do share the same concern – how the property in creativity and innovation can expand and, accordingly, how industry and economy can grow under certain institutions of property rights in innovation and creativity. Meanwhile, to a different extent, neither perspective endorses the absolute property rights in creativity and innovation. However, facing the harsh reality of copyright expansion, both groups do offer some rhetorical rationales for addressing certain concerns but fail to provide a realistic framework for exploring and explaining many issues surrounding the relation between copyright expansion and the growth of copyright industries.

In the real world, even if copyright expansion has already become a reality, the linear assumption of the copyright-growth relation behind copyright expansion is still too simple to comprehend the complex reality in the copyright industries. Moreover, it is also too ideological to achieve the goal of copyright protection. The mixed and inconclusive results of empirical assessment in Chapter 5 signify that this is the case with the UK book publishing industry in which legal change is, at most, a necessary condition for a real-world change. An attempt to enhance efficiency through a seemingly rational law would perhaps result in higher inefficiency and lower cost-effectiveness in economic development and industrial growth. As Joan Robinson, an eminent Cambridge economist, pointed out, 'It is impossible to understand the economic system in which we are living if we try to interpret it as a rational scheme. It has to be understood as an awkward phase in a continuing process of historic development'.[4] The growth of the UK book publishing industry is no exception.

As copyright expansion has become a seemingly rational but unwinnable game, Schumpeter's theoretical framework can offer a powerful perspective for exploring and explaining the relation between copyright expansion and industrial growth under the forces of creative destruction in the UK copyright industries. Chapters 2 and 4 examine Schumpeter's theoretical framework of creative destruction and its distinct applicability to investigating the dynamic copyright-growth interaction. Under Schumpeter's framework, the copyright-growth relation not only cannot be linearly assumed but also cannot be non-linearly perceived using a simple model. Rather, this issue should be further reframed under the following question: 'What is the relation between copyright expansion and the growth of copyright industries in general, and in the digital age in particular?' and 'What forces could affect the relation between copyright expansion and the growth of copyright industries?' Then, the complexity and dynamics of the copyright-growth relation can be assessed against empirical evidences in the larger context of creative destruction.

Schumpeter was way ahead of his time and scrutinised the complex and dynamic changes and interactions within the modern economic system under his innovative research method of non-mainstream economics. He conveyed the fundamental but brilliant message that the success of an economic system depended on creativity, innovation, evolution, and competition. The forces in the process of creative destruction are the moving forces behind the progress of industrial evolution and the advances in living standards.[5] In the process of creative destruction, entrepreneurs play a key role in prolonging industrial evolution and boosting living standards by throwing away 'old ways' and pursuing 'new things'. The Internet bubble in the recent decade in which old-fashioned models of economic structure vanished abruptly and new models of business operation emerged just as abruptly is shocking evidence of Schumpeter's theory of creative destruction.[6]

The forces of creative destruction, as indicated in Chapter 2, did creep into the UK book publishing industry for decades, even centuries. In the period from 1976 to 2006, as Chapter 5.2.2 shows, the business ratio data of 327 UK book publishing firms were recorded in the database of Key Note Inc. Among them, only 15 UK book publishing firms maintained their full records for that 30-year period. Certainly, some firms that survived the entire period might not have retained their full business data for the period, or Key Note Inc might have failed to collect the full business data from those firms that did indeed survive in that period. Nevertheless, considering the reliability of Key Note Inc as a leading UK data firm in compiling and preserving business data, it is safe to say that the 15 book publishing firms discussed in Chapter 5 survived the period from 1976 to 2006. Obviously, the overall survival rate in the UK book publishing industry was considerably lower during that 30-year period. Meanwhile, the empirical assessment and analysis in Chapter 5 estimate and evaluate the pattern and level of the interactions between the law and other complex and dynamic factors, particularly the forces of creative destruction, in the UK book publishing industry during the three decades. This assessment and analysis suggest that the impacts of creative destruction on the copyright-growth relations in the UK book publishing industry as a typical copyright industry were observable to differing extents during that period. Thus, 'creative destruction' was a real trend in the book publishing field in that period. As information technology advances and innovations proceed, the forces of creative destruction will continue to affect the growth of the UK copyright industries in general, and the UK book publishing industry in particular, under certain legal institutions.

In brief, under the pressure of creative destruction, for any types of entrepreneurs, seeking legal change is proposed to strengthen legal certainty.[7] Once legal change, such as copyright expansion, is enacted, ensuring certainty is always a fundamental requirement of a legal institution. For rational entrepreneurs in the copyright industries, the cost of copyright expansion as a legal change should be a minimum consideration in the first place, even for their own interests. No matter how many times copyright expansion proceeds and how long the term of copyright expansion reaches, the expansion can never catch up with the changes in the copyright industries under the forces of creative destruction in the information age.

In contrast, for Schumpeterian entrepreneurs in these industries, their mission is not to seek certainty under a legal institution from a legal change, such as copyright expansion, which has uncertain results. Rather, they need a strategic scheme of law and economics for coping with the dynamic changes in these industries and for balancing the complex interactions between short-term profit pursuit and long-term growth promotion, between private benefit and public responsibility, and between innovation and imitation under the forces of creative destruction. As a design of strategy formulation[8] on account of the economic impacts of legal actions or institutions on economic growth or industrial growth, a strategic scheme of law and economics in the copyright industries in the information age should be a realistic design of strategy formulation for the purpose of innovation and creativity in consideration of diverse legal and economic factors. In this regard, based on the assessment of the copyright-growth relation under the forces of creative destruction in Chapter 5, a realistic strategic scheme of law and economics should encompass the four key issues of policy implications concerning the copyright-growth interaction – complexity, competition, efficiency, and entrepreneurship – as explored in Chapter 3.2.4.

On the whole, as Chapter 2.1 indicates, the growth of the UK book publishing industry as a key sector of UK copyright industries has undergone a process of creative destruction for decades, or even centuries. Meanwhile, the copyright-growth relation under the forces of creative destruction, as shown in Chapter 3, has become more complex than expected for the 30-year period under consideration. As information technology advances, globalisation increases and competition becomes more open and cut-throat, the players in all UK copyright industries shall face more complex and dynamic challenges under the pressure of creative destruction in the future. This harsh reality will compel all players to further enhance entrepreneurship, strengthen competitiveness, boost innovation, and encourage creativity to promote growth and development. The copyright regime is not just a legal empire. Rather, it should be a creative institutional arrangement under which only Schumpeterian entrepreneurs who pursue innovation and creativity within a realistic and visionary strategic scheme of law and economics can survive and thrive in the future. In the long-term process of creative destruction, Schumpeterian entrepreneurs aggressively promote the growth of properties in creativity and fair play in the game of property rights in creativity.

Notes

1 L. Lessig, *Code and Other Laws of Cyberspace*, New York: Basic Books, 1999, p. 53.
2 Ibid, pp. 53–60.
3 See also W. Fisher, *Promises to Keep: Technology, Law, and the Future of Entertainment*, Stanford, CA: Stanford Law and Politics, 2004, Chapter III.
4 J. Robinson, *Economics: an Awkward Corner*, London: Allen & Unwin, 1966, p. 11.
5 P. Ormerod, *Why Most Things Fail: Evolution, Extinction and Economics*, London: Faber and Faber, 2005, Chapter XIV.
6 S. Garelli, *Top Class Competitors: How Nations, Firms and Individuals Succeed in the New World of Competitiveness*, Chichester, UK: John Wiley, 2006, Chapter II, Section 2.1.5.
7 P. Goldstein, *Intellectual Property: the Tough New Realities That Could Make or Break Your Business*, New York: Portfolio, 2007, p. 36.
8 For a brief introduction to the process of strategy formulation, see Grant, op. cit., 2002, pp. 4–33. For a systematic discussion of the strategic roles of intellectual properties in growing firms and industries, see P. Sullivan, *Value-Driven Intellectual Capital: How to Convert Intangible Corporate Assets into Market Value*, New York: John Wiley, 2000.

Appendices

Appendix A. Formulas

Formula 1: Instability index

Hymer and Pashigian's formula of instability index for measuring the level of competition is:[1]

$$I = \sum_{i=1}^{n} \left| s_{it} - s_{i,t-1} \right| \tag{1.1}$$

where
I — instability index
S_{it} — the market share of a specific firm ('firm i') at time t
$S_{i,t-1}$ — the market share of the same firm ('firm i') at a previous time $(_{i,t-1})$
n — refers to the number of firms for all firms in a group or an industrial sector.

Formula 2: Dynamism score

Vaaler and McNamara's formula of dynamism score for measuring the level of competition should be:[2]

$$DS = \frac{se}{\overline{Y}_t} \tag{2.1}$$

where
DS — the dynamism score
S_e — the standard error
$\overline{Y}_t$ — the average value (the mean value) of industry sales in the year t of four five-year periods.

Formula 3: Structure of intervention model of time series

Figure 5.2 shows the compositions of a typical time series model. To investigate the effects of the deterministic component, a sufficient scrutiny of the noise or stochastic component, particularly its systematic part, is necessary. One of the fundamental roles of a time series model is to inspect the noise or stochastic component, especially serial correlation or autocorrelation as the core element of its systematic part, in order to clarify the deterministic ('explained') component.

The formula for a general intervention model will be:[3]

$$Y_t = I_t + N_t \qquad\qquad (3.1)$$

where
Y_t — the tth observation of the time series
I_t — the intervention or deterministic component of the model
N_t — the noise or stochastic component of the model.

However, in this research, as Figure 5.1 illustrates, the four variables – the Copyright, Designs and Patents Act 1988 that endorses copyright expansion and all three forces of creative destruction (dynamic competition, concentrating industry structure, and technological innovation) – have been identified as the independent or explanatory variables and, following the rationale of time series analysis, as the deterministic component under the time series model. Among the four independent or explanatory variables, only technological innovation and copyright expansion are coded as the intervention variables. The other two variables (dynamic competition and concentrating industry structure) are still identified as part of the deterministic component of the model but will not be assessed as the intervention variables. Thus, for the research purposes of this book, the above formula for a general intervention model of time series can be revised and the intervention component (technological innovation and copyright expansion) is regarded as one part of the deterministic component of the model. Another part of the deterministic component of the model is the non-intervention component (dynamic competition and concentrating industry structure).

As illustrated in Figure 5.2, in a typical time series model, the noise or stochastic component of the model (N_t), or the serial error term of the time series, consists of two parts – systematic part and random part. s_t and a_t can be used to symbolise the two parts respectively. The random part is also termed as the unsystematic part, the error term of the serial error term, white noise, or random shock.[4] Accordingly, it is assumed that $N_t = s_t + a_t$ in the model.

In a general ARIMA model, the time series Y_t is stationary if the following conditions are held:[5]

1 $E(Y_t)$ = constant for all t
2 *Variance* (Y_t) = constant for all t
3 *Covariance* (Y_t, Y_{t+k}) = constant for all t and $k \neq 0$.

In a specific intervention model under an ARIMA model, for an inferential purpose, the following basic assumptions of the random shock or white noise should be held:[6]

1   Zero mean: $E(a_t) = 0$
2   Constant variance: $V(a_t) = \sigma^2$
3   No autocorrelation (independent shocks): covariance $(a_t a_{t+k}) = 0$
4   Normality, $a_t \sim N(0, \sigma^2)$.

Meanwhile, to detect the existence and/or the pattern of autocorrelation or serial correlation in the time series data of this research, a pooled time series or panel matrix is constructed as Table 1 of Appendix B indicates. In this matrix, the four independent variables – dynamic competition, concentrating industry structure, technological innovation, and copyright expansion are denoted as $\beta_1 X_{it}$, $\beta_2 X_{it}$, $\beta_3 X_{it}$, and $\beta_4 X_{it}$ respectively. Y_{it} represents the dependent or response variable as 'pre-tax profits (£'000 with natural logarithmic data transformation and 'mean replace of missing data' weighted by UK GDP Deflator) of the 15 firms over 30 years'. If using C_t to symbolise the non-intervention deterministic component (dynamic competition and concentrating industry structure) or the control variables (still the independent or explanatory variables) for distinguishing the effects of technological innovation and copyright expansion, the following formula can be derived:

$$Y_{it} = C_t + I_t + N_t \tag{3.2}$$

$$C_t = \beta_1 X_{it} + \beta_2 X_{it} + \beta_3 X_{it}, \tag{3.3}$$

$$I_t = \beta_4 X_{it} \tag{3.4}$$

In the matrix, n_{it} denotes the time serial and cross-sectional error term, the noise or stochastic component, of the model. It is assumed that $N_t = n_{it}$ and $n_{it} = s_{it} + a_{it}$. Accordingly, the formula for a specific intervention model for this research will be:

$$Y_{it} = \beta_1 X_{it} + \beta_2 X_{it} + \beta_3 X_{it} + \beta_4 X_{it} + n_{it} \tag{3.5}$$

Of course, for an inferential purpose, a pooled time series or panel model should hold the basic assumptions of a standard linear regression model:[7]

1   Linearity: $L(Y_{it}\ \&\ X_{it})$
2   Non-stochastic X: $E(n_{it} X_{it}) = 0$
3   Zero mean: $E(n_{it}) = 0$
4   Constant variance: $V(n_{it}) = \sigma^2$
5   No autocorrelation: $E(n_{it} n_{jt}) = 0$
6   Normality: $U_{it} \sim N(0, \sigma^2)$.

Formula 4: A revised distributed lag model

With no consideration of lagged effects of the independent or explanatory variables in the standard regression model for the panel data, or pooled time series data, in Table 1 of Appendix B, the formula will be:

$$Y_{it} = \beta_k X_{it} + n_{it} \tag{4.1}$$

where

Y — the dependent or response variable as pre-tax profits (£'000 with natural logarithmic data transformation and mean replace of missing data weighted by UK GDP Deflator)

X — the independent or explanatory variables (dynamic competition measured by the level of competition $\beta_1 X_{it}$, concentrating industry structure measured by the level of industrial concentration $\beta_2 X_{it}$, technological innovation measured by the stage of technological innovation $\beta_3 X_{it}$, and copyright expansion $\beta_4 X_{it}$ measured by the 1988 Copyright, Designs and Patents Act)

β — the regression coefficients in the UK book publishing industry as the population in this research, k denotes the number of the independent or explanatory variables $(1 \ldots K)$

i — the number of firms as cross-sections $(1 \ldots N)$

t — the number of time points $(1 \ldots T)$ as time series

n_{it} — the time serial and cross-sectional error term.

To list all independent variables, the formula will be:

$$Y_{it} = \beta_1 X_{it} + \beta_2 X_{it} + \beta_3 X_{it} + \beta_4 X_{it} + n_{it} \tag{4.2}$$

If applying a distributed lag model with one year lag, the formula will be:[8]

$$Y_{it} = \beta_1 X_{it} + \beta_2 X_{it} + \beta_3 X_{it} + \beta_4 X_{it} + \beta_1 X_{it-1} + \beta_2 X_{it-1} + \beta_3 X_{it-1} + \beta_4 X_{it-1} + n_{it} \tag{4.3}$$

In this research, on account of the operational model, the lagged effects of the level of competition $\beta_1 X_{it-1}$ and the level of industrial concentration $\beta_2 X_{it-1}$ are solely accounted. The contemporaneous effects of these two independent variables ($\beta_1 X_{it}$ and $\beta_2 X_{it}$) are omitted from the model because it is assumed that the level of competition and the level of industrial concentration in a specific year would have no impact on the pre-tax profits of the firms in the UK book publishing industry in the same year. Thus, a revised distributed lag model for this study will be:

$$Y_{it} = \beta_1 X_{it-1} + \beta_2 X_{it-1} + \beta_3 X_{it} + \beta_4 X_{it} + n_{it} \tag{4.4}$$

Table 5.2 presents the Eviews printout of a standard or regular regression analysis of the panel, or pooled time series, data over 30 years under the above formula.

Formula 5: Autocorrelation and partial autocorrelation functions (ACFs & PACFs)

In general, a stochastic process of any time series has a unique autocorrelation function (ACF) and partial autocorrelation function (PACF).[9] In particular, a sample of observed time series is circa a special realisation of a stochastic process.[10] The formula for an ACF in a sample of time series is:

$$ACF(k) = \frac{\sum_{t=1}^{N-k} \left(Y_t - \bar{Y} \right) \left(Y_{(t+k)} - \bar{Y} \right)}{\sum_{t=1}^{N} \left(Y_t - \bar{Y} \right)^2} \tag{5.1}$$

where

Y_t — the tth observation of a sample of time series
$\bar{Y}$ — the mean of observations in the sample of time series
t — the number of time points $(1 \ldots T)$ in time series
N — the number of observations $(1 \ldots N)$ in the sample of time series
k — the number of lags $(1, 2, 3, \ldots)$ in the sample of time series.

The ACF is a Pearson product–moment correlation coefficient that measures the correlation between a time series (Y_t) and the lags of the time series (Y_{t+k}). The PACF is solidly connected with the ACF.[11]

The numerator of the above ACF equation is the covariance between the time series (Y_t) and the lags of the time series (Y_{t+k}). In contrast, the denominator of the equation is the variance with the time series (Y_t).[12] Thus, the variation of ACFs and PACFs reflects the variation of the mean and variances in the sample of time series. Accordingly, inspecting the ACFs and PACFs can provide substantial information about the stationarity of the time series.

Formula 6: Formalisation of stochastic processes

A general intervention model can be considered as an example of a general time series model. As Formula 3 indicates, a general intervention model will be:

$$Y_t = I_t + N_t \tag{6.1}$$

where

Y_t — the tth observation of the time series
I_t — the intervention or deterministic component of the model
N_t — the noise or stochastic component of the model.

Both auto-regressive and moving average processes are a stochastic process of a time series and are, in other words, the process in which the stochastic component of a time series is assumed to proceed. Both auto-regressive and moving average models are constructed to depict auto-regressive and moving average processes respectively in a time series model.

To formalise a stochastic process, as a common practice, symbol N_t is replaced with symbol $\breve{z}_t$.[13] (Indeed, choosing which symbol does not matter for any model description.) That is, $N_t = \breve{z}_t$.

Also as Formula 3 indicates, the stochastic component (N_t) in a time series model consists of two parts – systematic part (s_t) and random or white noise part (a_t). Accordingly, in the model, it is assumed:

$$N_t = s_t + a_t \tag{6.2}$$

or

$$\breve{z}_t = s_t + a_t \tag{6.3}$$

In essence, both auto-regressive and moving average models are constructed to specifically describe s_t, the systematic part of the stochastic component $(N_t$ or $\breve{z}_t)$.

When formalising a stochastic process, $\breve{z}_t$ can be depicted as

$$\breve{z}_t = z_t - \mu \tag{6.4}$$

where z_t symbolises an observed time series (for example, a time series of Wiley & Sons' annual profit in the period of 1976 to 2006).

In Formula 3, symbol z_t is replaced with symbol Y_t. (Again, choosing which symbol does not matter for any model description.)

μ stands for different values in different patterns of a stochastic process of a time series. If the stochastic process is stationary, μ symbolises the mean of the time series. If the stochastic process is non-stationary, μ denotes a reference point of the time series.[14]

When specifying a stochastic process, z_t as an observed time series can be reckoned as to be generated from a series of independent 'shock' a_t:[15]

$$z_t\,(Y_t) = \mu + a_t + \psi_1 a_{t-1} + \psi_1 a_{t-2} + \ldots \tag{6.5}$$

This series is assumed as either an infinite or a finite time series.

Accordingly

$$\breve{z}_t = z_t - \mu = a_t + \psi_1 a_{t-1} + \psi_2 a_{t-2} + \ldots \tag{6.6}$$

If the stochastic component $(N_t$ or $\breve{z}_t)$ does not exhibit any systematic features: that is, the systematic part (s_t) does not exist and $\psi_1 = \psi_2 = \ldots = 0$, then

$$\breve{z}_t = a_t \tag{6.7}$$

In this situation, the stochastic process advances as a white noise process.

In the data set for this research, as Table 5.7 shows, the stochastic processes in the time series of six book publishing firms – B T Batsford Ltd, Blackwell Science Ltd, David & Charles Plc, Hodder & Stoughton Holdings Ltd, Ladybird Books Ltd, and Mills & Boon Ltd – have been identified as a white noise process.

Of course, the stochastic component (N_t or $\check{z}_t$) in many time series does exhibit certain systematic features; that is, the systematic part (s_t) does exist and $\psi_1 \neq \psi_2 \neq \ldots \neq 0$. In that case, diverse ARIMA models – auto-regressive models, moving average models, or mixed models – are identified and applied.

Also as Table 5.7 shows, the stochastic processes in the time series of four book publishing firms – Faber & Faber Ltd, Ian Allan Ltd, Marshall Cavendish Ltd, and Penguin Books Ltd – have been identified as first-order auto-regressive processes. The stochastic processes in the time series of A & C Black Plc and Wiley & Sons Ltd, after first-order differencing and second-order differencing respectively, have also been identified as first-order auto-regressive processes. Accordingly, a first-order auto-regressive model, along with various differencing procedures (first- or second-order differencing) – such as ARIMA (1, 0, 0), ARIMA (1, 1, 0), and ARIMA (1, 2, 0) models – has been constructed to describe this process. A first-order auto-regressive model is defined as:

$$\check{z}_t = \phi_1 \check{z}_{t-1} + a_t \tag{6.8}$$

The stochastic process in the time series of Frederick Warne & Co Ltd, after a second-order differencing, has been identified as a second-order auto-regressive process. Accordingly, a second-order auto-regressive model, along with a second-order differencing, ARIMA (2, 2, 0) model, has been constructed to describe this process:

$$\check{z}_t = \phi_1 \check{z}_{t-1} + \phi_2 \check{z}_{t-2} + a_t \tag{6.9}$$

The stochastic processes in the time series of two book publishing firms – Constable & Co Ltd and Thames & Hudson Ltd – have been identified as first-order moving average processes after first-order differencing. Accordingly, a first-order moving average model with a first-order differencing, ARIMA (0, 1, 1) model, has been constructed to describe this process:

$$\check{z}_t = a_t - \theta_1 a_{t-1} \tag{6.10}$$

Many other types of ARIMA models can be formalised following the same procedures.[16]

In the meantime, according to the operational model illustrated in Figure 5.1, some symbols in the above formula are interchangeable with some in Formulas (6.7) to (6.10). However, each formalisation in these formulas depicts a single time series. Thus, the i subscript is absent in these formalisations. If these formalisations are applied to the panel or pooled time series data for several firms, the i subscript should be included in formulas. For example, the general intervention model $Y_t = I_t + N_t$ is adapted as follows for a set of panel data:

$$Y_{it} = I_{it} + N_{it} \qquad (6.11)$$

Because copyright expansion $\beta_4 X_{it}$ is defined as an intervention variable in Figure 5.1, $\beta_4 X_{it}$ can replace I_{it}. Meanwhile, when considering the level of competition $\beta_1 X_{it}$, the level of industrial concentration $\beta_2 X_{it}$, and the stage of technological innovation $\beta_3 X_{it}$ as the control independent variables, these variables can be added into the above general intervention model for panel data and the following formula is obtained:

$$Y_{it} = \beta_1 X_{it-1} + \beta_2 X_{it-1} + \beta_3 X_{it} + \beta_4 X_{it} + N_{it} \qquad (6.12)$$

Interestingly, the above formula is very close to the revised distributed lag model as formalised in Formula (4.4). The only difference is that N_{it} replaces n_{it}.

Are the two symbols interchangeable? The interchangeability depends on which model of panel data will be applied and how the issues of autocorrelation will be dealt with under the panel data model.

Formula 7: Constant, fixed, and random coefficients models

To assess autocorrelation or serial correlation in panel data, the formalisations in Formula 6 are adapted by adding the i subscript into formula $N_t = \check{z}_t = s_t + a_t$ and obtain the formula $N_{it} = \check{z}_{it} = s_{it} + a_{it}$ to describe the stochastic process of panel data.

In the revised distributed lag model as formalised in Formula (4.4), N_{it} has been changed into n_{it}. The revised distributed lag model in Formula (4.4) is indeed a panel data model:

$$Y_{it} = \beta_1 X_{it-1} + \beta_2 X_{it-1} + \beta_3 X_{it} + \beta_4 X_{it} + n_{it} \qquad (4.4)$$

In this research, the constant, fixed, and random coefficients models are constructed under the revised distributed lag model in Formula (4.4).

Of course, the above formula can be rewritten in a matrix notation of the independent or explanatory variables $(\beta_1 X_{it-1} + \beta_2 X_{it-1} + \beta_3 X_{it} + \beta_4 X_{it}) - \boldsymbol{\beta}' \, \boldsymbol{x}_{it}$ – plus an intercept α^* with no subscript in order to express a standard or regular regression formula for a regression analysis under the constant coefficients model of panel or pooled time series data. From now on, bold type is used to signify vectors or matrices (in the same way as with most textbooks of econometrics).

The term n_{it} in Formula (4.4) can also be changed into u_{it}. Both are the common notations in most textbooks of panel data econometrics. The standard or regular regression formula will be:[17]

$$y_{it} = \alpha^* + \beta' x_{it} + u_{it} \text{ and } u_{it} = n_{it} = N_{it} = \check{z}_{it} = s_{it} + a_{it} \tag{7.1}$$

Table 5.2 reports the estimating results of the 30-year panel data for these 15 book publishing firms with no correcting for autocorrelation or serial correlation from Formula (7.1) under the constant coefficients model. Tables 5.11 and 5.12 respectively show the estimating results of the 30-year panel data for six firms and four firms groups respectively from the same formula under the same model.

Unlike the constant coefficients model under which all coefficients, both intercepts and slopes, are assumed to be the same for all cross-sections[18] (firms in this research), the fixed coefficients model considers the effects of excluded or omitted variables either as fixed constants over time[19] but specific to individual cross-sectional units, or as fixed constants over all cross-sectional units but specific to each time period.[20] For the former dimension, the general formula of a fixed coefficients (LSDV) model is:[21]

$$y_{it} = \alpha^*_i + \beta' x_{it} + u_{it} \tag{7.2}$$

where

y_{it} — the value of the dependent or response variable for i^{th} individual cross-sectional unit at time t

α^*_i — a 1×1 scalar unknown constant representing the effects of excluded variables that are specific to i^{th} individual cross-sectional unit but constant over time

t — the number of time points $(1 \ldots T)$

i — the number of individual cross-sectional units $(1 \ldots N)$

β' — a $1 \times K$ vector of constants

x_{it} — a $K \times 1$ vector of the independent or explanatory variables as $x'_{it} = (x_{1it} \ldots x_{Kit})$

u_{it} — the error term representing the effects of excluded variables which are specific to both the individual cross-sectional units and time periods.

The key assumption of u_{it} is that it is uncorrelated with the independent or explanatory variables $(X_{it} \ldots X_{iT})$ and can be defined as an independently, identically distributed random variable with mean zero and variance σ^2_u. Meanwhile, to further explore the fixed coefficients (LSDV) model defined in Formula (7.2), the intercept term α^*_i can be decomposed into two parts – $\alpha^*_i = \mu + \alpha_i$ where μ denotes a mean intercept and α_i symbolises the deviation of the ith individual from the common mean μ. Accordingly, Formula (7.2) can be rewritten as:[22]

$$y_{it} = \mu + \alpha_i + \beta' x_{it} + u_{it} \tag{7.3}$$

Of course, Formula (7.3) is still a formalisation of the fixed coefficients (LSDV) model. In this formula, μ and α_i are still fixed constants that consist of the intercept term α_i^*.

Meanwhile, Formula (7.2) can also be written in vector form:[23]

$$
Y = y_{it} = \begin{bmatrix} y_1 \\ \vdots \\ y_N \end{bmatrix} = \begin{bmatrix} e \\ 0 \\ \vdots \\ 0 \end{bmatrix} a_1^* + \begin{bmatrix} e \\ 0 \\ \vdots \\ 0 \end{bmatrix} a_2^* + \cdots + \begin{bmatrix} 0 \\ 0 \\ \vdots \\ e \end{bmatrix} a_N^* + \begin{bmatrix} x_1 \\ x_2 \\ \vdots \\ x_N \end{bmatrix} + \begin{bmatrix} u_1 \\ \vdots \\ u_N \end{bmatrix}
$$

(7.4)

where

$$
\underset{T \times 1}{y_i} = \begin{bmatrix} y_1 \\ \vdots \\ y_N \end{bmatrix}, \quad \underset{T \times K}{X_i} = \begin{bmatrix} x_{1i1} & x_{2i1} & & x_{Ki1} \\ x_{1i2} & x_{2i2} & \cdots & x_{ki2} \\ \vdots & \vdots & & \vdots \\ \vdots & \vdots & & \vdots \\ \vdots & \vdots & \ddots & \vdots \\ x_{1iT} & x_{2iT} & \cdots & x_{KiT} \end{bmatrix}
$$

$$
\underset{1 \times T}{\acute{e}} = (1, 1, \cdots, 1), \quad \underset{1 \times T}{\acute{u}_i} = (u_{i1}, u_{i2}, \ldots, u_{iT}), \, Eu_i = 0, \, Eu_i u_i' = \sigma_u^2 I_T,
$$

$$
Eu_i u_j' = 0 \text{ if } i \neq j .
$$

Nonetheless, due to the pattern of panel data of the six-firm and four-firm book publishing groups, a fixed coefficients (LSDV) model is inappropriate for analysing the panel data of the six-firm and four-firm book publishing groups. The error components model as one type of the random coefficients (effects) model shall offer a frame for estimating these panel data.

In an error components model, μ is still assumed as a constant. Yet, α_i is no longer considered as a fixed constant in the intercept term α_i^*. Rather, it is treated as a variable just as u_{it} and, together with u_{it}, as part of the general error term, denoted as v_{it}. In other words, $v_{it} = a_i + u_{it}$. Accordingly, for an error components model, the regression equation will be:

$$
y_{it} = \mu + \beta' x_{it} + \alpha_i + u_{it}
$$

(7.5)

This error components model contains solely the cross-sectional effects (α_i) in the general error term (v_{it}), it is defined as the one-way error components model.[24]

If one term – λ_t – is added to the general error term (v_{it}) for standing for the effects of those excluded and unobserved variables in the model that vary over time but stay constant over individual cross-sectional units,[25] the regression equation will be:

$$y_{it} = \mu + \beta' x_{it} + \alpha_i + \lambda_t + u_{it} \tag{7.6}$$

The error components model under Formula (7.6) is defined as the two-way error components model because this model incorporates both the cross-sectional and time effects (both α_i and λ_t) of excluded variables.

A pooled feasible or estimated generalised least squares (FGLS or EGLS) estimation can be conducted under either the one-way or two-way error components model.

To conduct a pooled FGLS or EGLS estimation, it is needed to transform Formula (7.5) into an equivalent formalisation to simplify the process. The first step is to encompass all three terms of error components – α_i, λ_t, u_{it} – into the general error term v_{it} and let

$$v_{it} = \alpha_i + \lambda_t + u_{it} \tag{7.7}$$

Then, Formula (7.6) is rewritten as

$$y_{it} = \mu + \beta' X + \alpha_i + \lambda_t + u_{it} = \mu + \beta' X + v_{it} \tag{7.8}$$

X denotes a $NT \times K$ matrix of the independent or explanatory variables.[26]

$$\underset{NT \times K}{X} = \begin{bmatrix} x_{1i1} & x_{2i1} & & x_{Ki1} \\ x_{1i2} & x_{2i2} & \cdots & x_{ki2} \\ \vdots & \vdots & & \vdots \\ \vdots & \vdots & \ddots & \vdots \\ x_{1NT} & x_{2NT} & \cdots & x_{KNT} \end{bmatrix}$$

Some assumptions of v_{it} in Formula (7.8) are expected:[27]

(1) Independent random variables α_i, λ_t, and u_{it}: $E(\alpha_i\lambda_t) = E(\alpha_i u_{it}) = E(\lambda_t u_{it}) = 0$ for all i and t
(2) Zero means: $E(\alpha_i) = E(\lambda_t) = E(u_{it}) = 0$
(3) No autocorrelation:

$E(\alpha_i\alpha_j) = \sigma_\alpha^2$ if $i = j$ and $= 0$ if $i \neq j$
$E(\lambda_t\lambda_s) = \sigma_\lambda^2$ if $t = s$ and $= 0$ if $t \neq s$
$E(u_{it}u_{js}) = \sigma_u^2$ if $i = j$ and $t = s$ and $= 0$ otherwise

(4) Diagonal variance–covariance matrix:

The variance–covariance matrix of v_{it} $Ev_iv_i' = \sigma_u^2 I_T + \sigma_\alpha^2 ee'$, is diagonal

(5) Homoscedastic v_{it} with variance of $y_{it} = \sigma_y^2 = \sigma_\alpha^2 + \sigma_\lambda^2 + \sigma_u^2$

(6) Homogeneity: $E(\alpha_i X) = E(\lambda_t X) = E(u_{it} X) = 0$.

(7) Normality: $\alpha_i \sim N(0, \sigma_\alpha^2)$, $\lambda_t \sim N(0, \sigma_\lambda^2)$, $u_{it} \sim N(0, \sigma_u^2)$

(8) Matrix of regressors X is nonstochastic.

Meanwhile, both the variance–covariance matrix (Ω) and idempotent (covariance) of transform matrix (a $T \times T$ Q) are introduced as follows for running the pooled FGLS or EGLS estimation on account of the generalised least squares (GLS) estimation.[28]

$$\Omega = E(v_{it}v_{it}') = \sigma_\alpha^2 (I_N \otimes J_T) + \sigma_\lambda^2 (J_N \otimes I_T) + \sigma_u^2 (I_N \otimes I_T) \tag{7.9}$$

where

$\otimes$ — Kronecker product
T — the total number of time points
I_N — a $N \times N$ identity matrix
I_T — a $T \times T$ identity matrix
J_N — a $N \times N$ unit matrix
J_T — a $T \times T$ unit matrix.

The generalised least squares (GLS) estimator is defined:[29]

$$\hat{\beta}_{GLS} = (X'\Omega^{-1}X)^{-1} X'\Omega^{-1} y_{it} \tag{7.10}$$

However, it is unrealistic to run a GLS estimation directly because the variance components (σ_α^2, σ_λ^2, and σ_u^2) on which Ω depends are unknown. Only after these variance components (σ_α^2, σ_λ^2, and σ_u^2) are estimated from empirical data, the pooled Feasible Generalised Least Squares (FGLS or EGLS) estimation can be conducted through an estimated Ω on account of these estimated variance components (σ_α^2, σ_λ^2, σ_u^2) and $\hat{\sigma}_u^2$). These estimators are defined:[30]

$$\hat{\sigma}_\alpha^2 = \frac{T}{T-1} \left(\frac{\frac{1}{T}\Sigma_i(\Sigma_t \hat{v}_{it})^2}{N-K} - \frac{\Sigma_i\Sigma_t \hat{v}_{it}^2}{NT-K} \right) \tag{7.11}$$

$$\hat{\sigma}_\lambda^2 = \frac{N}{N-1} \left(\frac{\frac{1}{N}\Sigma_i(\Sigma_t \hat{v}_{it})^2}{T-K} - \frac{\Sigma_i\Sigma_t \hat{v}_{it}^2}{NT-K} \right) \tag{7.12}$$

$$\hat{\sigma}_u^2 = \frac{\Sigma_i \Sigma_t \hat{v}_{it}^2}{NT - K} - \hat{\sigma}_\alpha^2 - \hat{\sigma}_\lambda^2 \qquad (7.13)$$

In Formulas (7.11), (7.12), and (7.13), $\hat{v}_{it}^2$ can be any residuals obtained by the consistent estimation of the model.[31] Based on these estimators, an estimated Ω, $\hat{\Omega}$, can be defined under Formula (7.8). Replacing Ω with the estimated $\hat{\Omega}$, the (pooled) FGLS or EGLS estimator can be defined:[32]

$$\hat{\beta}_{FGLS} = (X'\hat{\Omega}^{-1}X)^{-1} X'\hat{\Omega}^{-1}y_{it} \qquad (7.14)$$

Table 5.13 reports the estimating results of the 30-year panel data for the six-firm group of book publishing from Formula (7.14) with no correcting for autocorrelation or serial correlation under the two-way random coefficients (random effects or error components) model.

Formula 8: FGLS estimates under ARIMA models

The pooled FGLS or EGLS estimator underlined in Formula (7.14) can be applied to correct for autocorrelation or serial correlation under a specific ARIMA model, such as the ARIMA (1, 0, 0) model, which depicts the stochastic processes in the time series of four book publishing firms (Faber & Faber Ltd, Ian Allan Ltd, Marshall Cavendish Ltd, and Penguin Books Ltd), and a specific a panel data model.

Table 5.14 – under Pooled EGLS (cross-section SUR) – reports the estimating results from the seemingly unrelated regressions of the feasible generalised least squares (SUR FGLS) estimator under the ARIMA (1, 0, 0) model.

The SUR model assumes that the cross-sectional individuals are interdependent because the unobserved variables excluded from the proposed regression model may affect 'all (or part of) the individual at the same time'.[33] The interdependence could disturb the identified relation between the independent or explanatory and dependent or response variable in the proposed model. To correct for this interdependence, reflected as the contemporaneous correlation between the error components of these individuals, it is necessary to inspect the covariance structure of the residuals of the proposed model and include the contemporaneous correlation in the model for controlling it.

In the case of the panel data for four book publishing firms (Faber & Faber Ltd, Ian Allan Ltd, Marshall Cavendish Ltd, and Penguin Books Ltd), to correct for the potential interdependence and identified first-order autocorrelation, a one-way error components panel model as defined in Formula (7.5) is proposed:

$$y_{it} = \mu + \beta' x_{it} + \alpha_i + u_{it} \qquad (7.5)$$

This formula can be also rewritten as Formula (7.8):

$$y_{it} = \mu + \beta' X + v_{it} \text{ and } v_{it} = \alpha_i + u_{it} \qquad (7.8)$$

In vector form, Formula (7.8) can be rewritten as:[34]

$$y_{it} = Y = \mu l_{NT} + \beta' X + v = Z\delta + v \qquad (8.1)$$

$$v = Z_\alpha \alpha + u \qquad (8.2)$$

Under the SUR model, the focus is on assessing a SUR equation for each cross-sectional individual (each firm, in this research). The potential interdependence correlation among cross-sectional individuals is estimated through examining the error components of the set of SUR equations for all individuals in the panel. The error components of the set of SUR equations are the same error components of Formula (7.8). To clarify the process of formalisation, the error components of equations are singled out and a set of M equations are defined for estimation:[35]

$$y_j = \mu l_N + \beta' X_j + v_j = Z_j \delta_j + Z_\alpha \alpha_j + u_j = Z_j \delta_j + v_j \ (j = 1, \ldots, M) \qquad (8.3)$$

$$v_j = Z_\alpha \alpha_j + u_j \ (j = 1, \ldots, M) \qquad (8.4)$$

Assumptions of Formulas (8.1), (8.2), (8.3) and (8.4):
(1) Strict exogeneity of X, $E[vj \backslash X_1, X_2, \ldots, X_M] = 0$
(2) Homoscedasticity, $E[v_j \, v_j' \backslash X_1, X_2, \ldots, X_M] = \sigma_{jl} I_T$, $\Sigma_\alpha = \sigma^2_{ajl}$, $\Sigma_u = \sigma^2_{ujl}$
(3) Normality: $\alpha \sim N\ (0, \Sigma_\alpha \otimes I_N)$, $u \sim N\ (0, \Sigma u \otimes I_{NT})$.
   $\alpha' = (\alpha_1', \alpha_2', \ldots, \alpha_M')$, $u' = (u_1', u_2', \ldots, u_M')$.
   $Z_\alpha = (I_N \otimes l_T)$, $\alpha_j' = (\alpha_{1j}, \alpha_{2j}, \ldots, \alpha_{Nj})$ and $u_j' = (u_{11j}, \ldots u_1 T_j, \ldots u_{N1j}, \ldots, u_{NTj})$ are random vectors with zero means and covariance matrix that is defined in Formula (8.5).

$$E\begin{pmatrix} \alpha_j \\ u_j \end{pmatrix}(\alpha_l', u_l') = \begin{bmatrix} \sigma^2_{\alpha_{jl}} \times I_N & 0 \\ 0 & \sigma^2_{u_{jl}} \times I_{NT} \end{bmatrix} \text{ for } j, l = 1, 2, \ldots, M \qquad (8.5)$$

The variance–covariance matrix for Formulas (8.3) and (8.4), Ω_M, is:[36]

$$\Omega_M = E\ (vv') = \Sigma_\alpha\ (I_N \otimes J_T) + \Sigma_u (I_N \otimes I_T) \qquad (8.6)$$

The SUR GLS estimator will be:[37]

$$\hat{\beta}_{SUR\ GLS} = (X' \Omega_M^{-1} X)^{-1}\ X' \Omega_M^{-1} y_{it} \qquad (8.7)$$

Formula (8.7) depends on the known Σ_α and Σ_u. However, in empirical data, these two terms cannot be known directly and should be estimated. To estimate the two terms, Formula (8.6) should be rewritten through replacing J_T by $T\bar{J}_T$ and I_T by $E_T + \bar{J}_T$ as follows:

$$\Omega_M = E\,(vv') = (T\Sigma_\alpha + \Sigma_u) \otimes (I_N \otimes \bar{J}_T) + \Sigma_u \otimes (I_N \otimes E_T) = \Sigma_1 \otimes P$$
$$+ \Sigma_u \otimes Q \tag{8.8}$$

In Formula (8.8), Σ_1 can be estimated as

$$\hat{\Sigma}_1 = V'QV/N \text{ and } \Sigma_u \text{ as } \hat{\Sigma}_u = V'QV/N(T-1).^{38}$$

Accordingly, an estimated Ω can be defined as:

$$\hat{\Omega}_M = \hat{\Sigma}_1 P + \hat{\Sigma}_u \otimes Q \tag{8.9}$$

Therefore, the SUR FGLS estimator that can be applied directly to empirical data can be defined through replacing Ω_M by $\hat{\Omega}_M$ in Formula (8.7):

$$\hat{\beta}_{SUR\,FGLS} = (X'\hat{\Omega}_M^{-1}X)^{-1}\,X'\hat{\Omega}_M^{-1}y_{it} \tag{8.10}$$

where
$\otimes$ — Kronecker product
Y — a $NT \times 1$ vector
X — $NT \times K$ matrix as defined in Formula (7.8)
I_N — a $N \times N$ identity matrix
I_T — a $T \times T$ identity matrix
l_T — $\mathbf{e}$, a $T \times 1$ unit vector or a vector of ones ('1's) of dimension T
l_{NT} — a vector of ones ('1's) of dimension NT
V — $[v_1, \ldots, v_M]$ as the $NT \times M$ matrix of disturbance for all M equations
Z — $[l_{NT}, X]$

$$\delta - \begin{pmatrix} \mu \\ \beta \end{pmatrix}$$

$\delta' - (\mu', \beta')$

$$Z_\alpha - (I_N \otimes I_T) = \begin{bmatrix} l_T & 0 & 0 \\ 0 & l_T & 0 \\ & & \cdots & \\ 0 & 0 & l_T \end{bmatrix}$$

$$NT \times T$$

y_j — a $NT \times 1$ vector
Z_j — $[l_T, X_j]$, an $NT \times k'_j$ matrix
δ'_j — (μ_j, β'_j)
β'_j — a $k_j \times 1$ vector
k'_j — a $k_j + 1$ vector
T — the total number of time points
N — the total number of cross-sectional individuals or individual units
J_N — a $N \times N$ unit matrix
J_T — a $T \times T$ unit matrix

Z_α — a $I_N \otimes l_T$ selector matrix of ones and zeros (or a matrix of individual dummies that may be included in the regression to estimate α_i or α_j if they are assumed to be fixed parameters)

P — a $Z_\alpha(Z'_\alpha Z_\alpha)^{-1}Z'_\alpha$ matrix that averages the observations from individual means

Q — an $I_{NT} - P$ matrix that is defined in Formula (8.11).

$$Q = I_T - \frac{1}{T} ee'$$ (8.11)

where

e — a $T \times 1$ unit vector (all elements = 1)

e — l_T, a $1 \times T$ unit matrix (1, 1 . . . 1).

The role of Q is to define the variations in the dependent or response variable (y_{it}) and independent variables (X). That is, Q can get rid of the individual effects of a variable and obtain individual observations that 'are measures as deviations from individual means'.[39]

The SUR FGLS estimator in Formula (8.10) can be employed to deal with the potential interdependence 'across observations at a particular point in time'[40] in the panel data, such as those of four book publishing firms (Faber & Faber Ltd, Ian Allan Ltd, Marshall Cavendish Ltd, and Penguin Books Ltd). It has not yet been concerned with the identified first-order autocorrelation in the time series data of these firms. Although coping with the issue of autocorrelation is not the focus of the SUR model, some formal treatment of this issue in a SUR model is still relevant if the time series in the panel data is relatively long,[41] such as the case of the above four firms.

Indeed, the SUR model allows one to control for the first-order autocorrelation.[42] To correct for the identified first-order autocorrelation, it is needed to transform the error components of the set of SUR equations, v_i, as defined in Formula (8.4). The aim of transforming v_i is realised through transforming the first-order auto-regressive u_j, into a classic error term with no autocorrelation for satisfying Assumption (3) of Formula (7.8).[43]

Before transforming v_i, it is necessary to define a first-order auto-regressive process of u_j in v_i:

$$u_j = \rho u_{j,t-1} + \boldsymbol{\epsilon}_j$$ (8.12)

where $|\rho| < 1$ and $\boldsymbol{\epsilon}_j$ are independently, identically distributed with zero mean and variance $\sigma^2_{\boldsymbol{\epsilon}}$. That is, $\boldsymbol{\epsilon}_j$ is a white noise part of the error component, $E(\boldsymbol{\epsilon}_j) = 0$, and $E(\boldsymbol{\epsilon}_j) = \sigma^2_{\boldsymbol{\epsilon}}$.

Applying the Prais–Winsten (PW) transformation matrix is the first step. The PW matrix, C, is constructed as:

$$
C = \begin{bmatrix}
(1-\rho^2)^{1/2} & 0 & 0 & \cdots & 0 & 0 & 0 \\
-\rho & 1 & 0 & \cdots & 0 & 0 & 0 \\
\vdots & \vdots & \vdots & \cdots & \vdots & \vdots & \vdots \\
\vdots & \vdots & \vdots & \cdots & \vdots & \vdots & \vdots \\
0 & \vdots & \vdots & \cdots & -\rho & 1 & 0 \\
0 & 0 & 0 & & 0 & \rho & 1
\end{bmatrix}
$$

To control for the identified first-order autocorrelation, it is necessary to apply the PW matrix and pre-multiply the equation in Formula (8.12) by $(I_N \otimes C)$. As a result of the pre-multiplication, the transformed v_j, v_j^* will be:

$$
v_j^* = (I_N \otimes C)v = (1-\rho)\,(I_N \otimes l^\mu{}_T)\alpha + (I_N \otimes C)u \tag{8.13}
$$

where $Cl_T = (1-\rho)l_T^\mu$, $l_T^\mu = (\mu, l'_{T-1})$, $\mu = \sqrt{(1+\rho)/(1-\rho)}$.

The variance-covariance matrix of the transformed v_i, $\Omega^*{}_M$ will be:

$$
\begin{aligned}
\Omega^*{}_M &= E\,(v_i^* \, v_i^{*\,\prime}) = \sigma^2{}_\alpha(1-\rho)^2\,[(I_N \otimes l^\mu{}_T l^\mu{}_T] + \sigma^2 \boldsymbol{\epsilon}\,(I_N \otimes I_T) \\
&= \sigma^2{}_\mu(I_N \otimes \bar{J}^\mu{}_T) + \sigma^2{}_{\boldsymbol{\epsilon}}(I_N \otimes E^\mu{}_T)
\end{aligned} \tag{8.14}
$$

where $l^\mu{}_T\, l^\mu{}_T = d^2 = \mu^2 + (T-1)$, $J^\mu_T = l^\mu_T\, l^\mu_T$, $\bar{J}^\mu_T = l^\mu_T\, l^\mu_T/d^2$, $E^\mu_T = I_N - \bar{J}^\mu_T$.

Because $\sigma^2{}_\alpha$, $\sigma^2{}_{\boldsymbol{\epsilon}}$ and ρ are all unknown, they should be estimated as follows:

$$
\hat{\sigma}^2{}_{\boldsymbol{\epsilon}} = v_j^{*\,\prime}\,(I_N \otimes E^\mu{}_T)\,v_j^*/N\,(T-1) \tag{8.15}
$$

$$
\hat{\sigma}^2{}_\mu = v_j^{*\,\prime}\,(I_N \otimes \bar{J}^\mu{}_T)\,v_j^*/N \tag{8.16}
$$

$$
\hat{\rho} = (\tilde{Q}_1 - \tilde{Q}_2/(\tilde{Q}_0 - \tilde{Q}_1) \tag{8.17}
$$

where $\hat{v}_j$ symbolises the OLS residual of Formula (8.3),

$$
\tilde{Q}_s = \Sigma^N_{i=1} \Sigma^T_{t=s+1} \hat{v}_{jt}\, \hat{v}_{j,t-s}/N(T-s).
$$

The estimated variance–covariance matrix of the transformed v_i, $\hat{\Omega}_M^*$, will be:

$$
\hat{\Omega}_M^* = \hat{\sigma}^2_\mu\,(I_N \otimes \bar{J}^\mu_T) + \hat{\sigma}^2{}_{\boldsymbol{\epsilon}}\,(I_N \otimes E^\mu_T) \tag{8.18}
$$

Accordingly, the SUR FGLS ARIMA estimator that can be applied directly to empirical data can be defined through replacing $\hat{\Omega}_M$ by $\hat{\Omega}_M^*$ in Formula (8.10):

$$\hat{\beta}_{SUR\,FGLS\,ARIMA} = (X'\hat{\Omega}_M^{*\,-1}\,X)^{-1}X'\hat{\Omega}_M^{*\,-1}y_{it} \qquad (8.19)$$

Table 5.14 – under 'Pooled EGLS (Cross-section SUR)' – is the application of the SUR FGLS ARIMA estimator against the panel data of those four firms.

Notes

1 Mariana Mazzucato, *Firm Size, Innovation, and Market Structure: the Evolution of Industry Concentration and Instability*, Cheltenham, UK: Edward Elgar, 2000, p. 14, 30.
2 P. Vaaler and G. McNamara, 'Are Technology-Intensive Industries More Dynamically Competitive? No and Yes'. Online. Available <http:// www.business. uiuc. edu/ Working _ Papers/ papers/ 06–01 24.pdf. 2006> (accessed 10 June 2008), p. 23.
3 D. McDowall, R. McCleary and E. Meidinger, *Interrupted Time Series Analysis*, Newbury Park, CA: Sage Publications, 1990, pp. 12–13. T. Mills, *Time Series Techniques for Economists*, Cambridge University Press, 1990, pp. 236–239.
4 Cook and Campbell, op. cit., p. 239.
5 D. Asteriou and S. Hall, *Applied Econometrics: A Modern Approach using EViews and Microfit*, New York: Palgrave Macmillan, 2007, p. 231.
6 McDowall, McCleary, and Meidinger, op. cit., p. 15.
7 C. Ostrom, *Time Series Analysis: Regression Techniques*, Newberry Park, CA: Sage Publications, 1990, pp. 14–16. L. Sayrs, *Pooled Time Series Analysis*, Newbury Park, CA: Sage, 1989, pp. 10–14.
8 Ostrom, op. cit., pp. 58–60.
9 Cook and Campbell, op. cit., p. 241.
10 Mills, op. cit., p. 63.
11 Cook and Campbell, op. cit., p. 241. B. Bowerman, R. O'Connell, and A. Koehler, *Forecasting, Time Series, and Regression: an Applied Approach* 4th edn, Belmont, CA: Thomson Brooks/Cole, 2005, pp. 408–412.
12 McDowall, McCleary and Meidinger, op. cit., p. 24.
13 G. Box, G. Jenkins and G. Reinsel, *Time Series Analysis: Forecasting and Control* 4th edn, New York: John Wiley, 2008, pp. 10–14.
14 Ibid, p. 9.
15 Ibid, p. 8.
16 All of these formulas are derived from Box, Jenkins and Reinsel, op. cit., Chapters I & II.
17 C. Hsiao, *Analysis of Panel Data* 2nd edn, Cambridge University Press, 2003, pp. 15–16. Asteriou and Hall, op. cit., p. 345.
18 Asteriou and Hall, op. cit., p. 345. Sayrs, op. cit., p. 19.
19 Hsiao, op. cit., p. 34.
20 Ibid, p. 30.
21 Ibid, p. 30.
22 Ibid, p. 33.
23 Ibid, p. 31.
24 B. Baltagi, *Econometric Analysis of Panel Data* 3rd edn, Chichester, UK: John Wiley, 2008, pp. 17–42.
25 Hsiao, op. cit., p. 34.
26 For the logic of adapting x_{it} to X, see L. Mátyás and P. Sevestre (eds), *The Econometrics of Panel Data: A Handbook of the Theory with Applications* 2nd rev, The Netherlands: Kluwer Academic Publishers, 1996, p. 45. See also Hsiao, op. cit., pp. 34–35.

27 Baltagi, op. cit., p. 37. Hsiao, op. cit., p. 34. Mátyás and Sevestre (eds), op. cit., pp. 51–52.
28 Baltagi, op. cit., p. 37.
29 Formula (7.10) is derived from Mátyás and Sevestre, op. cit., p. 55. Some symbols are changed for the context of this research.
30 Formulas (7.11), (7.12), and (7.13) are derived from Mátyás and Sevestre, op. cit., p. 61. Some symbols are changed for the context of this research.
31 Mátyás and Sevestre, op. cit., p. 60.
32 Formula (7.13) is derived from Mátyás and Sevestre, op. cit., p. 62. Some symbols are changed for the context of this research.
33 Mátyás and Sevestre, op. cit., p. 29.
34 Baltagi, op. cit., pp. 13–14.
35 Formulas (8.3), (8.4), (8.5), (8.6) and related term definitions are derived from Baltagi, op. cit., pp. 13–14, 115–116. The same author, *A Companion to Econometric Analysis of Panel Data* 3rd edn, Chichester, UK: John Wiley, 2008, pp. 125–128. See also W. Greene, *Econometric Analysis* 6th edn, Upper Saddle River, NJ: Pearson/Prentice Hall, 2008, pp. 252–264. Some symbols are changed for the context of this research.
36 Baltagi, op. cit., pp. 115–116.
37 Greene, op. cit., p. 256.
38 Baltagi, op. cit., p. 116.
39 Hsiao, op. cit., p. 32.
40 Greene, op. cit., p. 263.
41 Ibid, p. 263.
42 Sayrs, op. cit., p. 39.
43 Mátyás and Sevestre, op. cit., pp. 71–72. Baltagi, op. cit., pp. 92–94. The following Formulas (8.12), (8.13), (8.14), (8.15), (8.16), (8.17), (8.18), (8.19), and related term definitions are derived from Baltagi, op. cit., pp. 13–14, 87–119. See also Greene, op. cit., pp. 252–264. Hsiao, op. cit., pp. 14–42. Some symbols are changed for the context of this research.

Appendix B. Tables

Table 1 Pooled time series matrix for 15 book publishing firms' annual profits (1976–2006)

Case 1		T	Y_{it}	$\beta_k X_{it}$				
	Firm	Time (Year)	Pre-tax profit (£'000)[a]	Natural log of pre-tax profit[b] $\beta_1 X_{it}$	Dynamics index[c] $\beta_1 X_{it}$	Concentration ratio (%)[d] $\beta_2 X_{it}$	Innovation[e] $\beta_3 X_{it}$	UK Copyright 1988[f] $\beta_4 X_{it}$
1	A & C	1976	32.3152	3.48	10.8765	13.7769	0.00	0.00
2	Black Plc	1977	75.8938	4.33	12.6806	15.1088	0.00	0.00
3		1978	90.9226	4.51	12.3640	18.2369	0.00	0.00
4		1979	20.0915	3.00	14.0410	19.9530	0.00	0.00
5		1980	−25.1260		13.9910	20.9865	0.00	0.00
6		1981	50.2030	3.92	13.2600	19.4480	0.00	0.00
7		1982	148.0700	5.00	12.5901	21.9161	0.00	0.00
8		1983	168.8006	5.13	11.7072	23.9022	0.00	0.00
9		1984	152.1936	5.03	10.8423	9.8097	0.00	0.00
10		1985	210.6504	5.35	9.0763	22.4238	0.00	0.00
11		1986	284.5687	5.65	7.3125	24.7500	0.00	0.00
12		1987	347.0625	5.85	11.3582	43.0416	0.00	0.00
13		1988	396.3414	5.98	15.3984	32.7216	0.00	0.00
14		1989	408.6992	6.01	15.2064	35.2512	0.00	1.00
15		1990	190.7712	5.25	16.1876	37.5258	0.00	1.00
16		1991	286.2262	5.66	15.2700	41.9925	0.00	1.00
17		1992	408.4725	6.01	14.9226	43.1970	0.00	1.00
18		1993	273.3192	5.61	14.3622	39.8950	0.00	1.00
19		1994	293.6272	5.68	13.1088	42.6036	0.00	1.00
20		1995	351.4797	5.86	13.5840	34.8090	1.00	1.00
21		1996	371.0130	5.92	13.0905	38.3988	1.00	1.00
22		1997	392.7150	5.97	18.7320	40.1400	1.00	1.00
23		1998	448.6760	6.11	18.2160	41.8968	1.00	1.00
24		1999	482.7240	6.18	17.5104	32.2560	1.00	1.00
25		2000	721.6128	6.58	15.9987	37.6440	1.00	1.00
26		2001	821.5803	6.71	15.5248	52.3962	1.00	1.00
27		2002	138.7529	4.93	17.0000	58.0000	1.00	1.00
28		2003	525.0000	6.26	17.4267	59.4558	1.00	1.00

(*Continued overleaf*)

Table 1 Continued

Case	I	T	Y_{it}			$\beta_k X_{it}$		
	Firm	Time (Year)	Pre-tax profit (£'000)^a	Natural log of pre-tax profit^b $\beta_1 X_{it}$	Dynamics index^c $\beta_1 X_{it}$	Concentration ratio (%)^d $\beta_2 X_{it}$	Innovation^e $\beta_3 X_{it}$	UK Copyright 1988^f $\beta_4 X_{it}$
29		2004	121.9869	4.80	16.7664	58.6824	1.00	1.00
30		2005	889.6671	6.79	16.1310	53.2508	1.00	1.00
31		2006	1106.5866	7.01			1.00	1.00
32	B T	1976	54.0004	3.99	10.8765	13.7769	0.00	0.00
33	Batsford	1977	67.6760	4.21	12.6806	15.1088	0.00	0.00
34	Ltd	1978	83.3682	4.42	12.3640	18.2369	0.00	0.00
35		1979	43.5831	3.77	14.0410	19.9530	0.00	0.00
36		1980	18.4750	2.92	13.9910	20.9865	0.00	0.00
37		1981	66.6630	4.20	13.2600	19.4480	0.00	0.00
38		1982	133.9260	4.90	12.5901	21.9161	0.00	0.00
39		1983	161.3398	5.08	11.7072	23.9022	0.00	0.00
40		1984	170.7300	5.14	10.8423	9.8097	0.00	0.00
41		1985	175.5420	5.17	9.0763	22.4238	0.00	0.00
42		1986	80.0850	4.38	7.3125	24.7500	0.00	0.00
43		1987	149.0625	5.00	11.3582	43.0416	0.00	0.00
44		1988	86.6810	4.46	15.3984	32.7216	0.00	0.00
45		1989	50.6864	3.93	15.2064	35.2512	0.00	1.00
46		1990	−129.9456		16.1876	37.5258	0.00	1.00
47		1991	15.4518	2.74	15.2700	41.9925	0.00	1.00
48		1992	73.2960	4.29	14.9226	43.1970	0.00	1.00
49		1993	14.1372	2.65	14.3622	39.8950	0.00	1.00
50		1994	−43.8845		13.1088	42.6036	0.00	1.00
51		1995	−798.8175		13.5840	34.8090	1.00	1.00
52		1996	4594.6415	8.43	13.0905	38.3988	1.00	1.00
53		1997	4722.9018	8.46	18.7320	40.1400	1.00	1.00
54		1998	4827.3501	8.48	18.2160	41.8968	1.00	1.00
55		1999	4929.0924	8.50	17.5104	32.2560	1.00	1.00
56		2000	689213.0304	13.44	15.9987	37.6440	1.00	1.00
57		2001	491415.1281	13.11	15.5248	52.3962	1.00	1.00
58		2002	−182827.8072		17.0000	58.0000	1.00	1.00
59		2003	−448375.0000		17.4267	59.4558	1.00	1.00
60		2004	100366.5159	11.52	16.7664	58.6824	1.00	1.00
61		2005	−922024.1562		16.1310	53.2508	1.00	1.00
62		2006	663359.4146	13.41			1.00	1.00
63	Blackwell	1976	201.1196	5.30	10.8765	13.7769	0.00	0.00
64	Science	1977	327.7452	5.79	12.6806	15.1088	0.00	0.00
65	Ltd	1978	212.3326	5.36	12.3640	18.2369	0.00	0.00
66		1979	243.2617	5.49	14.0410	19.9530	0.00	0.00
67		1980	485.1535	6.18	13.9910	20.9865	0.00	0.00
68		1981	603.2590	6.40	13.2600	19.4480	0.00	0.00
69		1982	829.6340	6.72	12.5901	21.9161	0.00	0.00
70		1983	1494.9578	7.31	11.7072	23.9022	0.00	0.00
71		1984	1499.9850	7.31	10.8423	9.8097	0.00	0.00
72		1985	1495.2048	7.31	9.0763	22.4238	0.00	0.00
73		1986	1780.5565	7.48	7.3125	24.7500	0.00	0.00

#	Name	Year						
74		1987	1418.0625	7.26	11.3582	43.0416	0.00	0.00
75		1988	1282.2810	7.16	15.3984	32.7216	0.00	0.00
76		1989	3358.7760	8.12	15.2064	35.2512	0.00	1.00
77		1990	1551.0528	7.35	16.1876	37.5258	0.00	1.00
78		1991	2313.3552	7.75	15.2700	41.9925	0.00	1.00
79		1992	3442.6215	8.14	14.9226	43.1970	0.00	1.00
80		1993	4380.1758	8.38	14.3622	39.8950	0.00	1.00
81		1994	5411.3578	8.60	13.1088	42.6036	0.00	1.00
82		1995	6072.6516	8.71	13.5840	34.8090	1.00	1.00
83		1996	5904.7950	8.68	13.0905	38.3988	1.00	1.00
84		1997	6150.7896	8.72	18.7320	40.1400	1.00	1.00
85		1998	11129.4840	9.32	18.2160	41.8968	1.00	1.00
86		1999	6788.1924	8.82	17.5104	32.2560	1.00	1.00
87		2000	–4128.7680		15.9987	37.6440	1.00	1.00
88		2001	5366.1522	8.59	15.5248	52.3962	1.00	1.00
89		2002	–4725.3610		17.0000	58.0000	1.00	1.00
90		2003	48.0000	3.87	17.4267	59.4558	1.00	1.00
91		2004	471.5460	6.16	16.7664	58.6824	1.00	1.00
92		2005	2276.0388	7.73	16.1310	53.2508	1.00	1.00
93		2006	1296.9324	7.17			1.00	1.00
94	Constable	1976	4.8898	1.59	10.8765	13.7769	0.00	0.00
95	& Co Ltd	1977	6.7676	1.91	12.6806	15.1088	0.00	0.00
96		1978	10.2524	2.33	12.3640	18.2369	0.00	0.00
97		1979	–2.7819		14.0410	19.9530	0.00	0.00
98		1980	–1.8475		13.9910	20.9865	0.00	0.00
99		1981	–5.7610		13.2600	19.4480	0.00	0.00
100		1982	6.6300	1.89	12.5901	21.9161	0.00	0.00
101		1983	17.7194	2.87	11.7072	23.9022	0.00	0.00
102		1984	20.4876	3.02	10.8423	9.8097	0.00	0.00
103		1985	26.3313	3.27	9.0763	22.4238	0.00	0.00
104		1986	14.4153	2.67	7.3125	24.7500	0.00	0.00
105		1987	10.1250	2.32	11.3582	43.0416	0.00	0.00
106		1988	33.4768	3.51	15.3984	32.7216	0.00	0.00
107		1989	54.5360	4.00	15.2064	35.2512	0.00	1.00
108		1990	–86.4000		16.1876	37.5258	0.00	1.00
109		1991	–147.8958		15.2700	41.9925	0.00	1.00
110		1992	66.4245	4.20	14.9226	43.1970	0.00	1.00
111		1993	17.2788	2.85	14.3622	39.8950	0.00	1.00
112		1994	–69.4173		13.1088	42.6036	0.00	1.00
113		1995	18.8439	2.94	13.5840	34.8090	1.00	1.00
114		1996	50.0910	3.91	13.0905	38.3988	1.00	1.00
115		1997	63.7071	4.15	18.7320	40.1400	1.00	1.00
116		1998	–60.6560		18.2160	41.8968	1.00	1.00
117		1999	4929.0924	8.50	17.5104	32.2560	1.00	1.00
118		2000	4987.5402	8.51	15.9987	37.6440	1.00	1.00
119		2001	5093.0708	8.54	15.5248	52.3962	1.00	1.00
120		2002	458650.1367	13.04	17.0000	58.0000	1.00	1.00
121		2003	149471.0000	11.91	17.4267	59.4558	1.00	1.00
122		2004	210877.4214	12.26	16.7664	58.6824	1.00	1.00
123		2005	219215.4405	12.30	16.1310	53.2508	1.00	1.00
124		2006	196390.6234	12.19			1.00	1.00
125	David &	1976	42.0948	3.74	10.8765	13.7769	0.00	0.00
126	Charles Plc	1977	36.2550	3.59	12.6806	15.1088	0.00	0.00

(Continued overleaf)

Table 1 Continued

Case I	Firm	T Time (Year)	Y_it Pre-tax profit (£'000)^a	Natural log of pre-tax profit^b $\beta_1 X_{it}$	$\beta_k X_{it}$ Dynamics index^c $\beta_1 X_{it}$	Concentration ratio (%)^d $\beta_2 X_{it}$	Innovation^e $\beta_3 X_{it}$	UK Copyright 1988^f $\beta_4 X_{it}$
127		1978	54.2298	3.99	12.3640	18.2369	0.00	0.00
128		1979	73.5658	4.30	14.0410	19.9530	0.00	0.00
129		1980	112.3280	4.72	13.9910	20.9865	0.00	0.00
130		1981	125.0960	4.83	13.2600	19.4480	0.00	0.00
131		1982	−139.2300		12.5901	21.9161	0.00	0.00
132		1983	−182.7896		11.7072	23.9022	0.00	0.00
133		1984	140.4864	4.95	10.8423	9.8097	0.00	0.00
134		1985	238.5306	5.47	9.0763	22.4238	0.00	0.00
135		1986	229.5770	5.44	7.3125	24.7500	0.00	0.00
136		1987	357.7500	5.88	11.3582	43.0416	0.00	0.00
137		1988	431.6116	6.07	15.3984	32.7216	0.00	0.00
138		1989	379.1856	5.94	15.2064	35.2512	0.00	1.00
139		1990	−181.0944		16.1876	37.5258	0.00	1.00
140		1991	637.2028	6.46	15.2700	41.9925	0.00	1.00
141		1992	66.4245	4.20	14.9226	43.1970	0.00	1.00
142		1993	−129.5910		14.3622	39.8950	0.00	1.00
143		1994	−141.2283		13.1088	42.6036	0.00	1.00
144		1995	4433.9102	8.40	13.5840	34.8090	1.00	1.00
145		1996	373.5600	5.92	13.0905	38.3988	1.00	1.00
146		1997	451.1859	6.11	18.7320	40.1400	1.00	1.00
147		1998	−184.6440		18.2160	41.8968	1.00	1.00
148		1999	1039.2228	6.95	17.5104	32.2560	1.00	1.00
149		2000	−827.5968		15.9987	37.6440	1.00	1.00
150		2001	353.8536	5.87	15.5248	52.3962	1.00	1.00
151		2002	264.8919	5.58	17.0000	58.0000	1.00	1.00
152		2003	559.0000	6.33	17.4267	59.4558	1.00	1.00
153		2004	1427.9643	7.26	16.7664	58.6824	1.00	1.00
154		2005	1898.7948	7.55	16.1310	53.2508	1.00	1.00
155		2006	0.0000				1.00	1.00
156	Faber &	1976	37.6302	3.63	10.8765	13.7769	0.00	0.00
157	Faber Ltd	1977	76.1355	4.33	12.6806	15.1088	0.00	0.00
158		1978	152.7068	5.03	12.3640	18.2369	0.00	0.00
159		1979	51.3106	3.94	14.0410	19.9530	0.00	0.00
160		1980	−22.5395		13.9910	20.9865	0.00	0.00
161		1981	96.2910	4.57	13.2600	19.4480	0.00	0.00
162		1982	−48.6200		12.5901	21.9161	0.00	0.00
163		1983	−142.6878		11.7072	23.9022	0.00	0.00
164		1984	186.3396	5.23	10.8423	9.8097	0.00	0.00
165		1985	152.8248	5.03	9.0763	22.4238	0.00	0.00
166		1986	258.4076	5.55	7.3125	24.7500	0.00	0.00
167		1987	218.2500	5.39	11.3582	43.0416	0.00	0.00
168		1988	366.4514	5.90	15.3984	32.7216	0.00	0.00
169		1989	460.6688	6.13	15.2064	35.2512	0.00	1.00
170		1990	223.2576	5.41	16.1876	37.5258	0.00	1.00

171		1991	196.4586	5.28	15.2700	41.9925	0.00	1.00
172		1992	710.0550	6.57	14.9226	43.1970	0.00	1.00
173		1993	685.6542	6.53	14.3622	39.8950	0.00	1.00
174		1994	882.4774	6.78	13.1088	42.6036	0.00	1.00
175		1995	830.7702	6.72	13.5840	34.8090	1.00	1.00
176		1996	371.0130	5.92	13.0905	38.3988	1.00	1.00
177		1997	−107.3421		18.7320	40.1400	1.00	1.00
178		1998	−559.2840		18.2160	41.8968	1.00	1.00
179		1999	233.1648	5.45	17.5104	32.2560	1.00	1.00
180		2000	−1510.5024		15.9987	37.6440	1.00	1.00
181		2001	−545.8380		15.5248	52.3962	1.00	1.00
182		2002	−274.5949		17.0000	58.0000	1.00	1.00
183		2003	452.0000	6.11	17.4267	59.4558	1.00	1.00
184		2004	118.9116	4.78	16.7664	58.6824	1.00	1.00
185		2005	952.5411	6.86	16.1310	53.2508	1.00	1.00
186		2006	312.9414	5.75			1.00	1.00
187	Frederick	1976	37.8428	3.63	10.8765	13.7769	0.00	0.00
188	Warne &	1977	62.6003	4.14	12.6806	15.1088	0.00	0.00
189	Co Ltd	1978	122.7590	4.81	12.3640	18.2369	0.00	0.00
190		1979	39.5648	3.68	14.0410	19.9530	0.00	0.00
191		1980	52.8385	3.97	13.9910	20.9865	0.00	0.00
192		1981	56.3755	4.03	13.2600	19.4480	0.00	0.00
193		1982	−65.4160		12.5901	21.9161	0.00	0.00
194		1983	−12.5901		11.7072	23.9022	0.00	0.00
195		1984	262.9242	5.57	10.8423	9.8097	0.00	0.00
196		1985	878.7426	6.78	9.0763	22.4238	0.00	0.00
197		1986	1231.1734	7.12	7.3125	24.7500	0.00	0.00
198		1987	1585.1250	7.37	11.3582	43.0416	0.00	0.00
199		1988	2390.0044	7.78	15.3984	32.7216	0.00	0.00
200		1989	3472.2285	8.15	15.2064	35.2512	0.00	1.00
201		1990	3740.6551	8.23	16.1876	37.5258	0.00	1.00
202		1991	3982.0226	8.29	15.2700	41.9925	0.00	1.00
203		1992	4131.9302	8.33	14.9226	43.1970	0.00	1.00
204		1993	1932.0840	7.57	14.3622	39.8950	0.00	1.00
205		1994	2393.7000	7.78	13.1088	42.6036	0.00	1.00
206		1995	3709.7904	8.22	13.5840	34.8090	1.00	1.00
207		1996	4286.6010	8.36	13.0905	38.3988	1.00	1.00
208		1997	4672.4358	8.45	18.7320	40.1400	1.00	1.00
209		1998	5300.2640	8.58	18.2160	41.8968	1.00	1.00
210		1999	6122.3976	8.72	17.5104	32.2560	1.00	1.00
211		2000	5472.4608	8.61	15.9987	37.6440	1.00	1.00
212		2001	3369.1380	8.12	15.5248	52.3962	1.00	1.00
213		2002	5162.9663	8.55	17.0000	58.0000	1.00	1.00
214		2003	3675.0000	8.21	17.4267	59.4558	1.00	1.00
215		2004	1989.7191	7.60	16.7664	58.6824	1.00	1.00
216		2005	1834.8729	7.51	16.1310	53.2508	1.00	1.00
217		2006	1755.0528	7.47			1.00	1.00
218	Hodder &	1976	259.1594	5.56	10.8765	13.7769	0.00	0.00
219	Stoughton	1977	323.8780	5.78	12.6806	15.1088	0.00	0.00
220	Holdings	1978	390.4006	5.97	12.3640	18.2369	0.00	0.00
221	Ltd	1979	219.4610	5.39	14.0410	19.9530	0.00	0.00
222		1980	296.3390	5.69	13.9910	20.9865	0.00	0.00

(Continued overleaf)

Table 1 Continued

Case 1		T	Y_{it}			$\beta_k X_{it}$		
	Firm	Time (Year)	Pre-tax profit (£'000)[a]	Natural log of pre-tax profit[b] $\beta_1 X_{it}$	Dynamics index[c]	Concentration ratio (%)[d] $\beta_2 X_{it}$	Innovation[e] $\beta_3 X_{it}$	UK Copyright 1988[f] $\beta_4 X_{it}$
223		1981	467.4640	6.15	13.2600	19.4480	0.00	0.00
224		1982	805.7660	6.69	12.5901	21.9161	0.00	0.00
225		1983	1562.5713	7.35	11.7072	23.9022	0.00	0.00
226		1984	2031.1992	7.62	10.8423	9.8097	0.00	0.00
227		1985	1300.0434	7.17	9.0763	22.4238	0.00	0.00
228		1986	1160.1647	7.06	7.3125	24.7500	0.00	0.00
229		1987	1306.6875	7.18	11.3582	43.0416	0.00	0.00
230		1988	866.2122	6.76	15.3984	32.7216	0.00	0.00
231		1989	545.3600	6.30	15.2064	35.2512	0.00	1.00
232		1990	−4064.9472		16.1876	37.5258	0.00	1.00
233		1991	9035.6240	9.11	15.2700	41.9925	0.00	1.00
234		1992	−4965.0405		14.9226	43.1970	0.00	1.00
235		1993	−11166.8172		14.3622	39.8950	0.00	1.00
236		1994	15379.5225	9.64	13.1088	42.6036	0.00	1.00
237		1995	4212.8406	8.35	13.5840	34.8090	1.00	1.00
238		1996	4594.6415	8.43	13.0905	38.3988	1.00	1.00
239		1997	6104.5365	8.72	18.7320	40.1400	1.00	1.00
240		1998	6300.1960	8.75	18.2160	41.8968	1.00	1.00
241		1999	−3617.6976		17.5104	32.2560	1.00	1.00
242		2000	7968.1536	8.98	15.9987	37.6440	1.00	1.00
243		2001	10176.1143	9.23	15.5248	52.3962	1.00	1.00
244		2002	12143.3045	9.40	17.0000	58.0000	1.00	1.00
245		2003	3541.0000	8.17	17.4267	59.4558	1.00	1.00
246		2004	11891.1600	9.38	16.7664	58.6824	1.00	1.00
247		2005	11599.2051	9.36	16.1310	53.2508	1.00	1.00
248		2006	32915.8432	10.40			1.00	1.00
249	Ian Allan	1976	18.9214	2.94	10.8765	13.7769	0.00	0.00
250	Ltd	1977	20.0611	3.00	12.6806	15.1088	0.00	0.00
251		1978	42.3586	3.75	12.3640	18.2369	0.00	0.00
252		1979	37.7102	3.63	14.0410	19.9530	0.00	0.00
253		1980	53.2080	3.97	13.9910	20.9865	0.00	0.00
254		1981	44.0305	3.78	13.2600	19.4480	0.00	0.00
255		1982	86.6320	4.46	12.5901	21.9161	0.00	0.00
256		1983	116.1087	4.75	11.7072	23.9022	0.00	0.00
257		1984	10.7316	2.37	10.8423	9.8097	0.00	0.00
258		1985	74.3472	4.31	9.0763	22.4238	0.00	0.00
259		1986	57.1273	4.05	7.3125	24.7500	0.00	0.00
260		1987	72.5625	4.28	11.3582	43.0416	0.00	0.00
261		1988	−157.2214		15.3984	32.7216	0.00	0.00
262		1989	−127.0368		15.2064	35.2512	0.00	1.00
263		1990	−165.8880		16.1876	37.5258	0.00	1.00
264		1991	−194.9870		15.2700	41.9925	0.00	1.00
265		1992	−58.7895		14.9226	43.1970	0.00	1.00
266		1993	89.5356	4.49	14.3622	39.8950	0.00	1.00
267		1994	104.5249	4.65	13.1088	42.6036	0.00	1.00

268		1995	−122.0757		13.5840	34.8090	1.00	1.00
269		1996	−299.6970		13.0905	38.3988	1.00	1.00
270		1997	42.7623	3.76	18.7320	40.1400	1.00	1.00
271		1998	132.9080	4.89	18.2160	41.8968	1.00	1.00
272		1999	224.0568	5.41	17.5104	32.2560	1.00	1.00
273		2000	338.2272	5.82	15.9987	37.6440	1.00	1.00
274		2001	116.6964	4.76	15.5248	52.3962	1.00	1.00
275		2002	164.9510	5.11	17.0000	58.0000	1.00	1.00
276		2003	54.0000	3.99	17.4267	59.4558	1.00	1.00
277		2004	−114.8112		16.7664	58.6824	1.00	1.00
278		2005	−239.9691		16.1310	53.2508	1.00	1.00
279		2006	−532.3230				1.00	1.00
280	Ladybird	1976	153.0720	5.03	10.8765	13.7769	0.00	0.00
281	Books Ltd	1977	99.8221	4.60	12.6806	15.1088	0.00	0.00
282		1978	191.0184	5.25	12.3640	18.2369	0.00	0.00
283		1979	315.9002	5.76	14.0410	19.9530	0.00	0.00
284		1980	351.7640	5.86	13.9910	20.9865	0.00	0.00
285		1981	583.5070	6.37	13.2600	19.4480	0.00	0.00
286		1982	674.9340	6.51	12.5901	21.9161	0.00	0.00
287		1983	786.1818	6.67	11.7072	23.9022	0.00	0.00
288		1984	1021.4532	6.93	10.8423	9.8097	0.00	0.00
289		1985	1265.9676	7.14	9.0763	22.4238	0.00	0.00
290		1986	1313.9279	7.18	7.3125	24.7500	0.00	0.00
291		1987	1521.5625	7.33	11.3582	43.0416	0.00	0.00
292		1988	1285.8678	7.16	15.3984	32.7216	0.00	0.00
293		1989	1287.0496	7.16	15.2064	35.2512	0.00	1.00
294		1990	1155.6864	7.05	16.1876	37.5258	0.00	1.00
295		1991	−19.8666		15.2700	41.9925	0.00	1.00
296		1992	1605.6405	7.38	14.9226	43.1970	0.00	1.00
297		1993	1591.2204	7.37	14.3622	39.8950	0.00	1.00
298		1994	1630.1097	7.40	13.1088	42.6036	0.00	1.00
299		1995	1362.4959	7.22	13.5840	34.8090	1.00	1.00
300		1996	886.3560	6.79	13.0905	38.3988	1.00	1.00
301		1997	899.7537	6.80	18.7320	40.1400	1.00	1.00
302		1998	−7225.2000		18.2160	41.8968	1.00	1.00
303		1999	1168.5564	7.06	17.5104	32.2560	1.00	1.00
304		2000	−2991.5136		15.9987	37.6440	1.00	1.00
305		2001	−1499.1723		15.5248	52.3962	1.00	1.00
306		2002	961.5673	6.87	17.0000	58.0000	1.00	1.00
307		2003	−726.0000		17.4267	59.4558	1.00	1.00
308		2004	−2447.9388		16.7664	58.6824	1.00	1.00
309		2005	−1794.0048		16.1310	53.2508	1.00	1.00
310		2006	−2630.4284				1.00	1.00
311	Marshall	1976	44.8586	3.80	10.8765	13.7769	0.00	0.00
312	Cavendish	1977	18.8526	2.94	12.6806	15.1088	0.00	0.00
313	Ltd	1978	45.8660	3.83	12.3640	18.2369	0.00	0.00
314		1979	−170.0050		14.0410	19.9530	0.00	0.00
315		1980	−141.8880		13.9910	20.9865	0.00	0.00
316		1981	167.4805	5.12	13.2600	19.4480	0.00	0.00
317		1982	300.5600	5.71	12.5901	21.9161	0.00	0.00
318		1983	259.2628	5.56	11.7072	23.9022	0.00	0.00
319		1984	354.1428	5.87	10.8423	9.8097	0.00	0.00
320		1985	414.0726	6.03	9.0763	22.4238	0.00	0.00

(Continued overleaf)

Table 1 Continued

Case I	Firm	T Time (Year)	Y_it Pre-tax profit (£'000)^a	Natural log of pre-tax profit^b β_1X_{it}	Dynamics index^c β_1X_{it}	β_kX_{it} Concentration ratio (%)^d β_2X_{it}	Innovation^e β_3X_{it}	UK Copyright 1988^f β_4X_{it}
321		1986	1311.7923	7.18	7.3125	24.7500	0.00	0.00
322		1987	2005.8750	7.60	11.3582	43.0416	0.00	0.00
323		1988	789.0960	6.67	15.3984	32.7216	0.00	0.00
324		1989	1792.6304	7.49	15.2064	35.2512	0.00	1.00
325		1990	2108.1600	7.65	16.1876	37.5258	0.00	1.00
326		1991	1824.0482	7.51	15.2700	41.9925	0.00	1.00
327		1992	−455.8095		14.9226	43.1970	0.00	1.00
328		1993	−7.8540		14.3622	39.8950	0.00	1.00
329		1994	1521.5953	7.33	13.1088	42.6036	0.00	1.00
330		1995	2480.0211	7.82	13.5840	34.8090	1.00	1.00
331		1996	927.9570	6.83	13.0905	38.3988	1.00	1.00
332		1997	2342.3268	7.76	18.7320	40.1400	1.00	1.00
333		1998	5087.9680	8.53	18.2160	41.8968	1.00	1.00
334		1999	4435.5960	8.40	17.5104	32.2560	1.00	1.00
335		2000	6701.8752	8.81	15.9987	37.6440	1.00	1.00
336		2001	5678.5974	8.64	15.5248	52.3962	1.00	1.00
337		2002	15991.5143	9.68	17.0000	58.0000	1.00	1.00
338		2003	2320.0000	7.75	17.4267	59.4558	1.00	1.00
339		2004	1610.4321	7.38	16.7664	58.6824	1.00	1.00
340		2005	1193.5581	7.08	16.1310	53.2508	1.00	1.00
341		2006	2891.7506	7.97			1.00	1.00
342	Mills &	1976	116.5048	4.76	10.8765	13.7769	0.00	0.00
343	Boon Ltd	1977	295.5991	5.69	12.6806	15.1088	0.00	0.00
344		1978	366.3884	5.90	12.3640	18.2369	0.00	0.00
345		1979	1081.2318	6.99	14.0410	19.9530	0.00	0.00
346		1980	1643.5360	7.40	13.9910	20.9865	0.00	0.00
347		1981	1324.2070	7.19	13.2600	19.4480	0.00	0.00
348		1982	1399.8140	7.24	12.5901	21.9161	0.00	0.00
349		1983	1493.0926	7.31	11.7072	23.9022	0.00	0.00
350		1984	780.9678	6.66	10.8423	9.8097	0.00	0.00
351		1985	551.9247	6.31	9.0763	22.4238	0.00	0.00
352		1986	442.0692	6.09	7.3125	24.7500	0.00	0.00
353		1987	666.0000	6.50	11.3582	43.0416	0.00	0.00
354		1988	852.4628	6.75	15.3984	32.7216	0.00	0.00
355		1989	1043.2416	6.95	15.2064	35.2512	0.00	1.00
356		1990	1115.5968	7.02	16.1876	37.5258	0.00	1.00
357		1991	1233.9366	7.12	15.2700	41.9925	0.00	1.00
358		1992	1596.4785	7.38	14.9226	43.1970	0.00	1.00
359		1993	1548.8088	7.35	14.3622	39.8950	0.00	1.00
360		1994	1112.2726	7.01	13.1088	42.6036	0.00	1.00
361		1995	1608.2859	7.38	13.5840	34.8090	1.00	1.00
362		1996	1813.4640	7.50	13.0905	38.3988	1.00	1.00
363		1997	2691.4068	7.90	18.7320	40.1400	1.00	1.00
364		1998	2089.0640	7.64	18.2160	41.8968	1.00	1.00

365		1999	2487.3948	7.82	17.5104	32.2560	1.00	1.00
366		2000	−3137.1264		15.9987	37.6440	1.00	1.00
367		2001	2748.9531	7.92	15.5248	52.3962	1.00	1.00
368		2002	3554.2089	8.18	17.0000	58.0000	1.00	1.00
369		2003	3031.0000	8.02	17.4267	59.4558	1.00	1.00
370		2004	1479.2193	7.30	16.7664	58.6824	1.00	1.00
371		2005	2161.8177	7.68	16.1310	53.2508	1.00	1.00
372		2006	2968.1040	8.00			1.00	1.00
373	Penguin	1976	424.1370	6.05	10.8765	13.7769	0.00	0.00
374	Books Ltd	1977	160.4888	5.08	12.6806	15.1088	0.00	0.00
375		1978	286.5276	5.66	12.3640	18.2369	0.00	0.00
376		1979	−182.6781		14.0410	19.9530	0.00	0.00
377		1980	−237.9580		13.9910	20.9865	0.00	0.00
378		1981	1111.0500	7.01	13.2600	19.4480	0.00	0.00
379		1982	1212.8480	7.10	12.5901	21.9161	0.00	0.00
380		1983	2407.5069	7.79	11.7072	23.9022	0.00	0.00
381		1984	2690.7048	7.90	10.8423	9.8097	0.00	0.00
382		1985	1368.1950	7.22	9.0763	22.4238	0.00	0.00
383		1986	4493.3024	8.41	7.3125	24.7500	0.00	0.00
384		1987	1764.5625	7.48	11.3582	43.0416	0.00	0.00
385		1988	1497.4890	7.31	15.3984	32.7216	0.00	0.00
386		1989	173.8736	5.16	15.2064	35.2512	0.00	1.00
387		1990	1179.8784	7.07	16.1876	37.5258	0.00	1.00
388		1991	−1494.4098		15.2700	41.9925	0.00	1.00
389		1992	5941.5570	8.69	14.9226	43.1970	0.00	1.00
390		1993	13627.4754	9.52	14.3622	39.8950	0.00	1.00
391		1994	5778.3918	8.66	13.1088	42.6036	0.00	1.00
392		1995	1154.3937	7.05	13.5840	34.8090	1.00	1.00
393		1996	−559.4910		13.0905	38.3988	1.00	1.00
394		1997	4245.6855	8.35	18.7320	40.1400	1.00	1.00
395		1998	10062.6520	9.22	18.2160	41.8968	1.00	1.00
396		1999	13049.9424	9.48	17.5104	32.2560	1.00	1.00
397		2000	9133.0560	9.12	15.9987	37.6440	1.00	1.00
398		2001	10036.8315	9.21	15.5248	52.3962	1.00	1.00
399		2002	405.5854	6.01	17.0000	58.0000	1.00	1.00
400		2003	−328.0000		17.4267	59.4558	1.00	1.00
401		2004	−3289.5459		16.7664	58.6824	1.00	1.00
402		2005	−6248.6277		16.1310	53.2508	1.00	1.00
403		2006	3385.3592	8.13			1.00	1.00
404	Thames &	1976	116.0796	4.75	10.8765	13.7769	0.00	0.00
405	Hudson	1977	149.6123	5.01	12.6806	15.1088	0.00	0.00
406	Ltd	1978	109.5388	4.70	12.3640	18.2369	0.00	0.00
407		1979	86.2389	4.46	14.0410	19.9530	0.00	0.00
408		1980	24.3870	3.19	13.9910	20.9865	0.00	0.00
409		1981	75.3045	4.32	13.2600	19.4480	0.00	0.00
410		1982	111.8260	4.72	12.5901	21.9161	0.00	0.00
411		1983	148.7497	5.00	11.7072	23.9022	0.00	0.00
412		1984	200.4858	5.30	10.8423	9.8097	0.00	0.00
413		1985	220.4601	5.40	9.0763	22.4238	0.00	0.00
414		1986	271.2212	5.60	7.3125	24.7500	0.00	0.00
415		1987	324.0000	5.78	11.3582	43.0416	0.00	0.00
416		1988	490.7938	6.20	15.3984	32.7216	0.00	0.00

(Continued overleaf)

Table 1 Continued

Case	I	T	Y_{it}			$\beta_k X_{it}$		
	Firm	Time (Year)	Pre-tax profit (£'000)[a]	Natural log of pre-tax profit[b] $\beta_1 X_{it}$	Dynamics index[c] $\beta_1 X_{it}$	Concentration ratio (%)[d] $\beta_2 X_{it}$	Innovation[e] $\beta_3 X_{it}$	UK Copyright 1988[f] $\beta_4 X_{it}$
417		1989	359.9376	5.89	15.2064	35.2512	0.00	1.00
418		1990	305.5104	5.72	16.1876	37.5258	0.00	1.00
419		1991	250.9078	5.53	15.2700	41.9925	0.00	1.00
420		1992	213.7800	5.36	14.9226	43.1970	0.00	1.00
421		1993	348.7176	5.85	14.3622	39.8950	0.00	1.00
422		1994	394.1626	5.98	13.1088	42.6036	0.00	1.00
423		1995	949.5687	6.86	13.5840	34.8090	1.00	1.00
424		1996	854.0940	6.75	13.0905	38.3988	1.00	1.00
425		1997	909.3534	6.81	18.7320	40.1400	1.00	1.00
426		1998	1050.7760	6.96	18.2160	41.8968	1.00	1.00
427		1999	1078.3872	6.98	17.5104	32.2560	1.00	1.00
428		2000	1500.3648	7.31	15.9987	37.6440	1.00	1.00
429		2001	1598.9289	7.38	15.5248	52.3962	1.00	1.00
430		2002	3780.2888	8.24	17.0000	58.0000	1.00	1.00
431		2003	1828.0000	7.51	17.4267	59.4558	1.00	1.00
432		2004	1954.8657	7.58	16.7664	58.6824	1.00	1.00
433		2005	2041.3092	7.62	16.1310	53.2508	1.00	1.00
434		2006	1488.3536	7.31			1.00	1.00
435	Wiley &	1976	144.1428	4.97	10.8765	13.7769	0.00	0.00
436	Sons Ltd	1977	114.0824	4.74	12.6806	15.1088	0.00	0.00
437		1978	179.9566	5.19	12.3640	18.2369	0.00	0.00
438		1979	225.6430	5.42	14.0410	19.9530	0.00	0.00
439		1980	269.7350	5.60	13.9910	20.9865	0.00	0.00
440		1981	320.9700	5.77	13.2600	19.4480	0.00	0.00
441		1982	235.5860	5.46	12.5901	21.9161	0.00	0.00
442		1983	465.8337	6.14	11.7072	23.9022	0.00	0.00
443		1984	438.0444	6.08	10.8423	9.8097	0.00	0.00
444		1985	821.9496	6.71	9.0763	22.4238	0.00	0.00
445		1986	1045.3762	6.95	7.3125	24.7500	0.00	0.00
446		1987	1090.6875	6.99	11.3582	43.0416	0.00	0.00
447		1988	1444.8826	7.28	15.3984	32.7216	0.00	0.00
448		1989	1449.3744	7.28	15.2064	35.2512	0.00	1.00
449		1990	1243.4688	7.13	16.1876	37.5258	0.00	1.00
450		1991	1677.6240	7.43	15.2700	41.9925	0.00	1.00
451		1992	2384.4105	7.78	14.9226	43.1970	0.00	1.00
452		1993	2749.6854	7.92	14.3622	39.8950	0.00	1.00
453		1994	4156.2611	8.33	13.1088	42.6036	0.00	1.00
454		1995	4491.4026	8.41	13.5840	34.8090	1.00	1.00
455		1996	5453.9760	8.60	13.0905	38.3988	1.00	1.00
456		1997	5266.7445	8.57	18.7320	40.1400	1.00	1.00
457		1998	4780.2280	8.47	18.2160	41.8968	1.00	1.00
458		1999	4336.3188	8.37	17.5104	32.2560	1.00	1.00
459		2000	8834.4576	9.09	15.9987	37.6440	1.00	1.00
460		2001	10116.8250	9.22	15.5248	52.3962	1.00	1.00

461	2002	14831.0355	9.60	17.0000	58.0000	1.00	1.00
462	2003	9264.0000	9.13	17.4267	59.4558	1.00	1.00
463	2004	7224.9048	8.89	16.7664	58.6824	1.00	1.00
464	2005	8599.0674	9.06	16.1310	53.2508	1.00	1.00
465	2006	12999.4352	9.47			1.00	1.00

a. Pre-tax profit (£'000) is weighed with mean replace of missing data and UK GDP Deflator. b. Natural logarithmic (ln) data transformation of pre-tax profits (£'000) with mean replace of missing data and UK GDP Deflator. c. Dynamics index with mean replace of missing data and UK GDP Deflator under one-year lag. d. Concentration ratio (%) with mean replace of missing data and UK GDP Deflator under one-year lag. e. Technological innovation is measured as technological innovation since 1995 and coded as Pre-1995 = 0 and Post-1995 = 1. f. The UK's Copyright, Designs and Patents Act 1988 is designed as an intervention variable and coded as Pre-1988 = 0 and Post-1988 = 1.

Table 2 List of UK book publishing firms in Keynote's *Business Ratio Reports* (1976–2006)

No	Name of firm	Starting year recorded in Business Ratio Reports
1	A & C Black Plc	1976–77
2	A Wheaton & Company Ltd	1979–80
3	Aberdeen University Press Ltd	1981–82
4	Academic Press Inc (London) Ltd (Owned by Harcourt Publishers Ltd)	1976–77
5	Academy Group Ltd	1990–91
6	Addison Wesley Longman Group Ltd (Owned by Longman Communications Limited)	1985–86
7	Adelph Comm Ltd	1996–97
8	Aladdin Books Ltd	1986–87
9	Alain Charles Publishing Ltd	1984–85
10	Alan Hutchison Ltd	1988–89
11	All Children's Co Ltd	1993–94
12	(G) Allen & Unwin (Publishers) Ltd	1976–77
13	Anaya Publishers Ltd	1990–91
14	Andre Deutsch Ltd	1976–77
15	Angus Hudson Ltd	1990–91
16	Antique Collectors' Club Ltd	1986–87
17	The Architectural Press Ltd	1984–85
18	Arrowhead (Holdings) Ltd	1996–97
19	Arms & Armour Press Ltd	1984–85
20	Associated Book Publishers Plc	1976–77
21	Aurum Press Ltd	1990–91
22	Autodata Ltd	1993–94
23	Award Publications Ltd	1990–91
24	B T Batsford Ltd	1976–77
25	Barrie & Jenkins Ltd	1990–91
26	Basil Blackwell Ltd	1985–86
27	Bailliere Tindall Ltd	1984–85
28	The Barefoot Child Ltd	1996–97
29	Belitha Press Ltd	1993–94
30	Bell & Hyman Ltd	1984–85
31	Berlitz Publishing Co Ltd	1993–94
32	Bison Books Ltd	1988–89
33	Blackie & Son Ltd	1981–82
34	Blackstone Press Ltd	1990–91
35	Blackwell Polity Ltd	1990–91
36	Blackwell Publishers Ltd	1993–94
37	Blackwell Science Ltd (Blackwell Scientific Publications Ltd)	1979–80
38	Blandford Press Ltd	1984–85
39	Bloomsbury Publishing Plc (Bloomsbury Publishing Ltd)	1988–89
40	The Bodley Head Ltd	1981–82
41	Boxtree Ltd	1990–91
42	Boydell & Brewer Ltd	1996–97
43	BPP (Letts Educational) Ltd	1990–91
44	Brassey's (UK) Ltd	1993–94

45	Breslich & Foss Ltd	1993–94
46	The Bridgewater Book Co Ltd	1993–94
47	The British Publishing Co Ltd	1985–86
48	Burke Publishing Co Ltd	1981–82
49	Butterworth & Co (Publishers) Ltd	1976–77
50	Cadogan Books Plc	1993–94
51	(John) Calmann & King Ltd (Laurence King Publishing Ltd)	1986–87
52	Campden Publishing Ltd	1996–97
53	Canongate Books Ltd	1996–97
54	Carlton Books Ltd	1993–94
55	Carnell Ltd	1996–97
56	Cassell Ltd	1976–77
57	Cassell Educational Ltd	1990–91
58	Cassell Publishers Ltd	1990–91
59	Century Hutchinson Pub Group Ltd	1984–85
60	Century Publishing Co Ltd	1984–85
61	Chadwyck-Healey Ltd	1985–86
62	Chambers Harrap Publishers Ltd	1990–91
63	Chartsearch Ltd	1981–82
64	Chatto & Windus Ltd	1984–85
65	Chivers Book Sales Ltd (BBC Audiobooks Limited)	1985–86
66	Christopher Helm (Publishers) Ltd	1986–87
67	Chronicle Communications Ltd	1993–94
68	Colins & Brown Ltd	1990–91
69	Colour Library Books Ltd	1986–87
70	Columbus Books Ltd	1985–86
71	The Conde Nast Publications Ltd	1990–91
72	Conegate Ltd	1985–86
73	Conran Octopus Ltd	1990–91
74	Constable & Co Ltd (Constable & Robinson Limited)	1976–77
75	Cornhill Publications Ltd	1990–91
76	Croner Publications Ltd	1988–89
77	Croom Helm Ltd	1981–82
78	The Crowood Press Ltd	1990–91
79	Current Medical Literature Ltd	1988–89
80	David & Charles (Holdings) Plc	1976–77
81	David Campbell Publishers Ltd	1990–91
82	Darton Longman & Todd Ltd	1986–87
83	Debrett's Peerage Ltd (SPG Market Solutions Limited)	1993–94
84	Dorling Kindersley Holdings Ltd	1990–91
85	DP Publications Ltd	1990–91
86	Duncan Baird Publishers Ltd	1993–94
87	Edinburgh University Press Ltd	1993–94
88	Edisea Ltd	1996–97
89	Edward Arnold (Publishers) Ltd	1976–77
90	Egmont Children's Books Ltd	1996–97
91	Egmont Publishing Ltd	1990–91
92	Element Books Ltd	1990–91
93	Elfande Ltd	1996–97

(Continued overleaf)

Table 2 Continued

No	Name of firm	Starting year recorded in Business Ratio Reports
94	Ellesmere Investments Ltd	1993–94
95	Elsevier Science Publishers Ltd	1984–85
96	Enid Blyton Ltd	1996–97
97	Europa Publications Ltd	1984–85
98	Evans Brothers Ltd	1979–80
99	Everyman Publishers Plc	1996–97
100	Exley Publications Ltd	1996–97
101	F A Thorpe (Publishing) Ltd	1976–77
102	Faber & Faber (Publishers) Ltd	1976–77
103	Fisk Publishing Co Ltd	1985–86
104	Financial Training Publics Ltd	1984–85
105	Folens Ltd	1993–94
106	The Folio Society Ltd	1993–94
107	The Foundry Creative Media Co Ltd	1996–97
108	Fourth Estate Ltd	1993–94
109	Francis Lincoln Ltd	1990–91
110	Frederick Warne & Co Ltd	1976–77
111	Futura Publications Ltd	1976–77
112	Gaia Books Ltd	1993–94
113	Geoffrey Faber Holdings Ltd	1988–89
114	George G Harrap & Co Ltd	1976–77
115	George Philip & Son Ltd	1976–77
116	George Weidenfeld Holdings Ltd	1976–77
117	Golden Standard Ltd	1996–97
118	Gollancz (Holdings) Ltd	1984–85
119	Graham Trotman Ltd	1986–87
120	Granada Publishing Ltd	1979–80
121	Grandreams Ltd	1984–85
122	Grenville Books Ltd	1993–94
123	Grisewood & Dempsey Ltd	1984–85
124	Grolier Ltd	1993–94
125	Grosvenor Press International Ltd	1986–87
126	Guinness Superlatives Ltd (Guinness Publishing Ltd or Guinness World Records Limited)	1976–77
127	H K Lewis & Co Ltd	1984–85
128	H Karnac (Books) Ltd	1996–97
129	Hamish Hamilton Ltd	1976–77
130	The Hamlyn Publishing Group Ltd (Octopus Publishing Group)	1976–77
131	Harcourt Publishers Ltd (Harcourt Brace Jovanovich Ltd)	1984–85
132	Harper Colins Publisher Ltd	1986–87
133	Harrap Ltd	1979–80
134	Haynes Publishing Group Plc	1981–82
135	Headline Book Publishing Plc	1988–89
136	Heinemann Group of Publishers Ltd	1976–77
137	Helicon Publishing Ltd	1993–94
138	Henry Kimpton Ltd	1976–77

139	Hm Publishers Holdings Ltd	1996–97
140	Hobsons Publishing Plc	1985–86
141	Hodder Headline Plc	1990–91
142	Hodder & Stoughton Holdings Ltd	1976–77
143	Holt Saunders Ltd	1976–77
144	Hove Publishers Ltd	1996–97
145	Hutchinson Publishing Group Ltd	1980–81
146	Ian Allan Ltd	1976–77
147	Intermediate Technology Publications Ltd	1996–97
148	International Book Distributors Ltd	1985–86
149	International System & Comms Ltd	1996–97
150	International Thomson Plc	1985–86
151	IOP Publishing Ltd	1986–87
152	Isismedne Ltd	1996–97
153	J L Design Ltd	1996–97
154	J M Dent & Sons (Holdings) Ltd	1976–77
155	Jane's Publishing Company Ltd	1981–82
156	Jessica Kingsley (Publishers) Ltd	1996–97
157	Jonathan Cape Ltd (Owned by The Random House Group Limited)	1976–77
158	Jordan Publishing Ltd	1996–97
159	Judy Piatkus (Publishers) Ltd	1996–97
160	Kelsey Publishing Ltd	1996–97
161	Kensington Publications Ltd	1996–97
162	Kevin Mayhew Ltd	1996–97
163	Kingfisher Publications Plc	1996–97
164	Kingscourt Publishing Ltd	1996–97
165	Kluwer Ltd (Kluwer Law International Limited)	1985–86
166	Kogan Page Ltd	1990–91
167	Kp Sales Ltd	1996–97
168	Labyrinth Publishing (UK) Ltd	1993–94
169	Ladybird Books Ltd	1977–78
170	Larousse Plc	1993–94
171	Lawrence Erlbaum Associates Ltd	1990–91
172	Lion Publishing Plc (Lion Hudson Plc)	1984–85
173	Little, Brown & Co (UK) Ltd	1990–91
174	Longman Group UK Ltd	1985–86
175	Longman Holdings Ltd	1976–77
176	M B O 4 (AWC) Ltd	1985–86
177	MCB University Press Ltd	1988–89
178	MacDonald & Co (Publishers) Ltd	1981–82
179	Macmillan Ltd	1976–77
180	Macmillan Publishers Ltd	1990–91
181	Malaby Holdings Ltd	1981–82
182	Marshall Cavendish Ltd	1976–77
183	Marshall Editions Ltd	1996–97
184	Marshall, Morgan & Scott Ltd	1984–85
185	Martin Dunitz Ltd	1996–97
186	Mary Glasgow Publications Ltd	1976–77
187	Maskell Wiles Ltd	1993–94
188	McGraw-Hill Book Co (UK) Ltd (McGraw-Hill International UK Ltd)	1984–85
189	Mechanical Engineering Publications Ltd	1984–85

(Continued overleaf)

Table 2 Continued

No	Name of firm	Starting year recorded in Business Ratio Reports
190	Medi Cine International Ltd	1996–97
191	Medicine Group (UK) Ltd	1988–89
192	Melbourne House (Publishers) Ltd	1984–85
193	Merehurst Ltd	1990–91
194	Metal Bulletin Books Ltd	1996–97
195	Methuen Publishing Ltd	1996–97
196	Michael Joseph Ltd	1976–77
197	Michael O'Mara Books Ltd	1993–94
198	Midsummer Books Ltd	1996–97
199	(Harlequin) Mills & Boon Ltd	1976–77
200	Minerva Press Ltd	1996–97
201	Mitchell Beazley International Ltd	1984–85
202	Mitchell Beazley London Ltd	1990–91
203	Mosby International Ltd	1996–97
204	Mosey-Year Book Europe Ltd	1988–89
205	Multiplex Techniques Ltd	1985–86
206	(John) Murray (Publishers) Ltd	1976–77
207	Musterlin Group Plc	1984–85
208	New English Library Ltd	1976–77
209	New Holland Publishers (UK) Ltd	1990–91
210	New Left Books Ltd	1986–87
211	Octopus Publishing Group Ltd	1977–78
212	Oliver Books Ltd	1996–97
213	Omega Books Ltd	1984–85
214	Open International Publishing Ltd	1996–97
215	Orion Books Ltd	1990–91
216	The Orion Publishing Group Ltd	1993–94
217	P P S Publications Ltd	1996–97
218	Pan Books Ltd	1976–77
219	Parkgate Books Ltd	1996–97
220	Parks Bookshops Ltd	1985–86
221	Parragon Book Service Ltd	1993–94
222	Patrick Stephens Ltd	1979–80
223	Pavilion Books Ltd	1990–91
224	Pearl & Dean Publishing Ltd	1988–89
225	Pearson Education Ltd	1996–97
226	Pen & Sword Books Ltd	1996–97
227	Penguin Books Ltd	1976–77
228	Pergamon Press Ltd	1976–77
229	Peter Haddock Ltd	1984–85
230	Phaidon Press Ltd	1990–91
231	Philip Wilson Publishers Ltd	1988–89
232	Phoenix Publishing & Media Ltd	1996–97
233	Pitman Ltd	1976–77
234	Plexus Publishing Ltd	1996–97
235	Prc Publishing Ltd	1996–97
236	Prion Books Ltd	1996–97
237	Profile Books Ltd	1996–97

238	Publishing Holdings Plc	1984–85
239	The Q Group Plc	1996–97
240	Quadrille Publishing Ltd	1993–94
241	Quadrillion Publishing Ltd	1993–94
242	Quartet Books Ltd	1984–85
243	Quarto Children's Books Ltd	1993–94
244	Quarto Publishing Ltd	1985–86
245	Ragged Bear Ltd	1996–97
246	Ramboro Enterprises Ltd	1990–91
247	Random House Group Ltd	1996–97
248	Random House Publishing Group Ltd	1990–91
249	Random House UK Ltd	1984–85
250	Ravette Books Ltd	1990–91
251	Reed Educational & Professional Publishing Ltd	1996–97
252	Reed International Books Ltd (Owned by Reed Elsevier UK Limited)	1986–87
253	RIBA Publications Ltd	1988–89
254	Robson Books Ltd	1990–91
255	The Rough Guides Ltd	1996–97
256	Routledge, Chapman & Hall Ltd	1985–86
257	Routledge & Kegan Paul Plc	1976–77
258	Routledge Publishing Holdings Ltd	1996–97
259	Sadie Fields Productions Ltd	1996–97
260	Sage Publications Ltd	1996–97
261	Salamander Books Ltd	1984–85
262	Schofield & Sims (Holding) Ltd	1976–77
263	Scholastic Publications Ltd (Scholastic Limited)	1984–85
264	Science Research Associates Ltd	1976–77
265	SCM Press Ltd	1990–91
266	Scope International Ltd	1993–94
267	Search Press Ltd	1986–87
268	Selectabook Ltd	1990–91
269	Setform Ltd	1993–94
270	Shaw & Sons Ltd	1988–89
271	Sidgwick & Jackson Ltd	1984–85
272	Simon & Schuster (UK) Ltd	1996–97
273	Sinclair-Stevenson Ltd	1990–91
274	Sphere Books Ltd	1977–78
275	Stancroft Securities Ltd	1985–86
276	Stanley Thornes (Publishers) Ltd	1996–97
277	Sterling Publications Ltd (SPG Media Limited)	1984–85
278	Stroudgate Plc	1993–94
279	Studio Editions Ltd	1988–89
280	Swapequal Ltd	1993–94
281	Summerhouse Publishing Ltd	1996–97
282	Sutton Publishing Ltd	1993–94
283	T H Brickell & Son Ltd	1984–85
284	T & T Clark Ltd	1986–87
285	Taylor & Francis Group Ltd	1993–94
286	The Templar Co Plc	1986–87
287	Tempus Publishing Ltd	1996–97
288	Teviot Scientific Publications Ltd	1984–85
289	Thames & Hudson Ltd	1977–78

(Continued overleaf)

Table 2 Continued

No	Name of firm	Starting year recorded in Business Ratio Reports
290	Thomas Nelson & Sons Ltd	1986–87
291	Thomas Telford Ltd	1988–89
292	Thomson Books Ltd	1990–91
293	Thorsons Publishing Group Ltd	1984–85
294	Three Monks Press Ltd	1990–91
295	Time-Life Entertainment Grp Ltd	1990–91
296	Times Mirror Intl Publishers Ltd	1990–91
297	Titan Books Ltd	1990–91
298	Tn & Sons Ltd	1996–97
299	Tolley Publishing Co Ltd	1993–94
300	Toucan Books Ltd	1996–97
301	Transworld Publishers Ltd	1976–77
302	Twin Books (UK) Ltd	1990–91
303	Two-Can Publishing Ltd	1990–91
304	Ulverscroft Group Ltd	1985–86
305	Unwin Hyman Ltd	1986–87
306	Usborne Publishing Ltd	1993–94
307	Van Nostrand Reinhold Co Ltd	1979–80
308	Ventura Publishing Ltd	1988–89
309	Victor Gollancz Ltd	1976–77
310	Virago Press Ltd	1984–85
311	Virgin Publishing Ltd	1990–91
312	Virtue & Co Ltd	1976–77
313	W B Saunders Co Ltd	1984–85
314	W H Allen & Co Plc	1984–85
315	W H Freeman & Co Ltd	1985–86
316	Walker Books Ltd	1985–86
317	Ward Lock Ltd	1979–80
318	Wayland (Publishers) Ltd	1984–85
319	Whitstable Litho Ltd	1984–85
320	(John) Wiley & Sons Ltd	1977–78
321	Wiley Heyden Ltd	1990–91
322	William Collins & Sons (Holdings) Ltd	1976–77
323	Wolfe Medical Publications Ltd	1977–78
324	The Women's Press Ltd	1990–91
325	Woodhead-Faulkner Ltd	1984–85
326	World Distributors (Man) Ltd	1976–77
327	World International Publishing Ltd	1979–80

Bibliography

Alcaly, R., *The New Economy*, New York: Farrar, Straus and Giroux, 2003.

Agre, P. and M. Rotenberg (eds), *Technology and Privacy: The New Landscape*, Cambridge, MA: The MIT Press, 1997.

Alikhan, S. and R. Mashelkar, *Intellectual Property and Competitive Strategies in the 21st Century*, New York: Kluwer Law International, 2004.

Allan, W. and P. Curwen, *Competition and Choice in the Publishing Industry*, London: Institute of Economic Affairs, 1991.

Alston, L., T. Eggertsso, and D. North (eds), *Empirical Studies in Institutional Change*, Cambridge University Press, 1996.

Amabile, T., *Creativity in Context*, Boulder, CO: Westview Press, 1996.

Andersen, E., 'Review of Richard Swedberg's "Schumpeter: A Biography"', *Journal of Economic Literature*, vol. 31, 1993, 1969–70.

—— 'The Limits of Schumpeter's *Business Cycles*', 2005. Online. Available <http://www.business.aau.dk/evolution/esapapers/esa05/businesscycles05.pdf> (accessed 12 November 2008).

—— *Schumpeter's Evolutionary Economics: A Theoretical, Historical and Statistical Analysis of the Engine of Capitalism*, London: Anthem Press, 2009.

Arena, R. and C. Dangel (eds), *Contribution of Joseph Schumpeter to Economics: Economic Development and Institutional Change*, London: Routledge, 2002.

Arrow, K., 'Economic Welfare and the Allocation of Resources for Invention', in *The Rate and Direction of Inventive Activity: Economic and Social Factors*, Princeton, NJ: Princeton University Press, 609–626, 1962.

Asteriou, D. and S. Hall, *Applied Econometrics: A Modern Approach using EViews and Microfit*, New York: Palgrave Macmillan, 2007.

Baddeley, M. and D. Barrowclough, *Running Regressions: A Practical Guide to Quantitative Research in Economics, Finance and Development Studies*, Cambridge: Cambridge University Press, 2009.

Baker, M. and B. Cunningham, 'Court Decisions and Equity Markets: Estimating the Value of Copyright Protection', *Journal of Law and Economics*, vol. 2, 2006, 567–596.

Baltagi, B. and B. Raj, 'A Survey of Recent Theoretical Developments in the Econometrics of Panel Data', *Empirical Econometrics*, vol. 17, 1992, 85–109.

—— *Econometric Analysis of Panel Data* 3rd edn, Chichester, UK: John Wiley, 2008.

—— *A Companion to Econometric Analysis of Panel Data*, Chichester, UK: John Wiley, 2009.

Barro, R., *Nothing is Sacred: Economic Ideas for the New Millennium*, Cambridge, MA: The MIT Press, 2002.

Barron, A., 'The Legal Properties of Films', *The Modern Law Review*, vol. 67(2), 2004, 177–208.

Baumol, W., 'Notes on Some Dynamic Models', *Economic Journal*, vol. LVIII, 1948, 506–521.

— *Business Behavior, Value and Growth* rev. edn, New York: Macmillan, 1959.

— *Economic Dynamics: an Introduction*, New York: Macmillan, 1959.

— 'Contestable Markets: An Uprising in the Theory of Industry Structure', *The American Economic Review*, vol. 72(1), 1982, 1–15.

— J. Ordover, 'Antitrust: Source of Dynamic and Static Inefficiencies?', in T. Jorde and D. Teece (eds), *Antitrust, Innovation, and Competitiveness*, Oxford: Oxford University Press, 1992, 82–97.

— 'Innovation and Creative Destruction', in L. McKnight, P. Vaale, and R. Katz (eds), *Creative Destruction: Business Survival Strategies in the Global Internet Economy*, The MIT Press, 2001, pp. 21–38.

— *The Free-Market Innovation Machine: Analysing the Growth Miracle of Capitalism*, Princeton University Press, 2002.

— R. Litan and C. Schramm, *Good Capitalism, Bad Capitalism, and the Economics of Growth and Prosperity*, New Haven, NJ: Yale University Press, 2007.

Beesley, M., D. Goyder, M. Matson, D. Sawers, W. Shew and I. Stelzer (eds), *Markets and the Media*, London: The Institute of Economic Affairs, 1996.

Bell, D. and I. Kristol (eds), *The Crisis in Economic Theory*, New York: Basic Books, 1981.

Bellaigue, E., *British Book Publishing as a Business since the 1960s*, The British Library, 2004.

Benkler, Y., *The Wealth of Networks: How Social Production Transforms Markets and Freedom*, New Haven, NJ: Yale University Press, 2006.

Bently, L. and B. Sherman, *Intellectual Property Law* 2nd edn, Oxford University Press, 2004.

Best, M., *The New Competition: Institutions of Industrial Restructuring*, Cambridge, UK: Polity Press, 1990.

Bettig, R., *Copyrighting Culture: The Political Economy of Intellectual Property*, Westview Press, 1996.

Biondi, Y. 'Schumpeter's Economic Theory and the Dynamic Accounting View of the Firm: Neglected Pages from the Theory of Economic Development', *Economy and Society*, vol. 37(4), 2008, 525–547.

Blair, J., *Economic Concentration: Structure, Behavior and Public Policy*, New York: Harcourt Brace Jovanovich, 1972.

Blaug, M., *The Methodology of Economics: Or How Economists Explain* 2nd edn, Cambridge University Press, 1992.

— 'Why Did Schumpeter Neglect Intellectual Property Rights?' *Review of Economic Research on Copyright Issues*, vol. 2(1), 2005, 69–74.

Bork, R., *The Antitrust Paradox: A Policy at War with Itself*, New York: Maxwell Macmillan, 1993.

Bowerman, B., R. O'Connell, and A. Koehler, *Forecasting, Time Series, and Regression: an Applied Approach* 4th edn, Belmont, CA: Thomson Brooks/Cole, 2005.

Box, G., G. Jenkins and G. Reinsel, *Time Series Analysis: Forecasting and Control* 4th edn, New York: John Wiley, 2008.

Boyle, J., *The Public Domain: Enclosing the Commons of the Mind*, Yale University Press, 2008.

Bresnahan, T. and M. Trajtenberg, 'General Purpose Technologies: Engine of Growth', *Journal of Econometrics*, vol. 65, 1995, 83–108.

Breyer, S., 'The Uneasy Case for Copyright: A Study of Copyright in Books, Photocopies, and Computer Programs', *Harvard Law Review*, vol. 84(2), 1970, 281–351.

Bronk, R., *The Romantic Economist: Imagination in Economics*, Cambridge University Press, 2009.

Brown, T. and J. Ulijn (eds), *Innovation, Entrepreneurship and Culture: the Interaction between Technology, Progress and Economic Growth*, Cheltenham, UK: Edward Elgar, 2004.

Burlamaqui, L., 'How Should Competition Policies and Intellectual Property Issues Interact in a Globalised World? A Schumpeterian Perspective', Presentation at the Seminar 'Contributions to the DevelopmentAgenda on Intellectual Property Rights', United Nations University, Maastricht, Netherlands, 23–24 September 2005. Online. Available <http://hum.ttu.ee/wp/paper6.pdf> (accessed 26 March 2011).

Case, J., *Competition: The Birth of a New Science*, New York: Hill and Wang, 2007.

Casey, B., R. Dunlop and S. Selwood, *Culture as Commodity? The Economics of the Arts and Built Heritage in the UK*, London: Policy Studies Institute, 1996.

Castells, M., *The Rising of the Network Society* 2nd edn, Malden, MA: Blackwell Publishing, 2000.

Cellini, R. and G. Cozzi (eds), *Intellectual property, Competition and Growth*, New York: Palgrave Macmillan, 2007.

Cheung, S., *The Theory of Share Tenancy*, Chicago: The University of Chicago Press, 1969.

— *Will China Go 'Capitalism'?* London: Institute of Economic Affairs, 1982.

— 'The Contractual Nature of the Firm', *Journal of Law and Economics*, vol. 26(1), 1983, 1–21.

Choi, S. and A. Whinston, *The Internet Economy: Technology and Practice*, Austin, TX: SmartEcon Publishing, 2000.

CIPIL, *Review of the Economic Evidence Relating to an Extension of the Term of Copyright in Sound Recordings for the Gowers Review*, Centre for Intellectual Property and Information Law, University of Cambridge, 2006.

Clark, Drew, 'How Copyright Became Controversial', in A. Thierer and W. Crews (eds), *Copy Fights: the Future of Intellectual Property in the Information Age*, Washington DC: Cato Institute, 2002, 147–161.

Clemence, R. and F. Doody, *The Schumpeterian System*, New York: A M Kelley, 1966.

Coase, R., 'The Market for Goods and the Market for Ideas', *American Economic Review*, vol. 64, 1974, 384–391.

— *The Firm, the Market and the Law*, Chicago: The University of Chicago Press, 1988.

— *Essays on Economics and Economists*, Chicago: The University of Chicago Press, 1994.

— 'The New Institutional Economics', *The American Economic Review*, vol. 88(2), 1998, 72–74.

Commission of the European Communities, Directorate-General for Enterprise, *Competitiveness of the European Union Publishing Industries: Final Report*, Luxembourg: Office for Official Publications of the European Communities, 2000.

Cook, T. and D. Campbell, *Quasi-Experimentation: Design & Analysis Issues for Field Settings*, Boston, MA: Houghton Mifflin, 1979.

Cook, T., L. Brazell, S. Chalton and C. Smyth, *The Copyright Directive: UK Implementation*, Bristol, UK: Jordans, 2004.

Cooter, R. and T. Ulen, *Law and Economics* 4th edn, Boston, MA: Addison-Wesley, 2004.

Cornish, W. (ed), *Cases and Materials on Intellectual Property* 5th edn, London: Sweet & Maxwell, 2006.

Costin, H. (ed), *Readings in Strategy and Strategic Planning*, Orlando, FL: Harcourt Brace, 1998.

Cronin, D., 'Proposed EU Copyright Term Extension Faces Vocal Opposition in Parliament', *Intellectual Property Watch* (27 January 2009). Online. Available <http://www.ip-watch.org/weblog/2009/01/27/eu-copyright-term-extension-meets-vocal-opposition-in-parliament> (accessed 10 March 2011).

Curwen, P., *The UK Publishing Industry*, Oxford: Pergamon Press, 1981.

Dam, K., *The Law-Growth Nexus: the Rule of Law and Economic Development*, Washington, DC: Brookings Institution Press, 2006.

D'Aveni, R. with R. Gunther, *Hypercompetition: Managing the Dynamics of Strategic Manoeuvring*, New York: The Free Press, 1994.

David, P., 'The Evolution of Intellectual Property Institutions and the Panda's Thumb', Presentation at the Meeting of the International Economic Association in Moscow, 24–28 August 1992. Online. Available <http://www.compilerpress.atfreeweb.com/Anno%20David%20Evolution%20of%20IP%20Institutions%20 1992.htm> (accessed 16 December 2006).

Davidson, J. and W. Rees-Mogg, *The Sovereign Individual: Mastering the Transition to the Information Age*, New York: Touchstone, 1997.

Davies, G., *Copyright and Public Interest* 2nd edn, London: Sweet & Maxwell, 2002.

Davis, L. and D. North, *Institutional Change and American Economic Growth*, Cambridge University Press, 1971.

Davis, P., 'The Effect of Local Competition on Admission Prices in the U.S. Motion Picture Exhibition Market', *Journal of Law and Economics*, vol. XLVIII, 2005, 677–708.

Deazley, R., *On the Origin of the Right to Copy: Charting the Movement of Copyright Law in Eighteenth-Century Britain (1695–1775)*, Oxford, UK: Hart Publishing, 2004.

—— *Rethinking Copyright: History, Theory, Language*, Cheltenham, UK: Edward Elgar, 2006.

DeLong, B., 'Creative Destruction's Reconstruction: Joseph Schumpeter Revisited', *The Chronicle Review*, vol. 54(15), 7 December 2007.

Derry, T. and T. Williams, *A Short Story of Technology: From the Earliest Times to A.D. 1900*, Oxford University Press, 1960.

Drahos, P., *A Philosophy of Intellectual Property*, Aldershot, UK: Dartmouth, 1996.

Drucker, P., 'Toward the Next Economics', in D. Bell and I. Kristol (eds), *The Crisis in Economic Theory*, New York: Basic Books, 1981, 7.

—— *Innovation and Entrepreneurship*, New York: HarperBusiness, 1985.

—— *Post-Capitalist Society*, New York: HarperBusiness, 1993.

—— *Adventures of a Bystander* Reissue edn, New York: John Wiley, 1998.

Dunn, W., *Public Policy Analysis: An Introduction* 2nd edn, Upper Saddle River, NJ: Prentice-Hall, 2004.

Easterbrook, F., 'Ignorance and Antitrust', in T. Jorde and D. Teece (eds), *Antitrust, Innovation, and Competitiveness*, Oxford University Press, 1992, 119–136.

Ebner, A., 'Institutions, Entrepreneurship, and the Rationale of Government: An Outline of the Schumpeterian Theory of the State', *Journal of Economic Behavior & Organization*, vol. 59, 2006, 497–515.

Economist, *The Economist Numbers Guide: the Essentials of Business Numeracy* 5th edn, London: Profile Books, 2003.

Einhorn, M., *Media, Technology and Copyright: Integrating Law and Economics*, Cheltenham, UK: Edward Elgar, 2004.

Eisenberg, C., R. Gerlach and C. Handke (eds), *Cultural Industries: The British Experience in International Perspective*, Berlin: Centre for British Studies at Humboldt University, 2006.

Ellig, J. (ed), *Dynamic Competition and Public Policy: Technology, Innovation, and Antitrust Issues*, Harvard University Press, 2001.

Epstein, R., 'The "Necessary" History of Property and Liberty', *Chapman Law Review*, vol. 6(1), 2003, 1–29.

Evans, D., 'Why Different Jurisdictions Do Not (and Should Not) Adopt the Same Antitrust Rules', *Chicago Journal of International Law*, vol. 46(1), 2009–2010, 161–187.

— and R. Schmalensee, 'Some Economic Aspects of Antitrust Analysis in Dynamically Competitive Industries', Cambridge, MA: National Bureau of Economic Research, 2001. Online. Available http://www.nber.org/papers/w8268 (accessed 20 March 2010).

Feather, J., 'The Publishers and the Pirates: British Copyright Law in Theory and Practice, 1710–1775', *Publishing History*, vol. 22, 1987, 5–32.

— 'Publishers and Politicians: the Remaking the Law of Copyright in Britain 1775–1842 Part I: Legal Deposit and the Battle of the Library Tax', *Publishing History*, vol. 24, 1988, 49–76.

— *A History of British Publishing* 2nd edn, London: Routledge, 2006.

Field, M., *The Publishing Industry – Growth Prospects Fade?* London: Comedia Publishing Group, 1986.

Fisher, W., *Promises to Keep: Technology, Law, and the Future of Entertainment*, Stanford, CA: Stanford Law and Politics, 2004.

Fisk, C., 'Assembly Line Creativity: The Transformation of Innovation within Corporations, 1875–1930', Paper to be presented at London School of Economics, 7 December 2006.

Fitzpatrick, S., 'Prospect of Further Copyright Harmonisation?' *European Intellectual-Property Review*, vol. 25(5), 2003, 215–223.

Fleischacker, S., *On Adam Smith's Wealth of Nations: A Philosophical Companion*, Princeton, NJ: Princeton University Press, 2005.

Floud, R. and D. McCloskey (eds), *The Economic History of Britain since 1700* Volume 1: 1700–1860 2nd edn, Cambridge University Press, 1994.

— Volume 2: 1860–1970s, Cambridge University Press, 1981.

— Volume 3: 1930–1992 2nd edn, Cambridge University Press, 1994.

Foley, D., *Adam's Fallacy: A Guide to Economic Theology*, Cambridge, MA: Belknap Press of Harvard University Press, 2006.

Foss, N. and V. Mahnke (eds), *Competence, Governance, and Entrepreneurship: Advances in Economic Strategy Research*, Oxford University Press, 2000.

Friedman, D., *Law's Order: What Economics Has to Do with Law and Why It Matters*, Princeton, NJ: Princeton University Press, 2000.

Friedman, M., *Essays in Positive Economics*, Chicago: University of Chicago Press, 1953.

Frith, S. and L. Marshall (eds), *Music and Copyright* 2nd edn, UK: Edinburgh University Press, 2004.

Furubotn, E. and R. Richter. *Institutions and Economic Theory: the Contribution of the New Institutional Economics* 2nd edn, University of Michigan Press, 2005.

Gabor, A., *The Capitalist Philosophers: the Geniuses of Modern Business – Their Lives, Times, and Ideas*, New York: Crown Business, 2000.

Ganley, P., 'Digital Copyright and New Creative Dynamics', *International Journal of Law and Information Technology*, vol. 12(3), 2004, 282–332.

Garelli, S., *Top Class Competitors: How Nations, Firms and Individuals Succeed in the New World of Competitiveness*, Chichester, UK: John Wiley, 2006.

Georgakopoulos, N., *Principles and Methods of Law and Economics*, Cambridge University Press, 2005.

Getzels, J. and I. Taylor (eds), *Perspectives in Creativity*, Chicago: Aldine, 1975.

Ghemawat, P., *Games Business Play: Cases and Models*, Cambridge, MA: The MIT Press, 1997.

Gibson, J., 'Risk Aversion and Rights Accretion in Intellectual Property Law', *The Yale Law Journal*, vol. 116, 2007, 886–933.

Giersch, H., 'The Age of Schumpeter', *AEA Papers and Proceedings*, vol. 74(2), 1984, 103–109.

Gilhooly, K., *Thinking: Directed, Undirected and Creative*, New York: Academic Press, 1982.

Godwin, M., 'The New Legal Panic over Copyright', in A. Thierer and W. Crews (eds), *Copy Fights: the Future of Intellectual Property in the Information Age*, Washington DC: Cato Institute, 2002, 177–183.

Goldstein, P., *Copyright's Highway: from Gutenberg to the Celestial Jukebox*, New York: Hill and Wang, 1994.

— *International Copyright: Principles, Law, and Practice*, Oxford University Press, 2001.

— *Intellectual Property: the Tough New Realities That Could Make or Break Your Business*, New York: Portfolio, 2007.

Gordon, W. and R. Watt (eds), *The Economics of Copyright: Developments in Research and Analysis*, Cheltenham, UK: Edward Elgar, 2003.

Gorman, R. and J. Ginsburg, *Copyright: Cases and Materials* 6th edn, New York: Foundation Press, 2002.

Gould, D. and W. Gruben, 'The Role of Intellectual Property Rights in Economic Growth', *Journal of Development Economics*, vol. 48, 1996, 323–350.

Grant, R., *Contemporary Strategy Analysis: Concepts, Techniques, Applications* 4th edn, Malden, MA: Blackwell Publishers, 2002.

Greene, J., 'Will Yahoo! Feel the Love?' *Business Week*, 18 February 2008, 26–28.

Greene, W., *Econometric Analysis* 6th edn, Upper Saddle River, NJ: Pearson/Prentice Hall, 2008.

Greenhalgh, C. and M. Rogers, *Innovation, Intellectual Property, and Economic Growth*, Princeton University Press, 2010.

Grossman, G. and E. Lai, 'International Protection of Intellectual Property', *The American Economic Review*, vol. 94(5), 2004, 635–1653.

Hadfield, G., 'The Economics of Copyright: An Historical Perspective', *ASCAP Copyright Law Symposium*, Number 38, 1992, 1–46.

Handke, C., 'Copyright and Digital Copying Technology', in C. Eisenberg, R. Gerlach and C. Handke (eds), *Cultural Industries: The British Experience in*

International Perspective, Berlin: Centre for British Studies at Humboldt University), 2006, 71–98.

Harris, R., Book Review of *Prophet of Innovation: Joseph Schumpeter and Creative Destruction*, 2008. Online. Available <http://www.historycooperative.org/journals/lhr/26.3/br_23.html> (accessed 16 November 2008).

Hausman, D., 'Economic Methodology in a Nutshell', *Journal of Economic Perspectives*, vol. 3(2), 1989, 115–127.

Heald, P., 'Property Rights and the Efficient Exploitation of Copyrighted Works: An Empirical Analysis of Public Domain and Copyrighted FictionBestsellers', *Minnesota Law Review*, vol. 92, 2008, 2008–1031.

Heilbroner, R., *The Worldly Philosophers: the Lives, Times, and Ideas of the Great Economic Thinkers* 6th edn, New York: Simon and Schuster, 1992.

— *21st Century Capitalism*, New York: W W Norton & Company, 1993.

Helmstadter, E. and M. Perlman (eds), *Behavioral Norms, Technological Progress, and Economic Dynamics: Studies in Schumpeterian Economics*, Ann Arbor, MI: University of Michigan Press, 1996.

Helpman, E. (ed), *General Purpose Technologies and Economic Growth*, Cambridge, MA: The MIT Press, 1998.

HMSO, *Gowers Review of Intellectual Property*, Norwich, UK: Crown Copyright, 2006.

Hodgson, G., *Economics and Institutions: A Manifesto for a Modern Institutional Economics*, Cambridge, UK: Polity Press, 1988.

—(ed), *A Modern Reader in Institutional and Evolutionary Economics*, Cheltenham, UK: Edward Elgar, 2002.

Hovenkamp, H., 'The Marginal Revolution in Legal Thought', *Vanderbilt Law Review*, vol. 46, 1993, 305–359.

— *The Antitrust Enterprise: Principle and Execution*, Harvard University Press, 2005.

Howitt, P., 'Growth and Development: A Schumpeterian Perspective', *Commentary* (CD Howe Institute), No. 246, 2007, 1–15. Online. Available <http://www.econ.brown.edu/fac/Peter%5FHowitt/publication/CDHowe%20commentary.pdf> (accessed 10 August 2009).

Hsiao, C., *Analysis of Panel Data* 2nd edn, Cambridge University Press, 2003.

Hutton, W. and A. Giddens (eds), *Global Capitalism*, New York: The New Press, 2000.

ICC Information Group, *Business Ratio Report - Book Publishers* 3rd edn, London, UK: ICC Business Publications Ltd, 1980.

— *Business Ratio Report – Book Publishers* 4th edn, 1981.

— *Business Ratio Report – Book Publishers* 6th edn, 1983.

— *Business Ratio Report – Book Publishers* 8th edn, 1985.

— *Business Ratio Report – Book Publishers* 9th edn, 1986.

— *Business Ratio Report – Book Publishers* 11th edn, 1988.

— *Business Ratio Report – Book Publishers* 12th edn, 1989.

— *Business Ratio Report – Book Publishers* 13th edn, 1990.

— *Business Ratio Report – Book Publishers* 15th edn, 1992.

— *Business Ratio Report – Book Publishers* 17th edn, 1994.

— *Business Ratio Report – Book Publishers* 20th edn, 1997.

— *Business Ratio Report – Book Publishers* 23rd edn, 2000.

— *Business Ratio Report – Book Publishers* 25th edn, 2002.

— *Business Ratio Report – Book Publishers* 27th edn, 2004.

— *Business Ratio Report – Book Publishers* 29th edn, 2006.
— *Business Ratio Report – Book Publishers* 32th edn, 2009.
Idris, K., *Intellectual Property: A Power Tool for Economic Growth*, WIPO Publication No. 888, Geneva: World Intellectual Property Organisation, 2002.
IIL, *The IViR Report*, Institute for Information Law, University of Amsterdam, 2006.
Jayaratne, J. and P. Strahan, 'Entry Restrictions, Industry Evolution, and Dynamic Efficiency: Evidence from Commercial Banking', *Journal of Law and Economics*, vol. 41(1), 1998, 239–273.
Jorde, T. and D. Teece (eds), *Antitrust, Innovation, and Competitiveness*, Oxford University Press, 1992.
Jones, H. and C. Benson, *Publishing Law* 3rd edn, London: Routledge, 2006.
Kallay, D., *The Law and Economics of Antitrust and Intellectual Property: an Austrian Approach*, Cheltenham: Edward Elgar, 2004.
Kamien, M., 'Market Structure and Innovation Revisited', *Japan and World Economy*, vol. 1, 1989, 331–339.
Katz, M. and H. Shelanski, 'Schumpeterian Competition and Antitrust Policy in High-Tech Markets', *Competition*, vol. 14, 2005. Online. Available <http://ssrn.com/abstract=925707> (accessed 30 March 2008).
Keklik, M., *Schumpeter, Innovation and Growth: Long-Cycle Dynamics in the Post- WWII American Manufacturing Industries*, Hampshire, UK: Ashgate, 2003.
Kent, T., 'Sound Recording and Copyright', 2008. Online. Available<http://www.copyright.mediarights.co.uk/> (accessed 30 April 2008).
Kerr, O., 'A Lukewarm Defence of the Digital Millennium Copyright Act', in A. Thierer and W. Crews (eds), *Copy Fights: the Future of Intellectual Property in the Information Age*, Washington DC: Cato Institute, 2002, 163–170.
Kingsford, R., *The Publishers Association 1896–1946*, Cambridge University Press, 1970.
Kirzner, I., 'The "Austrian" Perspective on the Crisis', in D. Bell and I. Kristol (eds), *The Crisis in Economic Theory*, New York: Basic Books, 1981, 113.
Koren, N. and E. Salzberger, *Law, Economics and Cyberspace: the Effects of Cyberspace on the Economic Analysis of Law*, Cheltenham: Edward Elgar, 2004.
Krecké, E., 'Economic Analysis and Legal Pragmatism', *International Review of Law and Economics*, vol. 23, 2004, 421–437.
Kretschmer, M., 'Digital Copyright: the End of an Era', *European Intellectual Property Review*, vol. 25(8), 2003, 333–342.
— et al., 'Creativity Stifled? A Joint Academic Statement on the Proposed Copyright Term Extension for Sound Recordings', *European Intellectual Property Review*, vol. 30(9), 2008, 341–347.
— et al., 'Copyright Extension is the Enemy of Innovation', *The Times*, 21 July 2008. Online. Available <http://www.timesonline.co.uk/tol/comment/letters/article4374115.ece> (accessed 10 March 2011).
Krugman, P., *Peddling Prosperity: Economic Sense and Nonsense in the Age of Diminished Expectations*, New York: Norton, 1994.
Ku, R., 'The Creative Destruction of Copyright: Napster and the New Economics of Digital Technology', *University of Chicago Law Review*, vol. 69, 2002, 263–322.
Kuznets, S., 'Schumpeter's Business Cycles', *The American Economic Review*, vol. 30(2), Part 1, 1940, 257–271.
Landes, W. and R. Posner, 'An Economic Analysis of Copyright Law', *Journal of Legal Studies*, vol. 18, 1989, 325–363.

— *The Economic Structure of Intellectual Property Law*, Harvard University Press, 2003.

Langlois, R., 'Schumpeter and the Obsolescence', Working Paper, Department of Economics, University of Connecticut, 2002. Online. Available <http://www.ifpi.org/content/library/liebowitz-study-aug2007.pdf> (accessed 26 March 2011).

Lazonick, W., *Business Organisation and the Myth of the Market Economy*, Cambridge University Press, 1991.

Le, N., 'Microsoft Europe and Switching Costs', Presentation at Annual Congress of the Society for Economic Research on Copyright Issues in Turin, Italy, 8–9 July 2004.

Lee, R., *Unobtrusive Methods in Social Research*, Philadelphia, PA: Open University Press, 2000.

Lee, Y., *Schumpeterian Dynamics and Metropolitan-Scale Productivity*, Hampshire, UK: Ashgate, 2003.

Lessig, L., *Code and Other Laws of Cyberspace*, New York: Basic Books, 1999.

— *The Future of Ideas: the Fate of the Commons in a Connected World*, New York: Vintage Books, 2001.

— *Free Culture: How Big Media Uses Technology and the Law to Lock Down and Control Creativity*, New York: The Penguin Press, 2004.

Leveque, F. and H. Shelanski (eds), *Antitrust, Patents and Copyright: EU and US Perspectives*, Cheltenham, UK: Edward Elgar, 2005.

Li, W. and L. Xu, 'The Impact of Privatisation and Competition in the Telecommunications Sector around the World', *Journal of Law and Economics*, vol. XLVII, 2004, 395–430.

Liebowitz, S., 'What are the Consequences of the European Union Extending Copyright Length for Sound Recordings?' 2007.

— and S. Margolis, 'Seventeen Economists Weigh in on Copyright: the Role of Theory, Empirics, and Network Effects', AEI-Brookings Joint Centre for Regulatory Studies, 2004.

Litman, J., 'Copyright and Information Policy', *Law and Contemporary Problems*, vol. 55(2), 1992, 185–209.

— *Digital Copyright*, Prometheus Books, 2001.

— 'Revising Copyright Law for the Information Age', in A. Thierer and W. Crews (eds), *Copy Fights: the Future of Intellectual Property in the Information Age*, Washington DC: Cato Institute, 2002, 125–145.

Lipsey, R., K. Carlaw and C. Bekar, *Economic Transformations – General Purpose Technologies and Long-Term Economic Growth*, Oxford University Press, 2005.

Lloyd, I., *Information Technology Law* 4th edn, Oxford University Press, 2004.

Long, C., 'Information Costs in Patent and Copyright', *Virginia Law Review*, vol. 90(2), 2004, 465–549.

Lundström, A. and L. Stevenson, *Entrepreneurship Policy: Theory and Practice*, Springer, 2010.

Machlup, F., 'Schumpeter's Economic Methodology', *The Review of Economics and Statistics*, vol. 33(2), 1951, 145–151.

MacQueen, H., *Copyright, Competition, and Industrial Design*, Edinburgh University Press, 1995.

— and C. Waelde, G. Laurie and A. Brown, *Contemporary Intellectual Property: Law and Policy* 2nd edn, Oxford University Press, 2011.

Man, J., *The Gutenberg Revolution: the Story of a Genius and an Invention that Changed the World*, London: Review, 2002.

Mandel, M., *The Coming Internet Depression*, New York: Basic Books, 2000.

Mankiw, G., *Principles of Economics* 3rd edn, Mason, OH: South-Western/Thomson Learning, 2004.

Mansell, R. and E. Steinmuller, *Mobilising the Information Society: Strategies for Growth and Opportunity*, Oxford University Press, 2002.

Martin, S., 'The Mythology of the Public Domain: Exploring the Myths Behind Attacks on the Duration of Copyright Protection', *Loyola of Los Angeles Law Review*, vol. 36, 2002, 253–322.

Maskus, K., *International Intellectual Property Rights and the Global Economy*, Washington, DC: Institute for International Economics, 2000.

— (ed), *The WTO, Intellectual Property Rights and the Knowledge Economy*, Northampton, NA: Edward Elgar, 2004.

Mathews, J., 'A Resource-Based view of Schumpeterian Economic Dynamics', *Journal of Evolutionary Economics*, vol. 106, 2002, 1–26.

Mattei, U., *Comparative Law and Economics*, Ann Arbor, MI: University of Michigan Press, 1996.

Mátyás, L. and P. Sevestre (eds), *The Econometrics of Panel Data: A Handbook of the Theory with Applications* 2nd rev, The Netherlands & Norwell, MA: Kluwer Academic Publishers, 1996.

May, C., *A Global Political Economy of Intellectual Property Rights: the New Enclosures?* New York: Routledge, 2000.

— and S. Sell, *Intellectual Property Rights: A Critical History*, London: Lynne Rienner Publishers, 2006.

Mayer-Schönberger, V., 'Schumpeterian Law: Rethinking the Role of Law in Fostering Entrepreneurship', 2007. Online. Available <http://works.bepress.com/cgi/viewcontent.cgi?article=1001&context=viktor_mayer_schoenberger> (accessed 14 March 2008).

Mazeh, Y. and M. Rogers, 'The Economic Significance and Extent of Copyright Cases: An Analysis of Large UK Firms', *Intellectual Property Quarterly*, 4th Issue, 2006, 404–420.

Mazzucato, M., *Firm Size, Innovation, and Market Structure: the Evolution of Industry Concentration and Instability*, Cheltenham, UK: Edward Elgar, 2000.

McCraw, T., *Prophet of Innovation: Joseph Schumpeter and Creative Destruction*, Harvard University Press, 2007.

— 'Alfred Chandler: His Vision and Achievement', *Business History Review*, vol. 82(2), 2008.

McDaniel, B., 'A Contemporary View of Joseph A. Schumpeter's Theory of the Entrepreneur', *Journal of Economic Issues*, vol. XXXIX(2), 2005, 485–489.

McDowall, D., R. McCleary and E. Meidinger, *Interrupted Time Series Analysis*, Newbury Park, CA: Sage Publications, 1990.

McKnight, L. and J. Bailey (eds), *Internet Economics*, Cambridge, MA: The MIT Press, 1998.

— and P. Vaaler and R. Katz (eds), *Creative Destruction: Business Survival Strategies in the Global Internet Economy*, Cambridge, MA: The MIT Press, 2001.

Menard, S., *Longitudinal Research* 2nd edn, Thousand Oaks, CA: Sage Publications, 2002.

Mendenhall, W., J. Reinmuth, R. Beaver and D. Duhan, *Statistics for Management and Economics* 5th edn, Boston, MA: Duxbury Press, 1986.

Mendenhall, W. and T. Sincich, *A Second Course in Statistics: Regression Analysis* 5th edn, Upper Saddle River, NJ: Prentice Hall, 1996.

Mercuro, N. and S. Medema, *Economics and the Law: From Posner to Post-Modernism* 2nd edn, Princeton, NJ: Princeton University Press, 2006.

Merges, R., 'Intellectual Property Rights and the New Institutional Economics', *Vanderbilt Law Review*, vol. 53(6), 2000, 1857–1877.

Mills, T., *Time Series Techniques for Economists*, Cambridge University Press, 1990.

Moore, G., *Living on the Fault Line: Managing for Shareholder Value in the Age of the Internet*, New York: HarperBusiness, 2000.

— *Dealing with Darwin: How Great Companies Innovate at Every Phase of Their Evolution*, Penguin Group, 2005.

Mowery, D. and N. Rosenberg, *Technology and the Pursuit of Economic Growth* Cambridge University Press, 1989.

Murray, A., 'Security vs. Privacy on the Internet', Presentation Given to London School of Economics Lawyers Alumni Group Simmons & Simmons, London, 13 November 2002. Text is available in LL4B5 course materials at London School of Economics from http://www.itlawweb.co.uk.

— and C. Scott, 'Controlling the New Media: Hybrid Responses to New Forms of Power', *The Modern Law Review*, vol. 65(4), 2002, 491–516.

— *The Regulation of Cyberspace: Control in the Online Environment*, London: Routledge-Cavendish, 2007.

Nadel, M., 'How Current Copyright Law Discourages Creative Output: The Overlooked Impact of Marketing', *Berkeley Technology Law Journal*, vol. 19(2), 2004, 785–856.

Negroponte, N., *Being Digital*, New York: Vintage Books, 1995.

Netanel, N., 'Copyright and a Democratic Civil Society', *The Yale Law Journal*, vol. 106, 1996, 283–387.

— 'Locating Copyright within the First Amendment Skein', *Stanford Law Review*, vol. 54(1), 2001, 1–86.

— 'Copyright and "Market Power" in the Marketplace of Ideas', in F. Leveque and H. Shelanski (eds), *Antitrust, Patents and Copyright: EU and US Perspectives*, Cheltenham, UK: Edward Elgar, 2005, 149–179.

— *Copyright's Paradox: Property in Expression/Freedom of Expression*, Oxford University Press, 2006.

Nielsen, K. and B. Johnson (eds), *Institutions and Economic Change: New Perspectives on Markets, Firms and Technology*, Northampton, NA: Edward Elgar, 1998.

North, D., *Institutions, Institutional Change, and Economic Performance*, Cambridge University Press, 1990.

— and R. Thomas, *The Rise of the Western World: A New Economic History*, Cambridge University Press, 1973.

Nowell-Smith, S., *International Copyright Law and the Publisher in the Reign of Queen Victoria*, Oxford University Press, 1968.

O'Hare, M., 'Copyright: When is Monopoly efficient?' *Journal of Policy Analysis and Management*, vol. 4(3), 1985, 407–418.

Ormerod, P., *Why Most Things Fail: Evolution, Extinction and Economics*, London: Faber and Faber, 2005.

Oser, J. and W. Blanchfield, *The Evolution of Economic Thought* 3rd edn, New York: Harcourt Brace Jovanovich, 1975.

Ostrom, C., *Time Series Analysis: Regression Techniques*, Newberry Park, CA: Sage Publications, 1990.

Pavlve, O., 'Dynamic Analysis of an Institutional Conflict: Copyright Owners against Online File Sharing', *Journal of Economic Issues*, vol. XXXIX(3), 2005, 633–663.

Phillips, P., *Marx and Engels on Law and Laws*, Totowa: Barnes and Noble Books, 1980.

Pira International, *Publishing in the Knowledge Economy: Competitiveness Analysis of UK Publishing Media Sector* (Crown), 2002.

Plant, A., 'The Economic Aspects of Copyright in Books', *Economica*, May 1934, 167–195.

Plant, M., *The English Book Trade: An Economic History of the Making and Sale of Books* 2nd edn, London: Allen & Unwin, 1965.

Png, I.P.L. and Q. Wang, 'Copyright Duration and the Supply of Creative Work', 2006. Online. Available <http://papers.ssrn.com/sol3/papers.cfm?abstract_id=932161> (accessed 26 March 2011).

— 'Copyright Duration and the Supply of Creative Work: Evidence from the Movies', 2009. Online. Available <http://www.comp.nus.edu.sg/~ipng/> (accessed 5 March 2012).

Popper, K., *The Logic of Scientific Discovery*, London: Hutchinson, 1959.

— *Conjectures and Refutations: The Growth of Scientific Knowledge*, London: Routledge & Kegan Paul, 1963.

Porter, A., 'Plan to Extend Copyright on Pop Classics', *The Sunday Times*, 5 June 2005. Online. Available <http://www.timesonline.co.uk/tol/news/uk/article530132.ece> (accessed 10 March 2011).

Posner, R., *The Problems of Jurisprudence*, Harvard University Press, 1990.

— *Economic Analysis of Law*, Boston, MA: Little Brown, 1992.

— *Overcoming Law*, Harvard University Press, 1995.

Post, D., 'His Napster's Voice', in A. Thierer and W. Crews (eds), *Copy Fights: the Future of Intellectual Property in the Information Age*, Washington DC: Cato Institute, 2002, pp. 107–124.

PwC, *The Impact of Copyright Extension for Sound Recordings in the UK: A Report for the Gowers Review of Intellectual Property prepared by PwC on Behalf of the BPI*, PricewaterhouseCoopers LLP, 2006.

Quah, D., 'Digital Goods and the New Economy', in D. Jones (ed), *New Economy Handbook*, Academic Press, 2003, pp. 289–321.

Ramello, G., 'Copyright and Antitrust Issues', in W. Gordon and R. Watt (eds), *The Economics of Copyright: Developments in Research and Analysis*, Cheltenham, UK: Edward Elgar, 2003, 118–147.

Raven, J., *The Business of Books: Booksellers and the English Book Trade 1450–1850*, New Haven: Yale University Press, 2007.

Reichman, J., G. Dinwoodie and P. Samuelson, 'A Reverse Notice and Takedown Regime to Enable Public Interest Uses of Technologically Protected Copyrighted Works', *Berkeley Technology Law Journal*, vol. 22, 2007, 981–1060.

Richards, D., *Intellectual Property Rights and Global Capitalism: the Political Economy of the TRIPS Agreement*, New York: M E Sharpe, 2004.

Ricketts, M., *Economics of Business Enterprise: an Introduction to Economic Organisation and the Theory of the Firm* 3rd edn, Cheltenham, UK: Edward Elgar, 2002.

Robbins, L., *A History of Economic Thought: The LSE Lectures*, S. Medema and W. Samuels (eds), Princeton: Princeton University Press, 1998.

Robinson, J., *Economic Philosophy*, Harmondsworth, UK: Penguin, 1964.

— *Economics: an Awkward Corner*, London: Allen & Unwin, 1966.

— and J. Eatwell, *An Introduction to Modern Economics*, UK: McGraw-Hill, 1974.

Roncaglia, A., *The Wealth of Ideas: A History of Economic Thought*, Cambridge University Press, 2005.

Rosenberg, N., *Schumpeter and the Endogeneity of Technology: Some American Perspectives*, New York: Routledge, 2000.

Ross, P., 'How Long is Long Enough? Copyright Term Extensions and the Berne Convention', *Progress on Point* 13–15 June 2006. Online. Available <http://www.pff.org> (accessed 20 May 2009).

Ryan, M., *Knowledge Diplomacy: Global Competition and the Politics of Intellectual Property*, Washington, DC: Brookings Institution Press, 1998.

Samuelson, P. 'Intellectual Property and the Digital Economy: Why the Anti-Circumvention Regulations Need to be Revised?' *Berkeley Technology Law Journal*, vol. 14, 1999, 519–566.

— 'Legally Speaking: The Dead Souls of the Google Booksearch Settlement', 2009. Online. Available <http://radar.oreilly.com/2009/04/legally-speaking-the-dead-soul.html> (accessed 10 March 2011).

— 'Google Book Search and the Future of Books in Cyberspace', 2010. Online. Available <http://www.ischool.berkeley.edu/ pam> (accessed 10 March 2011).

Samuelson, P. and W. Nordhaus, *Economics* 19th edn, New York: McGraw-Hill, 2010.

Sayrs, L., *Pooled Time Series Analysis*, Newbury Park, CA: Sage Publications, 1989.

Schroeder, L., D. Sjoquis and P. Stephan, *Understanding Regression Analysis: an Introductory Guide*, Newbury Park, CA: Sage Publications, 1986.

Schumpeter, J., *Business Cycles: A Theoretical, Historical, and Statistical Analysis of the Capitalist Process* 2 volumes, New York: McGraw-Hill, 1939.

— 'The Creative Response in Economic History', *Journal of Economic History*, vol. 7(2), 1947, 149–159.

— Translated by R. Opie, *The Theory of Economic Development: an Inquiry into Profits, Capital, Credit, Interest, and the Business Cycle*, Harvard University Press, 1962[1911].

— *Capitalism, Socialism and Democracy* 3rd edn, New York: Harper & Row, 1976[1942].

— *History of Economic Analysis* 11th edn, Oxford University Press, 1980[1950].

Schwartz, P. and W. Treanor, '*Eldred* and *Lochner*: Copyright Term Extension and Intellectual Property as Constitutional Property', *The Yale Law Journal*, vol. 112, 2004, 2331–2414.

Seipp, D., 'The Concept of Property in the Early Common Law', *Law and History Review*, vol. 12(1), 1994, 29–91.

Sell, S., *Private Power, Public Law: the Globalisation of Intellectual Property Rights*, Cambridge University Press, 2003.

Seville, C., *Literary Copyright Reform in Early Victorian England: The Framing of the 1842 Copyright Act*, Cambridge University Press, 1999.

Shadish, W., T. Cook and D. Campbell, *Experimental and Quasi-Experimental Designs for Generalized Causal Inference*, Boston, MA: Houghton Mifflin, 2002.

Shane, S., *A General Theory of Entrepreneurship: the Individual-Opportunity Nexus*, Cheltenham, UK: Edward Elgar, 2003.

Shavell, S., *Foundations of Economic Analysis of Law*, Harvard University Press, 2004.

Sherman, B. and L. Bently, *The Making of Modern Intellectual Property Law: the British Experience, 1760–1911*, Cambridge University Press, 1999.

Sherwood, R., *Intellectual Property and Economic Development*, Boulder, CO: Westview Press, 1990.

Shionoya, Y., *The Soul of the German Historical School: Methodological Essays on Schmoller, Weber and Schumpeter*, New York: Springer-Verlag, 2005.

Shy, O., *Industrial Organization: Theory and Applications*, Cambridge, MA: The MIT Press, 1995.

— *The Economics of Network Industries*, Cambridge University Press, 2001.

Singleton, R., B. Straits and M. Straits, *Approaches to Social Research*, Oxford University Press, 1993.

Siwek, S., 'The Measurement of "Copyright" Industries: The American Experience', *Review of Economic Research on Copyright Issues*, vol. 1, 2004, 17–25.

Smith, A., *Lectures on Jurisprudence*, R. Meek, D. Raphael and P. Stein (eds), Indianapolis, IN: Liberty Fund, 1982[1723–1790].

— *Wealth of Nations*, New York: Prometheus Books, 1991[1776].

Spar, D., *Ruling the Waves: Cycles of Discovery, Chaos, and Wealth from the Compass to the Internet*, New York: Harcourt Trade, 2001.

Spinello, R. and H. Tavani (eds), *Intellectual Property Rights in a Networked World: Theory and Practice*, Hershey, PA: Information Science Publishing, 2005.

Starr, P., *The Creation of the Media: Political Origins of Modern Communications*, New York: Basic Books, 2004.

Sterk, S., 'Rhetoric and Reality in Copyright Law', *Michigan Law Review*, vol. 94, 1996, 1197–1249.

Stigler, G., 'Two Notes on the Coase Theorem', *Yale Law Journal*, vol. 99, 1989, 631–633.

Stiglitz, J., *Economics* 2nd edn, New York: W W Norton & Company, 1997a.

— *Whither socialism?* Cambridge, MA: The MIT Press, 1997b.

Stryszowski, P., 'Intellectual Property Rights, Globalization and Growth', *Global Economy Journal*, vol. 6(4), 2006, 1–31.

Sturgeon, T., 'Modular Production Networks: A New American Model of Industrial Organisation Grasping Opportunity, Meeting Challenges of New Technology Revolution', *Industrial and Corporate Change*, vol. 11(3), 2002, 451–496.

Sullivan, P., *Value-Driven Intellectual Capital: How to Convert Intangible Corporate Assets into Market Value*, New York: John Wiley, 2000.

Swedberg, R., *Joseph Schumpeter: His Life and Work*, Cambridge, UK: Polity Press, 1991. Nanjing, China: Jiangsu Press, 2005.

Tang, P., 'Digital Copyright and the "New" Controversy: Is the Law Moulding Technology and Innovation?' *Research Policy*, vol. 34, 2005, 852–871.

Thierer, A. and W. Crews (eds), *Copy Fights: the Future of Intellectual Property in the Information Age*, Washington DC: Cato Institute, 2002.

Thomas, L., 'The Two Faces of Competition: Dynamic Resourcefulness and the Hypercompetitive Shift', *Organization Science*, vol. 7(3), 1996, 221–242.

Thurow, L., 'Needed: A New System of Intellectual Property Rights', *Harvard Business Review*, September–October 1997, 94–103.

— *The Future of Capitalism: How Today's Economic Forces Shape Tomorrow's World*, New York: Penguin Books, 1996.

— *Building Wealth: The New Rules for Individuals, Companies, and Nations in a Knowledge-Based Economy*, New York: HarperBusiness, 1999.

Torremans, P. (ed), *Copyright Law: A Handbook of Contemporary Research*, Cheltenham, UK: Edward Elgar, 2007.

Towse, R., *Creativity, Incentive and Reward: an Economic Analysis of Copyright and Culture in the Information Age*, Cheltenham, UK: Edward Elgar, 2001.

— (ed), *Copyright in the Cultural Industries*, Cheltenham, UK: Edward Elgar, 2002.

— 'Copyright Policy, Cultural Policy and Support for Artists', in W. Gordon and R. Watt (eds), *The Economics of Copyright: Developments in Research and Analysis*, Cheltenham, UK: Edward Elgar, 2003, 66–80.

— 'Copyright and Economics', in S. Frith and L. Marshall (eds), *Music and Copyright* 2nd edn, UK: Edinburgh University Press, 2004, 54–69.

— 'Economics and Copyright Reform: Aspects of the EC Directive', *Telematics and Informatics*, vol. 22, 2005, 11–24.

Tucker, R., *The Marx-Engels Reader*, New York: W W Norton & Company, 1972.

UNCTAD and UNDP, *The Creative Economy Report 2008*, United Nations, 2008.

Useem, J., 'Dead Thinkers' Society: Meet the New Economy's Oldest New Economist', *Business 2.0*, November 2001, 132–134.

Vaaler, P. and G. McNamara, 'Are Technology-Intensive Industries More Dynamically Competitive? No and Yes', 2006. Online. Available <http://www.business.uiuc.edu/Working_Papers/papers/06-0124.pdf> (accessed 10 June 2008).

Vaidhyanathan, S., *Copyrights and Copywrongs: the Rise of Intellectual Property and How It Threatens Creativity*, New York: New York University Press, 2001.

Vandaele, W., *Applied Time Series and Box-Jenkins Models*, Orlando, FL: Academic Press, 1983.

Varian, H., 'High-Technology Industries and Market Structure', in The Federal Reserve Bank of Kansas City, *Economic Policy for the Information Economy*, Kansas City, Missouri: The Federal Reserve Bank of Kansas City, 2001, 65–101.

Warsh, D., *Knowledge and the Wealth of Nations: A Story of Economic Discovery*, New York: W W Norton and Company, 2006.

Watt, R., *Copyright and Economic Theory: Friends or Foes?* Cheltenham, UK: Edward Elgar, 2000.

Weimer, D. and A. Vining, *Policy Analysis: Concepts and Practice* 2nd edn, Upper Saddle River, NJ: Prentice-Hall, 1992.

Weinreb, L., 'Copyright for Functional Expression', *Harvard Law Review*, vol. 111(5), 1998, 1149–1254.

Williamson, O., *The Economic Institutions of Capitalism*, New York: The Free Press, 1985.

— 'Antitrust Lenses and the Uses of Transaction Cost Economics Reasoning', in T. Jorde and D. Teece (eds), *Antitrust, Innovation, and Competitiveness*, Oxford University Press, 1992, 137–164.

Wu, T., 'Copyright's Communications Policy', *Michigan Law Review*, vol. 103, 2004, 278–366.

Yi, X., 'Steven Cheung, a Talent in Economics', a Postscript to the Chinese Edition of *The Theory of Share Tenancy*, Chicago: The University of Chicago Press, 1969 and Beijing: The Commercial Press, 2001.

Zajac, E., *Political Economy of Fairness*, Cambridge, MA: The MIT Press, 1995.

Index